The Masters of Sitcom

From Hancock to Steptoe

The Masters of Sitcom
From Hancock to Steptoe

Ray Galton and Alan Simpson

compiled by Christopher Stevens

Michael O'Mara Books Limited

First published in Great Britain in 2011 by
Michael O'Mara Books Limited
9 Lion Yard
Tremadoc Road
London SW4 7NQ

ISBN: 978-1-84317-633-6 in hardback print format
ISBN: 978-1-84317-773-9 in EPub format
ISBN: 978-1-84317-774-6 in Mobipocket format

1 3 5 7 9 10 8 6 4 2

Designed and typeset by e-type

Plate section designed by Deep Rehal

Printed and bound by CPI Group (UK) Ltd, Croydon, CR0 4YY

www.mombooks.com

Contents

To Dr Margaret 'Peggy' Shackles, who, as Assistant Physician at Surrey County Sanatorium in Milford, was our doctor in the late 1940s. Without her, we might not have survived to do any of this.

Compiler's Note

I n the basement of Ray Galton's home in west London, two rows of filing cabinets stand on the stone floor of a former pantry. These metal drawers contain all the scripts that Ray and his writing partner, Alan Simpson, have stockpiled since the beginning of their career in 1951, as well as innumerable newspaper cuttings.

The house is close to the Thames. The first time I saw the archive, an obvious question leapt into my head, and I asked it: 'What happens if the river floods?'

Alan and Ray glanced at each other, and then looked at me kindly, as if I was simple-minded. Speaking together, they said: 'They get wet.'

That incident tells you a lot about Galton and Simpson, the fathers of sitcom and two of the most influential scriptwriters in television history. They are effortlessly funny; they seem to share thoughts before they speak; they have always known the importance of preserving their work, even when the BBC was busily wiping their tapes; they regard life with an amused nonchalance.

Nonchalance is much healthier, of course, than neurosis, but it is also less effective in staking out a literary reputation. When I began to compile the extracts and conduct the interviews for this book, three years ago, it was one of my contentions that Galton and Simpson were, alongside Wodehouse, the greatest comic writers of the twentieth century. They had changed the way the nation spoke, and created a new genre of comedy. Ray and Alan refused to admit as much, and sometimes looked uncomfortable when I claimed it for them.

Since the day we embarked on the book, I have been insisting it should be called *The Men Who Invented Sitcom*. I believe that's an accurate summary of their achievement. Ray and Alan, whose genuine modesty and absence of ego are plain to anyone who meets them, have been arguing with me for three years that sitcom began with Shakespeare, if not earlier. Which of us is right, the reader will have to decide.

All the excerpts in this book are taken from the scripts, and not the broadcasts. Ray and Alan kept copies of all their 600 scripts, sometimes in multiple drafts: the typed originals with their pencil annotations, the clean copies, the rehearsal scripts, the copies that had been adorned with doodles by TV production staff. Where possible, I used final drafts, the versions that Tony Hancock and Sid James, or Harry H. Corbett and Wilfrid Brambell, would have worked from. In every case, I have transcribed what is on the page; in some cases, this is different from what was actually broadcast, if the performer ad libbed, or fluffed, or skipped a line.

The sheer scale of Galton and Simpson's output, and the impossibly high standards of writing they maintained throughout their career, have meant many harsh decisions have been made in the editing. If an extract from your favourite episode of *Hancock's Half Hour* or *Steptoe and Son* has been omitted, I am sorry. I have been guided in my selection by three principles:

- to demonstrate how the sitcom genre developed, from comic sketches in radio variety shows to dramatic, emotional confrontations on television;
- to illustrate the many different elements of the *Hancock* and *Steptoe* characters;
- to include as much unseen material as possible – especially the development of Hancock before the *Half Hours*; the many lost episodes of Tony Hancock's radio and television shows; the extraordinary film script, *The Day Off*, that Hancock refused to make; the sixteen *Comedy Playhouses* that expanded the boundaries of sitcom; and a lost *Steptoe* Christmas Special.

These criteria meant limitations had to be imposed on other material. In order to focus on the early development of situation comedy, we decided – reluctantly – not to include extracts from Galton and Simpson's Hollywood movies, nor from the seventies TV series such as *Clochemerle* and *Dawson's Weekly*, and to reproduce only token extracts from the later, better known *Steptoes* and from Ray and Alan's last two series of *Playhouse*-style programmes.

The commentaries that link the extracts are based on extensive conversations with Alan and Ray, as well as on numerous interviews with surviving actors from the shows and with others who knew the stars, and also with contemporary sitcom writers and aficionados. The opinions expressed in these commentaries are, of course, my own.

Christopher Stevens

Introduction

When I discovered Tony Hancock, I was eight years old. His face peered out from a record sleeve in a stack of my father's LPs: on the front cover, a man with basset hound features – all bloodshot eyes and drooping jowls – stared at the camera with an air of grievance. He looked like he'd had rotten luck and was expecting it to get worse. It did; by 1972 he had been dead for four years.

I already knew a little bit about another comedy by Hancock's scriptwriters, because on Monday evenings my parents allowed me to stay up to hear the music that opened *Steptoe and Son*. I couldn't watch the show: I was always sent to bed. *Steptoe* contained 'language', and I was too young for that. But *Hancock* contained language too – wonderful language – and I first encountered it on the back sleeve of that album. Below the titles, 'The Blood Donor' and 'The Radio Ham', there were two columns of notes. I had never read anything quite like it:

> *Record lovers already entranced by the breathtaking translucency of* This Is Hancock *and the overwhelming poignancy of* Pieces of Hancock *will surely be dead chuffed by the addition of this, the third of the trilogy of three records made by this Grand Old Man of English Television. Over a period of six tremendous years he has endeared himself to the hearts of dozens of viewers with his cheerful banter and unpleasant manner, qualities which surely must earn him a place in the top 10,000 comedians of the post-war years. Mr Hancock gives a strong, savage portrayal of a man torn between the noble desire to give a pint of his blood and the primitive desire to hang on to it... Another strong, powerful performance, rich in realism, showing an emotional depth rarely captured on record before, and calculated to batter the listener into a state of complete indifference.*

The top 10,000... no wonder the figure on the cover wore his hat like a badge of defeat. But the manufacturers must have cared about him, because a footnote at the bottom emphasized what a high fidelity recording this was:

Technical data: Recorded by a Grindley Gibbons Mark Two Panovistic microphone incorporating ecliptical suspension bars with two overhead valves, Sansom and Margrave condensers with hand-ground tappets, disc brakes and twin exhaust pipes. Three hundred megacycles on a frequency of two thousand bicycles providing an output of 0000.003 volts to the square inch with a noise ratio of ten to one at half volume giving an annual fall out of 97 units. For best results wipe the surface after every playing with a piece of best quality emery cloth.

When I got to the bit about twin exhaust pipes, I stopped and read it again. I loved that record before I ever played it. I've still got the cover, framed and on the wall, signed by the men who wrote those notes on the back: Ray Galton and Alan Simpson.

'The Blood Donor' was probably the best known and most loved of all the 600 scripts from their 60-year career. It marked a high point for Galton and Simpson, and the edge of a precipice for the performer. After he broke from them, the best work Tony Hancock could muster was arguably a series of commercials for the Egg Marketing Board. For Ray and Alan, there was an astonishing proposal from the BBC: they were invited to write a series of half-hour plays, on any subjects they chose, to star whichever actors they chose, in whatever roles they decided to create.

With *Hancock's Half Hour*, Galton and Simpson invented modern sitcom. With the *Comedy Playhouse* programmes that followed, and the ragged figures of Albert and Harold Steptoe who emerged from them, they set the patent on their invention. By presenting rounded characters, trapped in lifelike situations by poverty, class and their own flaws, and telling their stories in language that was rich and earthy, the writers realized a dream they had followed for more than a decade. Almost fifty years on, *Hancock* and *Steptoe* remain the apogee of brilliant sitcom.

Ray Galton and Alan Simpson met as teenagers in Milford Sanatorium, near Godalming, Surrey, where both were recovering from pulmonary tuberculosis. Ray, the younger by eight months, had been admitted in January 1947, when he was not expected to survive more than a few days. Alan arrived the following summer, and during the long and painful treatments a friendship began that would endure for more than sixty years. Listening to US Forces radio broadcasting from Germany, they discovered US comics such as Jack Benny and a type of streetwise wit that was unknown in Britain's music-hall tradition.

Both voracious readers, they also shared a love of American writers, including James Thurber and Damon Runyon. By the time they were discharged at the start of the fifties, they had already begun writing sketches together for the hospital's radio network and, soon after, for an amateur concert group at the local church hall. 'We realized straight away,' Ray said, 'that we laughed at the same things, at the same moment. It was almost telepathic. I didn't have to tell Alan what I was thinking – he got the joke without a word being said.' They were bound by more than a sense of humour: the experience of the sanatorium had shaped their personalities. Other teenagers were doing National Service or beginning careers, but Ray and Alan had been aged by years of debilitating disease on wards where deaths were commonplace.

These were the components that made their partnership so different from the other two-man teams writing comedy after the war. Together they had survived an experience that few their age could comprehend. Each shared an ability to see a joke as fast as the other thought of it. They believed American comedy was decades ahead of British humour, and they wanted sketches and situations that reflected a post-war, post-empire London, with radio stars who used language the way their working-class audiences did.

Those ideals quickly evolved into great ambitions. In 1951 they were gag-merchants paid by the line; within two years they were the BBC's most versatile and admired scriptwriters. As they climbed, they began to formulate a truly alternative comedy: believable characters and credible stories, true-to-life situations in ordinary settings, with dialogue written as everyday speech. It would star their favourite performer, Tony Hancock, the obsessive and anxious compère of their hour-long variety show, *Star Bill*. In *Hancock's Half Hour*, though, there would be no joke-telling, punchlines or music-hall patter. The writers were intent on getting rid of catchphrases, songs, running gags, musical interludes and sketches. This was a type of comedy as radical as the realist theatre that would sweep the English stage in the late fifties: natural, honest and unflinching.

Tony Hancock's widow, Freddie, would see the writers at work not only on the *Half Hours* but also, as Harry H. Corbett's agent, on *Steptoe*. She is now living in New York, and when we talked, she pinpointed their gift for weaving reality into fantasy: 'What's so clever about Galton and Simpson, they have the most amazing talent for filing. They will file away something you said in total earnestness and they will bring it out, out of context and out of synch, and it will be the most hysterical thing. I think they don't even consciously do it; they do it instinctively. That's my personal opinion, and of course they'll deny it – but many times I watched Tony doing a read-through, and he'd come to a line that echoed something he'd been saying, completely seriously, about history or politics or philosophy. And they'd mirrored it, and made it hysterically funny. He'd look at them and just say, "Cheeky buggers!"'

Having created a genre, Galton and Simpson soon revelled in the freedom it gave them to create better, funnier sitcoms. It is astonishing that when they completed 'The Blood Donor' in 1961 they had already written more than 150 *Half Hours* for Tony Hancock. Most of the classic situation comedies that followed had nowhere near as many episodes: there were 57 *Steptoes*, for example, 64 editions of *Only Fools and Horses* (created and written by John Sullivan), 21 of *Porridge* (Dick Clement and Ian La Frenais), 25 of *Blackadder* (Richard Curtis and Ben Elton), 80 of *Dad's Army* (Jimmy Perry and David Croft) and just 12 of *Fawlty Towers* (John Cleese and Connie Booth). Most long-running series will reach a peak before sliding into a gradual decline: *Hancock's Half Hour* simply kept getting better.

The greatest sitcoms, like the best murders, are set in locked rooms from which there seems no means of escape. The shabby rooms at 23 Railway Cuttings, and later the squalid bedsit in Earl's Court, were Hancock's cell. The house and the rag-and-bone yard in Oil Drum Lane, Shepherd's Bush, were Harold Steptoe's prison. His favourite word for the ramshackle building was 'rat-hole': 'What's the point of decorating this rat-hole? You can't disguise the sordidness of this place.'

Steptoe and Son's success stemmed from the writers' genius for inverting expectations. Every plot explored unseen facets in the characters or revealed surprises in their family history. The dialogue was breathtakingly inventive – in an episode set around a funeral, for instance, Harold and Albert appear dressed in black suits and bowler hats. One burly and pompous, one slight and anxious, their resemblance to Laurel and Hardy is so blatant that some reference seems unavoidable... and so the line that Harold actually says is even more shocking: 'Oh, this is ridiculous. Can't we go out separately? We look like a couple of pox doctors' clerks.'

Galton and Simpson's partnership was faithful to the precepts they had started with when they left the sanatorium. The relationship was perfectly equal: not a word could be added to the script without the approval of both. 'I did all the typing,' said Alan, 'but if Ray left the room for a minute and heard the keys clacking, he'd be back in there like a shot – "What are you changing? Show me!" And it was always nothing, I was just tidying up the typescript, amending the date or something like that.'

The parity of egos was so absolute that, somewhere during the sixties, the writing credits were reversed, from 'Alan Simpson and Ray Galton' to 'Galton and Simpson'. Both men insist the change was imposed and not requested, and that neither of them cared – the standard of the scripts mattered far more than the politics of billing. 'Both versions were alphabetical,' pointed out Ray, 'A comes before R and G comes before S. That's all it was.' Such indifference is rare in television, where insecurities often erupt in comical ways. The order of billing for the *Steptoe* stars, for instance, depended on which actor appeared first each week.

The absence of petty rivalries between Ray and Alan was a significant factor in the partnership's longevity. So too was their refusal to argue: when there was a difference of opinion, they simply left a pause. 'I'd go moody, more often than Alan,' Ray admitted. 'I'd come up with a brilliant suggestion – at least, it would seem brilliant to me at the time – and if he didn't think much of it, he wouldn't comment. He'd never say, "What a bloody stupid idea," even if he was thinking it. He just wouldn't comment. And sometimes I would see straight away that it wasn't as clever as I'd imagined, and sometimes I'd get the hump and think, "Right! Let's see him come up with something better." Usually, after a time, one of us would have a flash of inspiration, and the silence would immediately be forgotten.'

'Once or twice we went for days without talking,' Alan agreed. 'The usual friendly pleasantries in the morning – "Do anything good last night?" "Yeah, we went to the pictures, how about you?" – but then we'd start work and nothing would be said for hours... both of us thinking, "It must be his turn to suggest something."'

Self-deprecating humour pervades all of their conversation. Both men prefer to underplay their achievements, partly perhaps because of natural modesty – the first words that anyone who knows them uses to describe both Ray and Alan are 'likeable', 'decent', 'friendly', 'nice' – and partly because they know the worth of their achievements. They can afford to be offhand. It would be unwise to take their self-effacing jokes at face value: the notion for instance that long and unproductive silences were common is belied by the scale of their output over three decades. During the late fifties they were writing forty Hancock shows annually, and throughout the sixties and seventies almost every year produced a fresh series, a movie script, or more. 'We didn't know we were so prolific,' Ray claimed. 'It never felt like it at the time. We even used to have holidays, and I don't do that any more.'

Such productivity demanded self-discipline. They regarded them-selves as craftsmen, not artistes, and imposed office hours – 11 a.m. to 7 p.m., eight hours a day and five days a week. They socialized outside the office, but work was left on their desk: it was not allowed to follow them into the restaurant or the pub. During each new season of broadcasts, they attended the recordings and some, though not all, of the rehearsals: they observed each episode as it developed and were on hand to help if cuts or minor rewrites were required. 'Our biggest fault was overwriting,' Alan said. 'Every show had a plot, and the script would develop that... and then we were also writing what we felt was funny dialogue. Obviously we didn't want to cut that, because it could mean losing our favourite lines. But even when we were overwriting, that didn't mean the stuff was flowing easily.'

'Sometimes it did,' Ray remarked. 'But mostly we had to sweat it out, a line at a time – constantly working at each phrase, improving and changing. Even the most famous bits of dialogue, like that one everybody quotes, from "The Blood Donor"... "A pint... that's very nearly an armful!" It started off as, "A pint... that's an armful!" and then one of us said, "Nearly an armful," and the other one said, "Very nearly an armful." It's funnier, because it's more precise. And that's what we were always trying to do: make it funnier. Not that we were falling off our chairs, holding our splitting sides. Most of the time, if you came up with a great line, it was worth a nod and a smile. Not laugh-out-loud reactions. Our work was much too serious for that.'

'One of the things I'm proudest of,' Alan said, 'is that people can't tell which scripts were comparatively easy to write – the three-day produc-tions – and which ones had to be dragged out of us over three weeks, or even three months, such as the ones we had to tear out of our flesh, word by word. There's no discernible difference in the result. And that's the craftsmanship, that's what we spent years learning. All those years writing for *Star Bill* and Frankie Howerd with his guests, we were serving our apprenticeship.'

Sixty years after they first met, Galton and Simpson get together once a week to talk. They sit in Ray's front room, at either end of a long sofa beneath a wall hung with paintings of sailing ships, and drink fresh coffee. Alan insists that he only drops round because on Mondays his cleaning lady needs him out of the way – but as the afternoon becomes evening, the coffee pot is replaced by a bottle of red wine, and the conversation carries on. They talk of remakes and DVD releases – several classic scripts have been re-recorded for radio, while the Les Dawson and later *Comedy*

Playhouse series have been restored and repackaged, as well as the complete *Hancock* and *Steptoe*. They talk too of classic American radio, and current stand-up comedians, and favourite movies, writers, actors... everything except football, because Ray has a lifelong disdain for all sport, while Alan is a dedicated fan, the president of Hampton and Richmond Borough FC. And when they talk, they still finish each other's sentences, and start to chuckle before the punchline. It is a friendship that has deepened but not altered in six decades.

The story of how those seminal shows were written, and of the evolution of situation comedy, was unravelled for me in a series of long interviews at Ray's home between 2008 and 2011. I first approached Galton and Simpson to ask about Kenneth Williams – whose comedy career they had helped to launch with *Hancock's Half Hour* – for my biography of Williams, *Born Brilliant*. My first visit to the splendid Georgian house in west London set the pattern: I would walk up the steps at about noon, be greeted by three delirious dogs and their laconic owner, and stand chatting in the kitchen for a few minutes while the coffee brewed. By the time we had drunk half a mug, Alan Simpson would arrive; with him would be their manager, Tessa Le Bars, who started work at their script agency in the sixties as an office assistant and who has worked for them with dedication ever since.

More coffee would be poured, and we'd move from the kitchen table to the capacious sofas in the front room, a space so vast that there stood, quite literally in a corner, a grand piano. Ray and Alan always took the sofa facing the long windows and the garden, and would stretch out at opposite ends, with the dogs vying to occupy the space between them. Alan was economical in his movements, his hands folded on his stomach; Ray was more restless, constantly shifting his posture as he rolled thin cigarettes. Both appeared to have near-perfect recall of all the 600 scripts filed in their archive, in the stone cellar below the kitchen. During the many hours of interviews that we taped, they were in agreement about everything but the most insignificant sequence of events. They seemed to be drawing from a common well of memory.

Everything that's funniest in sitcom history had its beginning with Galton and Simpson. They didn't only invent the genre – they created the characters whose genes would be passed down through all the classic sitcoms. Ricky Gervais's pompous, hapless manager in *The Office*? That's Hancock. John Cleese's apoplectic *Fawlty Towers* hotel manager? A nephew of Hancock. The idiot Baldrick and his marginally less stupid master, Blackadder? Direct descendants of Bill and Tony. And Father Ted, trapped on a rain-blasted island with a drunk, a half-wit and his own pretensions? Harold Steptoe would have recognized him as a brother.

Galton and Simpson's characters are worthy of comparison with Dickens's comic originals. Hancock is as much an archetype as Mr Micawber, Old Man Steptoe the equal of Fagin. Galton and Simpson's language has been just as influential. They took working-class wit and let it into tens of millions of homes – coarse, direct, streaked with black comedy, revealing its profoundest meanings when it paused or stumbled over its own words.

'I went to see *The Caretaker* by Pinter when it first came out [in 1960],' Galton said, 'and I told Hancock, "You must go and see it, it's very funny." Because I started laughing, I couldn't not, and then people around me started laughing. He did go and see it and I think they had to drag him out... he was falling about on the floor laughing.'

'And then he told us,' Simpson added, 'I don't understand it... you've been writing this stuff for ages!'

1 A Bodyful of Good British Blood and Raring to Go

Everyone has their favourites. My own is the episode of *Hancock's Half Hour* where Tony clears out a drawerful of junk, and Bill Kerr ties his own fingers together as he tries to roll up a ball of string. Bill himself cites 'Sunday Afternoon At Home', where nothing happens at all. The best-loved episode of *Steptoe and Son* is, perhaps, the one where Harold and Albert cut their house in two. Hancock's most quoted line might be, 'Does Magna Carta mean nothing to you? Did she die in vain?' The abiding image of Old Man Steptoe is probably one of Albert in his tin bathtub, fishing pickled onions out of the dirty water. And then there's 'The Blood Donor', of course, and 'A Death in the Family', and so many classic moments that they threaten to overshadow the wealth of under-rated or forgotten material, especially the hundreds of episodes that were either lost or were preserved in such poor recordings that they are rarely repeated.

So here are those most famous scenes, at the outset, plucked out of chronological order. Whether these shows are 'The Best of Galton and Simpson' is a matter of opinion; they are, at least, 'The Best Loved'. The first of them will be new to almost every reader, because it hasn't been heard or reprinted since it was broadcast almost 60 years ago – but it happens to be a personal favourite of Ray and Alan's. In their first full script for their friend Frankie Howerd, they took the opportunity to send up his special guest: Richard Burton, already a Hollywood star (in *My Cousin Rachel* and *The Robe*), was then enjoying a triumphant season at the Old Vic in *Hamlet* and *The Tempest*. Burton, frustrated as Howerd steals the show, launches into a parody of every melodramatic movie cliché:

THE FRANKIE HOWERD SHOW, first series, episode one

First broadcast: Sunday 22 November 1953

RICHARD: I must have been mad to come here in the first place.
FRANKIE: Think of the honour. You'll be able to leave here tonight and
    tell everybody that you have acted with Frankie Howerd.
RICHARD: If that leaks out, I'm finished. I'll be back bashing that gong for
    J. Arthur Rank.
FRANKIE: Come on then, we can't stand here chit-chatting all night.
RICHARD: Stand away… not one step nearer, or I'll run you through. You
    filthy scum. Filthy scum, I say. Don't worry, darling, I shall protect you.
    Who is that? Ah, what is that lurking in the shadows? Set sail! We will
    make the Caribbean by nightfall. Oh darling, your eyes, your lovely,
    lovely eyes. Please, please don't leave me – I… I can't see, it's so
    dark… where are you? But soft… step back. Lower the drawbridge…
    Filthy scum… Filthy scum, I say… Fire the cannons. Now is the time
    to charge – follow me, men. You understand… it was… it was your…
FRANKIE: Show me that in the script. Go on, show me.
RICHARD: Well, if you think I'm going to stand here all night with nothing
    to say, you've got another think coming, mate.

When *Hancock's Half Hour* began in 1954, it made a household name not only of its star but also of a young character actor named Kenneth Williams: hired to play a variety of types, he quickly established himself with an ingratiating, self-satisfied whine that the writers dubbed his 'Snide' voice. When he appears in this scene, with a nasal 'good evening', the audience burst out cheering. What follows is domestic sitcom at its finest, a perfect parody of working-class family and friends bickering around a television. With this and many other episodes in the same vein, Galton and Simpson set the benchmark for situation comedy (forty years later, Caroline Aherne and Craig Cash would base a successful series, *The Royle Family*, around this scenario):

HANCOCK'S HALF HOUR, second series, episode nine

'THE TELEVISION SET'
First broadcast: Tuesday 14 June 1955

    EFFECTS: (Door bell)

TONY: *(Annoyed)* Oh who's this!
ANDREE: Go and see, you're nearest the door.

TONY: But me telly play. I don't want to miss any of it.

EFFECTS: (Door bell)

BILL: Go and answer it.
TONY: Oh all right. Perishing people. Right in the middle of a play...

EFFECTS: (Door open)

TONY: *(Upstage)* Yes?
KENNETH: *(Snide)* Good evening.
TONY: Oh, cor blimey, it's him.
KENNETH: I'm your next-door neighbour.
TONY: Well, make the most of it, I'm moving tomorrow.
KENNETH: I've just come round to borrow a pint of milk. My Tibby hasn't
    had anything to drink all day.
TONY: Well, I'm very sorry to hear it, I...
KENNETH: 'Course, he only gets fed when I come home from work, you
    see... and he does like the top off the milk...
TONY: Yes, well, look, here's a quart. Must go.
KENNETH: You haven't any fish as well, have you? Any old little bits'll do,
    he's not fussy – cod fillet, bit of plaice, anything like that. Nice cat he is.
TONY: Yes, I've seen him, digging up me rhubarb. Now look, I must go,
    it's been very nice...
KENNETH: Ooooooohhh. You've got a telly.
TONY: Yes, we're watching the play, so if you don't mind...
KENNETH: You don't mind if I step inside for a minute and watch it, do you?
TONY: Well, I...
KENNETH: Thanks. *(Downstage)* Good evening all.
ALL: *(Good evenings)*
KENNETH: I'll sit down here, shall I?
TONY: No, well, that's my seat, you see, and...
KENNETH: You can sit behind me, can't you?
TONY: Yes... but I can't see the screen... and the play...
KENNETH: Oh dear.
TONY: What?
KENNETH: You haven't bought one of *those* sets, have you?
TONY: Well, yes... and we're trying to watch the play, you see...
KENNETH: You've bought trouble there, you have.
TONY: Yes, well...
KENNETH: I'll give it three weeks and you'll need a new tube. Have you
    had any trouble with the valves yet?
TONY: No.

KENNETH: You will. They go in bunches. Cost you a fortune. *(Laughs)*

TONY: Yes, well, let's see if they last till the end of the play, shall we? I've been waiting all week to see this, and...

KENNETH: You've got it too bright, you know.

TONY: Oh cor...

KENNETH: Of course, it's nothing to do with me – but quite frankly, I think you've bought a lot of rubbish there.

SIDNEY: Oi... pimples!

KENNETH: Are you talking to me?

SIDNEY: Yes – and if you keep on, I'll probably be the last person to do so.

KENNETH: Oh.

SIDNEY: Shut your cakehole and watch the play.

'Sidney' was Sid James, of course, and Hattie Jacques' arrival completed the greatest line-up of any radio comedy. The following scene contains the seed of Tony Hancock's first cinema film, and his only big-screen success, *The Rebel* (1961). In the movie, he plays a sculptor who can only produce one work – whether his model is his landlady or a shipping tycoon's wife, the statue is always a misshapen boulder. It was no easier on radio:

HANCOCK'S HALF HOUR, fourth series, episode six

'MICHELANGELO HANCOCK'
First broadcast: Sunday 18 November 1956

TONY: Keep still, Miss Pugh. How can I carve with you flopping all over the place?

BILL: What's she doing hanging from the ceiling on a pulley?

TONY: She's a descending angel. Keep that trumpet higher. Stop flapping those wings about, you're not trying to cross the Channel.

HATTIE: Well, hurry up. I can't hold this pose much longer.

TONY: Oh, stop moaning. It was a mistake using you as a model.

BILL: Oh, I don't know. At least you don't have to alter the shape of the rock so much.

TONY: We're on the last knockings now... few more bashes on the nose here...

EFFECTS: *(Three or four more thumps of chisel)*

TONY: There we are... finished. Crank her down.

EFFECTS: *(Ratchet winch being unwound)*

HATTIE: Careful! Careful!

TONY: Cor dear, it's like unloading at the docks, isn't it?

HATTIE: Is the statue ready now?

TONY: Yes. What do you think?

HATTIE: Is that supposed to be me? It doesn't look anything like me.

TONY: Well, it's got to go up in a public place. We've got to be careful.

HATTIE: It's an insult. Look at it, it's repulsive.

TONY: Look dear, that's how I see you.

HATTIE: It's hideous. My nose isn't as flat as that.

TONY: It will be if you don't shut up.

HATTIE: Well, I think it's crude and vulgar. Look, it hasn't even got any clothes on. Why didn't you carve my clothes in?

TONY: Because I wanted a nude.

HATTIE: Why didn't you ask me then?

TONY: Oh no. Look, dear, be content in the knowledge that you have been connected with a masterpiece. When it wins the first prize you'll be proud to know it's you.

HATTIE: That? Win a prize? They wouldn't even consider it. It looks as if it's been worn away by the wind. Why not forget about it?

TONY: I don't expect you to recognize genius. In years to come this will be hailed as a typical example of the Hancock romantic period. Museums all over the world will be fighting for this. 'Course, I've started a new trend, you see. When he sees this, Henry Moore'll turn it in and go back to carving door knockers.

When they were struggling to find a good idea for a *Half Hour*, Galton and Simpson would use three good ideas instead (a productivity trick which works for only the most creative writers). In this episode, Tony browses through his diary and fantasizes about the adventures masked by his mundane jottings. When he reaches the third entry, he wanders into a daydream that became one of his most famous scenes – as a test pilot:

HANCOCK'S HALF HOUR, fourth series, episode twelve

'THE DIARY'
First broadcast: Sunday 30 December 1956

TONY: (*Reading*) July fourth. Ah. Went to fair on Common. Had threepenny go on roundabout. Little bus was full up, had to sit in aeroplane instead…

GRAMS *[recorded music]: (Hancock chords)*

    EFFECTS: *(Door opens)*

TONY: Wing Commander Hancock reporting, sir.

BILL: *(RAF top brass)* Come in, Hancock. You know why I've sent for you?

TONY: I can guess, sir. P.64?

BILL: P.64 it is. According to specifications it should top well over 2,000 miles an hour.

TONY: *(Casually)* Jolly good show.

BILL: Quite frankly, no one knows exactly what will happen when you get up there. All we know is at that speed, metal does peculiar things. Once you've gone through the heat barrier, metal can turn to jelly.

TONY: What flavour, sir?

BILL: *(Short laugh)* Same old Hancock. Does nothing frighten you?

TONY: Nothing in the air, sir.

BILL: Here is a scale model of the aircraft. As you can see, the design is quite revolutionary. No wings. Vertical take-off. You lie flat on your stomach in the cockpit. And you will notice it is approximately half the size of anything else we have.

TONY: I'm a bit worried about that, sir.

BILL: Ah, so you are human after all. What's worrying you?

TONY: Will there be enough room for my moustache?

BILL: You're a cool customer. No different now than you were when you destroyed the German Air Force in '43.

TONY: A little older, sir.

BILL: Good luck, Hancock. England is proud of you. It's in the hangar waiting for you. Everything depends on you.

TONY: If… if anything should go wrong, sir, promise me…

BILL: Anything, Hancock.

TONY: Don't abandon the project, sir. Keep 'em flying. Melt all my medals down and build another one, there are plenty of other good chaps willing to have a crack. Goodbye, sir.

BILL: Goodbye, Hancock. Sergeant James.

SIDNEY: Sir.

BILL: Show Wing Commander Hancock to the plane.

    GRAMS: *(Dam Busters March)*

SIDNEY: There she is, sir. All ready for you. We've been up all night polishing it. We put your favourite white wall tyres on for you.

TONY: Thank you, James, you're a good egg. Oh well, time to put her through her paces. I want eggs for tea when I get back, James.

SIDNEY: Oh, that I had his moral fibre.

TONY: *(Slightly off)* Ready to start engines.

    EFFECTS: (Engines start)

SIDNEY: Don't forget it's a vertical take-off, sir.

TONY: *(Off)* I know, don't bother to open the hangar door, I'll go out through the fanlight.

    EFFECTS: (Rocket taking off)

    GRAMS: (Dam Busters March)

    EFFECTS: (Jet plane travelling. Radio static)

TONY: H for Hancock calling Control Tower. Levelling out at eighteen hundred miles per hour. Everything going to plan. Fine plane, tell the designer chappie.

HATTIE: Control Tower, Control Tower to Hancock. We're worried about possible sabotage. The mechanic who was working on your aircraft is missing. Think you should come down. Land immediately, repeat, land immediately.

TONY: Nonsense, she's going beautifully. I don't know a thing about any mechanic. Taking her up to two thousand, four hundred miles an hour.

    EFFECTS: (Knocking, knuckles on glass)

TONY: Hancock to Control Tower. Something strange is happening. There is a peculiar knocking sound on the windscreen. It seems to be coming from outside the plane. Am slowing down to eighteen hundred miles an hour. Will slide cockpit open to see what's wrong.

    EFFECTS: (Cockpit cover being slid back)

KENNETH: *(Snide)* Good evening. It ain't half cold out here, can I come in?

TONY: What's that?

KENNETH: Can I come in?

TONY: There's no room, get off.

KENNETH: Oh, don't be like that. Move over, I'll sit on your lap.

TONY: Get your boot off me joystick, do you mind? Who are you?

KENNETH: I'm the mechanic. I was working on the tail when you took off. Frightened the life out of me. I mean, I wasn't expecting it. I was sitting there, singing happily to myself, and the next minute, whoosh... I was up here.

TONY: Sit still, I can't control the plane with you jumping about.

KENNETH: I'm only trying to get comfortable. All these knobs and levers here, sticking in me. What's this one?

TONY: Don't touch it.

EFFECTS: (Ejector seat going off – suggest sound of firework rocket)

KENNETH: Oooh, it's the ejector seat. Come back, where are you?

TONY: *(Off)* I'm out here, sitting on the tail.

KENNETH: Oh no, stop messing about. No, come back in. It's no use sitting out there sulking. I can't drive the thing.

TONY: *(Off)* Well, go into a dive, so I can slide down.

KENNETH: All right, I'll try this lever.

EFFECTS: (Ejector seat again)

KENNETH: Hallo. You might have told me there was another ejector seat.

TONY: All right, we're both out here, now what do we do?

KENNETH: Oooh look, we're going up.

TONY: Well, what do you expect when we're both sitting on the tail?

KENNETH: Isn't life funny? In the papers this morning, the stars said this was my lucky day.

TONY: If we keep going up at this rate, you'll be able to tell them they're wrong.

KENNETH: Well come on, we've had a little skylark, and a little giggle, let's go down now.

TONY: How can we go down? Look, we're finished, the engine's falling off.

KENNETH: That's all right, they've got plenty more down there.

TONY: We want one up here. We're going into a dive. We're out of control. We can't get back to the cabin. Give me a piece of string.

KENNETH: Oooh, I'm scared. Oooh.

TONY: Don't panic, man. This is the RAF. Where's that stiff upper lip?

KENNETH: Just above this loose, flabby chin.

TONY: Give me that string, I'll get you down safely.

GRAMS: (Link)

BILL: Well, Hancock, you've done it again. Saved the plane. How did you manage it? Sitting on the tail like that?

TONY: Quite simple. I took a piece of string, lasso'ed the controls, and steered it home. Lucky I was a cox at Oxford, eh, sir?

BILL: Brilliant work, Hancock. You've won another medal. You're a brave man, Hancock. You will go down in history as the most courageous and decorated pilot in the RAF.

GRAMS: (Hancock chords)

TONY: *(Reading from diary)* July the fifth. Last time I go on the roundabouts. Been in bed all day with dizzy spells. *(Stops reading)* No, well, it wasn't my fault, that bloke cranking the handle got a bit worked up. I remember Mother walking round holding my hand had a job keeping up with me.

Asked to name his favourite of the *Half Hours*, Bill Kerr does not hesitate: 'Well, of course! "Sunday Afternoon". That's a lot of people's favourite. If you can imagine the four of us, with Hattie, bored to death – Sunday was the most boring bloody day in the world. And Alan and Ray captured that to the *n*th degree. There was hardly anything said – we just sat around, and Tony sighing. Once every year I'll put that in the car radio and listen to it. And I've got to stop myself from crashing into a wall, I'm laughing so much.'

HANCOCK'S HALF HOUR, fifth series, episode fourteen

'SUNDAY AFTERNOON AT HOME'
First broadcast: Tuesday 22 April 1958

TONY: Oh dear. Oh dear oh dear. Cor dear me. Stone me, what a life. What's the time?

BILL: Two o'clock.

TONY: Is that all? Cor dear, oh dear. Oh dear me. I don't know. *(Yawns)* Oh, I'm fed up.

SIDNEY: Oi.

TONY: What?

SIDNEY: Why don't you shut up moaning and let me get on with the paper?

TONY: Well, I'm fed up.

SIDNEY: So you just said.

TONY: Well, so I am.

SIDNEY: Look, so am I fed up, and so is Bill fed up, we're all fed up, so shut up moaning and make the best of it.

TONY: Are you sure it's only two o'clock?

BILL: No, it's, er… one minute past two now.

TONY: One minute past two. Doesn't the time drag? Oooh, I do hate Sundays. I'll be glad when it's over. It drives me up the wall, just sitting here looking at you lot. Every Sunday it's the same. Nowhere to go, nothing to do. Just sit here waiting for the next lot of grub to come up. There must be something we can do. Bill, haven't you got any bright ideas?

BILL: No.

TONY: It was a waste of time asking, really, wasn't it? *(PAUSE) (Yawns)* Oh, I'm fed up.

HATTIE: Why don't you men go out for a walk while I wash up the dishes?

TONY: *(Mimics her)* Why don't you men go for a walk? Why don't *you* go for a walk? Go on, hoppit. It'll be one less to look at all day. *(PAUSE)* Have you finished with that paper yet?

SIDNEY: No.

TONY: Well hurry up, I haven't seen it yet. I want to know what my stars say.

SIDNEY: What are you?

TONY: June the twenty-first.

SIDNEY: What sign is that?

HATTIE: The crab.

TONY: And what of it?

SIDNEY: It says, 'Today looks like being a very exciting day.'

TONY: Well, good luck to *him*. Who is he? Arnold the gipsy. Look at him, spotted handkerchief round his head, great cartwheel earrings. A right fake if ever I saw one. The nearest he's ever been to a caravan was at the motor show.

SIDNEY: Why don't you turn it in?

ALL: *(PAUSE) (A few clearing of throats, sighs, etc)*

HATTIE: Oh look, it's started raining.

TONY: That's all we wanted. You watch, it'll go dark in a minute and we'll have to switch the lights on. I think I'll go to bed.

HATTIE: You've only been up an hour.

TONY: That's by the way and nothing to do with it. I might just as well be in bed – there's nothing else to do. I wish I hadn't got up now. Your dinner wasn't worth getting up for, I'll tell you that for a start.

HATTIE: I don't know, I ate all mine.

TONY: That's neither here nor there. You also ate Bill's, Sid's and mine. I thought my mother was a bad cook, but at least her gravy used to move about. Yours just sort of lies there and sets.

HATTIE: That's the goodness in it.

TONY: That's the half a pound of flour you put in it.

...

SIDNEY: Why don't you sit down and relax? It's a day of rest. Have a kip or something, anything, but do me a favour and shut up.

TONY: Oh dear. What a life. It's Sunday, I've had a rotten dinner, it's raining and I've got nothing to do.

HATTIE: There's plenty of odd jobs you can do around the house.

TONY: Oh shut up. It's a day of rest. I'm not mending your bed again.

SIDNEY: *(Wearily)* Read the paper, will you?

TONY: Well… it makes you sick. I hate Sundays.

SIDNEY: So do I, but there's one a week, there always has been, and there's nothing we can do about it.

TONY: It's not like this on the Continent, it's their big day over there. All the cafés open, football matches, race meetings, everybody's gay. Not over here though. Everything's shut up.

SIDNEY: I wish you would.

…

(EFFECTS: Rustle of newspaper. Little bit of singing from Tony which tails off and dies away into an embarrassed silence.)

(PAUSE)

TONY: Have you noticed when you look at that wallpaper long enough, you can see faces in it?

BILL: Honest?

TONY: Yes, yes, you can, you can see faces after a time. It's the pattern, it makes little faces. There's a lovely one of an old man with a pipe.

BILL: Where?

TONY: Come over here. Look at it from where I'm sitting. Screw your eyes up, now stare hard, squint a bit, that's it, now concentrate on that bit by the serving hatch. See it?

BILL: No.

TONY: Yes, look, it's there, plain as eggs. Look, see, look along me finger. There's his nose, that's his pipe, and there's his hat. See it?

BILL: No.

TONY: *(Gets a bit annoyed)* Of course you can see it. There's dozens of them all over the room. Look, there's Churchill over there, Charlie Chaplin over the mantelpiece, concentrate, squint, man, squint… don't shut them… can't you see them?

BILL: No.

TONY: Oh, go and sit down. You wait till you want me to see anything.

When the idea of this anthology was first discussed, Alan and Ray immediately suggested this extract from one of the last radio *Half Hours*. 'We didn't usually laugh out loud at what we were writing,' Ray said, 'but with the tortoise we couldn't help it. Just the idea of Tony peering inside this shell, and there's nothing there…'

HANCOCK'S HALF HOUR, sixth series, episode nine

'SID'S MYSTERY COACH TOURS'
First broadcast: Tuesday 24 November 1959

SIDNEY: Hallo Hancock. I haven't seen you for days. How's the tortoise I sold you?

TONY: It hasn't moved since I put it in the garden.

SIDNEY: Hasn't moved?

TONY: Not a step. I haven't even seen it yet. I haven't seen its head or its legs. I picked it up and shook it this morning, there's nothing in there.

SIDNEY: Of course there's something in there.

TONY: I don't care about something in there, is there a tortoise in there?

SIDNEY: Well, there should be.

TONY: Well, I don't think there is. I looked in through the front and I could see right out through his leg holes.

SIDNEY: Well, perhaps he was curled up.

TONY: They don't curl up.

SIDNEY: Well, give him a chance, he's only a baby, he's still growing. He hasn't filled the shell up yet.

TONY: The shell grows with them. There's nothing in it. I've been poking sticks in through every hole and there's nothing in there.

SIDNEY: Oh well, if you've been doing that, that explains it. He must have got a bit niggly. He probably lifted his shell up and ran for it.

TONY: Well, I'm not satisfied, I want my money back.

SIDNEY: No, I'm sorry, I never return money, you ought to know that.

TONY: Well, give me another one then. And no cheating. I want one with a head and four legs poking out.

SIDNEY: You're too late, mate. I'm not in the tortoise trade any more. They live too long. There's no replacement trade worth talking about.

BILL: Why don't you sell old ones?

TONY: Why don't you sell old ones? What a poltroon this man is. How can you tell how old a tortoise is?

BILL: You count the rings on its back.

TONY: That's a tree.

BILL: Oh. You count its teeth?

TONY: That's horses.

BILL: Well, you can't be right all the time.

TONY: No, no, you're quite right, William. I wish I hadn't taken him in…
Look, I wish to speak to Sidney. You amuse yourself. Stand there and
count the nails up the side of the shed.
BILL: One, two, three, four…
TONY: No, no, to yourself, eh? Quietly. That's a good lad.

Tony Hancock's brother, Roger, believed the star was eventually
destroyed by his obsessive self-analysis, a constant examination of his
psyche for which he was not mentally equipped nor sufficiently well
educated: 'Tony was an intelligent man, but he was not an intellectual.'
Galton and Simpson saw the same pretentions in Hancock and frequently
mocked them – most lethally in this episode, which many fans regard as
the best of them all. It co-starred Warren Mitchell as Gregory, and Fenella
Fielding as Greta: 'I was very much in awe of Tony Hancock,' she said. 'I
could hardly speak to him, I was so shy. So I didn't enjoy doing it very
much. But he hardly spoke to me – he just got on with it.'

'The Poetry Society' was remarkable for its construction. It takes place
in 'real time', a half-hour slice of Hancock's life, without segues or
musical links:

HANCOCK'S HALF HOUR, sixth series, episode eleven

'THE BEATNIKS' (also known as 'THE POETRY SOCIETY')
First broadcast: Tuesday 8 December 1959

SIDNEY: Oh blimey, I've seen some birds but… look at it. All lank hair and
wooden beads. How do you do, pleased to make your acquaintance.
BILL: Hiya doll, how about you and me sloping off down the pub? There's
a piano down there, it's talent night tonight in the saloon bar… are
you musical?
GRETA: *(Low and husky)* I only listen to Bartok and Weber.
BILL: Well, that's all right, sing a couple of their songs, the lads won't
mind.
GRETA: What an intriguing little savage you are.
TONY: Bill, come away… I must apologize, Greta, he's not one of us, he's
very suburban in his musical taste… he doesn't appreciate the finer
points of classical music like we Gilbert and Sullivan fans. By the way,
dear, I know it's against all group ethics to consider such things
important, but I must say I like your turnout tonight.
GRETA: Oh thank you, do you like it?
TONY: Oh yes, very individual. The elongated eyebrows touching the

earholes certainly gets me going, I might tell you. And the blue
lipstick sets it off marvellously. I think without a doubt you are the
weirdest looking one here tonight.

GRETA: Oh, that's very kind of you, I do my best.

GREGORY: Well, shall we start? We have many important new works to
read.

TONY: By all means... I'll get some chairs.

GREGORY: That won't be necessary. We don't use chairs – chairs are a
symbol of unproductive work, the furnishings of a decadent society.

TONY: Of course, of course, I hadn't realized... Bill, take the chairs out
and burn them... horrible suburban bric-a-brac. Well then, what do
we do, stand around?

GREGORY: My dear fellow, haven't you read your handbook? It definitely
states, at cultural meetings such as poetry reading, the members
shall adopt postures in keeping with the intellect of the individual
without sacrificing the mood of the work. We are thus irrevocably
united as a group in relation to the poem being read.

TONY: I see. Well, you start, and I'll sort of stand loosely so I can sort of
slide into something as it comes over me.

GREGORY: We will commence with a work by myself. I have entitled it
'Tin-can'.

TONY: Tin-can. Hmm... let's see. I think I'll lean up against the fireplace
with one arm up suggesting the lid's been opened.

GREGORY: Quiet please, I can't get in the mood with talking going on.
Right, 'Tin-can' by Gregory.

> Splish, splash, splonk,
> Wooden shoes, red socks,
> Coffins, tombstones and tranquillizers.

TONY: Very good, very significant that is.

GREGORY: I hadn't finished, had I?

TONY: Oh, I'm very sorry.

GREGORY:

> Aspirins and driving tests,
> Jet planes and skeletons,
> Frog singing to egg timer,
> Calendars and candle, upside-down,
> Plastic apples on coconut palms,
> Splish, splash, splonk.

TONY: Is that it?

GREGORY: Yes, that is it.

TONY: Marvellous, I wish I could write like that. Are you all right? By Jove, you look washed out.

GREGORY: It's just the emotional strain of reading it. The vibrations sap my energy.

TONY: Yes, I know how it is. It's a pity we burnt the chairs, we could have had a sit-down.

GREGORY: Did you like the poem?

TONY: Sensational. What an emotional experience. I haven't heard anything like that since 'The Road to Mandalay'. Who's next?

SIDNEY: Oh no, we haven't got another one… Let's get the booze out.

TONY: Do you mind? If you can't appreciate the delicacy of the works, you might at least have the courtesy to keep your cakehole closed. Bill, what are you doing?

BILL: I've adopted a pose. In readiness for the next one.

TONY: Very funny, now come out of the sideboard.

…

BILL: I've just written a poem. Can I read it?

TONY: I somehow don't think the sort of poems you write will be suitable for this gathering. We are not interested in young ladies from various parts of the country.

BILL: No, no, I've written an abstract poem.

TONY: Don't be ridiculous, one has to be sympathetic with the symbolism of existence to turn out that sort of stuff. Get back in the sideboard.

GRETA: No, let's hear what the little savage has written. It might provide some light relief after the intensity of the last two offerings.

TONY: Oh, very well, make it quick and don't take the mickey.

BILL: Thank you. Ahem. 'Incandescent', by William.

> *Hic, haec, hoc.*
> *Rinky tinky on purple grass,*
> *Shafts of light, hob-nailed boots*
> *Tramping down the bamboo*
> *That grows upwards, downwards, sideways,*
> *Into the concrete cosmos.*
> *Life is mauve, I am orange.*
> *Hic, haec, hoc.*

TONY: What a load of rubbish. You buffoon. Rinky tinky on purple grass. What does that mean? You're orange and life is mauve. I have never heard such unadulterated codswallop in my life. Get back in the sideboard this minute.

GREGORY: Wait! How dare you speak to a genius like that?

TONY: I beg your pardon?

GREGORY: A genius.

TONY: What, him? A genius? He doesn't know how to spell it.

GREGORY: That was without a doubt the most inspired, stimulating piece of poetry I have ever heard. Transcending anything anyone in this group has ever created. I'll never be able to write such masterpieces as that.

TONY: Yes, but he's a dolt. He can't do anything.

GREGORY: Can't do anything! In a few brilliantly conceived lines he has summed up the human capacity for suffering and its struggle for survival.

TONY: Oh come now, Gregory… surely it was empty, devoid of any symbolism… you made a mistake, he fooled you for a moment – analyse it, bamboo, hob-nailed boots… well, it doesn't mean anything to me. My aura of perception didn't even wobble. Greta, what did you think?

GRETA: It was like a revelation. It transported me to another plane. For the first time I saw the fifth dimension, like a golden flash cleaving the skies… I was transported to the heights of delirium.

TONY: See what you've done now, she's off. Why don't you keep quiet when there's ladies present?

GREGORY: Life is mauve, I am orange… it says everything. I suggest we call it 'The Last Poem'… there's nothing left to write about now…

TONY: Don't make any hasty decisions. Listen to mine. A little gem, this is. Taken me four years to complete, this has. All my soul has been poured into this little number. Listen.

Life is cream, I am puce…

GREGORY: Maudlin sentimental rubbish.

TONY: I object! You haven't given me a fair hearing. The rest of it is a knockout. Revelations you've never dreamt of, unfolding before your eyes. Cop this.

Steel rods of reason through my head.
Salmon jumping, where jump I?
Camels on fire, and spotted clouds,

Striped horses prance the meadow, wild,
And rush on to drink at life's
Fountains deep. Life is cream, I am puce.
Ching, chang, chollah.

GREGORY: How dare you revile the group with such shallow, trivial
    nonsense?

…

SIDNEY: I shall now read an abstract poem I've just written. 'Limbo', by
    Sidney.
TONY: Oh, this is getting farcical.
GREGORY: Quiet please, Sidney's going to read to us.
SIDNEY: 'Limbo', by Sidney.

Mauve world, green me,
Black him, purple her,
Yellow us, pink you.

GRETA: Beautiful, beautiful.
SIDNEY:

Lead pipes, fortune made,
Six to four, came in second,
Green country, blue Harringay and White City.
Hic, haec, hoc.

GREGORY: I can't take any more… all this sensuous excitement in one
    evening. What an experience to hear such beauty, such translucent
    symbolism. How you must know life, Sidney.
SIDNEY: Oh I do, boy!
GRETA: How you must have suffered to produce work like that.
SIDNEY: Suffered, I've been in agony sometimes.
GRETA: Sidney, Sidney, I feel the vibrations between us growing stronger
    and stronger, some red, some yellow…
SIDNEY: Yeah, all right love, we'll sort them out later, eh?

This speech to the jury, from Hancock's BBC television series, has
become one of the most quoted passages in the Galton and Simpson
canon:

HANCOCK'S HALF HOUR (TV), fifth series, episode two

'TWELVE ANGRY MEN'
First broadcast: Friday 16 October 1959

TONY: *(Adopts a barrister pose for his final address)* I will not go
through the facts of this case again, save to suggest to you that
there is some element of doubt as to this boy's guilt. As
Shakespeare said in *The Merchant of Vienna*, when Portion accused
Shylock Holmes of pinching a pound of meat… 'The quality of
mercy is not strained… it droppeth as the gentle rain from heaven…
(points up) upon the place beneath… *(flutters his hand down to the
ground).'* Take the Thomas who was sent to Coventry for looking
through a keyhole at Lady Godiva. Can anybody prove he was
looking at her? Can anybody prove it was he who shouted out at
her, 'Get your hair cut'? Of course not. Sheer supposition. Does
Magna Carta mean nothing to you? Did she die in vain, that brave
Hungarian peasant girl who forced King John to sign the pledge at
Runnymede and closed all the boozers at half past ten? Is all this
forgotten? No. My friends, it is not John Harrison Peabody who is on
trial here today but the fair name of British justice. I ask you to send
that poor boy back to the loving arms of his poor white-haired old
mother… a free man. I thank you.

Long before their release on video, and later as part of the Hancock DVD
boxed set, 'The Radio Ham' and 'The Blood Donor' were available on
LP: this has helped to make them the best known of all Ray and Alan's
work. And they are quintessential Hancock: in both stories, he is
desperate for something to give his life meaning, but trapped by his own
failings. He spends most of 'The Radio Ham' trying, unsuccessfully, to
take down an emergency message on his new short-wave radio set. His
pencil breaks, he loses the signal, his neighbours hammer on the door…
as the catalogue of interruptions grows, there is a sense that Galton and
Simpson's ingenuity is never-ending. They are playing with the character,
thwarting him whenever he moves, as if he is a piece on a board to be
flicked from one side to the other:

HANCOCK, first series, episode three

'THE RADIO HAM'
First broadcast: Friday 9 June 1961

TONY: *(Holding up two large radio set valves)* Aha, you little beauties. We'll soon have you fixed in. We'll soon have the watts throbbing through you, and your filaments glowing red hot, carrying the thoughts and words of mankind to the four corners of the Earth. Oh, there's nothing like a DS 19/87B. Look at you. A triumph of technological engineering. A work of art. They can keep their Sistine Chapels, give me the inside of a wireless set any day.

...

TONY: This is G.L.K. London calling HB 24 D Tokyo area. G.L.K. London calling HB 24 D Tokyo. Come in, Tokyo.

(He adjusts some dials)

TONY: Hallo, hallo, HB 24 D Tokyo. Yoki? How are you? No, no, no, how… are… you. No… how… are… you. How are you. No, no… how are you. *(Tries Japanese accent)* How are you. This is Rondon GLK, how getting are you? Oh never mind, how's the weather out there? No, no, what is the weather like? No, no, is it raining? Raining. Pitter patter. Water. Wet. Ugh, nasty. Hallo, hallo. Yes, listening, go ahead. Sorry, what was that? Yes I can hear, no understand. I… cannot… understand. No comprendi. Say it slowly. Slowly. Not so fast. No, no, I can't understand. Can you put it another way? Put it another way. Say it differently. No, in English. Fool. Slowly now. Slowly. It… is… are… raining… not. Oh good, good. Very good. It is are raining not here also. Yes. Cor, this is hard work. Well, what have you been getting up to then? Getting up to. No, no, not when are you getting up. Getting up to. What have been doing. Doing. You. What have you been doing. What… have… you… doing… been. No, no, no, no, what… have… what time is it over there? Time. O'clock. Big hand. Little hand… Whereabouts? I know it's not raining, you told me. Start again. Here in London ten o'clock, what time in Tokyo? What time… this is G.L.K. London signing off. Goodbye Tokyo, it's been very nice, same time Monday. Eh? Oh yes, Sayonara.

(He twists a dial)

TONY: It's marvellous to be able to converse with people all over the world. People different to yourself, with something new to say, it broadens your outlook, increases your knowledge of things. I bet there's not many people round here who know it's not raining in Tokyo. I suppose I must lead what the social workers call a full life. The world is my oyster... I can dip in and have a basinful anywhere I fancy. Oooh, these headphones don't half make your ears hot.

(He takes off his headphones which have great padded earpieces)

TONY: *(Fingers his ear tenderly)* Dear oh dear, like two braised lamb chops under there, they are.

...

TONY: I think a quick glass of cold milk before we go back on the air.

(Picks up a bottle of milk, looks at the foil cap on it. There is about an inch missing off the top of the milk.)

TONY: Hallo, the blue tits have been at the top of the milk again. Look at my gold top, pecked to ribbons it is. They must have beaks like pneumatic drills, some of them. I will not have great feathered heads stuck in my milk bottles guzzling the cream. It's that landlady. It's her who encourages them round here. Her and her coconut shells and bits of bacon rind hanging all over the place.

(He catches sight of a loaf of bread. It has been nibbled away in bits. He picks it up.)

TONY: They've been at my farmhouse as well. Look at it, great feetmarks all over it. It's not good enough. Birds have no right to be in towns. Why don't they stay in the country where they belong? Wait till they perch on my aerial with a lump of bread in their mouth. I'll shove a few hundred volts through it, that'll make their feet tingle.

...

(He carries on turning the dial. A quick mélange of languages, symphony orchestra, singing and atmospherics.)

YACHTSMAN: *(Faintly, getting stronger then fading away again against a background of atmospherics)* Mayday. Mayday. Mayday.
TONY: Mayday. What's he talking about? That was three weeks ago. It's nearly June.
YACHTSMAN: Mayday. Mayday. Mayday.
TONY: Mayday. That's a code word. *(Picks up his book)* It's a code name for a typhoon, isn't it? No, that's girls' names. Alice, Gloria, Elsie... Mayday, Mayday... it rings a bell. Where are we? *(He is flicking through the manual)* Mayday. 'emergency distress signal. Help me.' *(He puts the

book down dramatically and feverishly gets a line on the signal) Hallo
Mayday… Hallo Mayday… I am receiving you. Come in Mayday.
YACHTSMAN: *(Over crackle)* Thank God you've answered. I've been
calling for six hours, I thought I'd never reach anybody.
TONY: Where are you, where are you located?
YACHTSMAN: Listen carefully, I cannot keep on the air much longer, my
batteries are almost finished. My radio is damaged and I can only
transmit on this one wavelength.
TONY: I understand, go ahead.
YACHTSMAN: Please keep tuned in on this waveband. You are my only
contact with the outside world.

(TONY draws himself up with pride)

TONY: At last. My bread pudding days are over.
YACHTSMAN: I beg your pardon.
TONY: Nothing, carry on, I am waiting your instructions.
YACHTSMAN: Listen carefully. I am the Motor Yacht *Billet Doux*, out of
Sierra Leone. I am holed beneath the waterline and am shipping
water fast. I have run out of fuel and am drifting in the Atlantic Ocean
three hundred miles off the African coast. I can only keep afloat for
another two or three hours. It is imperative you radio for help.
TONY: Roger. Will do. What is your exact position?
YACHTSMAN: My position is…
TONY: Hang on, I haven't got a pencil. Hold on, don't sink yet, I've got
one somewhere. I was writing the Flying Doctor's wavelength down
just now… hang on… ah, here it is. Go ahead.
YACHTSMAN: My position is Longitude…

(TONY presses on the pencil and breaks it)

TONY: Hang on, I've broken it.
YACHTSMAN: For heaven's sake hurry, man, this radio can't last much
longer.
TONY: Wait a minute, I've got another somewhere, you can never find
things when you want them, can you? *(He is looking for his pencil)*
What's the weather like out there?
YACHTSMAN: Oh for heaven's sake.
TONY: It's not raining in Tokyo. *(He finds pencil)*
YACHTSMAN: Will you please hurry up, my battery is going fast. My
position is Longitude…

(The voice fades and atmospherics drown it. Then we hear…)

ACTOR: If he should find us here, Desdemona, what shall we do…
ACTRESS: Tell him the truth, Clive. We have nothing to be ashamed of. We love each other.
TONY: Oh for crying out loud.

(He bangs the set. Atmospherics drown the play.)

TONY: Hallo, hallo, Mayday. Are you still there, Mayday?
JAPANESE VOICE: How it is weather in San Francisco, it is are raining not here in Tokyo.
TONY: Will you get off the air, you Oriental fool! I've got a bloke here somewhere drifting helplessly with a great hole in his boat. Please keep this wavelength clear. Emergency. Mayday. Mayday. Mayday.
AUSTRALIAN VOICE: Come in Mayday. This is Sydney Australia, am receiving you loud and clear, what's wrong?
TONY: Not me, I've got a mayday waiting for me to help him.
AUSTRALIAN VOICE: You lucky blighter, I've never had a mayday since I started. Where is he?
TONY: You keep out of this, he's mine. Anyway, I don't know, I've lost him.

(He turns the dial slowly, trying to pinpoint the emergency call)

TONY: *(While turning)* Hallo Mayday… are you receiving me… come in Mayday… *(Victor Sylvester music)* Get off. Come in Mayday… Hallo Mayday, where have you gone? Oh, he's probably drifting about. *(Fiddles with the dial)* Why can't he chuck his anchor overboard, how does he expect me to find him if he keeps moving about?
YACHTSMAN: *(Over crackle)* … three degrees west. Did you get that?
TONY: Get what?
YACHTSMAN: My position, I just gave it to you.
TONY: No, no, I lost you, would you mind repeating it?
YACHTSMAN: Oh, of all the incompetent… Is there anyone else there? This is an emergency.
TONY: No there isn't anybody else here, I'm quite capable of dealing with it.
YACHTSMAN: Well, pull yourself together for heaven's sake.
TONY: Now listen, my good man, don't you take that attitude with me. I'm doing my best. It's not my fault you've got a hole in your boat, you should learn to steer it better, shouldn't you… Now… give me your position again and don't let's have so much of it.
YACHTSMAN: I'm sorry. Here is my position.

(Banging on the door)

TONY: Hang on, there's somebody at the door.

...

TONY: Hallo Mayday... are you still there, Mayday... come in Mayday.
YACHTSMAN: Hallo, is that you? This is Mayday.
TONY: Thank heavens you're still alive.
YACHTSMAN: Now listen. This might be my last chance of speaking to you. Here is my position. Longitude ten degrees, thirty-three minutes west, latitude...

(The radio goes dead and the lights go out)

TONY: Oh no.

(He gets up from the set. Takes out some change. Sorts through it. Goes out into the corridor. Puts the shilling in the meter. The lights and the radio come back on. TONY sits at the radio again.)

YACHTSMAN: ... south-southeast by north-northwest. Did you get that?
TONY: No.
YACHTSMAN: Why not?
TONY: I had to go out and get a shilling for the meter.
YACHTSMAN: You're doing this on purpose. You want me to drown. You're mad.
TONY: Now calm down, pull yourself together. How can you expect me to help you if you panic? Save your strength, you might be days out there yet. Now... clearly and concisely... give me your position.
YACHTSMAN: Right.
TONY: Yes.
YACHTSMAN: Longitude ten degrees, thirty-two minutes west, latitude five degrees, twenty-two minutes south. Will you repeat that?

(TONY reads from the pad)

TONY: Latitude ten degrees...
YACHTSMAN: No, no, longitude ten degrees.
TONY: Oh. Longitude ten degrees, twenty-two minutes west.
YACHTSMAN: No, no, thirty-two minutes west.
TONY: No, you're wrong there.
YACHTSMAN: Look, I know where I am. I've got the compass in front of me.
TONY: You said twenty-two degrees west.
YACHTSMAN: No, no, that was the latitude, five degrees twenty-two minutes south.

TONY: No, no, thirty-two minutes south. I've got it down on my pad. Thirty-two minutes south.

YACHTSMAN: I didn't say that.

TONY: You did. No, wait a minute, I tell a lie... twenty-two degrees south, you're right. Yes, I can't read my own writing, it's a game, isn't it?

YACHTSMAN: Look, let's start again.

TONY: Yes, right.

YACHTSMAN: Longitude ten degrees thirty-two minutes west.

TONY: Longitude ten degrees thirty-two minutes west.

YACHTSMAN: Correct.

TONY: Now we're getting somewhere, we'll have you out of this in no time at all. Carry on.

YACHTSMAN: Latitude five degrees...

(A valve on top of the set blows up in a flash and a cloud of smoke. Then another one goes the same. PAUSE. Then a third one goes. A LONGER PAUSE. Then a couple of bits fall off. TONY sits there and watches all this.)

TONY: *(PAUSE)* I wonder if a longitude without a latitude is any good.

The following episode, 'The Blood Donor', is one that, more than anything created by any other comedy writer, defines sitcom. Filmed a few days after Tony Hancock suffered concussion in a car accident, it is not his most relaxed performance – he had been relying on cue cards throughout the series, and for this show was unable to remember a word of dialogue. Throughout the performance, his eyes are darting around, looking for the next line. In a strange way, this enhances his acting: he is in a hospital, about to give blood for the first time, and he looks terrified, unable even to meet the nurse's eye. The script, in any case, is indestructibly sublime: 'One of our better ones,' Alan and Ray agreed:

HANCOCK, first series, episode five

'THE BLOOD DONOR'
First broadcast: Friday 23 June 1961

(Shot of the outside of a large London hospital. Dissolve to a door reading 'Blood Donor Dept'. Dissolve into the room. There are several donors awaiting attention. A nurse is sitting at a reception desk. At the end of the room are some screens behind which the

blood donations are taken. The waiting donors are reading
magazines, etc. TONY enters. Goes up to the reception desk.)

NURSE: Good afternoon, sir.

TONY: Good afternoon. I have come in answer to your advert on the wall next to the Eagle Laundry in Pelham Road.

NURSE: An advert. Pelham Road.

TONY: Yes. Your poster. You must have seen it. There's a nurse pointing at you, a Red Cross lady actually, I believe, with a moustache and a beard. Pencilled in, of course. You must know it, it's one of yours – next to Hands Off Cuba, just above the cricket stumps. It says, 'Your blood can save a life.'

NURSE: Oh, I see – you wish to become a blood donor.

TONY: I certainly do. I've been thinking about this for a long time. Something for the benefit of the country as a whole. What should it be? I thought. Become a blood donor or join the Young Conservatives? But as I'm not looking for a wife and I can't play table tennis, here I am. A bodyful of good British blood and raring to go.

NURSE: Yes, quite. Well now, if you'd take a seat, I'll just take a few particulars.

(TONY sits down opposite her. She takes a form and a pen.)

NURSE: Can I have your name?

TONY: Hancock. Anthony Hancock. Twice candidate for the county council elections, defeated; Hon Sec British Legion, Earl's Court Branch; treasurer of the darts team and the outings committee.

NURSE: I only want the name…

TONY: We're going to Margate this year… by boat. If there are any young nurses like yourself who would care to join us, we would be more than happy to accommodate you.

NURSE: Thank you, I'll bear it in mind. Date of birth?

TONY: Er, yes. Shall we say the twelfth of May, nineteen er… I always remember the twelfth of May, it was Coronation Day, you know, 1936.

NURSE: You're only twenty-five?

TONY: No, no, the Coronation was in 1936, I was born a little before that in er, nineteen er… *(makes a quick mental calculation)* Is all this really necessary?

NURSE: I'm afraid so. The twelfth of May…

TONY: Yes. I always remember that, the Coronation, we all got a day off at our school, did you? And we got a cup and saucer in a box and a bar of soap. Very good, I've still got that, and a spoon for the Silver Jubilee and a biscuit tin with their pictures on...

NURSE: How old are you?

TONY: *(Disgruntled)* Thirty-five.

NURSE: Thank you. Nationality.

TONY: You've got nothing to worry about there. It's the blood you're thinking about, isn't it? British. British. Undiluted for twelve generations. One hundred per cent Anglo-Saxon, with perhaps just a dash of the Viking, but nothing else has crept in. No, anybody who gets any of this will have nothing to complain about. There's aristocracy in there, you know. You want to watch who you're giving it to. It's like motor oil, it doesn't mix, if you get my meaning.

NURSE: Mr Hancock, when a blood transfusion is being given, the family background is of no consequence.

TONY: Oh come now, surely you don't expect me to believe that. I mean, after all, east is east, really...

NURSE: *(Slightly needled)* Mr Hancock, blood is blood the world over. It is classified by groups, not accidents of birth.

TONY: I did not come here for a lecture on Communism, young lady.

NURSE: I happen to be a Conservative.

TONY: Then kindly behave like one, madam.

NURSE: Have you had any of these diseases?

(She hands him a printed list. TONY reads it. He tries to remember a couple. Looks uncomfortable at another one. Looks completely puzzled at another one.)

TONY: *(Hands the list back)* No I haven't. Especially that one. I told you before, you have nothing to fear from me. I am perfectly healthy.

NURSE: Just one more thing. Have you given any blood before?

TONY: Given, no. Spilt, yes. Yes, there's a good few drops lying about on the battlefields of Europe. Are you familiar with the Ardennes? I well remember Von Runstedt's last push. Tiger Harrison and myself, being in a forward position, were cut off behind enemy lines. 'Captain Harrison,' I said. 'Yes sir,' he said. 'Jerry's overlooked us,' I said, 'where shall we head for?' 'Berlin,' he said. 'Right,' I said, 'last one in the Reichstag is a cissy.' So we set off... got there three days before the Russians...

NURSE: You've never been a blood donor before.

TONY: No. So there we were, surrounded by storm troopers. 'Kamerad, Kamerad,' they said...

NURSE: *(Has not taken any notice. Hands him a card.)* If you will just sit over there with the others, Doctor will call you when he's ready.

TONY: Thank you. So we started rounding them up and…

(She gets up, puts some papers under her arm and leaves him)

TONY: Oh.

(He makes his way over to where the other donors are waiting their turn and sits down between two of them. He looks at the people round him.)

TONY: Well… it's a grand job we're all doing. *(PAUSE)* Yes, I think we can all be very proud of ourselves. *(PAUSE)* Some people, all they do is take, take, take out of life, never put anything back. Well, that's not my way of living, never has been. You're only entitled to take out of life what you are prepared to put into it. Do you get a badge for doing this?

MAN: No, I don't think so.

TONY: Pity. We should have something for people to pick us out by.

MAN: It's not really important, is it? As long as we give the blood and help someone, that's the main thing.

TONY: Oh well, quite, quite. As long as they get their corpuscles, quite. That's reward in itself, I agree, no names no pack drill, quite… I just think we ought to get a badge as well. I mean, nothing grand, a little enamelled thing, a little motto, that's all, nothing pretentious… he gaveth for others so that others may live. I mean, we are do-gooders, we should get something for it.

MAN: What do you want, money?

TONY: Don't be vulgar. I'm a great believer in charity. Help others, that's my motto. I contribute to every flag day that's going. The lapels of my suits are always the first thing to go. Covered in holes they are. Yes, I always give what I can. *(Brings out his diary)* Here, you look at this, it's all in my diary. Congo relief, two and six. Self-denial week, one and eight. Lifeboat day, sixpence. Arab refugees, one and two, it's all down here… yes, yes… I do what I can. My conscience is clear. When I'm finally called, by the Great Architect, and they say, 'What did you do?' … I'll just bring my book out, I'll say, 'Here you are, add that lot up!' I've got nothing to fear, I could go tomorrow. Ah yes.

(He takes out a pencil from the spine of the diary and makes an entry)

TONY: 'June, 1961. Gave blood for the needy.' How much do you reckon that's worth? Three quid? Just to keep the book straight. Just for my own benefit, I'm not trying to put a price on it.

(The man reacts in disgust. TONY puts the diary back and relaxes, very pleased with himself.)

TONY: Do you come here often?

MAN: This is my twelfth time.

TONY: Well, there's no need to boast about it, old man. How much did you give to the Arab refugees?

MAN: Oh really!

TONY: No, come on, how much? You're shouting about how much blood you've given, how much did you give to the Arab refugees?

MAN: If you must know… I gave five pounds.

TONY: Oh. Well, some people are better placed than others. I would have given more, but I have commitments, I can't afford to go around chucking fivers all over the place. I have to send my mother thirty bob a week.

…

(He settles back in his chair. Looks around for something to do. Hums to himself. Crosses his legs. Bangs his knee with the side of his hand to make his leg jump up. It doesn't work. Bangs it harder. It still doesn't work. Bangs it quicker, hurts his knee and the side of his hand, but his knee still doesn't jump up. He stops doing it. A slight pause and his knee jerks up. He looks puzzled at this. He takes his pulse. He can't find it. He feels all round his wrist. On the side of his temple. On the other wrist. He still can't find it. Puts his hand over his heart, smiles in relief as he feels it beating. Looks at the posters round the room.)

TONY: Drink-a pint-a milk-a-day.

(The reception desk nurse comes back and sits at her desk, a few yards away from TONY. He hasn't noticed her.)

TONY: *(Recites)* Coughs and sneezes spread diseases. *(Sings to the tune of Deutschland Uber Alles)* Coughs and sneezes spread diseases, trap the germs in your handkerchief, coughs and sneezes spread…

(He catches sight of the nurse who is looking at him coldly. He smiles in embarrassment.)

TONY: I, er, felt rather lonely sitting here by myself. It's funny what you do when you're on your own, isn't it?

…

DOCTOR: *(At his desk, in the blood clinic)* Hold out your hand, please.

(TONY holds his hand out. The doctor takes the needle.)

DOCTOR: Now this won't hurt. You'll just feel a slight prick at the end of your finger.

(Shot of TONY wincing in readiness. Eyes screwed shut. Cut to the doctor as he jabs the needle in. TONY yells in agony. He has a look at the end of his finger. He beams proudly.)

TONY: Well, that's that, I'll have my cup of tea and my biscuit now. Nothing to it, is there, really? I can't understand why everybody doesn't do it… here you are… *(Offers another finger)* … have ten if you like. *(Holds both hands out)*

DOCTOR: *(Busy smearing the drop of blood from the needle on to a slide)* Hmm… oh no, I don't need any more.

TONY: *(Gets up)* Well, I'll bid you good day, thank you very much, whenever you want more, don't hesitate to get in touch with me.

DOCTOR: Where are you going?

TONY: To have my tea and biscuits.

DOCTOR: I thought you came here to give some of your blood.

TONY: You've just had it.

DOCTOR: This is just a smear.

TONY: It may be just a smear to you, mate, but it's life and death to some poor wretch.

DOCTOR: No, no, no, I've just taken a small sample to test.

TONY: A sample. How much do you want then?

DOCTOR: Well, a pint, of course.

TONY: A pint? Have you gone raving mad? Oh, you must be joking.

DOCTOR: A pint is a perfectly normal quantity to take.

TONY: You don't seriously expect me to believe that. I came here in all good faith to help my country. I don't mind giving a reasonable amount, but a pint… that's very nearly an armful. I don't mind that much. *(Holds out his finger)* But not up to here, mate, I'm sorry. *(Indicates just below his shoulder)* I'm not walking around with an empty arm for anybody. I mean, a joke's a joke…

DOCTOR: Mr Hancock, obviously you don't know very much about the workings of the human body. You won't have an empty arm, or an empty anything. The blood is circulating all the time. A normal healthy individual can give a pint of blood without any ill effects whatsoever. You do have eight pints of blood, you know.

TONY: Look, chum, everybody to his own trade, I'll grant you, but if I've got eight pints, obviously I need eight pints, and not seven, as I will have by the time you've finished with me. No, I'm sorry, I've been misinformed, I've made a mistake... I'll do something else, I'll be a traffic warden...

Within twelve months of the last *Hancock* show, Galton and Simpson had created another seminal sitcom, *Steptoe and Son*. Despite the writers' aversion to catchphrases, the show quickly acquired one, through Harry H. Corbett's uniquely disgusted delivery. Though it wasn't used often, it was the line that everyone could imitate: 'You dirty old man!' Ray and Alan accepted it as an inevitable consequence of the show's popularity, and believed that viewers seized on it, not just because Harold's adenoidal voice was easily imitated, but also because the line summed up Albert's appeal: 'Old Man Steptoe is a much more obvious comic figure,' Ray said. 'His appearance never changed. It's a bit like Dickens. Some of these figures pass into everyday use, like Scrooge.'

STEPTOE AND SON, second series, episode two

'THE BATH'
First broadcast: Thursday 10 January 1963

> *(HAROLD comes into the living room, taking off his coat. He hangs it up.)*

ALBERT: Did you have a good day, son?
HAROLD: No, I didn't, I...

> *(He turns and sees ALBERT in the bath)*

HAROLD: Oh cor blimey – what are you doing?
ALBERT: I'm having a bath.
HAROLD: What day is it? It's not your birthday, is it? What do you want to have a bath tonight for? Of all the days you could have picked, what do you want to go and pick tonight for?
ALBERT: What's wrong with tonight then?
HAROLD: I told you this morning. I got a bird coming round tonight. Delia. I've asked her round for a cocktail before we go down the bingo. And it ain't customary for a bird to meet a bloke's father in the bath. You'll just have to get out.
ALBERT: I only just got in.

HAROLD: Well, you'll have to get out again, won't you? There's no point in arguing about it, I just don't want Delia to see my father stuck in front of the fire in a tin bath. People don't live like this any more, Dad. Not tin baths in the front room, those days have gone.

ALBERT: If you're ashamed of your home, why do you want to bring her back here?

HAROLD: Look, I told her not to expect a palace, but I didn't say nothing about scruffy old gits having a bath in front of the fire in the dining room. I mean, it brings the whole tone of the place down straight away. It's a social stigma these days. We may not have much, but we have got atmosphere. You might as well have the horse sitting in the armchair and have done with it. I mean, surely you see my point of view, Dad. When I introduce her to you, and you shake hands, whether you sit down or stand up, it's going to be rude either way.

ALBERT: I'm not getting out till I've finished my bath. When's she coming?

HAROLD: About a quarter of an hour. Do you reckon you'll be finished?

ALBERT: I might be. If you give me a hand.

HAROLD: You're not being very helpful, are you? All right… what do you want me to do?

ALBERT: Go and fetch another kettle of hot water, it's a bit parky in here. Go on, it's on the gas.

HAROLD: All right, but hurry up. *(Goes to the kitchen)* What a way to live.

(ALBERT stops washing himself. He takes a soap rack and lays it across the bath. From the side away from the audience, he picks up a plate on which is his dinner and puts it on the soap rack. He then picks up a bottle of beer, and a knife and fork, and puts them on the rack. He takes a bottle of sauce, shakes some on his dinner and gets stuck into it with great relish, swilling it down with beer from the bottle. Then he takes a jar of pickled onions, tips it up in order to spear one out and they fall into the bath. He picks one out and pops it into his mouth. He then fishes in the water for the others and puts them back in the jar.)

(HAROLD returns, carrying a tin kettle. He watches Albert fishing the pickled onions out of the water.)

HAROLD: Oh, you dirty old man. What are you doing?

ALBERT: I'm having my dinner.

HAROLD: What are you doing with them onions?

ALBERT: Oh. They fell in the water.

HAROLD: Well, don't you put them back in the jar.

ALBERT: Well, you don't think I'm going to leave them in the water, do you? I can't wash myself in a bathful of pickled onions, can I?

HAROLD: You shouldn't be eating your dinner in the bath. A bath is for washing in. You wash in the bath and you eat at the dinner table. Oh, you have got some filthy habits. You're getting worse. Give us them here.

(He snatches the jar of onions from ALBERT. ALBERT finds another onion in the water and offers it to HAROLD.)

ALBERT: There's another one in here.

HAROLD: I don't want it. Throw it away.

(ALBERT tosses it over his shoulder)

HAROLD: Not on the floor.

ALBERT: Dah, you're worse than your mother, you are.

HAROLD: We got a dustbin outside. That's to put all your scraps and rubbish in. What do you think they come round every Tuesday for? To empty it. They don't bother now… there's never anything in ours. It's all in here. *(Indicates the room with his arm)*

ALBERT: You're getting finicky all of a sudden, aren't you?

HAROLD: Yeah, I'm finicky. Yeah, when it comes to things like this, I am finicky. You wouldn't have told me about those onions, would you? You wouldn't have told me they'd been in your bathwater. You would have sat there and watched me eat them, you wouldn't have said nothing.

ALBERT: It's not going to do you any harm, is it, a bit of soap and water. They weren't in there more than a couple of seconds.

HAROLD: What's that got to do with it? I fail to see your reasoning. *(Points to the label on the jar)* Look. Pickled onions in vinegar. Not soap and water. If I wanted my onions to taste of… look, this is beside the point. It's irrelevant. Whichever way you look at it, to fish pickled onions out of your bath and put them back in the jar is an act of extreme dirtiness. Dirty, dirty.

When *Steptoe and Son* returned to TV in 1970 after a four-year break, the *Radio Times* celebrated by putting Corbett, co-star Wilfrid Brambell and the carthorse Hercules on their front cover. Their reunion lasted no longer than the credits of the first episode:

STEPTOE AND SON, fifth series, episode one

'A DEATH IN THE FAMILY'
First broadcast: Friday 6 March 1970

(The door opens and HAROLD is standing there. He has the horse's collar and harness round his neck.)

ALBERT: You're back late. I held up getting your dinner ready. I was expecting you back about four.

(HAROLD stands at door. ALBERT carries on laying the table.)

ALBERT: Has the horse been put away?
HAROLD: *(Quietly)* Yeah, he's been put away.
ALBERT: What have you got that stuff hanging round you for? Are you going to clean it? It's about time. That horse looks a disgrace. You don't look after him.

(HAROLD closes his eyes in anguish)

ALBERT: Did you notice I've cleaned the stables out? And I've creosoted it. I've got another two sackfuls you can take round to old Mother Butler. By the way, has he started going in the street? Because if he is, you can take a bucket round with you and pick it up. Don't leave it there. We don't want them all nipping out of their gardens and picking it up free of charge, do we? It's a nice little by-product, that is. Pays for his oats. In one end and out the other, and it don't cost us a penny. That's good economics, that is. That's what you're always spouting about, you and your Party.

(HAROLD walks to look at the horse show rosettes above his desk.)

ALBERT: *(Continuing)* Harold Wilson don't do that, do he? *(PAUSE)* I said, Harold Wilson don't do that, do he?
HAROLD: Not now, Dad.

(HAROLD sits wearily in chair)

ALBERT: What's the matter with you? You look like you've lost two bob and found a tanner.
HAROLD: Dad. I want to talk to you. Sit down, Dad.
ALBERT: I haven't got time to sit down, I'm getting the dinner.
HAROLD: Don't worry about the dinner, Dad, I couldn't eat. *Please* sit down.
ALBERT: I don't want to sit down.
HAROLD: *(Testily)* Sit down.

(ALBERT sits down)

HAROLD: Dad, I've asked you to sit down because I've got something to tell you.

ALBERT: Go on then.

HAROLD: There comes a time in every man's life when he has to face the prospect of carrying on with the people and the things that he's gathered around him not being there any more.

ALBERT: Where are you going?

HAROLD: I'm not going anywhere.

ALBERT: You've got a bird and you want to clear off and shack up with her. You dirty little toe-rag.

HAROLD: It's got nothing to do with a bird. *(HAROLD goes over to the old man and puts his arm round his shoulder)* I wouldn't leave you, Dad... not now. What I'm trying to say is, none of us are getting any younger, and the time comes when we all have to shuffle off this mortal coil.

ALBERT: *(Puzzled)* What?

HAROLD: Snuff it, die.

ALBERT: I'm not making out a will.

HAROLD: I'm not talking about you. Oh gawd. Look... when that time comes, as come it must, to everybody and everything, we must face it bravely, and carry on the best way we can.

ALBERT: I know that.

HAROLD: Even in the midst of life there is death.

ALBERT: I know.

HAROLD: I know you know... but even when you know... when it happens, the shock and the grief can sometimes be too much to bear. That is why we've got to be ready for it. Because it does sometimes happen to... somebody close.

ALBERT: I've only got you.

HAROLD: Are you sure?

ALBERT: Well, there's only you... *(A dreadful thought wells up.)*

HAROLD: Exactly...

ALBERT: *(Frightened)* The horse. What's wrong with him?

HAROLD: *(Quickly)* Nothing. Well, I say nothing... that's not quite true.

ALBERT: Why?

HAROLD: He's dead.

The seventies series of *Steptoe* were shot in colour, a technical advance that Ray and Alan viewed with misgiving. Much of the appeal of the sitcom lay in its claustrophobic set: the sitting room and kitchen of a tumbledown house in a junk yard. The background clutter included a stuffed bear, a skeleton and an array of bottles upside-down on the sideboard, their dregs draining into optics. The writers were concerned that the oppressive, seedy atmosphere would be compromised by colour. 'We needn't have worried,' Alan said. 'If anything, it looked even grottier.'

Even so, many of the episodes did not survive in colour – the BBC wiped their tapes, and the shows were only salvaged many years later from videocassettes recorded in black and white on Ray Galton's own television system at home. The minority that do exist in colour are now repeated much more often than the rest, and 'Divided We Stand' is one of the most frequently shown. But that doesn't fully explain why it is so loved; perhaps it is the sheer absurdity of the comedy, achieved with a surreal flourish that seems to transpose the limitless imagination of Galton and Simpson's radio sitcoms onto the television. Harold and Albert, unable to bear living together and both refusing to move out, decide to split the house... literally. The hallway is divided into two alleys, a turnstile is installed into the kitchen, and the sitting room is cut in half by a plywood version of the Berlin Wall. And they only have the one telly:

STEPTOE AND SON, seventh series, episode six

'DIVIDED WE STAND'
First broadcast: Monday 27 March 1970

> *(HAROLD starts setting up for a night's television viewing. He moves his chair into position, sits down, picks up the Radio Times, chooses a programme. He leans forward to switch the set on and only then realises all the knobs are on the old man's side. HAROLD goes over to the partition and knocks on the hatchway.)*

ALBERT: *(OFF)* Who is it?
HAROLD: Next door.

> *(The hatchway slides open. ALBERT peers through.)*

HAROLD: Would you mind switching the television set on?
ALBERT: What programme?
HAROLD: BBC2.
ALBERT: Hang on.

(The hatchway slides shut. HAROLD reacts.
Cut to ALBERT: he looks at the TV programmes in the newspaper.)

ALBERT: *(Reads)* Royal Festival Hall. Margot Fonteyn and Rudolf Nureyev. 'Les Sylphides'… dirty devils.

(He switches the set on.
Cut back to HAROLD: settling back in his chair, watching his half of the screen.)

HAROLD: I hope they don't dance too far apart.

(HAROLD starts humming the music, leaning to one side, hoping to see more of the screen.
Cut to ALBERT: he is fed up. Reacts in disgust.
Cut back to HAROLD enjoying it.)

ALBERT: *(OFF)* Harold, you want to come round this side, her drawers have just fallen down.
HAROLD: Liar.

(Cut to ALBERT: he cackles and watches for a few more seconds.)

ALBERT: Oh gawd, I can't watch this all night. *(Picks up the TV programmes)* ITV – 'Blood Of The Ripper'. Ah, that's more like it.

(Cut back to HAROLD, enjoying the ballet. Suddenly the music stops, and a ghoulish screaming rings out. HAROLD gets up and goes over to the partition. He knocks on the hatchway. It slides open and ALBERT peers through.)

ALBERT: What do you want now? I'm trying to watch the television.
HAROLD: That is not BBC2.
ALBERT: I know it's not.
HAROLD: I specifically want to watch Rudolf Nurryevv and Margaret Fontana.
ALBERT: I'm not watching that rubbish.
HAROLD: We agreed that Mondays, Wednesday and Fridays should be my choice of programmes, and Tuesdays, Thursdays and Saturdays your choice, with us each having every alternate Sunday.
ALBERT: That's right.
HAROLD: Today is Wednesday. I want BBC2 on.
ALBERT: Well, I don't.
HAROLD: That is a very unfair attitude to adopt. We made an agreement. We shook hands on it. I've got the law of contract on my side.

ALBERT: I've got the knobs on my side.

(*HAROLD reaches through and grabs ALBERT by the scruff of the neck, and pulls his head through the partition.*)

ALBERT: *(Yells)* Oh, let go, you're hurting me.
HAROLD: Are you going to put BBC2 on?
ALBERT: No.

(*HAROLD squeezes. ALBERT yells.*)

ALBERT: You're strangling me.
HAROLD: Put the ballet back on.
ALBERT: All right, all right, let go.

(*HAROLD lets go. ALBERT retreats and rubs his neck.*)

ALBERT: I'm not putting the ballet on.
HAROLD: You wait till you come out of there, I'll murder you.

(*ALBERT is worried about this.*)

ALBERT: *(Wheedling)* I don't want to watch the ballet, Harold, it drives me round the twist. I'll tell you what, let's compromise. We'll watch BBC1 tonight, then you can have another turn tomorrow.
HAROLD: What's on BBC1?
ALBERT: Football. European Cup.
HAROLD: Hmm. That's not bad. All right then, we'll watch BBC1.

(*ALBERT goes over and turns on BBC1. A football match is on. He sits down.
Cut to HAROLD: he is also sitting down, watching. He gets interested. He follows the part of the ball as it goes over to ALBERT's side of the screen.*)

HAROLD: *(Calls)* Was that a goal?
ALBERT: No, he saved it.
HAROLD: Oh gawd.

(*He is now getting very interested in the game. Urging the players on.*)

HAROLD: Man on! Turn! Man up your back!

(*Suddenly the set starts moving into ALBERT's side of the room. There is only a few inches left on HAROLD's side when he jumps up and grabs it to pull it back.*)

HAROLD: Leave it alone.

ALBERT: You've got more screen than I have.

HAROLD: *(Pulling)* I haven't. It's split right down the middle. Let go.

ALBERT: It's a twenty-one inch screen, and I'm entitled to ten-and-a-half inches.

HAROLD: You've got ten-and-a-half inches.

ALBERT: I haven't. I've only got nine inches. Let go.

HAROLD: Oh all right then, have the bleeding lot.

> *(HAROLD lets go. ALBERT falls over. HAROLD is gleeful. ALBERT picks himself up, and sits on his chair to watch the whole of the TV screen. HAROLD gets an evil thought. He picks up the flex, follows it to the wall socket and pulls out the plug.)*

HAROLD: *(Laughs)* Normal service will be resumed tomorrow. In the meantime, we are going to bed. From all of us here at the three-pin plug, goodnight everybody, goodnight. *(He sings the first three phrases of the National Anthem. Yawns, and looks at his watch. Goes over to the door and switches out his light, on his way into the hall.)*

2 Early Years

Alan Simpson was born on 27 November 1929 at 33 Concannon Road, Brixton. His father Frank was a milkman; Alan was an only child, though he had numerous cousins. His mother Lil's family worked at the Chelsea football ground, in the Tote booths, on the turnstiles or selling programmes; his grandfather was a groundsman. Alan's early memories are of Saturdays and the pub opposite Stamford Bridge: 'It was called the Sun. After the game I'd be stuck outside, because children weren't allowed in the bar in those days. Every five minutes one of my uncles would come out and say, "You all right, son?" and give me a bottle of lemonade or an arrowroot biscuit.'

Ray Galton was born at 25 Enbrook Street, Paddington, on 17 July 1930, the son of a bus conductor named Herbert Galton and his wife, Christina. Ray's older brother was a merchant seaman, and their father had served in the Royal Navy throughout the First World War and into the twenties; he remained a reservist, and when war loomed again he volunteered. By then Herbert and Christina had separated, and Ray regrets that he did not have an opportunity to question his father more closely about his war service. 'He was one of the few men who fought right through both world wars.'

Pubs evoked a strong childhood memory for Ray too, though his parents rarely drank: 'My folks just were not pub-goers. The only time I can remember them drinking anything at home was Christmas, when I had to go out with a jug and get some stout for the Christmas pudding. The big pub close to us was called the Rose, and I remember the way the young men used to dress. The code of that time was double-breasted waistcoats and hats, always a hat.'

In 1940, Alan was evacuated to Weston-super-Mare in Somerset. 'The first night I got there, it was bombed. I never got bombed in London. The Luftwaffe had been bombing the Cardiff docks, and on their way back they unloaded the racks, dropping incendiaries – they burned one of the schools down. There were more air raids down that part of the world than in London, and I hated it. I was there ten months, billeted with eleven kids, sleeping on a piano stool at one stage – I couldn't stand sharing a bed with all these other children, like sardines; half of them used to wet the bed; they were aged only eight or nine. I got permission from the woman to stay downstairs in the front room, and I used to sleep lying down on the long piano stool. I wasn't six foot four as I am now. My mother came down to visit me, and she was horrified that her son was sleeping on the piano stool. I managed to get taken home, just in time for the Blitz.'

Ray's mother decided from the outset that he was safer staying in the city: 'Whenever the German aircraft came over, you got air-raid sirens. When that happened, I'd be taken to the air-raid shelter.'

After leaving school in 1944, Ray was apprenticed to a plasterer, and worked as a labourer on bomb sites around Wimbledon before taking a job behind a desk at the Transport and General Workers' Union, off Millbank in Westminster. Two years later, his brother Bert, on leave, was the first to realize that the sixteen-year-old Ray was ill – an x-ray the next day revealed advanced tuberculosis of the lungs. This was six years before mass vaccination virtually wiped out the disease in Britain: 50,000 people were being struck down by TB every year, most of them living on inadequate food rations in overcrowded housing. Ray's condition was so severe that he was admitted to the Milford sanatorium within ten days: 'They didn't let me out of bed for more than a year after that. That was very hard for a young man.'

Though his great ambition was to be a sports reporter, Alan's first job, at sixteen, was as a postal clerk for a firm of shipping agents in Leadenhall Street in the City. He began coughing up blood on his bus journey to work one day in 1947, and within thirty-six hours suffered a haemorrhage at St George's Hospital, so serious that he was given the last rites. That same week, his father died from leukaemia.

The demand for sanatorium beds was high, and it was thirteen months before Alan was admitted to Milford. Until the following summer he was confined, first to his bedroom and then to Cumberland House, a cottage hospital in Mitcham, with his widowed mother borrowing countless books to keep him occupied: he would work his way through three novels a day. By the time he left his room, he was short-sighted.

'When I first went into the sanatorium, I was the youngest person there,' Ray said. 'I was like a mascot. Nearly all the people in there were ex-servicemen, straight out of the army, navy and air force.'

'The main thing about the sanatorium,' Alan agreed, 'was that you were mixing with people so much older than yourself. You grew up talking about things that as teenagers you don't normally discuss with each other. You didn't have a teen age.'

Though they were among the youngest patients at Milford, they were initially kept on different wards. The first that Ray Galton saw of his future writing partner was a shadow in the corridor that led to the washrooms. With the glass-panelled doors behind him, his room went dark as the figure walked by. 'I thought, "Who the hell is that? Six foot four at least" – and in the sanatorium, everybody else was about three-stone-nothing in their pyjamas. So I asked around, and the nurses told me this was the one bloke in the place who didn't want to get out of bed. Everyone else was dying to get up; we were all bored to tears. But Alan reckoned he'd get well faster if he just lay there. So every now and then I'd see this shadow go by. Years later, Spike Milligan used to call him "He Who Blocks Out The Sun".'

The illness was horrific; the treatments were more hideous still. When Ray was diagnosed with TB in both lungs he was given just six weeks to live and, as he fought on, the doctors remained pessimistic. After nine months, Bert Galton received a letter from the hospital, warning that the prognosis was still grim: 'The line of treatment he has had so far,' wrote Dr Margaret Shackles, 'has helped to control the activity of the disease, but the outlook for the future is not at all good.' To smother the TB bacilli, Ray was given an artificial pneumo-thorax, a procedure in which air was pumped behind the pleural wall to create a pocket that collapsed the lung.

'That didn't hurt,' Ray said. 'I didn't look forward to having the air replenished once a week, because the nurses had to use quite a big needle between the ribs. But on top of that I got fluid on that lung, and that had to be drained off by what was called an aspiration – again through the rib cage, pulling it out by syringe. And unfortunately I had to be conscious all through this, because the patient had to co-operate, and roll onto one side or the other so that the syringe could find the liquid. It would sometimes take half an hour, and I would be practically delirious, from the pain of it. It's terrible now even to think about it.' The only concession to pain relief was a local anaesthetic, administered with a small needle; a larger needle was used to begin siphoning off the fluid, and after a few minutes a still broader bore was inserted.

Alan, whose lung capacity was larger, had a different treatment – a phrenic crush, in which a nerve in the neck was compressed, pulling up the diaphragm and paralysing it to deflate the lung. The effects lasted for months.

The treatment all the patients dreaded, though, was thoracoplasty, which fortunately Ray and Alan avoided: 'That was the biggest operation known to mankind,' Ray said. 'It was so bad that they could only do it in three stages, and it would take three years because you had to recover each time. They took your bloody ribs out and they were never replaced, so blokes used to walk all lopsided, which compressed the lung. By comparison, there was a more minor operation, if you got away with it... they just took one of the lungs away.'

One of the worst torments of TB was the prospect of the years ahead, years of painful and fitful recovery. 'Some buggers had been there fourteen or fifteen years,' Alan said. 'They were chronic, they weren't getting worse and they never got better. They just stayed there until they died.'

The institution had become a way of life to so many patients that some, with no homes or family to return to, would be permitted to stay even when they were fully recovered. Male and female wards were separate, but relationships were commonplace: men and women met at the movie screenings on Mondays, Wednesdays and Saturdays, and at the twice-weekly card schools. The romances, like the treatments, were often painful, as many marriages fell apart, with a husband or wife stranded outside when a patient faced years of treatment. One macabre story did the rounds: a man whose wife was on one of the women's wards wanted to marry his mistress, and decided murder would be quicker and cheaper than divorce. He brought his wife chocolates laced with strychnine, but as he handed the ribboned box over, the superintendent, Dr Allison, walked past. The doctor dipped in, swallowed a chocolate and collapsed vomiting.

Without drugs, the cure consisted mostly of bed rest and the brutal surgical methods. For his first twelve months, Ray was not allowed to stand up, even to climb into a wheelchair, and when at last he was permitted to go to the bathroom once a day, he had to be supported: his legs would no longer hold him. Health was regained via a rigid hierarchy of advances, called promotions, as if the ranks of beds at Milford were fostering a tubercular army. Commode promotion was the lowest level, where a patient was permitted to go down the corridor to the bathroom once a day. A further promotion meant two daily visits, then three, and then patients were allowed to use the washroom, to shower and brush their teeth. The next level, confusingly, was called 'Bed': there was no limit on bathroom visits, and an hour at the whist drives and movie screenings was now sanctioned. Physiotherapy did not exist but, as longer spells out of bed were awarded, patients were expected to walk laps around the site. At six hours, it was one circuit, or 'round'; at eight hours, four rounds, and at ten hours, six rounds. At that point, physical work would be introduced, in six gradual stages, until patients proved they could work on the farm or in the boiler rooms all day without triggering a relapse.

During the long months of total bed rest, their only distractions were reading and radio. Ray remembers seeing, when he first arrived, another patient laughing over a book, one of Thorne Smith's Topper fantasies. Wanting to escape, he began to read comic novels too, and in the sanatorium library discovered more American authors – James Thurber, Damon Runyan, Mark Twain and the Canadian humorist Stephen Leacock, all of whom seemed much more real and relevant than the upper-class English antics of Wodehouse and Waugh. Alan remembered reading Orwell's *1984* shortly after its publication in 1948: the novel's hallucinogenic nightmares were probably inflamed by the author's own TB fevers. 'We used to read all sorts of things,' Alan said. 'It was a bit of both escapism and education – I don't think it was consciously educating yourself.'

Radio was their other escape. Ray had been moved into a cubicle with a man called Tony Wallis: 'When I saw it, I said, "How are you going to get me in this bloody room?" The whole two-bedded cubicle was a workshop. You couldn't move for equipment. All the walls were covered in boxes. The locker by his bed had a fixed electric drill. And he had this 1155 radio, salvaged from a Lancaster bomber, which looked beautiful.'

Ray and Tony listened to American comedy shows on the forces station AFN Radio Stuttgart. Tony ran a wire out through the wall from the radio to Alan's bed, so that he too could listen on headphones. So many patients asked to be included in the private network that Tony and another man scrambled over the roofs of the wards and the buildings in their dressing gowns and pyjamas, wiring up all the dormitories. Ray, unable to leave his bed, sat drilling blocks of wood for the plugs to be mounted to the walls.

'They allowed us to do this,' Alan said, 'because you were there for so long, and you could treat the cubicle more or less as your home. It was not like being in a hospital where you'd be in and out in two weeks. It was three years or more. You were allowed to make it more personal, so Tony did it by turning his room into a garage workshop. He'd have had a car in there if there had been room.'

When they were placed on the same ward, the two teenagers began a friendship based on an addiction to US radio comedies – especially the Jack Benny show, Burns and Allen, and the Phil Harris show. These acts were funnier, sharper and more believable than the music-hall humour of the BBC's most popular output, such as *It's That Man Again* with Tommy Handley or Kenneth Horne's *Much Binding in the Marsh*. They shared their tastes in comic novelists too, as well as similar views on politics and music.

As they earned promotions, they began bending the rules. 'When I was allowed to be up two hours a day,' Ray said, 'we used to sneak down to the railway station in Milford and get the train into Guildford, and go to the pub. If we'd got caught they would quite possibly have thrown us out. We couldn't be out too long.'

'Drinking wasn't banned, and nor was smoking,' Alan explained. 'Most of the doctors used to smoke cigarettes or pipes. Patients were allowed two hours smoking every day. But the nurses used to come round every night at 9 p.m. with cocoa, so they'd know if you weren't in bed. Even those who were allowed up had to be in bed with lights out by ten o'clock. They used to come round and, irrespective of whether you were asleep, shine a torch in your face to make sure you were there.'

Meanwhile, Tony Wallis's radio ambitions expanded. He converted a linen cupboard into a studio to broadcast in-house to the patients for an hour a day. A radio committee was set up to decide the programming, which consisted mostly of record requests. Ray and Alan suggested movie commentaries, inspired by the BBC's *Seat in the Circle*, where a reporter described what was happening on the cinema screen at the Leicester Square Odeon for listeners at home: for Radio Milford, it would be a running commentary on the weekly film shown in the sanatorium canteen. And when the committee appealed for comedy sketches, Ray and Alan volunteered to write a series called *Have You Ever Wondered?* Alan explained: 'The idea was: have you ever wondered what this place would be like if the doctors swapped places with the patients? Or if the BBC paid us a visit?'

The shows earned Ray and Alan their first fan letter. Mr F. W. Robins on ward F21 wrote to the *Milford Bulletin*, the hospital's newsletter: 'A bouquet to the team of *Have You Ever Wondered?* Slick, up-to-the-minute and with a dash of satire, it was a worthy effort indeed. The next programme will be eagerly awaited after such an encouraging start.'

The first 15-minute episode was broadcast on Saturday 7 May 1949, at 10.30 a.m., billed as 'a new comedy series by Ray Galton and Alan Simpson'. 'We were going to do six of them,' Alan said, 'but we got to four and after that we dried up.'

The dry period was temporary. Alan and Ray left Milford a few months apart, in 1950 and 1951. Alan's amateur church concert group needed material, and he asked Ray if he'd be willing to try writing together again. That proved to be fun and they decided to send a letter applying for jobs as office boys with the most successful script team in the country, Frank Muir and Denis Norden. A polite reply suggested that, if they had material they believed was good enough, they should send it to a script editor and talent spotter at the BBC called Gale Pedrick.

They didn't yet have the material, but they had the belief. At Alan's mother's house in Streatham Vale, south London, the twenty-one-year-old writers began a working pattern that lasted throughout their professional lives. Alan, who had started learning to type at the shipping agents' office, sat at the borrowed typewriter, with Ray at his shoulder. Nothing was committed to paper until both men agreed the line was right. Their first sketches were based on the format of Muir and Norden's *Take It from Here*, which featured every week a pastiche of a popular movie, book or play. Ray and Alan built a story around the privateer Captain Henry Morgan, and worked up a scene where pirates were playing cards.

'Where's the crew?' demands Morgan.
The bo'sun replies, 'They're in the hold, playing Jane Russell pontoon.'
'Jane Russell pontoon? What's that?'
'The same as ordinary pontoon, only you need 38 to bust!'
Attackers came swarming up the sides of the ships and over the bulwarks. 'Bulwarks to you too!'

Taking their mentors' advice, they sent the script to Gale Pedrick. 'A couple of weeks later, we got a reply,' said Ray. 'He told us, "Don't read more into this letter than appears on the surface, but we've read your script and were highly amused. Please make an appointment with my secretary, and hopefully I can help you." We got drunk on that letter. We showed it to everyone. If that had been the end of our writing careers, we'd still be dining out on it now – "Look at this, a letter from the BBC, we could have made it!"'

'It was the pontoon gag that caught his eye,' Alan said. 'The bulwarks line was never used.'

Gale Pedrick passed the script to several producers, and a few days later the comedian Derek Roy, star of the BBC's *Happy-Go-Lucky*, invited them to supply one-liners for the show and for his stage act, at five shillings a joke. This was a pittance even in the early fifties; it's about £5 or £6 at today's prices. To make matters worse, it was clear that Roy's radio show was dying on its feet. Within weeks, the producer of *Happy-Go-Lucky* had suffered a nervous breakdown and collapsed, and a young executive named Dennis Main Wilson was brought in to rescue the programme. He called a crowded meeting at Roy's flat in Bryanston Street, close to Marble Arch, and announced that the script team had been fired. 'We were standing at the back, just about in the hallway of this little apartment,' Alan said, 'and Dennis looked round the room, pointed to us and said, "You two tall blokes! Are you writers? Right then, you're doing the last three shows of the series."'

'We had to say yes,' Ray agreed, 'or we'd have been finished before we ever started. The one big consolation was *Happy-Go-Lucky* was so bad, nothing we could do would make it any worse. And we were going to get 46 guineas a show, which was a fortune compared to five shillings between us, per joke.'

With their first pay cheque, they invested in their own typewriter. Ray would arrive at the house in Streatham Vale at nine every morning, after a twenty-minute bus journey from Rose Hill near Cheam, and they would work at the script all day and into the night. 'If our doctors from the sanatorium had seen us, they would have despaired. We were supposed to be resting,' Alan said. 'But we got the energy to do it, because we were so fired up.'

'Sometimes, Dennis would come round in the evening, usually after closing time, with fish and chips for us,' Ray remembered. 'He'd say he'd come to help with the scripts... most times he'd just doze off and we'd still be there till the small hours, writing away.'

HAPPY-GO-LUCKY, episode twelve

First broadcast: Monday 12 November 1951

This was the first episode (the twelfth in the series) to feature Galton and Simpson as co-writers. Also credited were E. K. Smith and Ralph Petersen, who wrote the Boy Scouts sketch, and Rona Ricardo, who was married to Derek Roy. The announcer, Phillip Slessor (the host of *Variety Bandbox*), played the straight man to Roy's joker.

As Phillip tries to introduce a selection from the Rodgers and Hammerstein hit, *South Pacific*, Derek Roy cuts in:

DEREK: Phillip, Phillip, wait a minute. All these American musicals... Why can't they give a British composer a break? You haven't read *my* musical play yet.
PHILLIP: Your musical play? Original?

DEREK: Absolutely. It's all about a tropical island, an elderly planter...
then there's a native girl in a flimsy grass skirt.

PHILLIP: Wait a minute! Girl in a flimsy... this sounds strangely like *South Pacific*!

DEREK: Certainly not.

PHILLIP: What's your play called?

DEREK: *North Atlantic*.

This was Ray and Alan's first run-in with the BBC censors – Derek Roy's original line was, '*South South Atlantic*. I would have made it just *South Atlantic*, but the native girl looked more interesting further south.'

DEREK: Anyway, this girl has a parrot called Ben Hur.

PHILLIP: Ben Hur?

DEREK: Yes, for years she called it 'Ben' – then one day it laid an egg. Set the scene, Phillip. Stanley, a little Hawaiian music, please...

ORCHESTRA: *('Aloha' guitars and girls)*

PHILLIP: *(Over music)* Somewhere on the tropical island of Bally Low, we find the unconscious body of a castaway. He's been there for weeks. Yes, he's been washed up for a long time. *(To audience loudly)* That's so true.

One of the co-stars of *Happy-Go-Lucky* was Tony Hancock, then twenty-seven years old. He was best known for *Educating Archie*, as the tutor to a ventriloquist's doll voiced by Peter Brough. Ventriloquism, which relies on a lifelike doll and a deadpan face, is the epitome of stage humour, and ought to have been impossible on radio. In fact, fourteen-year-old schoolboy Archie Andrews, hyperactive and sarcastic, was one of Britain's favourite radio characters in the early fifties, and much of his success was due to his earnest, frustrated, pompous teacher. As that teacher, Hancock lectured and scolded the puppet as if it were a real boy, and he insisted that Brough must always speak his lines with Archie in his arms, even at rehearsals.

In *Happy-Go-Lucky*, Hancock was a scoutmaster, with Peter Butterworth, Bill Kerr and Graham Stark in his Eager Beaver patrol. The scripts for their segment had already been bought and paid for, so Ray and Alan were not yet writing for Tony Hancock. But during rehearsals at the Paris Cinema in London's Lower Regent Street, they were spectators in the stalls, and the comedian nodded to the twenty-one-year-old writers as he walked down the stairs. 'Did you write that? Very funny,' Hancock remarked, gesturing at the stage as Derek Roy wound up a sketch with Benny Hill and Frances King as squabbling children at a party. The date of that first encounter was 11 November 1951; the show was broadcast the following day, and sixty years later the gag about film stars adopting orphans is more relevant than ever – just substitute Madonna or Angelina for Jane Russell:

HAPPY-GO-LUCKY, episode twelve

First broadcast: Monday 12 November 1951

PHILLIP: One of our most eminent politicians commented recently on how much smarter are the children of this generation. The modern child is learning to write at an earlier age... this much we know because nowadays rude words on walls are written much lower down. So tonight we should like to dedicate the rest of the programme to that 'Happy-Go-Lucky' age – the kiddies... bless them... let's go over to little Dewek Woy's house where he is giving a birthday party.

(Gradual fade) (Crossfade intro)
EFFECTS: (Doorbell)

HARRY NOBLE: Hello – there's another one of Derek's charming little playmates.

EFFECTS: (Door opens)

HARRY: Hallo, little man, how do you do?
BENNY: *(American)* Who wants to know?
HARRY: Well, I...
BENNY: Hey, Mac – you the butler?
HARRY: No I am not! I'm Derek's father. Who are you?
BENNY: Benny Hill – I'm a Were-wolf Cub. I run the protection rackets in the Vampire Patrol Mob.
HARRY: Well – er – come on in, Benny. Leave your knuckledusters on the hallstand, son – you'll find Derek and Graham in the drawing room.
BENNY: Thanks, buster – I'll find my own way around.
HARRY: Hmmm. That little – er – boy... needs watching. Oh, here comes someone else up the garden path.
PEGGY COCHRANE: *(Approaching mike)* Come along, Frances dear... here we are... Why *Harry*, how *are* you, darling?

HARRY: Lady Ariadne! This *is* a pleasure… and who is this pretty little girl?

PEGGY: This is little Frances. She is the daughter of Dawn Levere, the famous Hollywood film star. Say hello to Uncle Roy, dear.

FRANCES: Hallo… I like you… would you do me a favour and marry my mummy? I haven't had a daddy for two whole weeks now.

HARRY: Well, I don't know, Frances – I'll have to think about it. Come on in and meet Derek's other little friends.

DEREK: Hallo, Frances. Woo wee zam!!!

HARRY: Stop that, Derek – why, you're acting like a fifteen-month-old child…

DEREK: I know – I want to be adopted by Jane Russell!

FRANCES: Oh Derek, you are funny!

DEREK: And you're very pretty, Frances – it must be thrilling to have a famous film star as your mummy. Have you any brothers or sisters?

FRANCES: No – but I've got three Poppas by my first Momma, and four Mommas by my last Poppa.

HARRY: Oh, kiddies! Tea's ready – come up to the table…

EFFECTS: *(Scramble of feet, chairs, plates, etc.)*

BENNY: OK, Mac, make with the jelly!

HARRY: Just you wait your turn, Benny!

BENNY: I don't want to wait. Slap it in the middle, Mac – then everyone'll have a bit!

GRAHAM: I say, fellows – can I smell anything burning?

FRANCES: *(Scream)* Benny's set my pigtails on fire! Help! Put it out! *(Weeps)*

BENNY: Say – she looks cute with an urchin cut, doesn't she?

HARRY: *(Slyly)* Oh, Benny…

BENNY: What do you want?

HARRY: Come over here.

EFFECTS: *(Swish; breaking of vase)*

BENNY: Maaaa… missed me.

GRAHAM: I say – do let's play some jolly games.

HARRY: OK – what do you want to be, Benny? Al Capone? Mmmmm?

BENNY: No, I want to be a saint.

HARRY: *(Amazed)* A saint?

BENNY: Yeah – a Saint Bernard… I'm a *dog*.

HARRY: And what do you want to be, Graham?

GRAHAM: I'd like to portray Einstein working on his theory of relativity.

HARRY: And what do you want to be, Frances?
FRANCES: I want to be a fairy on a Christmas tree.
HARRY: And what do you want to be, Derek?
DEREK: I want to be sick.

Hancock wasn't the only one who was impressed by the sketch. Producer Dennis Main Wilson saw that his stop-gap writers could be better than he had ever hoped. He commissioned them to write an hour-long Christmas special about a similar crowd of children – 'a fantasy about kids getting lost in the chimney, looking for Father Christmas,' Alan said. It featured Hattie Jacques as her character Sophie Tuckshop, the greedy schoolgirl from the forties radio staple *It's That Man Again*. Galton and Simpson, who weeks earlier had been limited to writing one-liners for just one comic, were now producing sketches for a range of experienced radio comedians with established styles, easily recognized by the listeners. It was a tough apprenticeship, which would instil the confidence they needed to expand the comedy genre until it crossed over into straight drama; tough, too, because *Happy-Go-Lucky* was Derek Roy's show and he regarded his chief scriptwriters as a pair of naifs who had previously been glad to get five bob a joke. The pair of naifs knew what Roy thought of them, as the tag to this sketch makes clear:

HAPPY-GO-LUCKY, episode thirteen, with Dick Emery

First broadcast: Monday 26 November 1951

DEREK: My family have always been connected with the sea… my
    mother was in the Navy.
DICK: In the Navy?
DEREK: Yes… she was tattooed on Father's stomach. And even before I
    joined the Navy, my job had always led me towards the sea… I used
    to be a sewer inspector. But the most famous of all my ancestors was
    the notorious Welsh pirate captain, HenRoy Morgan.
DICK: Oooh… I'd like to hear about him.
DEREK: And so you shall, Dick.
ORCHESTRA: (Stirring naval music)
DEREK: (Narration) My story begins in the little village of Llanfechech…
    Flanflapech… Chlanfech… (Take) The story begins in Wales,
    birthplace of HenRoy Morgan. He came of a sea-faring family – the
    son of Ebediah and Florence Waters, known as Ebb and Flo. Then

came his first trip and, once aboard, he realized how ignorant he was... he thought a windlass was a girl with indigestion. He was discouraged and thought he had nothing to give the sea... soon they struck rough weather and he realized his mistake. Then came the day he became master of his own ship...

MORGAN: Now look you, men... today we sail from Dover in search of Spanish gold. This trip is going to be dangerous. Some of you might not come back... so if there is any man amongst you who does not want to go with me, let him raise his right hand.

EFFECTS: *(Machine-gun fire)*

NARRATION: And so Morgan put to sea with the best left-handed crew in the business. Dawn found them well out to sea... Dawn was swimming the Channel. As they peered through the mist and fog, the only sound to be heard was the clanging of the ship's bell... bing bong... bing bong... bing bong... the lapping of the waves... lap lap... lap lap... and the flapping of the sails... flip flop... flip flop... bing flip... bong lap... flap flop... flop bing... lap bloop... bloop bleep... *(Aside)* This is what comes from having three-year-old scriptwriters.

No recordings survive of *Happy-Go-Lucky*, so it's impossible to know whether Roy managed to get the laughs from that inspired onomatopoeia. It was to be a trademark of Galton and Simpson scripts, though they didn't pioneer it – Spike Milligan, for instance, was using nonsense noises and vocal silliness to stoke the chaos on *The Goon Show*. Ray and Alan used gibberish almost as a Freudian tool, to expose the fantasies within the characters' minds: Harold Steptoe in his flea-ridden armchair, screaming through the gears in an imaginary racing car, or Hancock at the bridge of a Navy destroyer in his bathtub, whooping and pinging as he hunted U-boats.

In April 1952, Hancock invited Galton and Simpson to write a five-minute slot for his appearance on the BBC radio show *Worker's Playtime*. He offered them 25 guineas (worth about £450 today), which was half his fee. Within weeks they were writing his regular radio show with Charlie Chester, *Calling All Forces*, which they had taken over from Ted Ray. The original writers were Bob Monkhouse and Denis Goodwin – but, as Monkhouse recalled in his autobiography, Hancock loathed their material and would tear pages from the script to use as toilet paper. Galton and Simpson were drafted in for the last six episodes, and stayed as the show's main writers for two years as its name gradually contracted – from *Forces All-Star Bill*, to *All-Star Bill*, and then *Star Bill*. Here's their first sketch with Hancock, experimenting with the wide-boy persona that would eventually belong to Sid James:

CALLING ALL FORCES, episode eleven

First broadcast: Monday 23 June 1952

CHARLIE: Tell me, how did you enjoy the party last night?

TONY: Taking things all round, I had quite a successful evening.

CHARLIE: You did? How?

TONY: Taking things all round.

CHARLIE: Tony, you don't mean…

TONY: Uh-huh. Care to buy a hot grandfather clock?

CHARLIE: Don't be ridiculous. What good is an old grandfather to me?

TONY: I can see you're not an old grandmother.

CHARLIE: I don't understand, Tony. How did you manage to smuggle that huge grandfather clock out of the house without being seen?

TONY: Well, I must admit it was a bit tricky, Charles. After all, it's not easy, carrying a grandfather clock under one arm.

CHARLIE: *One* arm! Why didn't you use the other one?

TONY: What, and drop the piano?

CHARLIE: Anthony Hancock, I'm disgusted with you. Just you take those things back to that house this minute.

TONY: *(PAUSE)* What house?

CHARLIE: *(Shocked) Tony*!

TONY: *(Musing)* I wonder where I can get rid of 20,000 second-hand bricks in a hurry.

The show centred each week on the parody of a cinema spectacular, such as this swords-and-sandals epic, also from their first script for Hancock and Chester:

ORCHESTRA: *(Link music segueing into Egyptian theme – hold under next speech)*

CHARLIE: *(Dramatic)* Egypt! Eternal mystery land of the East, where once reigned the great king Tutankhamen – with his half-brother One-Ton Khamen. It is to this desolate land that Mark Antony, along with his army and Cleopatra, has fled. And we find Mark, completely overcome with love for Cleopatra, sitting all day long on the banks of the Nile, idly throwing passing Egyptians to the crocodiles.

CAROLE CARR: *(Loud scream off mike)*

EFFECTS: *(Loud splash)*

TONY: *(PAUSE)* She loves me.

CAROLE: *(Loud scream off mike)*

EFFECTS: *(Loud splash)*

TONY: She loves me not.

CAROLE: *(Loud scream off mike)*

EFFECTS: *(Loud splash)*

TONY: She loves me. Ah Cleopatra, me proud beauty, what fun it is sitting here by your side, watching the hot sun streaming through my magnifying glass and setting fire to your beard.

EDNA FRYER: Oh Mark. I'm glad I won't be in Rome when Caesar finds out I've fled with you to Egypt. He'll probably throw thousands of Christians to the lions, pillage cities by the score, burn down all the temples, and inflict hideous tortures on the poor slaves.

TONY: Yes, that's Caesar. Anything for a laugh. Quite frankly, Cleo, I never could understand what you ever saw in Caesar. After all, take away his manly physique, his good looks and his blond, wavy hair, and what have you got?

EDNA: You.

TONY: Cleo, me darling. *(Breathes)* Can't you see we were made for each other?

EDNA: Made for each other? How do you know?

TONY: Look at the way me aristocratic Roman nose turns down and your proud Egyptian nose turns up. Every time I kiss you, we lock bumpers.

EDNA: *(Hot and sexy)* Oh Mark, Mark. Stop this idle chitter-chatter. Look into my eyes. Don't you realize you're a man and I'm a woman?

TONY: *(Nervous)* Well, now we've picked sides, shall we get on with the game?

EDNA: *(Sexy)* Mark, stop backing away from me. I'm only a woman hungering for love. Kiss me. Kiss me.

EFFECTS: *(Kiss – the full thing)*

TONY: *(Breathless)* My word. That's what I call a really hot kiss. The Roman eagle on me breastplate just laid an egg.

'Charlie Chester was the top banana on that show,' Ray said. 'He must have made a fortune in the music halls, and radio helped him to keep his name up there in lights, all the time. He insisted on performing a monologue at the start of *Calling All Forces* every week, and he wouldn't allow us to write that. He wrote it himself. And that meant he took 23 guineas, which was a third of the fee for the whole script. Meanwhile, he was earning God knows how much a week. We thought that was a bit underhand.'

CALLING ALL FORCES, episode twelve

First broadcast: Monday 30 June 1952

CHARLIE: Tony, what's the matter with you? You look as if you got out of the wrong side of the gutter this morning.

TONY: I've had a dreadful experience, Charles. They – they took me along to see a psychiatrist.

CHARLIE: A psychiatrist?

TONY: Yes, you know, Charles. He probed into my thoughts, examined my mind, raked up my past.

CHARLIE: He sounds more like a sewer inspector. But tell me, Tony, what did this psychiatrist say?

TONY: Well, after a thorough examination, he said that I was a kleptomaniac.

CHARLIE: Why, that's ridiculous, Tony. You've never been up in one of those things in your life.

TONY: *(Sarcastic)* Charles, do you ever find you can put your finger in one ear and beckon with it out of the other? No, Charles, a kleptomaniac is someone who can't help stealing things – and I don't mind telling you I felt very insulted by what he said. Me – a kleptomaniac. I never thought I'd live to hear someone call me that. What utter nonsense.

CHARLIE: Tony, what's that you're hiding behind your back?

TONY: *(Right on mike)* Can I interest you in a second-hand psychiatrist's couch?

CHARLIE: Oh Tony! What are you? A thief, a crook, a rogue, a cheat, a robber, a swindler…

TONY: I don't know, Charles. You make everything sound so good.

CHARLIE: Tony, you're incorrigible.

TONY: Thank you, Charles. I think you're rather nice-looking too.

CHARLIE: It's obvious that quack didn't do you any good, Tony. But don't

worry, I'll cure you. Now lie down on this couch. That's it. Now I'll test
your reflexes with this hammer. First your left leg.

ORCHESTRA: *(Single note on xylophone)*

CHARLIE: Now the other leg.

ORCHESTRA: *(Different note on xylophone)*

CHARLIE: Now your arm.

ORCHESTRA: *(Another note on xylophone)*

CHARLIE: Now the other arm.

ORCHESTRA: *(Yet another note on xylophone)*

CHARLIE: *(Thoughtful)* Mmmmmmmmm.

ORCHESTRA: *(Xylophone plays 'Colonel Bogey')*

TONY: Oh Charles. Listen. You're playing our tune.

CHARLIE: Right now, Tony. Relax. Let yourself go. Send your mind back.

TONY: Why?

CHARLIE: The guarantee's up next week.

From the same show, a sketch that uses an extended sound effect for the
climax. Galton and Simpson didn't employ nonsense sound effects, as the
Goons did with their raspberries and exploding army boots, but they
revelled in the surreal images that could be conjured with mundane
sound effects such as car engines and train whistles:

CHARLIE: Mmmm. It says, 'Dear Mr Hancock, in reply to your
advertisement for a wife, we are sending a suitable young lady by the
name of Deirdre Laverne round today. Signed: the Golders Green
Matrimonial and Lonely Hearts Society.' Tony! What have you been
doing?

TONY: Well, Charles, I thought it was time I settled down and got married.
You see, I've always had a hankering to hear hordes of little
Hancocks howling their hearts out.

CHARLIE: Here, Tony, there's a girl coming up the path, holding a copy of
the *Matrimonial Times*.

TONY: That must be her, Charles. Let me have a look – oh no! *Charles*,
look. She's so big – she must be about eleven feet tall. Look, she's…
she's bent over to light her cigarette!

CHARLIE: What's wrong with that?

TONY: From a lamp post? This is terrible. She's ugly, too. What am I going
to do? She'll be here any minute and she'll expect me to marry her.

EFFECTS: (Door opens)

JENNIFER RAMAGE: *(Horsey, sporting type)* Hallo there. My name is Deirdre Laverne. Who are you?

TONY: Hiram P. Gluckenheimer.

JENNIFER: Well, which one of you is Tony Hancock?

TONY: He is!

CHARLIE: Why, you double-crossing…

JENNIFER: I've waited so long for this moment. Mr Hancock – Tony, darling… I will!

CHARLIE: Go away. *I'm* not Hancock. *He* is.

TONY: Oh, well. Goodbye.

> EFFECTS: *(Very fast running footsteps – quick door open and shut – more very fast running footsteps – quick car door open and shut – powerful car starting up and racing away – dissolve into express train racing along at full speed – dissolve into jet plane hurtling past and fading into distance – slide whistle down – terrific crash.)*

CHARLIE: What happened?

TONY: *(Right on mike)* My braces were caught in the door.

By 1952, the two writers had shares in a flat in Richmond – a bohemian bolthole which they shared at £6 a week with a collective of chancers, artists and their girlfriends, who were often nurses. Nobody really lived there: it was a place to stage parties and sleep off the effects. 'It used to get pretty wild,' Ray said. 'We'd be up half the night, music blaring out. The flat was next door to a police station, but the police didn't stop us. They would just bang on the wall and call out, "Oi!" They'd look out of the window and we would look out of the window, sideways. All very friendly. So we'd invite them in for a drink, and they'd come in and get pissed. And knock off the nurses during the day.'

A year later, as their success grew, they both bought sports cars. 'We both had the same model, Austin A40s, with dropheads, and bodies by Jensen,' Alan said. 'I got mine first, and then Ray found another one – his was apple-green, an unusual colour. That made a lot of difference to life. We started getting out of the city.'

Bath was a favourite destination: with little traffic on the roads and no speed cameras, they could rise late after a party and still be at the Hole in the Wall restaurant, reckoned by many to be the best in Britain, for lunch. Recalling the thrill of fifties motoring is one of the few things that makes them nostalgic: 'In those days,' Ray said, 'you could park the car anywhere you liked. If you were going shopping on Oxford Street, or in Piccadilly, you'd just pull up.'

When they were socializing, they did not discuss their work. They shared an identical sense of humour, which was a keystone of their almost telepathic understanding, but they never worked on comedy scripts outside the office. They were proud of being professional writers, craftsmen who could lay down their tools at the day's end. That self-discipline prevented their friendship from becoming claustrophobic; it also meant they returned fresh to the work each day.

As they became more confident at writing for Tony Hancock, they began to see him as a grandiose fantasist, with a childlike yearning to be the romantic hero of his own life:

CALLING ALL FORCES, episode thirteen

First broadcast: Monday 7 July 1952

TONY: *(Sings)* The Wheel of Fortune has come away in my hand. *(Shouts)* Right men, break out those top gallants, batten down the hatches, hoist the top sail, raise the ensign, secure the rigging, make fast the bow rope, weigh the anchor, lower the gangplank – and the last one up on deck's a cissy. Well, Chester, we're almost there. All we have to do is navigate this tricky coral reef.

CHARLIE: What's a coral reef?

TONY: It's a barrier of rock built by millions of little insects who work at terrific speeds. But look, there's a gap. We'll go through.

EFFECTS: (Terrific crash)

TONY: *(PAUSE)* Fast little devils, aren't they?

CHARLIE: I say, Captain, look. The natives are lined up on the shore to greet us.

TONY: Yes, and they're making frantic signals to us. What do you make of it?

CHARLIE: Either they're being very rude or we've only got two minutes before the tide goes out.

TONY: Right, quickly. Throw a line out.

CHARLIE: Which one?

TONY: That last one. It didn't get a laugh.

Both over 6ft 3ins tall, both articulate with strong London accents, both clean-shaven (the beards came, and went, later), Galton and Simpson were alike in almost everything. Alan was the more soberly dressed, though: it was Ray who seized on fashions and improved them, or simply improvised. 'In the fifties, most men were expected to dress like their fathers,' he said. 'I was one of the first people to start wearing Edwardian styles, even before the kids on the street caught onto it. I had my clothes made – I still get dressed up to the nines in whichever way I like, cowboy styles or whatever.' He had his clothes made by a friend from the sanatorium, who was a tailor at a Wimbledon department store called Elys. Alan preferred conventional suits.

'I really hate old men's clothes,' Ray said. 'They're generally brown. And cheap-looking. Beige.'

'Beige is serviceable,' Alan retorted. 'Doesn't show the dirt!'

CALLING ALL FORCES, episode fifteen

First broadcast: Monday 21 July 1952

TONY: *(Humming to himself)* Piece of chiffon here. Pin a strip of satin there. Few inches of silk just over there...

CHARLIE: *(Coming on)* Ah, there you are, Tony. What are all these bits of cloth doing all over the floor? Look at the mess you're making.

TONY: Mess, Charles? Mess? I don't think you quite comprehend. You are now witnessing the birth of a new epoch in the female fashion world. *I* am opening a dress designing house.

CHARLIE: You? A dress designer? Ha, ha, ha! Just think – Tony Hancock...

TONY: Ah, ah, ah, ah, ah! Not *Tony* Hancock. From now on it's... Antoine Hancock.

CHARLIE: *(Scornful)* Antoine Hancock. You couldn't even design a *salad* dressing.

TONY: Oh no, birdbrain? It so happens I've just finished my latest creation. Here you are. Just cast your mince pies over this little lot. I've called it 'Beautiful Morning in the Champs-Élysées'.

CHARLIE: Looks more like a 'Filthy Night in Clapham High Street'. Just look at that colour scheme. Bright green bodice, black skirt with a tweed cap. What debutante would wear an outfit like that?

TONY: Agatha Stinkweed. She's reserve goalkeeper for Scunthorpe United.

CHARLIE: No, but honestly, Antoine, you'll never get anywhere in this business unless you get famous people among your clientele. Are there any film stars wearing anything of yours?

TONY: Yes. Ralph Richardson's got a pair of my old socks, Larry begged a few of my cast-off vests. Dame Edith Evans…

CHARLIE: I didn't mean that. I meant, do you make any dresses for film *actresses*?

TONY: No, but I have a few designs on Diana Dors. Ha, ha, ha, ha! Dresses. A few designs. Oh my word. Listen to old Hancock. I just snatched that one out of the air.

CHARLIE: Put it back, it needs all the air it can get. Now look, Tony – I mean Antoine. How can you open a dress designing shop? You haven't even got a model.

TONY: That's just where you're wrong, Chester. The agency are sending a girl round for me to interview. I've asked for a girl who's tall, slim, graceful and as beautiful as the day is long.

EFFECTS: (Door opens)

MIRIAM KARLIN: *(As potty Ada)* Hallo. Antoine Hancock?

CHARLIE: Short day, wasn't it?

MIRIAM: My name is Ada Spludgebucket. My name is Ada Spludgebucket. Pleased to meet you. Pleased to meet you. Nice day. Nice day.

TONY: Pardon my curiosity, but why do you say everything twice?

MIRIAM: Two heads.

CHARLIE: So this is the girl who wants to become a model?

MIRIAM: That's right.

CHARLIE: With that face and that figure, there's only one suit *she* could model.

TONY: What's that?

CHARLIE: A diving suit.

Potty Ada Spludgebucket was a character who kept turning up in Galton and Simpson scripts: she is the half-mad aunt at the Steptoe family funeral, for instance, who starts lifting up her skirt to flash her bloomers after a glass of sherry. In *Steptoe and Son*, they took stereotypes ('Tart-with-a-Heart', 'Bible-Bashing Conman', 'Vague Vicar', and others) and subtly, with great craft, revealed the real characters within the stock figures. At the start of their careers, though, they were more intent on sending them up. Here, they cast Eric Barker as the absent-minded-professor-with-a-beautiful-daughter of Tarzan adventures:

CALLING ALL FORCES, episode sixteen

First broadcast: Monday 28 July 1952

ERIC: And so Professor Chester, my daughter Jane and myself began to get ready for our arduous journey to Africa.

EDNA: Shall I help you to pack, Father?

ERIC: Ah, thank you, Jane. Let's see now. Four sleds, two teams of huskies, six pairs of snowshoes, four pairs of skis and eight fur coats.

CHARLIE: What are you taking all that to Africa for?

ERIC: So we can travel across the snows.

EDNA: But Father, there isn't any snow in Africa.

ERIC: I know. I've thought of that. I'm taking eight boxfuls with us.

CHARLIE: But why?

ERIC: We'll sprinkle it under the sled to make it go faster.

EDNA: But Father, you've forgotten something. The snow will melt in Africa.

ERIC: I know. That's why I'm taking the refrigerator. We can store the snow away every night. I'm not silly, you know. Right. We fly to Africa tomorrow.

ORCHESTRA: (Bridge)

EFFECTS: (Plane taking off. Merge into…)

ORCHESTRA: ('The Campbells Are Coming')

CHARLIE: This isn't Africa. Back into the plane.

EFFECTS: (Plane taking off. Merge into…)

ORCHESTRA: (Hawaiian music)

CHARLIE: This isn't Africa. Back into the plane.

EFFECTS: (Plane taking off. Merge into…)

ORCHESTRA: (Chinese music)

CHARLIE: Ah, here we are. Unpack, everybody.

Calling All Forces changed its name and its format in autumn 1952, becoming *Forces All-Star Bill*, with the series going out back-to-back. It used a variety of compères and didn't always feature Tony Hancock, but he was an audience favourite, and his return caused some rejoicing:

FORCES ALL-STAR BILL, series two, episode thirteen

First broadcast: Sunday 8 March 1953

MICHAEL HOWARD: Well, well, Tony Hancock, in the flesh... and so much
of it.

TONY: Hullo, hullo, back on the programme ten seconds, and old
spectacle mush here starts insulting me. You shouldn't talk to me like
that – the prodigal son has returned, you should kill the fatted calf.

MICHAEL: Looks like the fatted calf has returned, we should kill the
prodigal son.

TONY: *(On mike)* And that, listeners, gives Howard the lead by two
wheezes to one. Howard leading, two wheezes to one. And now
back to the contest for a smashing rejoinder from the boy. *(Normal)*
Tell me, how would you like to appear in a new musical play I'm
presenting?

MICHAEL: What's it called – Porky and Bess?

TONY: Ha! Ha! Ha! Ha! Oh my word yes that one backfired, didn't it?
Three insults in a row, eh? They're really rolling off your tongue,
aren't they? *(Nasty)* Be careful your teeth don't follow suit.

Galton and Simpson were drafted in to write the entire second series of
Forces All-Star Bill. Its target audience was unique to its time. In the
1950s, all young men who passed the National Service medical were
required to spend two years in the British armed forces, and in the early
fifties that meant huge numbers were called up to serve in the army, navy
and air force. The BBC's directive to its writers was simple: keep the
troops entertained.

FORCES ALL-STAR BILL, series two, episode fourteen

First broadcast: Sunday 15 March 1953

GRAHAM: I'm Alfred Hackett, Regimental Sergeant Major of the 3rd
Golders Green Life Guards and blanco taster to the trade.

BONAR: And what are you doing here?

GRAHAM: I have been detailed to the BBC, me being the herbert what
has been lumbered with the Forces Edificational Broadcasts on
account of I've copped hold of some epidemic cerstificates which
henables me to talk about that what which they wouldn't
comprehend too good enough hotherwise... won't they... yus... eh!

Now, it's my job to try and educate our charlie boys overseas and this week my lecture is entitled, 'What National Service men should know before being posted to a camp what contains members of the opposite... if you'll pardon the expression... sex.' Lesson one is the vultures and the locusts.

BONAR: Don't you mean the birds and the bees?

GRAHAM: No, this is an advanced course. Now then, the first hint is on the art of proposing... to wit: to woo... as drawn up by the Army Council. First of all you must sort out the objective, surround her and with a quick pincer movement cut off her line of retreat. You should then consolidate your position by digging in... and if no resistance is encountered you are, to coin a phrase, on to a bit of all right.

BONAR: Yeah? And then what happens then?

GRAHAM: You moves in to mop up. By then she should be utterly routed and you moves in to press your suit. You do this by taking two paces smartly forward and with the top lip a-quivering and nostrils diluted you gaze down into her upturned minces and in a voice a-throbbin' with passion you says, 'Ermintrude, how about changing your moniker to 1609523?'

Graham Stark, from Hancock's Eager Beaver patrol on the Derek Roy show, was a versatile comic on *Forces All-Star Bill*: 'He did an American voice, like the cat Sylvester in the Tweetie-Pie cartoons,' said Alan, 'but playing it as a swaggering six-year-old kid. And he had this catchphrase, "I'm a dog." Graham used to idolize that character – he still talks about it.'

FORCES ALL-STAR BILL, series two, episode fourteen

First broadcast: 15 March 1953

TONY: *(Calls)* Oh, Sylvester.

GRAHAM: Yeah? What do you want?

TONY: Look, supposing I told you old Hancock was in a hole...

GRAHAM: *(Vicious)* Impossible, they don't dig them that wide.

TONY: Yes, but supposing I *was* in a hole, what would you do?

GRAHAM: *(Vicious)* Shovel the dirt in.

JOAN HEAL: *(Sarcastic)* My, my, what a charming little boy. I wonder where he comes from.

BONAR COLLEANO: Out of a basket every time you blow a flute. Now listen, kid, we're entering you for a beautiful child contest.

GRAHAM: Oh yeah?

JOAN: Now come on, Sylvester, we've got to try and get you groomed up ready for the contest. Now let's comb your hair out of your face and see what you look like. There.

TONY, JOAN and BONAR: *(All scream)*

BONAR: Gee, I've seen better looking faces on a Japanese television set.

GRAHAM: Listen, moe – one more crack like that and I'll bash you over the head so hard you'll have to wear open-toed shoes to see where you're going.

TONY: Now come on, let's get on. The baby contest starts in a minute.

JOAN: I think we'd better give him a good wash first. Put him under the tap.

GRAHAM: No, no, let me go. Help!

TONY: Hand me the scrubbing brush, Colleano. Fine. Now for his neck.

(Effects: Scrubbing noise)

GRAHAM: *(Shouts)* Hey Mac, take it easy with the scrubbing brush. You're almost down to my skin.

TONY: Come on, Colleano, let's do his hair. You hold his head while I cut it off. What sort of hairstyle shall we give him?

BONAR: How about a bang over the eyes?

GRAHAM: Hey, Hancock – I hope you know what you're doing with those scissors.

TONY: Certainly. Hancock haircuts come in three different styles. Short, very short and ''Iggins – put this one in the incubator'.

EFFECTS: (Scissors snipping)

JOAN: *(Worried)* Now watch out, Tony, don't go mad with those scissors.

BONAR: Hey, Sylvester – can you hear what I'm saying?

GRAHAM: Yeah.

BONAR: That's strange. Your ears hit the ground five minutes ago.

TONY: Right. There we are. That's your hair cut. Now just put your Little Lord Fauntleroy suit on. That's it. Now, let's get him down to the contest.

ORCHESTRA: (Link)

EFFECTS: (Door open and shut)

TONY: Why, Sylvester.

GRAHAM: Hello Piggy. I'm back.

BONAR: Good, did you win?

GRAHAM: Of course I did.

TONY: Good. Excellent. And... er... did you get the five hundred pounds?

GRAHAM: No.

JOAN: You didn't? Then what did you get?

GRAHAM: Five hundred bags of bones.

TONY: Five hundred bags of... Didn't you win the beautiful child contest?

GRAHAM: No, that was yesterday. I just won Crufts first prize for the most beautiful Cocker spaniel of 1953.

TONY: You don't mean...

GRAHAM: Yeah. I'm a dog!

Another regular was Geraldine McEwan, about to experience her first starring role on television in a detective series called *Crime On Our Hands*. Decades later, she would be the definitive version of Miss Marple. When this show went out, she was not quite twenty-one, and Hancock's yearning for her was a running gag:

FORCES ALL-STAR BILL, series two, episode sixteen

First broadcast: 12 April 1953

TONY: *(Clark Gable type)* Ah Geraldine, my darling. Don't try and fight this thing, it's bigger than both of us. From now on, it's just you and me, Geraldine. *(Kissing noises)* It's no use denying it, kid, you love me. You know you love me. *(Kissing noises)* Now come on, admit it. You're fascinated by me, Geraldine. You're crazy about me. You just can't resist me. *(Kissing)* Ah, why do you cheapen yourself like this, Geraldine? Why do you throw yourself at me? Do I mean so much to you? Yeah, of course I do. *(Kissing)* Oh Geraldine, Geraldine...

EFFECTS: *(Door opens)*

GERALDINE: Hallo, Anthony.

TONY: Hallo, Geraldine.

GERALDINE: Anthony, why are you sitting on the couch kissing that floor mop?

TONY: *(Clutching at straws)* Floor mop, Geraldine? Floor mop? Ha, ha! Ah, but it isn't a floor mop. No, it's me dinner. Ah, that's it, me dinner. Yes, I'm eating me dinner.

GERALDINE: Your dinner?

TONY: Yes, spaghetti bolognese on a giant chopstick.

3 The Emergence of Hancock

T he next series in the Galton and Simpson canon was simply called *Star Bill*, each episode a full hour, with a packed programme of songs from the musicals and chart hits between the sketches. By now, in the rhythm of the lines and the precision of the wordplay, the mature Galton and Simpson style was emerging.

'We had different guests every week,' recalled Graham Stark, 'and they [Galton and Simpson] wrote as if they had been writing for them all their lives. They could write for anybody at all, and everything they wrote was incredible class. I adore them; they're my favourite people. This extraordinary partnership that they have... When you meet them, they don't seem to have any particular chemistry, but by God they have. Just extraordinary. They are so inventive, there's not an ounce of cliché in anything they write. Look at Charlie Chaplin, all the greats – you don't know why they are so great but they just are. Alan and Ray are faultless, I've never read a bad script of theirs in my life.'

STAR BILL, series one, episode one

First broadcast: Sunday 7 June 1953

ROBIN: Ladies and gentlemen. We have great pleasure tonight in presenting the very first broadcast of a very unusual act. Straight from their sensational overnight success at the Chipping Sodbury Working Men's Sewing Circle and Ballet Class, here are those tiddly trapeze artists – Antonio and Grahamina, the two Gorgonzolas.
ORCHESTRA: (Chord)
GRAHAM & TONY: We bring you somersaults from out of the sky, my brother and I.
ROBIN: In their death-defying act, Antonio and Grahamina will swing backwards and forwards across the stage on a trapeze suspended 500 feet off the ground. What gives them this amazing courage? Is it

their confidence in their own ability? Is it their great artistry? Is it their nerves of steel?

TONY: *(On mike)* Or is it because their hands are glued to the bar?

ROBIN: And now to Grahamina to tell you about the act.

GRAHAM: Thank you. For our first trick on the trapeze tonight, Antonio will do a treble back somersault through a flaming hoop with his hands tied behind his back, his eyes blindfolded, while he balances upside down with his head wedged between the handlebars of a large motorbike.

TONY: *(Heavy drama)* No, no, I can't do it. I can't do it, I tell you. I can't do it.

GRAHAM: Why?

TONY: I haven't got a driving licence.

The first show was broadcast five days after the coronation of Elizabeth II. In two sketches, the writers first imagined Hancock's view of the pageantry, and then parodied the BBC coverage:

GERALDINE: Hello Anthony. What did you think of the Coronation? Wasn't it wonderful?

TONY: I didn't see it.

GERALDINE: But you camped out in the Mall all Monday night.

TONY: I know, that's the trouble. I didn't wake up till Wednesday.

GERALDINE: Oh Anthony, you are the limit. After all the trouble I went to – hiring your sleeping bag with the picture of Marilyn Monroe so you needn't get cold. Making your cocoa just the way you like it – 90 per cent proof. Didn't you wake up at all?

TONY: Yes, I must admit I woke up once. There were a lot of brass bands going by, so I opened me eyes, but I couldn't see a thing.

GERALDINE: Why not?

TONY: I'd climbed into me sleeping bag head first.

GERALDINE: So what did you do?

TONY: I took me shoes off, and me feet had the time of their lives. Ah yes, best Coronation plates on view.

GERALDINE: Complete with mug.

...

ROBIN: Another feature of the Coronation was the sterling work done by the BBC commentators. We take up the commentary as Wynford Vaughan Stark is describing the scene from his vantage point on top of a guardsman's busby.

EFFECTS: *(Crowd noise in background)*

GRAHAM: *(Fading in)*... and the people all round me in the Mall are restless and impatient as they wait for the procession to come round the corner. This really is a momentous occasion and the air of expectancy is... No thanks, Gilbert, I'm on the wagon till after the broadcast. Er... the air of expectancy is apparent everywhere. *(Excited)* And now I believe... Yes! Yes! A great cheer goes up as the procession turns the corner and proceeds majestically up the Mall. What a glorious sight. I can see the glittering coaches, looking magnificent in the morning sunlight... It's a really... *(Panicky and disjointed)* I... where... here... I say, I've dropped my microphone. Where is it? Sir, will you please take your feet *off* my microphone? Shan't be long, listeners. Ah, I've got it. And as I straighten up I can just see the procession... *(Despondent)* disappearing round Admiralty Arch. Oh, I wish you could have seen this, listeners. You might have been able to tell *me* what was going on. But now for another eye-witness description of what they tell me is a simply glorious sight, and so over to Audrey Bustle in Whitehall.

GERALDINE: Audrey Bustle here, and in the distance I can hear the strains of the military bands heralding the approach of the procession. It should be coming into view any moment now, and I expect you're all dying to hear what this glorious pageant looks like and so I will... *(Annoyed)* Well, of all the nerve. Just look at that Joan Heal over there. Wearing the same dress as me. If that isn't the limit. She distinctly told me she would be wearing her emerald green square neck today, and there she is in that duck egg blue thing. I've never been so... oh, she's seen me. *(Calls very sweetly)* Hallo *darling*! You look ravishing *darling*! Goodbye *darling*! Look after yourself *darling*! *(Undertone)* Two-faced cat.

GRAHAM: *(Urgent whisper)* The commentary, the commentary.

GERALDINE: *(Disgruntled)* Oh yes, the commentary. Well, as the procession disappears in the distance, let somebody else get on with it.

TONY: *(RAF type)* Hallo listeners. Raymond Glenn Hancock here and – well, quite frankly, I can't see a dickey bird. I've left my glasses at home, and the rain has sort of curled my moustache right up around my eyes and sort of blacked out the whole issue. But I must say it *sounds* first class. The glorious sort of jingle-jangle of the harnesses, the splendid sort of clip-clop of the horses, the majestic sort of trundle-trundle of the wheels. And the overall sort of picture one gets in one's mind is a sort of jingle-jangle, clip-clop, trundle-trundle. I can't describe it any more except to say it *sounds* really wonderful. I do wish I could see it – don't you? But now to the last sort of few yards of the procession. I understand Wynford Vaughan Stark has sort of nipped round to a new vantage point outside the Coach and Horses near Westminster Bridge. So let's sort of go over to the Coach and Horses for some more graphic descriptions.

GRAHAM: *(Slightly drunk)* Thank you, landlord. And as I lift my glasses up to my eyes and look down them I can see – the perishing things are empty. Fill 'em up again, landlord.

Hancock's persona as a comedian who did not tell jokes was now becoming established with the audience. It was Hancock's instinctive ability to weigh a line that made this lack of overt humour possible; he could time his delivery to perfection even at first sight. Other comics would scan a page, counting the gags and looking for the punchlines, and might demand rewrites if the bellylaughs were not obvious. Tony Hancock, by contrast, could see that his biggest laughs often came where there were no words at all, in the pauses. By pacing his run-up, Hancock would prime the audience to laugh in anticipation, between lines, as they relished his performance.

By the time *Hancock's Half Hour* made him Britain's best-loved comic, the gales of laughter before a line could bring the show to a halt. Hancock would chide the audience – 'wait for it, wait for it!' – and then coast into his next remark on the surge of laughter. Galton and Simpson gave him the scope to do this, by cutting him free from gags and set-ups. It was a technique developed by US comics, especially Jack Benny, but Hancock did it far better than any other British comedian, and by the beginning of *Star Bill* the writers were already talking to him about their ideal, of moving away from stand-up routines altogether. In the meantime, if Hancock had to tell jokes, he did it as badly as possible:

STAR BILL, series one, episode two

First broadcast: Sunday 14 June 1953

TONY: *(To himself)* Let's see now. Why did the chicken cross the road? Oooh, that's a hard one. Let me think. Why did the chicken cross the road? Yes… um… er… ah! I've got it! When it's ajar. No. No. That's when is a pickle pot not a pickle pot. Yes. Why did the chicken… no, I give up. Don't know that one. Let's see. Answers – turn to page 74. Ah, here we are. Why did the chicken cross the road? To get to the other side. *(Laughs)* To get to the other side. Must jot that one down. Be a sensation.

GERALDINE: Hallo Tony, what are you reading?

TONY: Me new gag book. Half a million jokes, all new, ninepence... *(Emotional)* Geraldine, I have a confession to make. When I'm up in front of this microphone, you know me as gay, laughing, hilarious old Hancock... but I've been living a lie. *(Dramatic)* Geraldine, I have never said a funny thing in my life.

GERALDINE: When do we get to the lie?

TONY: All those funny things you hear me say aren't me at all. I employ a ventriloquist. He stands off stage thinking up funny jokes while I stand here opening me mouth. *(Emotional)* Yes, Hancock the funny man is nothing but a great big dummy.

GERALDINE: When do we get to the lie?

TONY: Quiet. That's why I've had to learn a few jokes. Me ventriloquist hasn't turned up tonight. Still, I'm not worried now. As soon as Charlie Chester gets here, I'll dart forward, confront him with it, and stand back while he totters around the stage in a right two-and-eight.

GERALDINE: Well, I hope it works.

TONY: Of course it'll work. I'll say, 'Why did the chicken cross the road?' and he's bound to say, 'I don't know,' and then I'm in. Bash! Big laugh. He won't know what's hit him.

ROBIN: Oh, excuse me Hancock, our guest comic has arrived.

TONY: Good. Bring him on, Mr Boyle. Lead him to his doom. *(To himself)* What an answer. Demoralize him.

EFFECTS: (Applause)

TONY: Good evening, Mr Chester, it's a great pleasure to have you on the programme and I bet you're just dying to know why the chicken crossed the road.

CHARLIE: No thanks, not now, I'm busy.

TONY: I insist on you knowing why the chicken crossed the road.

CHARLIE: Look, I'm not interested. Some other time.

TONY: Very impatient chicken. Can't wait to nip across that road.

CHARLIE: I don't care. I hate chickens.

TONY: Better hurry up. It's halfway across.

CHARLIE: I don't care where it is. Run away.

GERALDINE: Is Anthony annoying you, Mr Chester?

CHARLIE: Yes he is... hallo! A female. All over, too. Careful where you tread – my tongue's around there some place. *(Growls)* Come to Char-lee.

GERALDINE: Please! Mr Chester! Can't you control yourself?

CHARLIE: Yes, but it's more fun this way. Oh Geraldine, where have you been all my life?

GERALDINE: I don't know, but I'm glad.

TONY: And there's this beautiful stretch of empty road, see, when who should come walking round the corner but this chicken. 'Oooh,' he said to himself, 'I think I'll nip a bit smartish across this road,' so…

CHARLIE: Stop interrupting me. Nobody cares about the chicken. Oh Geraldine, the night is so young and so beautiful…

TONY: So this chicken was dodging in and out of the traffic, trying to find a zebra crossing…

CHARLIE: Why don't you come out with me after the show tonight, Geraldine?

GERALDINE: But I'm going out with Anthony.

CHARLIE: Hancock? Why bother with the dandelion when the rose is in bloom?

TONY: Well, by now it was winter time and this poor little chicken was feeling dead parky waiting to cross this perishing road.

CHARLIE: Are you still on about this chicken?

GERALDINE: Oh, let him tell you, Charlie, it's the only joke he knows. He's been rehearsing it all evening. If he doesn't get a laugh tonight, they'll throw him off the show.

CHARLIE: Oh all right, let's have it.

TONY: Ah, me big chance. Bring the house down. Biggest laugh of the evening. Come on, you say to me, 'Why did the chicken cross the road?' Ready? Go!

CHARLIE: Why did the chicken cross the road?

TONY: Stand by for blasting. Here it comes. The chicken crossed the road be… the chicken… forgotten it. Me gag. Only one I know. Me belter gone for a burton. Don't go away, I'll think of something. Ha! Ha! Why did the chicken cross the road? Because it saw Evelyn Laye! No, that's not it. Try again. Because it saw Gregory Peck! No! Worse still. Ha! Ha! Boo! No! Applause! That's me lot. Don't know any more. Because it couldn't drive a steamroller. Doesn't make any sense. Who cares? That's it. Goodnight all. Don't throw things at the boy. He's doing his best. Aaaah! Help!

(Musical Break)

TONY: I'd like to have a little farm of me own, where I can settle down and potter about amongst the animals. I can even experiment on me livestock. Why, who knows, I might be able to cross a Buff-Orpington with a Rhode Island Red.

CHARLIE: Just a minute. Why should you cross the Rhode with a Buff-Orpington?

TONY: To get to the other side! I've done it. I've got it in. That's the one – success. All go home now.

Galton and Simpson only ever worked together and never collaborated with other writers. 'The way other partnerships worked, one person might write one episode, the other one might write the next, and then hand it to each other to go over and amend,' said Alan. 'We never did that. We always sat next to each other and started from scratch. Sometimes one would start the joke, the other would finish it. Fifty-fifty.'

Together, they were developing a persona for Hancock, which reflected, with exaggerations and distortions, the comedian's off-stage personality. His earnest insistence on high professional standards could seem like pomposity. That same eagerness could make him oblivious to other people's sarcasm, so that sometimes he appeared gullible. And his insecurities made him uneasily aware of his fame. The character who appeared in *Star Bill*, though far from the mature Hancock of the sitcoms, was already big-headed, flat-footed and thick-skinned:

STAR BILL, series one, episode three

First broadcast: Sunday 21 June 1953

GERALDINE: I don't know what we're going to do with Tony, Graham. I told you it was a mistake, showing him that fan letter.

GRAHAM: You mean, he's gone big-headed on the strength of one fan letter?

GERALDINE: Well, it's the only one he's ever had. From some woman. She said he was the most beautiful, most talented man she'd ever seen.

GRAHAM: I thought people in those places were only allowed to write to near relatives.

GERALDINE: This is serious, Graham. That letter has really turned his head. He even went to the beauty parlour today for a mudpack.

GRAHAM: I thought I'd noticed an improvement.

GERALDINE: Graham, the mudpack doesn't come off till tomorrow morning.

GRAHAM: Well, where's lover boy now?

GERALDINE: He's having all the walls and ceilings of his room lined with mirrors. He says he doesn't want to miss one glorious inch.

GRAHAM: Sssssssh. Here he comes now.

TONY: *(Comes on singing)* A I'm Adorable, B I'm so Beautiful, C I'm a Cutie full of Charm, D I'm so…

GRAHAM: *(Sarcastic)* Geraldine, come quickly. Look who's here. Miss Biscuit Factory 1953.

TONY: Ah, what an exhilarating time I've had strolling round me boudoir, drinking in the sheer beauty of all the pin-up photos stuck on the wall.

GRAHAM: Pin-up photos? Who of?

TONY: Me. Ah, it does a man like me good to occasionally come back to you plain, dull, ordinary people.

GERALDINE: *(Sotto)* See what I mean, Graham? He's like this all the time.

TONY: Where's me engagement book? Ah, let's see. Monday. Farewell ride round the park with the Queen of Tonga. Better take me umbrella just in case. Tuesday…

GRAHAM: Oh, this is ridiculous. Tony, I want to talk with you.

TONY: Talk? Let's have a look at me book. No, I don't think so. Not today. Full right up. I can manage Thursday at four. Yes, I'll grant you an audience on Thursday.

GRAHAM: *(Firmly)* Now!

TONY: Now? All right, you'll just have to ring up Douglas Fairbanks and tell him I can't come to his party. Ava Gardner will just have to dance with somebody else, that's all.

GRAHAM: Tony, this has got to stop.

GERALDINE: Yes, you're getting far too much above yourself.

GRAHAM: Just because some stupid woman sends you a letter.

TONY: Stupid woman? She's me fan.

GRAHAM: Look, Lady Windermere, you've been acting like a temperamental ham ever since we showed you that letter.

TONY: I have not! That letter has not made any difference to me at all. I'm still the same old modest, unaffected Hancock that I've always been.

GERALDINE: Oh good, then we can all go down to the Palais tonight.

TONY: Er, no, not tonight. I'm expecting somebody.

GRAHAM: Who?

TONY: My new butler.

GRAHAM: Oh no! What do you need a butler for?

TONY: *(Airily)* What you don't seem to understand, Starky, is that a man in

my position, the heart-throb of countless millions, has a certain
position to uphold. Yes, I've got a great weight on my shoulders.
GERALDINE: Don't worry, it's only your head.

Hancock himself was under increasing pressure. As well as hosting this hour-long weekly radio special, he was appearing nightly in a long-running spectacular at the Adelphi Theatre, called *London Laughs*. A command from Buckingham Palace to appear before the new queen at the Royal Variety Performance heightened his anxieties. 'He is a worrier,' commented a profile in *Television Mirror*. 'He worries when he has the audience convulsed with laughter. He worries as much over a box-office sell-out as when the auditorium is only partly full. And he worries himself sick over every broadcast he does.' After nine weeks of *Star Bill*, he quit the show, forcing Galton and Simpson to rewrite quickly for another presenter.

The format, with its musical interludes and guest stars, was easily adapted. 'It was an hour-long show. You used to have a guest musician, a guest singer, a guest comedian and sometimes a guest actor,' Alan explained, 'and you'd do a sketch with each of them, and then you'd finish up with the big sketch where everyone took part.'

Alfred Marks, like Hancock an RAF wartime veteran who had been working as a variety comedian since demob, took over. His first guest was Terry-Thomas, already in his forties, though he had not yet found international fame as the caddish star of films such as *School for Scoundrels*. Ray and Alan admired his work, and were alarmed to discover that he didn't like theirs. 'We wrote this sketch for him on *Star Bill*,' Ray said, 'and he told us, "I don't think this is at all funny. In fact, it's a load of shee-ite. What are you trying to do to my career, ruin me? It's bloody awful!" And he went on for the whole rehearsal until Josef Locke, who was the guest singer, a big Irish guy, picked him up by the scruff of his neck and held him against the frame of the door. "If you don't shut up," he said, "and if you don't go on and do these lads' script, I'll knock you right through this fucking door." He went on, and the sketch went like a bomb, but did he say a word to us afterwards? No, he didn't – he just sloped off.'

Alan took up the story: 'Fifteen years later, we were in Hollywood, and we were invited to a party in Terry's house. We brought the subject up, and he was good enough to be shame-faced about it. "Sorry," he said, "what a right shit I was." I don't know if he really remembered the incident, but we got on well with him after that!'

STAR BILL, series one, episode ten

First broadcast: Sunday 9 August 1953

GRAHAM: Good evening, Mr Terry-Thomas. Welcome to *Star Bill*. May I say how elegant you look, in that close-fitting black suit. Though I'm sure you are a lot thinner than when I last saw you.

TERRY: *(Acidly)* When you've finished talking to my cigarette holder, perhaps *I* can come in.

GRAHAM: Oh, of course. Mr Marks won't keep you long. He's just getting changed. Oh, here he is now.

ALFRED: Good evening.

TERRY: Good evening, I'm Terry-hyphen-Thomas.

ALFRED: I'm Alfred-question-Marks.

TERRY: Good heavens. I thought you were a coal sack with legs.

ALFRED: *(Indignant) This* is my new evening dress.

TERRY: You must spend some pretty sordid evenings.

GERALDINE: As a matter of interest, Mr Terry-Thomas, what would you wear with a suit like that?

TERRY: An ankle-length overcoat buttoned up to the neck.

ALFRED: There's nothing wrong with this suit. It fits me right down to the ground.

TERRY: Yes, especially the shirt tail. I like the way it pokes out of the bottom of your trouser legs.

ALFRED: It saves wearing spats.

GERALDINE: I must say, Alfred, that suit does look a trifle lumpy.

ALFRED: That's because I'm buying it on the never-never.

GRAHAM: So what?

ALFRED: The tailor doesn't trust me, so he's in here with me.

GRAHAM: The… er… top hat's a bit on the large size, isn't it?

TERRY: Oh, I don't know, perhaps it can be taken in a bit round the shoulders.

ALFRED: *(Icily)* Anything else?

TERRY: Well, I don't like to appear unduly critical, but is the suit *supposed* to have four legs?

ALFRED: It has *not* got four legs. My shoulder pads have slipped and the sleeves are dragging. All it needs is a slight alteration. There. That's it. Latest-style Edwardian turn-back cuffs. Everybody's wearing them.

TERRY: Yes, but not to the elbows.

ALFRED: All right. All right. So I admit the evening dress is a failure. But wait till you see me new games outfit. That's the one. I'll just nip out and put it on.

EFFECTS: (Door opens and shuts twice, quickly)

ALFRED: There you are, sportsman of the year. Like it?
TERRY: Oh yes. Sou'wester, oilskin cape, gum boots and inflated water
    wings. Very chic. I didn't know you were keen on fishing.
ALFRED: I'm not.
TERRY: Then what are you dressed up like that for?
ALFRED: I'm umpiring in the fifth test match at the Oval. *(Goes off)* Play...
    how's that... not out... no ball...

The *Star Bill* format was adapted at the end of 1953 to give Frankie Howerd his own show. Howerd's popularity helped the producers to attract the biggest names in theatre. 'We had remarkable guest stars,' Ray remembered: 'Sir Donald Wolfit, Robert Newton, Claire Bloom, they all came to see Frank. We did it at the Woolwich Theatre, where the audience were always soldiers. Of course they used to roar with laughter at anything.'

One of the guests was Tony Hancock: Ray and Alan had been writing for him for eighteen months, and by now the dislike the three shared for gags and punchlines had become a principle, a tenet of humour between them. 'We didn't think in terms of jokes at all,' Ray said. 'Hancock didn't tell jokes. It was life, the character and the situation and the relationships.'

'We very seldom did jokes,' Alan emphasized, 'because someone has to give the feed line, "And then what happened?" Once in a while we couldn't avoid it, and if ever we wrote a joke in, Tony would do it in a music-hall voice, "I Say, I Say!" So that was another reason not to put them in, unless it was deliberate... as *A Joke.*'

This next sketch shared the news with the audience: stand-up comedy between a gagman and a stooge was too old and arthritic to raise even a wheezy laugh. It was fit only to be mocked – by comics like Hancock, who guested on the first in the series of Frankie Howerd's variety show. This extract is the only surviving trace of a perfect pairing, a double act between two of Britain's most loved comics:

THE FRANKIE HOWERD SHOW, series one, episode one

*Script by Galton and Simpson with Eric Sykes, featuring bandleader
Billy Ternent*
First broadcast: Sunday 22 November 1953

FRANKIE: Read out the name of our next guest.
BILLY: Let's see. Our next guest is a sack of potatoes.
FRANKIE: Billy, the other side. That's the shopping list. Now who is it?
BILLY: Tony Hancock.
FRANKIE: Ladies and gentlemen, our next guest is a sack of potatoes.
TONY: And pray silence for King Edward Hancock.

    (Applause)

TONY: Thank you, thank you. And tonight I should like to present the first
    in a new series entitled 'A Book At Breakfast Time' – it's for the night
    workers. The first book to be read is a story of hate and violence,
    published by Codham Press at Height and Sixpence. It is a thrilling
    novel that I personally couldn't put down till I'd finished it, which will
    give you some idea how hungry I was. Written by Somerset Brown,
    this novel is entitled *Love Lies A-Bleeding*. Chapter 1. Liza Bleeding
    stirred in her sleep, and on doing so she spilt the hot chocolate down
    her nightdress and woke up. There was a movement from behind the
    curtains. Her big eyes filled with horror as she saw a big pair of army
    boots poking out from underneath them. She was unable to tear her
    eyes away from the sinister-looking boots as they slowly walked
    across the room. She screamed with terror... there was nobody in
    them!
FRANKIE: Is there much more of this?
TONY: Suddenly a man crawled out from under the bed – he drew
    himself up to his full height and leaned over the terrified girl, when
    the door burst open and the lodger rushed in and said...
FRANKIE: Hancock, come away and let me have a go.
TONY: ... and said, 'Hancock, come away and let me have a...' No he
    didn't. I wasn't there. Alibi. Yes. Somewhere else. Doing me
    needlework. *(On mike)* And if you're listening, Warder, I hope the
    mailbags proved satisfactory.
FRANKIE: Now listen, Mr Hancick.
TONY: Kock, Kock.
FRANKIE: Listen, cock. You've got a lot to say for a man who's been hired
    as my stooge.

TONY: *(Emotional)* Stooge? Hancock a straight man? Not getting any laughs? *(Breath)* Funny old Hancock? The only comic who ever got a laugh on *Workers Playtime* from an onion factory. No, Mr Howerd, I still can't do it. My public are waiting for me to be funny.

FRANKIE: Still.

TONY: I'm sorry, Mr Howerd. I cannot see my way clear to saying all the straight lines while you get all the laughs. *(Gradually raises voice)* I have my reputation as a comic to think of, my professional integrity. It would do my career untold damage. All I have worked for over the years…

FRANKIE: You'll get paid for it.

TONY: And then what happened, you don't say, what did you do then? My word, really? Well, well, well, amazing. How do you mean? What? Go on, get away? Tell me more… Now I am surprised…

FRANKIE: That's it. Yes. You've got the idea. You're going to be the best stooge I've had since Derek Roy. That reminds me, whatever happened to him? He had the makings. What's that, Billy? Oh. Can we have two minutes' silence, please. That's the second time he's died in Scunthorpe.

TONY: Well, quite frankly, Mr Howerd, I don't know why you need me. I thought Billy Ternent was your stooge.

FRANKIE: Well yes he is, but I'm getting rid of him. He's been getting a bit past it, you know… his eyes are going.

TONY: Why doesn't he wear spectacles?

FRANKIE: He does, but he can't see as far as the glass… and another thing… he's getting too cheeky. He keeps slipping little jokes in. He's full of little cracks, you know.

TONY: Yes, I noticed his head as I came in. Anyway, what have you brought me here for?

FRANKIE: Brought? Brought? Your big chance? You must be mad… I mean… can't you see it… Howerd and Hancock.

TONY: Yes. Yes. I like that. Hancock and Howerd.

FRANKIE: In this act… Howerd and Hancock.

TONY: 'Ancock and 'Owerd.

FRANKIE: In spite of you, Tony, there are too many haitches. I'll tell you what – Howerd and Tony.

TONY: Sounds like a man and a horse.

FRANKIE: Precisely. Now look. Let's start and don't forget – I get all the funny lines.

TONY: Right.

ORCHESTRA: *(Fanfare)*

BILLY: And now, ladies and gentlemen, direct from their successful tour of the corporation dustcarts, here are your friends and my friends – Howerd and Hancock.

ORCHESTRA: *(Corny music-hall play on – 'Happy days are here again')*

TONY: Thank you. A little monologue. In a little old log cabin, to the south of 'Ackney Wick, lives a grizzled old prospector by the name of Dirty Dick...

FRANKIE: Here.

TONY: Where?

FRANKIE: Here.

TONY: Oh.

FRANKIE: What's yellow and got twenty-two legs?

TONY: A Japanese football team.

FRANKIE: A Japanese... No. You're supposed to say, 'I don't know'. *I* get the funny answers. I'm going to have some trouble here, I can see that. I should have left him hanging up in the butcher's shop. Now come on, let's start again, and remember this time – I get the funny answers. Go.

TONY: A little monologue. Jake was a creep, a great big fellow with Edwardian trousers...

FRANKIE: Here, I say.

TONY: Oh, it's you again. I'm very sorry about this, ladies and gentlemen. What do you mean by coming on here and interrupting my monologue?

FRANKIE: You're clever, aren't you?

TONY: Yes, I'm clever.

FRANKIE: Well answer me this then. Why has a rabbit got a shiny nose?

TONY: I have no idea. Tell me, why *has* a rabbit got its powder puff at the other end?

FRANKIE: Because it's got its powder puff at the... Aah, he's done it again. Oh frantic Francis. Fran-ever-so-cis. Control yourself. Press on – don't take any notice. Just press on – where's his windpipe? Now look, Porky, let me explain. You're supposed to feed me the straight line. Got that? Feed me. Feed me.

TONY: How would you like a nice handful of wild berries?

FRANKIE: I think it might be as well to let me show you the hang of things. Wait a minute, I'll go and get the rope. Now listen, I'll give you one more chance. When I ask you the question, you don't know it.

TONY: I don't know it.

FRANKIE: That's it. Whatever it is, you don't know the answer.

TONY: I don't know the answer.

FRANKIE: Good. Start again. Go.

TONY: A little monologue. There's a green-eyed yellow monster that sits on *What's My Line...*

FRANKIE: I say, you there.

TONY: What can I do for you?

FRANKIE: Are you any good at riddles?

TONY: Am I any good at riddles?

FRANKIE: That's what I said.

TONY: I know the answer to every riddle there is... except the one you're just going to ask me. Carry on.

FRANKIE: Why did the Kaiser wear red, white and blue braces?

TONY: I don't know.

FRANKIE: You don't?

TONY: No. I haven't the slightest idea.

FRANKIE: You're sure?

TONY: Positive.

FRANKIE: You've got no idea?

TONY: No idea at all. For the life of me I can't think why the Kaiser wore red, white and blue braces. Inexplicable. I can't wait to hear why he did such a remarkable thing.

FRANKIE: Then I shall tell you. The Kaiser wore red, white and blue braces...

TONY: *(Quickly)* I've just remembered. To keep his trousers up.

FRANKIE: *(Slight pause) (Calls)* Billy. Forward with the cosh. Ladies and gentlemen, the next part of this programme is considered unsuitable for children. Where are you going, Hancock?

TONY: Home to tuck me teddy bear in.

FRANKIE: Come back. Francis wants to tuck your teeth in.

TONY: *(Panics)* No, don't hit old Hancock. Didn't mean it. Start again. Who, what, when, why. Then what happened? No. Keep off. Play the music. Good old Billy. Play boy. That's it. Taxi. Goodnight all.

ORCHESTRA: *(Coda of music-hall version of 'When You're Smiling')*

(Applause)

FRANKIE: Yeees, there he goes. Tony Hancock. Good old Tony. Very funny man, isn't he? Yes. Very funny. Last time I have him on this programme.

When Spike Milligan (*The Goon Show*) and Eric Sykes (*Variety Bandbox, Educating Archie,* Frankie Howerd's *Fine Goings On*) decided in 1954 to set up a scriptwriting agency, on the third floor of an office over a greengrocer's in Shepherd's Bush Green, they turned to Galton and Simpson as partners. For Ray and Alan, it was not only confirmation of their success as a writing team, but also a guarantee of future security; though this proposal to found a co-operative company was a surprise, they welcomed it. Over the next fifteen years, Associated London Scripts took in writers such as Johnny Speight, Terry Nation and Barry Took. The offices were not always above a greengrocer's, but that shop marked the beginning for shows such as *Till Death Us Do Part* and *Round the Horne*, as well as television's arch aliens, the Daleks of *Doctor Who*.

The millions who tuned in to the shows, though, were mostly unaware that professional scriptwriters existed – when Ray and Alan first tried to open a bank account, the manager assumed they were sign writers. Most people imagined the comedians were improvising their lines, around situations that developed together with whatever sound effects were to hand. The idea that all the jokes were written and honed and rehearsed seemed vaguely insulting to the stars, as if implying that they couldn't be that funny without assistance.

American audiences, Alan and Ray believed, were more sophisticated, which was why early US comedies on television depicted the backstage life of the stars. 'Americans knew about directors, for instance,' said Alan. 'English people would think that the only reason writers were employed was because Hancock hadn't got time to write his own stuff. It didn't occur to them that he *couldn't* write his own stuff, and without us he wouldn't have any stuff to do.'

Ray agreed: 'I still have to say to people that Hancock's view was, "You're the writers, you write it; I'm the actor, I'll perform it." And he did not add anything. But people do not believe that. Even now, if a newspaper wants to use a gag from one of our shows, they don't credit us – they attribute it to Hancock, or Steptoe, because they don't want to have to explain to readers that Galton and Simpson actually wrote the line.'

This injustice applies only to comedy. It was rooted in the BBC's determination to shield its artistes. Radio's light entertainment stars had become national sensations, and corporation executives feared that, if the public ever guessed their idols were reciting other people's jokes, the illusion of comic repartee would be destroyed. This insecurity seems bizarre: Hollywood producers, for example, did not pretend that their starlets and romantic leads were improvising their dialogue. But when Eric Sykes suggested he deserved some kind of a credit on *Variety Bandbox*, a name check at least, the BBC scolded him for letting his own ego put Frankie Howerd's career at risk.

The illusion was more easily maintained when the cast were simply telling gags, swapping repartee or performing monologues. But Galton and Simpson were now filling *Star Bill* with tightly constructed sketches that plunged listeners into a detailed and often surreal situation. It must have been obvious to any but the most naïve radio fan that Madame Hancock's Waxworks, for example, was not a spur-of-the-moment invention:

STAR BILL, series two, episode three

First broadcast: Sunday 14 March 1954

ROBIN BOYLE: One of the most fascinating ways of spending an afternoon's leisure is to pay a visit to the waxworks. Come with us now to the smallest and most obscure waxworks of the lot... a dingy, unpainted, dilapidated warehouse situated in the back streets of Shepherd's Bush.

(Crossfade)

MOIRA LISTER: Well, here we are, Alfie. This is the place. 'Madame Hancock's Waxworks. See the great and the infamous in lifelike detail. Admission 2d. People with hammers not admitted.' Come on, Alfie, let's go in – you can learn a lot in these places.

GRAHAM: No, I don't want to. I'm going down to the youth club. I want to try my knife out on their new settees.

MOIRA: You're coming in here. Go on, open the door.

EFFECTS: (Door open. Tinkle of shop bell.)

GRAHAM: Well, it can't be much good – there's no one here.

MOIRA: Now don't touch anything, Alfie. Alfie... where are you?

GRAHAM: Look, Mum, I've found a waxwork. Cor, it ain't half a rotten one. Dirty old clothes, cobwebs, falling to bits... and its face looks as though it's melting. It don't look very lifelike to me.

MOIRA: Who is it?

TONY: The proprietor. What can I do for you?

MOIRA: Well, Mr, er...

TONY: Ancock. Hanthony Ancock. Haitch-Hay-Hen-C-Ho-C-K.

MOIRA: Well, we'd like to see the waxworks.

TONY: Certainly, madam – admission is twopence a head... that'll be twopence for you and fourpence to Alfie. I think that's fair, don't you?

MOIRA: Here – do yer run this place by yourself?

TONY: By myself. Oh my word, no. I couldn't possibly run an establishment like this on me Jack. I've got Higgins.

MOIRA: Who's Higgins?

TONY: He's me model-maker. Been with us many years now, has Higgins. He's a bit old now... bit past it. He don't know much what's going on. We had a staff of a hundred here once. There's only me and Higgins here now. Very mysterious – each day the staff got smaller, and the waxworks got bigger. I don't know, the other day he had *me* try on Henry VIII's hat for size... I'm watching him.

GRAHAM: Here, Fatty.

TONY: Fatty? Fatty? *Mr* Fatty, if you please.

GRAHAM: I want to see the Chamber of Horrors.

TONY: The celebrated Chamber of Horrors. Here they are. Look around. Murderers, rogues, vagabonds, every one of them. Feast your eyes on its gruesome contents.

GRAHAM: Cor, smashing. I'd love to spend the night in here.

TONY: Yes, that's right... I'd have Crippen and the boys asking for a transfer. And now, as a final treat, I will take you next door to our workshop... the place where all these models are made. This way.

EFFECTS: (Door open)

TONY: Here we are. Notice the odd limbs of anatomy piled about the place awaiting assembly – while over here we have a hot vat of boiling wax.

EFFECTS: (Bubbling cauldron)

GRAHAM: Cor, look at all the steam rising.

MOIRA: Don't get too near, Alfie.

TONY: Oh, no danger, madam. Get as near as you like. Have a good look. Go on, stand on the edge and see how it bubbles. Go on – both of you – that's it. *(Sotto)* All right, Higgins – now!

EFFECTS: (Slide whistle. Moira yells. Loud splash.)

TONY: Well done, Higgins. Get 'em set up – Madonna and Child.

Alan and Ray's determination to create new comedy made them resistant to traditional British humour – variety acts, Blitz spirit and seaside postcard innuendo. Even the great comics, such as the belligerent, chain-smoking Jimmy James, could not raise a laugh from them. While they were recording a show in Blackpool, Graham Stark and co-star Pat

Kirkwood persuaded them to watch James, who was performing at the Winter Gardens. 'We had nothing but disdain for the music hall,' Ray said. 'When we got there it was crowded – they were hanging on the chandeliers. We were standing at the back because there was no room. And Jimmy James had everybody falling out of their seats with laughter. They just adored him. We stood through the whole thing with not a smile on our face. And we went back to the hotel with Pat and Graham, and we argued all night with them, until breakfast time. We argued about what comedy was, and that this man didn't have a clue and wasn't funny. We were convinced that he was a load of rubbish.'

James was a household name, though, and when two years later Main Wilson booked him for *Star Bill*, the writers were convinced they could fit a funny sketch to his style. By now, more confident and more experienced, they recognized James was a great comic technician, though outmoded. What they had not expected was that James would be as little impressed by their jokes as they had been by his. 'He came down, no rehearsal, just got out of the taxi,' Ray remembered, 'and he said, "I've read the script, lads, and I don't think it's very funny, but I'll do me best." We were absolutely mortified. My God!'

They assured him the sketch would work well, but as James walked onto the soundstage all their certainty had drained away. Jimmy James had been performing comedy in front of the toughest audiences long before they were born. 'If he thought he couldn't get a laugh with this material,' Alan said, 'he ought to know. But he did it… and it went like a bomb. He came off and we thought he'd say it was still bad, but he'd rescued it. Instead, he said, "There you are, lads – forty years in the business and I know fuck all!"'

STAR BILL, series two, episode five, with Jimmy James

First broadcast: Sunday 28 March 1954

JIMMY: Excuse me.
TONY: Who are you?
JIMMY: I'm him. I'm the bloke.
TONY: What bloke?
JIMMY: The one they're all talking about.
TONY: Who are?
JIMMY: The people in the bus queues.
TONY: Oh – *you're* the one?
JIMMY: That's right. I knew you'd recognize me.

TONY: Why yes. Of course I knew you the minute I set eyes... I... er...
how do you do?

GRAHAM: *(Sotto)* Who *is* he?

TONY: He's the one they're all talking about.

GRAHAM: Oh. I see. Yes.

MOIRA: Who is it, Graham?

GRAHAM: The one they're all talking about.

MOIRA: Is it? Oh!

JIMMY: Would you believe it? This one hasn't got any salt in it.

TONY: Hasn't it? Ah, well, no, you see, it's... *what hasn't?*

JIMMY: Me bag of crisps. I bought them to eat on the train coming down.
There should be one for every packet but here's a packet without
one. Can't be a shortage of salt, they're going full blast in Siberia.

TONY: Siberia? What are you talking about?

JIMMY: Salt. There's a blue packet of salt missing out of my packet of crisps.

TONY: I don't like crisps... with or without salt.

JIMMY: You're welcome to a packet because I've got one over and it'll
only go to waste. Funny thing, I thought it was there when I came.

TONY: It wasn't there – what's more it won't be there when you go out. In
fact, I don't think it was ever there.

JIMMY: My salt?

TONY: Your brain.

JIMMY: Somebody's knocked my salt off. Do you realize at this very
minute there's a bloke walking around Stockton-on-Tees with a
couple of packets of salt in one packet of crisps? I'll call in the police
station when I get back to see if he's handed one packet in.

TONY: Yes – and on the way out have a look on the board – see if *you're*
missing.

JIMMY: No, it can't be me – I was talking to my mother this morning.

TONY: Look, who are you – what's your name?

JIMMY: Oh, me name. Didn't I tell you? Wait a minute. It's on the tip of me
tongue. Charlie Brown – no, that's the wife's lodger – he's not a bit
like me.

TONY: I suppose he only acts like you.

JIMMY: Yes – except on pay days. Just a minute. I've got me card here.
Ah yes, that's it. Look – there you are – Jimmy James, that's me.

(Applause)

JIMMY: Yes, Jimmy James. I knew I'd get it. Mind you, I know who you are.

TONY: Do you really?

JIMMY: Yes. You're him. You're the bloke.

TONY: Yes, all right, we've done all that. Look – what are you doing here?

JIMMY: What am I doing here? Me? I've come here to perform. I'm going to do me turn. I've got the bears outside.

TONY: Oh good. Well, bring them in here... and... Bears?

JIMMY: Yes – that's the act. Jimmy James and his Performing Bears. I've got 'em doing the dancing. The band strikes up. I blow the whistle and they're at it – the Charleston.

TONY: What's he talking about? Mr James – has anybody hit you over the head with a big hammer today?

JIMMY: No.

TONY: The night is young. Performing Bears? What do you think this is – a circus?

JIMMY: Yes – that's why I'm here. I've been booked to appear at the circus this week. Here – the man with the two left ears hasn't been on yet, has he? I'm following him.

TONY: Look – Mr James – Harry. This is not the circus.

JIMMY: But it must be. I saw the performing monkeys lined up as I came in.

TONY: *That* was the band. This, Mr James, is a radio show.

JIMMY: Radio show? Oh, you should have told me that before. What must you think of me?

TONY: I'll tell you afterwards.

JIMMY: Radio? Well, of course. You won't be wanting the performing bears, will you?

TONY: No.

JIMMY: I'll go and get the horses.

TONY: I should think so too, I... what horses?

JIMMY: Well, I presume it's a Wild West Radio.

TONY: Here is a police message. At five past ten tonight Mr Jimmy James will probably meet with a nasty accident. Will any witnesses who see a rather stout-looking gentleman nipping away from the scene of the crime – please keep their mouths shut.

One other characteristic was attaching itself to the Hancock character in *Star Bill's* second series: he liked a drink. Both Alan and Ray insist that, throughout their years with Tony Hancock, they never saw his performance affected by alcohol, though by their last series of *Hancock* on TV his face was losing its mobility. The post-war years were a hard-drinking era, and it wasn't unusual for radio and television stars to perform when they were too drunk to stand, and almost too drunk to speak: Gilbert Harding, for instance, made a career of it on *What's My Line?* By those standards,

Tony Hancock was comparatively abstemious; his drinking a cause for amused comment rather than alarm.

In the following two sketches, Galton and Simpson send up his keen nose for a free round. The first also features Richard Greene, in a spoof of *Dial 'M' For Murder*, called... 'Dial "A" For 'Ancock'.

STAR BILL, series two, episode eight

First broadcast: Sunday 18 April 1954

EFFECTS: *(Chink of two glasses)*

RICHARD: Another drink, Hancock?
TONY: Don't mind if I do. I'll have a little scotch and soda.

EFFECTS: *(Very long pouring noise. Not less than 90 seconds.)*

RICHARD: Soda?

EFFECTS: *(Shortest squirt possible)*

TONY: Don't drown it. *(Tastes drink with loud smack of lips)* Mmmmm.

EFFECTS: *(Starts pouring again)*

TONY: Big glass this, isn't it?
RICHARD: Yes.
TONY: Hasn't got a stem on it either.
RICHARD: No – but then goldfish bowls seldom do.
TONY: *Goldfish* bowl? I wondered why that slice of orange kept jumping out of me mouth.

For series two of *Star Bill*, Moira Lister had replaced Geraldine McEwan. Well known for her role in *The Cruel Sea* with Jack Hawkins, she stayed on as Tony's love interest for the first run of *Hancock's Half Hour*. 'Moira Lister had the personality and the stardom to outshine anyone,' Alan said. 'She was a big name. I don't know how we ever got her!'

STAR BILL, series two, episode ten

First broadcast: Sunday 2 May 1954

MOIRA: Well, he's never been as late as this before.
GRAHAM: I wonder what's holding him up?

MOIRA: Last time I saw him – a lamp post.

GRAHAM: Well, I hope for his sake he gets here. We're holding a party after the show to celebrate the end of the series. And what's more – all the drinks are free.

EFFECTS: (Speeding car. Pulls up with squeal of brakes. Fast running footsteps up stairs. Door bursts open.)

TONY: *(On mike)* Not too much soda in mine.

GRAHAM: Don't let him stand too near the beer barrels, Moira. You know what happened last time.

MOIRA: Ah yes, I remember. Someone had chalked on his back – 'Stout and Bitter'.

TONY: *(Wooden)* Ha, ha, ha, ho, ho, ho, hee, hee, hee. Pardon me while I roll about the stage clutching me sides with helpless laughter.

GRAHAM: Well, now you're here, perhaps you'll explain why you're so late. You know this is the last show of the series. Where have you been?

TONY: Down at the Labour Exchange.

GRAHAM: Any luck?

TONY: No, hopeless. Hopeless. They kept offering me work. Well, I told them, work's not my trade at all.

MOIRA: But Tony, what are you going to do between now and next winter?

TONY: *(Airily)* Oh, I don't know. I might go to Spain – might go to the South of France. Maybe the Swiss Alps – Monte Carlo – Madeira – a world cruise. Then again, I might do what I did last year.

GRAHAM: What?

TONY: Stay in bed.

MOIRA: But Tony, you can't stay in bed all summer.

TONY: Oh, I don't. Every Friday morning I get out and sit on the chair while Mum changes the sheets.

Britain's comic tradition made the kind of comedy that Galton and Simpson were planning – comedy without punchlines and musical numbers – seem subversive. Variety dated back to at least the eighteenth century, when the licensing laws of 1737 had forbidden dialogue on the stage except with musical accompaniment (with only the Theatres Royal exempt). Actor-managers such as Robert Elliston tried to sidestep the censors in the Regency period by staging Shakespeare as dramatic dances, but many productions were obliged to rely on mime.

As the music halls emerged, the comedians were dancers and singers, and even by the first half of the twentieth century most of the popular turns featured comic songs, not spoken routines. Florrie Forde and Harry Champion were Edwardian stars famous for numbers like 'What Happened to the Manx Cat's Tail?' and 'Any Old Iron' – copies of the sheet music sold in millions and the songs were preserved on cylinder, but any patter linking the numbers was quickly forgotten.

Pantomime troupes toured Britain throughout the Victorian era. The Martinetti brothers were among the most acclaimed, staging silent melodramas with titles such as 'A Duel in the Snow', 'Remorse' and 'A Terrible Night'. Spectacular acrobatic comedies were popular at the circus too, crossing over into the music halls – in 1880, for instance, the six Hanlon brothers, with 'Professor' John Lees, staged an entertainment entitled *Voyage En Suisse* at the Gaiety Theatre on the Strand. According to a review in *The Theatre*, '… it included a bus smash, a chaotic scene on board a ship in a storm, an exploding Pullman car, a banquet transformed into a wholesale juggling party after one of the Hanlons had crashed through the ceiling onto the table, and one of the cleverest drunk scenes ever presented on the stage'.

Generations of comedy fans had been brought up on mime, song and slapstick, and the emphasis on laughter without language intensified with the arrival of motion pictures. For thirty years the only dialogue in the movies appeared on script-boards, printed in ornate lettering. Moviegoers were assumed to be slow readers, so even the shortest bursts of dialogue would be frozen on screen for several seconds. Audiences were adept at reading faces, though, and the best silent actors could mime a series of emotions far faster than any script could convey them. Charlie Chaplin, easily the greatest actor of the time, seems hard to fathom now, his movements a spasmodic sequence of convulsions. But if a classic Chaplin tableau, such as the gambling scene in 1917's *The Immigrant*, is broken down frame by frame, a narrative flashes by – the Little Tramp is confident, triumphant, alarmed, anxious, smug, frightened, cunning, cocky, cowardly, timid, terrified, resigned, reckless, desperate and selfless, all in a blur of gestures and expressions.

Spoken comedy made a tentative return to the British theatre by the turn of the century. The best-loved comic was Dan Leno, who in the 1880s had been the world champion clog dancer. His friend and biographer John 'Hickory' Wood described Leno's comedy clogging routine: 'He danced on the stage; he danced on a pedestal; he danced on a slab of slate; he was encored over and over again; but throughout his performance, he never uttered a word.' Later, the dancer became a celebrated monologist. He would start his act by running to the front of the stage, drumming his feet on the boards, raising a leg and holding his foot high in the air, and then bringing it down with a resounding slap before launching into a song. After a verse, his comic monologue would begin, but it wasn't wordplay that earned the laughter, it was Leno's ability to conjure, in gestures, a scene to accompany lines like these: 'The Baron said, "Now we will go to the meet." I couldn't see any meat. I looked round, but only saw a lot of empty plates; I think they must have eaten all the meat for breakfast.'

Dan Leno died, aged forty-three, in 1904. It was more than twenty years later, and an ocean away, that comic dialogue began to challenge slapstick and pantomime for popularity. The *Chicago Tribune*'s WGN radio station presented a weekly slot starring 'Sam 'n' Henry', two country boys who had migrated to the big city. This was just before the Great Depression, and the characters were trying to stay out of trouble with the police while they hunted for work. The idea had grown out of the minstrel shows, in which white musicians caked their faces in black make-up: Sam 'n' Henry were African Americans, played by white actors in excruciating, burlesque voices. In 1926, the routines proved so popular with Midwestern radio audiences that the actors, Freeman Gosden and Charles Correll, ditched their sponsors and relaunched the show with nationwide syndication. The characters were renamed 'Amos 'n' Andy'. By 1930, they had 40 million listeners.

The show survived for thirty years, though as the civil rights movement gathered strength it came under attack for its blatant racism. Its roots were so deep in discrimination, stereotypes and mockery that it could never be called a sitcom: it dealt in travesty, not reality. Amos 'n' Andy did make one significant contribution to radio comedy, though: their caricatured banter took place against a backdrop of ordinary situations. They got drunk in cheap bars and woke up on hard floors, bought their food in cheap stores, ran their taxi business from a bare room, and saw incompetent, alcoholic doctors when they were sick. In one early episode, when the duo were still Sam 'n' Henry, they go to a dentist who breaks off as many teeth as he pulls. 'If you've got soft teeth, I'll have to cut your jaw,' he warns. Henry starts to groan at the sight of the pliers, just as Hancock would three decades later when the needle appeared.

The success of *Amos 'n' Andy* inspired a slew of radio comedies. Among the best in the thirties was *Fibber McGee and Molly*, starring a vaudeville husband-and-wife act called Jim and Marian Driscoll Jordan. The show built a cast of recurring characters, all of them with their own catchphrases and running jokes. Fibber was a fantasist, an optimist in pursuit of the American dream, and every scheme led him into a series of quick-fire gags. Billy Mills and his orchestra provided a musical break in the first half of every show: this was a variety show, with cardboard cut-outs instead of characters, but it did have storylines.

Another hit show, *The Goldbergs* – which centred on a Jewish matriarch in New York – featured credible characters in ordinary situations. Written and starring Molly Berg, it ran on radio for fifteen years before transferring to television – but, despite its catchphrases and running jokes, *The Goldbergs* is usually regarded as a soap, not a sitcom. It was endearing and sentimental – *Life* magazine compared it to a comfortable pair of slippers – but it simply wasn't very funny. Nor did Molly Berg mean it to be: when the show launched on CBS TV in 1949, she insisted there could be no laughter track.

Ray Galton and Alan Simpson agree that one of the biggest influences on their writing, and on the development of the Hancock character, was the Chicago-born comic Jack Benny. His show, launched first on radio in 1932 and eighteen years later as a television series, featured Benny as a pompous, petty, stingy braggart: the cast included his wife Mary, the bandleader Phil Harris and the astonishing voice artiste Mel Blanc. Benny could play out a pause as though the radio audience could see a clock ticking, and the archetypal Jack Benny joke featured a gap that seemed to stretch on for minutes. Accosted by a mugger who demands, 'Your money or your life,' Benny says nothing and just lets the audience laugh it out. When the mugger finally repeats his threat, Benny snaps, 'I'm thinking it over.'

Comedy routines, punchlines, songs, running gags and ludicrous characters were the basis of the show – it was vaudeville, not sitcom, just as vaudeville was the basis for the two biggest American television comedies of the early fifties. *I Love Lucy* and *The Burns and Allen Show* both starred married couples, with storylines that pretended to take viewers behind the scenes of the show. This was a make-believe version of a make-believe world. *I Love Lucy* in particular was scripted and produced with a polish that nothing in Britain came close to matching.

'Comedy in Britain at that time was so far behind America, it was ridiculous,' said Ray Galton. But with *Hancock's Half Hour*, everything changed.

4 Hancock's Half Hour

The launch of *Hancock's Half Hour* in autumn 1954 was an experiment in comedy that had been simmering for eighteen months. Galton and Simpson discussed their ideas over and over with Hancock before they took the proposal to producer Dennis Main Wilson. He sent an enthusiastic memo to the Head of Variety, Michael Standing, on 1 May 1953: Hancock and his writers envisioned a half-hour show, 'based on reality and truth rather than jokes, merry quips, wheezes [and] breaks for crooners who have no reason to be on the show anyway'. Nine months later, Main Wilson was still firing off memos: 'The comedy style will be purely situation in which we shall try to build Tony as a real-life character in real-life surroundings. There will be no "goon" or contrived comedy approaches at all.'

Even at his most impassioned, Main Wilson could not have imagined that *Hancock's Half Hour* would not only keep its star famous long after his death, but also establish the careers of a trio of actors – Sid James, Kenneth Williams and Hattie Jacques – who would go on to found another British institution: the *Carry On* films.

Jacques didn't appear until the fourth series, and Williams played only a minor role in the beginning, but Sid James was a mainstay from the start. Ray Galton and Alan Simpson had seen him in a bit part in an Ealing comedy, *The Lavender Hill Mob*, and they told the BBC this was the actor they wanted to play Hancock's crooked friend. To discover his name, they had to go back to the cinema and sit through the film again until the credits came up. 'It turned out Sid had never done radio before,' said Alan, 'and he was shaking like a leaf at the first recording, in front of an audience. He kept the script up in front of his face and his hat down over his eyes... until he realized he was getting the laughs. Then he relaxed.'

The cast also included Australian comedian Bill Kerr as Hancock's inseparable stooge. Like Graham Stark (who was bitterly disappointed to be left out of the line-up), Kerr had been an Eager Beaver on *Happy-Go-*

Lucky. But in *Hancock's Half Hour*, Kerr was always more than just a straight man, feeding the star laughs. He was a psychological necessity – there had to be a good reason for Hancock to flatter himself that he was cultured, intelligent and quick-witted, and the reason was Bill Kerr. Another cornerstone of sitcom was laid down: like Basil Fawlty with his hapless Manuel, or Edmund Blackadder with the idiot Baldrick, Tony Hancock was saddled with the boy from Wagga-Wagga. 'Billy the Kerr' Hancock sometimes called him – or that might have been 'Billy the Cur', because as the series evolved, he was treated like a mongrel, fed on scraps and expected to sleep on the floor.

The signature tune for Hancock became one of the best known themes on the radio – as unmistakable as the opening bars of *The Archers*, it reflected the show's personality. All the music was composed by Wally Stott, who had worked with producer Dennis Main Wilson on *Happy-Go-Lucky*. Stott, who became known as Angela Morley after a trans-gender operation in the seventies, had not met Hancock when he wrote the tune for tuba and piccolo: he based the idea on Main Wilson's impersonation of a petulant and pompous blunderer. Like so much about the show, it was immediately right.

In the very first scene of the first episode, Galton and Simpson introduced one of their signature techniques: the long silence, punctuated by the sound of frustration:

HANCOCK'S HALF HOUR, first series, episode one

'THE FIRST NIGHT PARTY'
First broadcast: Tuesday 9 November 1954

> EFFECTS: *(Typewriter clacking. Very slow and deliberate. One finger.)*

TONY: *(Testy)* Hurry up, Kerr. Haven't you finished typing out those invitations yet?
BILL: Don't rush me, don't rush me.

> EFFECTS: *(Typewriter continues slow clacking. Ding of bell. Carriage slides back. Slight pause. Slow clacking again.)*

TONY: It might help if you took those gloves off.
BILL: My hands are cold.

> EFFECTS: *(More slow clacking. Seven keys struck.)*

BILL: Anyway, what's wrong with typing in gloves?

EFFECTS: *(More slow clacking. Six keys struck.)*

BILL: I like typing in gloves.

EFFECTS: *(More slow clacking. Five keys struck.)*

BILL: Lots of people type in gloves.

EFFECTS: *(More slow clacking. Four keys struck.)*

TONY: Not in boxing gloves.

Radio Times announced *Hancock's Half Hour* by warning that the stories were 'based on the life of the lad 'imself from the files of the *Police Gazette*'. It was true that many of the character's foibles were rooted in the person-ality of the comedian, but many more were jokes – like his name, Anthony Aloysius St John Hancock the Second. In fact, he was simply Anthony John Hancock. 'Tony was an intelligent, serious-minded man, somebody who thought deeply,' said Ray Galton. 'We took that, and made him the sort of deep thinker who never reads anything heavier than the newspaper.'

It was the hapless, vulnerable side of Tony Hancock's personality that made audiences love him and forgive his cantankerous outbursts. That part of him, the clumsy optimist, was real. He was a magnet for minor disasters. Just after the war, when he was first trying to make his name as a comic, Hancock was offered a week in cabaret at Sidmouth. The engagement would pay £10, with free board; the return fare was £2; Hancock had five shillings. Determined to seize his opportunity, he borrowed the rest from friends, took a train to Devon, and arrived at the hotel to see a poster advertising the week's cabaret. His name was not on the bill. When he read his booking again, he realized he had turned up a week early. He travelled back that night with just enough money in his pocket for one cup of tea.

The character he projected on the air, the defeated dreamer, stumbled through mishaps like that every week:

HANCOCK'S HALF HOUR, first series, episode six

'THE NEW CAR'
First broadcast: Tuesday 7 December 1954

SIDNEY: Ah yes, here's one. Just the car you're looking for – a lovely
    model. One of the finest cars in the yard.
TONY: Bit old, isn't it?

SIDNEY: Old? It's in beautiful nick. Look at those headlights. Look at the workmanship.

MOIRA LISTER: Yes, they're lovely. Do they still make the wicks for them?

SIDNEY: Well anyway, it hasn't been used much. They're the original tyres.

TONY: Yes, those solid ones last forever, don't they?

SIDNEY: I'll start her up and take you for a ride in her. You'll be amazed at the performance.

MOIRA: What's its fuel consumption?

SIDNEY: Well, let's see now... on a long run I should say... oooh, round about ten miles to the gallon... of water... and a hundredweight of coke.

TONY: Look, I don't think we'll bother, I...

SIDNEY: Wait till you get in and see it go. You'll be intoxicated by the exuberance of your own velocity.

TONY: Really?

SIDNEY: I'll just get her going. Got a match?

BILL: Here you are.

SIDNEY: Right, you work the bellows – Hancock, take this brush and give the chimney a clean-out. Ah, she's getting up steam a bit now.

EFFECTS: *(Steam being got up)*

SIDNEY: We'll go for a ride round the block.

TONY: Bags I the tiller.

SIDNEY: Right – let her go.

MOIRA: Aren't you coming with us, Mr James?

SIDNEY: No, I'd better walk in front with the red flag.

Sid James usually contrived to be out of the way when catastrophe struck. Kenneth Williams did the opposite – his appearance signalled an approaching disaster:

POLICE RADIO: Calling all cars. News has just been received of the whereabouts of Butcher Collins, who escaped from Wandsworth prison three days ago. He is reported to be in the area of the Dog and Duck and is believed to be armed. Take no chances. This man is dangerous. Here is his description: five feet six tall... dressed in prison clothes... one ear missing... large scar on left cheek... shaven head... broken nose... three front teeth missing... patch over one eye... walks with a distinctive limp.

TONY: Could be anybody.

POLICE RADIO: He also speaks with a broad Cockney accent.
KENNETH: Oi, you – Fatty.
TONY: Oh, good evening.
KENNETH: Who are you?
TONY: Anthony Hancock at your service. How do you do?
KENNETH: Charmed, I'm sure.
TONY: Here – are you by yourself?
KENNETH: Yus.
TONY: You want to be careful – there's a dangerous escaped convict at
    large round here.
KENNETH: Is there now?
TONY: Yes there is. Here, just a minute. Let's have a look at you. Hallo –
    suit with arrows on it... one ear missing... large scar on left cheek...
    shaven head... broken nose... three front teeth missing... a patch
    over one eye, and you walk with a limp.
KENNETH: Well?
TONY: You want to watch out, somebody might mistake you for him.

Though he was never credited as a performer, Alan Simpson made more
than sixty appearances on *Hancock's Half Hour*. His experience on stage
had begun during his teens, in church halls with amateur societies, and
he had also occasionally spoken lines on *Star Bill*, as a voice in the crowd
– mainly, he says, to save Main Wilson the expense of hiring a utility actor.
Sometimes he helped out as the warm-up man, with a ten-minute routine
of jokes and stories to get the audience laughing before a recording. Ray
never performed, and even disliked saying odd lines (a very sharp ear
might hear him once, in a 1958 episode, as a voice in the crowd, heckling
Hancock). Even today, Ray is uncomfortable speaking in public, whereas
Alan is a relaxed after-dinner raconteur – though in private conversation
they are equally animated and witty.

A monologue featured in many early episodes, with Hancock telling a
long shaggy-dog story to a monosyllabic friend, played of course by Alan:

HANCOCK'S HALF HOUR, first series, episode thirteen

'A HOUSE ON THE CLIFF'
First broadcast: Tuesday 1 January 1955

TONY: 'Course, this isn't the first time I've been on the building lark.
    (ALAN interjects: I didn't think it was) You can tell by the expert

way I slice these bricks in half with me trowel, can't you? Mind you, me fingers aren't as long as they used to be. No, I come from a long line of builders, me. Me great-grandfather helped to build Tower Bridge. Yes, he was the bloke who sawed it in half. Then there's the Leaning Tower of Pisa. *(Your family built that?)* Every stone. My Uncle Fred designed it. Well, I say he designed it. That isn't exactly true. It was a rough sketch of me mother's wedding cake. The Italians liked it, so we put it up. *(Does it really lean?)* Well, strictly speaking… no. Between you and me, it's dead straight. It's the way they hold their cameras, that's what does it. Well anyway, me biggest job, and that's the one I want to tell you about, undoubtedly was the Forth Bridge. That's right, it *was* the Forth Bridge. I remember distinctly, because me other three fell down. Well anyway, I was in charge and I'd decided that we'd start building from both sides and we'd meet in the middle. You follow me? 'Cos you know the Forth Bridge. It's got all those big arches that go up and down, up and down, all the way across. How those trains get up and down those things I'll never know. Still, that's their worry. I was only building it. So anyway, there we were. We'd started from either side. We had a race to see who could get to the middle first. Well, we were going along like a house. We built the first twenty-seven yards in three seconds. Well, we had to, there was a train behind us. Well, we were doing very well until the fog sprang up. Well, I don't know how it happened, but the long and the short of it was… we passed each other. Well, I felt a right Toby, I can tell you. There was the other half of the bridge, twenty yards past me and six feet on the other side. Well, I blamed it on the crane driver. The bloke who was lifting the big girders about. 'It's your fault,' I said. 'Cos I was annoyed, see. Me whole face was red with anger. I clenched me fists until the muscles on me arm stood out like marbles. I looked up at him and I shook me fist. 'It's your fault,' I said. 'You weren't looking where you were going,' I said. 'Undo all those girders and go back and start again.' Well, I don't know whether it was the authority in my voice or the sense of shame he must have felt, but he did it without a murmur. 'Cos he could see I meant it. First he picked up one girder, then another, then another, until he had five huge iron girders in his crane. That was more than he'd ever carried before. 'Cos he was eager to rectify his mistake, see. He picked these five girders up and swung them into the air, high up above, gently as a lamb. A sort of sheepish, apologetic smile on his face. Then, as he swung them slowly across the middle of the bridge, do you know what he did? He dropped them on me head.

Alan Simpson's role was to put in just a word or two – but on one occasion, as he described to Ray Galton in a conversation during the research for this book, he overstepped the mark:

AS: One time, I said something like, 'Really? I don't believe it!' And Tony said, 'It says here, interrupt. Not take over.'
RG: Element of menace behind that?
AS: Oh yeah, absolutely. He meant it. I mean, he got a laugh, but he meant it.
RG: Were you rebuffed?
AS: I felt embarrassed, I suppose, I didn't realize that…
RG: You'd transgressed.
AS: Yeah, I'd transgressed.

This story shines a sidelight on the relationship between Hancock and his writers. The comedian fully respected their talent but, in most ways, they were his juniors: younger, less experienced, less celebrated. They each had their parts to play in this professional relationship, but Hancock took the dominant role. The gradual shift, over eight years, towards equality and parity with them would be one of the catalysts for his eventual split from Galton and Simpson: though they never resented Tony's fame, his own insecurities were to tear him apart.

Listening figures for *Hancock's Half Hour* quickly climbed from 4.5 million to 6.75 million, with repeats every week. A second series was inevitable. But when the show returned, the emphasis began to move from the surreal to the domestic. If Hancock had a screwdriver in his hand, he would be trying to fix the television rather than build a bridge. He wouldn't have needed the screwdriver if he had bought a good quality set – but Hancock's meanness with money was a joke that echoed right through the show's run:

HANCOCK'S HALF HOUR, second series, episode nine

'THE TELEVISION SET'
First broadcast: Tuesday 14 June 1955

KENNETH: What sort of prices did you have in mind?
TONY: Well, I want something good.

KENNETH: Naturally.

TONY: I mean, if you're buying a TV set, there's no point in getting a cheap one.

KENNETH: Of course not.

TONY: They're more trouble than they're worth.

KENNETH: Quite.

TONY: Always buy quality. It's cheaper in the long run.

KENNETH: I agree.

TONY: So taking everything into consideration, I'm quite willing to go up to... oooh... anything up to about fifteen quid.

KENNETH: Fifteen pounds.

TONY: Sssshhh – not so loud. Cor dear, I don't want everybody to know I've got that much money on me. I might be attacked.

Kenneth Williams had a favourite story about his mother, Louie. Hearing that her friend had just bought a new television, a top-of-the-range, fifteen-inch console, Louie retorted, 'Fifteen inches? That would console anyone!' A gag like that might have edged its way into a *Steptoe* script, but never into a *Hancock's Half Hour*. The star had no time for double entendres, which partly explains why he never had even a walk-on in a *Carry On*.

The penultimate episode of series two introduced another new sitcom element... suburban one-upmanship. Hancock was a gardener, obsessed with growing a marrow that would beat his neighbour's entry in the municipal vegetable show. It was a theme which foreshadowed comedies such as *The Good Life*, by John Esmonde and Bob Larbey, twenty years later:

HANCOCK'S HALF HOUR, second series, episode eleven

'THE MARROW'
First broadcast: Tuesday 28 June 1955

ANDREE: What about the man next door? He's entered for the competition – and his marrow is nearly as big as ours.

TONY: Never. Not in the same class. He don't half get annoyed, you know. I often lean over the fence and ask him how his cucumber's getting along. Still, he takes it in good part. He turns his hose on me.

BILL: I wouldn't be so cocky if I were you, Tub. There's three more weeks till the competition. A lot can happen in that time. Next door's determined to win, you know. He's been telling everyone he's going to beat you.

TONY: Mine's twice the size of his, he hasn't got a chance.

BILL: I know, but he's trying to sabotage your one. You want to watch him when he's pretending to weed his garden. A crafty look round, and half a dozen snails come sailing over the fence.

TONY: Ah, he's been doing that for years. But what he doesn't know... is that I sharpen their teeth up and throw them back. *(Sotto)* Hallo – look, speak of the devil. There he is, looking out of his bedroom window. *(Calls)* Morning. Five foot four, eight stone seven... and still growing. Har har har. That's narked him.

Hancock's timing was so perfectly weighted that, like Dan Leno in his monologues on the music-hall stage, he could conjure up scenes of physical comedy with just an inflection of his voice. Galton and Simpson used this talent more and more from the third series on. 'Hancock possessed an incredible ability to get it right on the first reading,' Alan said. 'He was a wonderful sight-reader. Every intonation, every rhythm: perfect from the moment he picked up the script. Even Laurence Olivier couldn't do that.'

The first episode of the third series was recorded just three months after the last show of the second, and listening figures were steadily climbing; by February 1956 they would crash through the 7 million mark. The success was intoxicating for Ray and Alan, who were inspired to fresh heights of invention while simultaneously developing Hancock's character.

HANCOCK'S HALF HOUR, third series, episode three

'THE BEQUEST'
First broadcast: Wednesday 9 November 1955

TONY: Here's an orchid. For your dress. A Corssige.

ANDREE: Why, it's beautiful. Just like the ones growing in the park greenhouse.

TONY: Oh, ha ha, yes, most odd... ha ha... pin it on.

ANDREE: I... I can't quite manage... I...

TONY: *(Intense)* Allow me, I have so much more experience in these things, I... *(Yells in agony)*

ANDREE: What's wrong?

TONY: Me finger... jabbed it... the pin... oooh.

ANDREE: Well, put your finger in your mouth and suck it.

TONY: *(With finger in mouth)* Darling, you're so beautiful... *(sucking noises)* You fascinating, you lovely creature... *(sucking noises)* There's something about you that drives a man to madness... *(sucks)*... I love you to distraction, don't you understand, I love you, I... it's still bleeding.

Hancock's intuitive timing was so good that, Ray said, 'he could say a line and get a laugh without understanding the joke himself. He'd come over to us sometimes and say, "Tell me, I got a laugh here, what was so funny?" He was marvellous to write for because he never tried to insert his own material into the scripts.'

HANCOCK'S HALF HOUR, third series, episode thirteen

'HANCOCK'S HAIR'
First broadcast: Wednesday 11 January 1956

TONY: *(Fade in)* ... seven, eight, nine, ten, eleven... six up on the bathroom floor and four more on the carpet... two in the fireplace... good grief – when is it going to stop? That's twenty-three already this morning.

BILL: What's wrong, Tub?

TONY: Me hair's falling out. I'm going bald.

BILL: Oh – there's nothing to worry about, cheer up Tub. *(Pats TONY on back)*

TONY: Stop patting me on the back. That's another three jumped out. What am I going to do? Hairless at my time of life. Patch where there was thatch.

BILL: Stop exaggerating. What's a few hairs falling out? You've still got enough there to stuff a sofa. I can't see any difference.

TONY: Ah, this is only the start. I've got me diary here somewhere... Monday it was two hairs, Tuesday it was six, Wednesday twelve, Thursday eighteen, today twenty-three. When I jump out of bed on Sunday morning I'll be knee deep in 'em. I'll only have a few strands left. I'll have to arrange 'em in a pattern across the middle of me head.

By this stage, every trace of stand-up comedy had been erased from the *Half Hours*. There were no routines, and no joke-telling – but the scripts were packed with one-liners:

GRAMS: *(Street noises)*

BILL: Is this the place?

TONY: Yes, 'Maison James'.

BILL: Funny Christian name, isn't it?

TONY: Of course it isn't. It's French. It's the male half of the name. Like, Josephine and Joseph, Geraldine and Gerald, Maisy and Maison. Perfectly normal.

BILL: What does that next bit say?

TONY: 'Maison James'… tonsorial artist.

BILL: What does that mean?

TONY: What does that mean? Use your common sense. It's obvious what it means… he paints tonsils as well.

Elements of social comment were adding depth to the scripts. 'We were committed socialists,' said Ray. 'Politics was one of the many things Alan and I agreed on. We were left-wingers.' No other BBC comedy would have dreamed, in 1956, of criticizing modern architecture:

HANCOCK'S HALF HOUR, third series, episode eighteen

'THE GREYHOUND TRACK'
First broadcast:Wednesday 15 February 1956

TONY: The only way you could possibly evict me from this land is if you were building houses on it.

SIDNEY: Yeah – that's what we're building.

TONY: A likely story. Show me the plans, then.

SIDNEY: Here you are.

EFFECTS: *(Rustle of paper, thick parchmenty sound)*

TONY: Funny shaped house, isn't it?

SIDNEY: Yes… well… It's a circular block of flats.

TONY: Oh? Then what's that big green path going all round the inside?

SIDNEY: That's so's the tenants can exercise their dogs.

TONY: Oh – you allow dogs in these flats then?

SIDNEY: Certainly. We wouldn't get the tenants in if we didn't have the dogs.

TONY: Well, I must say that's very good-hearted of you. 'Cos most places don't like dogs running about, you know.

SIDNEY: Oh, we encourage it. We even give them something to chase.

TONY: Very good idea... keeps them amused. Most humane... and... here – what's this little wooden box with the six doors stretching across the grass path?

SIDNEY: Oh, that... it's, er... let's see now... Oh yes, I remember – bicycle sheds.

TONY: Oh, yes, very thoughtful, very good planning, I... hallo, hallo, what's this?

SIDNEY: What?

TONY: What's this marked here... Tote?

SIDNEY: Tote? That's the name of the architect. Harry Tote.

TONY: Wait a minute, wait a minute... I'm no mug. What's this after his name? Two-and-six, and five bob?

SIDNEY: That's not two-and-six and five bob. That's the scale of the plans. Two sixths of an inch to every five foot.

TONY: Yes, of course... silly of me. You know, for a moment I... you'll laugh at this, it's funny really, but do you know what I thought? I thought... it's so ludicrous... I thought it might be a greyhound track you were building.

SIDNEY: Now Hancock – what on earth gave you that idea?

TONY: Oh, nothing really... it's just that I noticed all the flats have got turnstiles instead of front doors. Still, this modern architecture... they've got funny ideas, haven't they?

SIDNEY: Hilarious.

TONY: I must admit, Sid, this is a wonderful thing you're doing. Building all those flats for homeless people all over the borough, it's a really noble scheme and I wish you every success with it.

SIDNEY: Then you'll move out?

TONY. No. Then *I'll* be homeless and I'm not moving into one of *those* horrible things.

With the launch of series four came the classic Hancock line-up, and probably the greatest cast of any sitcom:

ANNOUNCER: This is the BBC Light Programme. We present Tony Hancock, Sidney James, Bill Kerr, Hattie Jacques and Kenneth Williams in...

TONY: *(Breath)* Hancock's Half Hour.

In her first appearance, Hattie Jacques reprised the typewriter scene which Bill and Tony had played in the very first *Half Hour*. Kenneth

Williams claimed, in his autobiography, that Hattie was hurt by frequent jokes about her size, but she gamely played up to them throughout her career. In 1963's *Carry on Cabby,* she complains that all she ever sees of her husband is his legs, sticking out from beneath a cab's engine: 'He knows I can't get under there!' Her husband in the movie, of course, is Sid James. In the *Half Hours,* no matter how much she tried to flirt with Hancock, it was always Sid who fancied her:

HANCOCK'S HALF HOUR, fourth series, episode five

'THE NEW SECRETARY'
First broadcast: Sunday 11 November 1956

> EFFECTS: *(Very slow, painful, one-finger typing. Ding of bell. Roller back. PAUSE. One-finger typing again. Ding of bell. Roller back. PAUSE. One-finger typing again. Ding of bell. Roller back. PAUSE. One tap.)*

HATTIE: *(Hums tunelessly over the typing)* Oh bother, I haven't put any paper in.

SIDNEY: Hallo ducks.

HATTIE: Oooh. How did you get in here?

SIDNEY: Through the window.

HATTIE: Do you usually make a habit of climbing in through people's windows?

SIDNEY: Yes.

HATTIE: Who *are* you?

SIDNEY: I'm Sid James. A friend of the family. Has Hancock told you about me?

HATTIE: No.

SIDNEY: That's a relief.

HATTIE: Well, what are you doing here?

SIDNEY: Oh, I was just passing by, saw the window open, so I thought I'd creep in and see if he was out. I didn't expect to find anybody else here. You're new, aren't you?

HATTIE: I'm Mr Hancock's private secretary.

SIDNEY: Oh, pleased to meet you, Miss er...

HATTIE: Pugh. But you can call me Grizelda.

SIDNEY: And what do you have to do here?

HATTIE: I look after Mr Hancock's business affairs.

SIDNEY: Do you now... Grizelda Pugh... what a lovely name.

HATTIE: *(Bell-like laugh)*
SIDNEY: Cor blimey. Tell me, Grizelda...
HATTIE: Yes, Mr James.
SIDNEY: Sidney.
HATTIE: Yes... Sidney.
SIDNEY: What business affairs do you look after?
HATTIE: Well, I answer the phone, reply to his fan mail, make up his
    expense sheets, file his... oooh, cheeky! File his correspondence,
    sign his cheques, look after his contracts...
SIDNEY: You sign his cheques?
HATTIE: Yes.
SIDNEY: Just you? Doesn't he have to sign them as well?
HATTIE: No, he doesn't like to be bothered. I do it all.
SIDNEY: What a lovely girl you are.
HATTIE: Oh, get away with you.
SIDNEY: No, I mean it. Standing there in the half light, regal, upright, you
    look like some mysterious Eastern princess.
HATTIE: Yes, I suppose I do, really. It's the split up my skirt that does it.
SIDNEY: You sign his cheques, eh?
HATTIE: Yes.
SIDNEY: I bet you've got lovely handwriting.
HATTIE: Have you noticed the way I smoulder?
SIDNEY: Yes, very attractive. Where's his chequebook?
HATTIE: Of course, my beauty comes from within.
SIDNEY: It must do.
HATTIE: Men can sense the unplumbed depths of my desire.
SIDNEY: Of course they can.
HATTIE: It must be the way my eyelids droop when I'm worked up.
SIDNEY: Here it is. Lancashire Cotton Mill and Farmers' Bank.
HATTIE: I do symbolic dances in front of the mirror, you know.
SIDNEY: *(As if writing)* Pay cash, one hundred pounds. Do you?
HATTIE: Yes. Guess what this one is. *(Sings Waltz from 'Swan Lake')*
SIDNEY: Very good. Sign just here.
HATTIE: That was a Greek goddess prancing in the meadows while the
    shepherd boy blissfully sleeps.
SIDNEY: The best thing he could have done. Here's the pen.
HATTIE: What's this for?
SIDNEY: Hundred nicker. Didn't Mr Hancock tell you? He pays me
    hundred nicker a week.
HATTIE: What for?
SIDNEY: Well, it's, er... I'm his brother.

HATTIE: What's the hundred for?

SIDNEY: To keep quiet about it.

Sid could wheedle his way around Grizzly, but Hancock barely had a civil word for her:

HANCOCK'S HALF HOUR, fourth series, episode six

'MICHELANGELO HANCOCK'
First broadcast: Sunday 18 November 1956

TONY: Oi, Miss Pugh… Grizzly!

HATTIE: What do you want?

TONY: I've got some work for you.

HATTIE: I don't want it. I'm busy enough as it is.

TONY: Doing what?

HATTIE: I'm knitting myself a jumper.

TONY: Of course. I saw the lorry bringing the wool in this morning. Listen here, missis, you're going to do some work for *me*, so put that in your pipe and smoke it. That reminds me, stop using my tobacco. Now… work. I've decided to enter for the council statue competition.

HATTIE: You? What do you know about statues?

TONY: Quite a lot, since I've watched the rate you work at. There's an entry form in the paper, I want you to fill it in.

HATTIE: Show me. Oh yes… so and so and so and so… conditions. All entries should be not less than ten foot high.

TONY: What? Show me. Oh, well, that's coalboxed that. I'm only five foot six. It's discrimination against the little man. It's not fair…

HATTIE: Look, Henry Moore, the *statue* has to be ten foot high.

BILL: That's just as bad, where are we going to get a ten-foot model?

TONY: Where are we going to find a… I don't know why you ever left the bush. You'd have been much happier blowing poison darts about. What a stupid remark to make. Where are we going to find a ten-foot model? There's dozens of them about. Any circus'll lend us one. Take a letter to Bertram Mills… 'Dear Bert…'

HATTIE: Honestly, you're just about the most stupid man I've ever come across.

TONY: You can't put that, he'd set his lions on me.

HATTIE: Mr Hancock, you don't need a ten-foot model. Haven't you ever heard of proportion? All you have to do is get an ordinary size model and make the statue twice as big.

TONY: Oh, that's how it's done. So old Nelson *wasn't* fifteen feet tall.

HATTIE: No.

TONY: I'm not surprised. When I saw his cabin on the *Victory*, I thought to myself at the time, he'd have to bend up a bit to get in that hammock. Oh well, it's easy now. All we need is the lump of rock, hammer and chisel, and we're away. Phone up the quarry and ask them to send down a twenty-foot boulder. Then there's a little job I want you to do.

HATTIE: *(Pleased)* You want me to be your model.

TONY: No. When it arrives I want you to carry it through to the back garden.

Hancock's character was stubbornly unromantic, and that extended into real life – even though he was married. 'Hancock was very awkward around women if it was about sex,' Ray said. 'He couldn't be serious, he could only be a buffoon, comedic. If Sid and he went out with two girls, he was very awkward about putting his arms around her or anything like that. Now whether that was deliberate, him being a character, or his own natural inhibitions... I can't think he was inhibited with women really. We used to kid him about being unromantic and he'd go along with it. It was not his style, he'd say, to be in any way associated too closely with a woman.'

Alan agreed. 'When you think about it, that's very difficult for any comedian. Michael Caine could play in a comedy and play a straight love scene, but comedians find it difficult – it's not just Hancock. If they did that, it wouldn't be funny and people would be saying, "Hmm, what's he on about? What's he doing here?" Because you can't really stop to think about that, or you shouldn't.'

Here's Hancock trying to back out of marriage with Hattie:

HANCOCK'S HALF HOUR, fourth series, episode eight

'*SID IN LOVE*'
First broadcast: Sunday 2 December 1956

GRAMS: *(Hancock, rising chromatically)*

TONY: *(As if writing)* Dear Grizelda, the nearer our wedding day gets, the more I think you ought to know something about my past. It is not generally known that I am weak in the head. Centuries of inbreeding among the aristocratic Hancocks have unfortunately resulted in a long line of congenital idiots of which I am the most recent and most congenital. I will therefore not hold you to your bond. Hoping this finds you as it leaves me, hanging upside-down from the chandelier in tropical kit, I am, yours…

GRAMS: (Hancock, rising chromatically)

HATTIE: Dear Anthony, I am in receipt of yours of the 23rd instant. Much as I was shocked by the contents, I feel now, more than ever, that it is my duty to marry you, and look after you till death us do part. Your ever loving and devoted future wife…

GRAMS: (Hancock, rising chromatically)

TONY: Dear Grizelda, forgive the spidery writing, but I'm not well again. I'm laying in bed in the throes of another attack of the plague. I knew those three years playing the piano in the opium dens of Shanghai would catch up on me sooner or later. It's our bad luck it should happen on the eve of our wedding but I'm sure you will understand that I can no longer hold you to our bond…

GRAMS: (Hancock, rising chromatically)

HATTIE: Dearest darling Anthony, how could I desert you in your hour of need? I will send a stretcher to bring you to the ceremony. Have patience, my darling…

GRAMS: (Hancock, rising chromatically)

TONY: Dearest Grizelda, surprise, surprise, my wife and fifteen children whom I thought dead arrived today from Afghanistan. Of course, I can now no longer hold you to our bond. I am yours truly…

GRAMS: (Hancock, rising chromatically)

HATTIE: Dear Mr Hancock, if you don't marry me tomorrow, I shall sue you for every penny you've got.
TONY: Dear Miss Pugh, see you in church.

'It gives us a lot of pleasure,' said Alan, 'to know that a lot of the members of the Tony Hancock Appreciation Society weren't even born when the shows were first broadcast. We never imagined at the time that the repeats would still be popular half a century later.' One of the episodes which regularly features in fans' Top Ten lists is 'The Wild Man of the Woods':

HANCOCK'S HALF HOUR, fourth series, episode sixteen

'THE WILD MAN OF THE WOODS'
First broadcast: Sunday 27 January 1957

KENNETH: *(Newspaper reporter)* Well come on, hurry up with this important announcement, I've got a dog show to report at eleven o'clock.

TONY: You wait here till I've finished. Now then, where's me scroll?

EFFECTS: (Parchment unrolls and rustles)

TONY: Right... my proclamation. I, Anthony Hancock, philosopher, guide, advisor and wicker bottom chair repairer... you'd better put me address after the last one... I, after sitting up all night thinking, have decided that... put down 'hedge trimmer' as well... have decided that civilization has failed us. I therefore come to the conclusion that I, to be honest with my principles, must from henceforth renounce the world. You can put down 'antique furniture for sale' as well.

HATTIE: Did you say you were going to renounce the world?

TONY: I did. I am cutting myself off from society. I am having nothing more to do with the world.

BILL: Oh no... this is going to set civilization back a thousand years.

TONY: There is no happiness in the world today for a man of my intellect, so I have decided the only solution is to become a recluse. I am going back to nature. I am going to renounce all my worldly goods and live in the woods.

SIDNEY: Where?

TONY: Clapham Common. It's the easy living and false comforts of modern civilization that are ruining mankind.

KENNETH: Why have you picked Clapham Common?

TONY: So I'll be near the shops. It's the wild woods for me. The trees will be my home, the ditch my bed, the clouds my blanket...

HATTIE: Oh shut up, don't be so stupid. You couldn't live in the open.

TONY: Of course I could. I've been practising in the back garden all week.

BILL: And you've been nipping in every night.

TONY: I stayed out all night Saturday.

BILL: Only because you lost your key.

TONY: Words, words. I have decided. I am leaving this house... leaving society. I shall become a hermit.

SIDNEY: Look, Hancock, have you really thought about this?

HATTIE: Quiet, he might change his mind.

KENNETH: What are you going to live on, Mr Hancock?

TONY: Nature is bountiful, young man. I will eat the food she has provided. Berries, herbs, grass… that's a point, isn't it. I hadn't thought of that.

BILL: Take your bow and arrow with you, and shoot some wildlife.

TONY: That's it, me little bow and arrow. I'll take the suction pad off it and sharpen the point up.

SIDNEY: What are you going to do with yourself in the woods?

TONY: I'll be free. For the first time in my life I shall be free to express the beauty of me artistic soul… the intellect which for so long has been straining inside this enormous chump of mine. I shall write poetry.

BILL: You don't mean that rubbish you scribble down in your diary every day?

TONY: Rubbish? Rubbish? Philosophical gems, matey. Listen to this. Sonnet by A.H. – 'O wondrous moon with silvery sheen, who throws its light upon East Cheam, from lofty height and through the mist… two o'clock Friday, chiropodist.' How did that get in? Where's the last line of me poem?

HATTIE: I rubbed it out to make room for the chiropodist appointment. You know you can't get your boots on if you leave your corn more than a week.

KENNETH: Well, I'd better be going to the dog show.

TONY: Are you going to print my decision?

KENNETH: No, I don't think so. Not very interesting, is it? I might print something when you get arrested. Cheerio.

Hattie Jacques returned for the fifth series, though it would be her last. Her character gave Hancock a depth that he was never to regain. 'Hattie Jacques was a terrific actress,' said Ray. 'She went on to work with Eric Sykes on television, of course, and Eric was one of the directors at Associated London Scripts. He and Spike Milligan both had offices on the same floor as us, and sometimes they'd stick their heads round the door, to try out a line – "How does this work, do you think it's funny?"'

'Ray and I were lucky, because we never had to do that,' Alan explained. 'We were able to bounce ideas off each other, and I think we always knew if something was genuinely funny.'

HANCOCK'S HALF HOUR, fifth series, episode five

'HANCOCK'S CAR'
First broadcast: Tuesday 1 April 1958

HATTIE: You must be hungry after all the work you've done. I've made a
    nice big dishful of cauliflower cheese.
TONY: Ugh. I don't like cauliflower cheese.
BILL: Neither do I.
SIDNEY: Neither do I.
HATTIE: *(Surprised)* Don't you really?
TONY: You know we don't like cauliflower cheese. You've always known it.
HATTIE: Oh, never mind, I'll just have to eat it all myself.
TONY: You planned that. You made it on purpose. You're always doing
    that. You've made a list of everything we don't like, then you
    deliberately go and make dirty great binfuls of it. Oooh, you gannet.
BILL: I think I'll have some cauliflower cheese.
SIDNEY: Yeah, I might as well have some too.
HATTIE: *(Worried)* But you don't like it. You said you don't like it. You told
    me you didn't.
TONY: Hallo, that frightened her. She didn't expect that. I'll have some
    too. Har, har, har. It's worth making yourself ill just to see her face. It
    drops two inches every spoonful we take. Where's me blindfold, I
    can't look at it and eat it.

Hancock's address was 23 Railway Cuttings, East Cheam – 'Twenty-three
is a funny number, whereas twenty-two and twenty-five aren't,' Ray said.
'And there was a note of pretentiousness about East Cheam. Cheam was a
good area, but East Cheam sounds like it's on the wrong side of the tracks.'

It's one of the most famous addresses in comedy, but that didn't stop
the writers from selling it, redeveloping it, knocking it down or, on one
occasion, blowing it up:

HANCOCK'S HALF HOUR, fifth series, episode six

'THE UNEXPLODED BOMB'
First broadcast: Tuesday 25 February 1958

TONY: Put that light on.

    EFFECTS: (Light switch)

TONY: Ah, that's better. So this is the cellar. I've never seen it before.

BILL: Haven't you? Well, let me show you around. That's the floor you're standing on, and they're the walls...

TONY: And don't tell me – that thing above me is the roof.

BILL: Are you sure you haven't been down here before?

TONY: No, no, I used to work for an estate agent. They taught me all about it. It's very roomy, isn't it? Almost as big as a bedroom.

BILL: Yeah.

TONY: So you can move your bed down here tomorrow. I'm letting your room. What's that up there in the ceiling?

BILL: That's the manhole. You remember, when you bought the place, it was just a jagged hole and you put a cover on it.

TONY: Oh yes. Well, what's that thing stuck in the floor underneath it?

BILL: What thing?

TONY: That thing. The big metal thing with the fins. What's this chalk writing on the side? '1942, Gott Straff England, Heil Hitler.' Is this yours?

BILL: No, I don't know what it is. I just use it to strike my matches on when I'm having a smoke.

TONY: Look, there's big dents all over it.

BILL: Oh yeah, that was me. I was trying to break it open with a pickaxe.

TONY: You hit it with a pickaxe? You fool, fancy doing a thing like that. It's not ours, you might have damaged it. Someone might come and ask for it back.

BILL: No, no, Tub, they can't. 1942. If it's not claimed within six months, it becomes the property of the people who find it. It's ours, Tub.

TONY: Oooh good. I've always wanted a metal thing with fins on. Buffoon, what good is it to us? Dig it up, and see how much you can get from the rag-and-bone man for it.

BILL: You can't move it, I've tried. It's embedded too far in the ground.

SIDNEY: *(Off mike)* Oi, you two, where's that wine? Me tongue's hanging out up here.

KENNETH: Can I give you a hand to decant it?

EFFECTS: (Footsteps coming downstairs)

TONY: No, no, stay there, Vicar, don't bother to come down, we're – er – we're just trying to select a bottle to suit your palate.

KENNETH: *(On mike)* Ah, there now. *(Horrified)* Good heavens!

TONY: What?

KENNETH: Stand back.

TONY: What is it? What's wrong?

KENNETH: Over there, sticking out of the floor. An unexploded bomb.

TONY: Yes, it's ours, we're claiming it, treasure trove, you know, it's – it's a what?

KENNETH: A bomb. An unexploded bomb.

TONY: *(Almost speechless)* You me... I've be... that's be... since... here in... down... all these years?

KENNETH: I'm afraid so.

TONY: What... here... down in the... all the... since... with me upstairs?

KENNETH: Yes, yes.

TONY: *(Groans)*

KENNETH: Oh dear, I don't think Mr Hancock is feeling well. Perhaps he ought to sit down.

BILL: Yeah, come on, Tub, sit down, have a rest, come on old son, over here.

TONY: Yes, thank you... not on the bomb! Go and reserve me a bunk in the underground station – we're getting out of here.

KENNETH: Come now, this is no time to panic.

TONY: It's a good enough time for me, mate. I'm off.

The original script for 'Sunday Afternoon At Home', one of the most inventive and influential episodes of any sitcom, suffered several long cuts. The comedy was rooted in the boredom of the characters, expressed in long sighs, grumblings and silences. As the pauses grew, the episode overran. As ever, Ray and Alan were on hand throughout the day's rehearsals and recording, to advise and rewrite if necessary. Most cuts, however, were proposed by Main Wilson, to keep the show within bounds, or by Hancock when he felt a line didn't work. The writers accepted excisions as a necessary evil of the broadcast medium: timings had to be adhered to, no matter how good the material that was lost. They accepted too that they almost always overfilled a script, as if their creativity, like a good pint of beer, was at its best when it foamed over.

One exchange lost to time constraints was an argument between Tony and Sid:

HANCOCK'S HALF HOUR, fifth series, episode fourteen

'SUNDAY AFTERNOON AT HOME'
First broadcast: Tuesday 22 April 1958

SIDNEY: What's on the telly?

TONY: The dinner plates. Why don't you clear them off, Miss Pugh? Too lazy to take them out to the kitchen. You'll ruin that veneer.

SIDNEY: What programme's on?

TONY: *Gardening Club* on one and *Free Speech* on the other.

SIDNEY: Oooh good, let's have *Free Speech* on.

TONY: No, I want *Gardening Club* on.

SIDNEY: What's wrong with *Free Speech*?

TONY: I prefer *Gardening Club*.

SIDNEY: Why? You never do any.

TONY: I intend to do some.

SIDNEY: How? You haven't got a garden.

TONY: I have a window box, and a few pots of cacti hanging about somewhere.

SIDNEY: There's nothing in the window box.

TONY: I know that. I'm letting it lie fallow this year. Obviously you know nothing about farming. Have you never heard of soil exhaustion and the rotation of crops? You keep planting stuff in that, it'll become a dust bowl. I saw *The Grapes of Wrath*, I know what I'm doing.

SIDNEY: I want to see *Free Speech*.

TONY: You're not seeing *Free Speech*. We're having *Gardening Club*.

SIDNEY: We'll toss for it.

TONY: All right.

SIDNEY: Heads, *Free Speech*. Tails, *Gardening Club*.

TONY: Tails. *Gardening Club*. Well done. We're having *Gardening Club*.

HATTIE: You're not.

TONY: I beg your pardon?

HATTIE: Didn't I tell you? The television set's broken.

TONY: You've been sitting there listening to us arguing about what programme to see and you knew it was broken? Why didn't you say so?

HATTIE: Well, I was getting quite interested in who was going to win. It passed a few minutes, didn't it?

TONY: Stone me. No television, it's raining, a rotten dinner and it's only twenty-five past three. Oooh, I'll hit somebody in a minute.

Galton and Simpson continued to draw their inspiration from domestic minutiae, with an episode spent clearing out a drawerful of clutter. Junk would be the background for eight series of *Steptoe and Son*: here, it provided the props for a sequence of comic genius:

HANCOCK'S HALF HOUR, fifth series, episode sixteen

'THE JUNK MAN'
First broadcast: Tuesday 6 May 1958

EFFECTS: *(A load of assorted stuff being tipped onto the table)*

BILL: Look at it all, how can anyone get so much stuff into one drawer?

TONY: I can't understand it, we cleared it out five years ago.

HATTIE: I don't know why you don't tip it all straight onto the fire. It's junk.

TONY: I know, it's amazing, isn't it? Still, we might as well sort it out first. Most of it can go, there might just be one or two things in there we ought to keep. All the things we want to keep we'll put back in the drawer. Let's see now, what have we got here?

BILL: What about all this string here? That can go.

TONY: No, no, we're always looking for string in this house – undo all the knots, roll it up into a ball and put it back. Let's see, hair grips, an elastic band, bit of billiard chalk, a German stamp, two drawing pins, a pipe cleaner, matchbox, a couple of fivestones, a doorknob, some curtain runners, half a pair of sunglasses, a domino, a bit of glass, a toy soldier with his head off, and a nail. Right, we'll put all that lot in the cigar box and put them back.

HATTIE: Why? I thought we were clearing it out.

TONY: We are, but we've got to discriminate. You never know when that stuff might come in handy... We must only get rid of the useless stuff. Put it back – now we know where it is when we need it. Now what else have we got? A couple of screws. We'd better keep those, they must have fallen out of something. We've just got to wait till something or other falls to bits, then we know where they've come from. You'll be glad then we kept it.

HATTIE: All right then, but please throw out something.

TONY: I intend to. That's the idea of having a clear-out. Now, there's some marbles here.

HATTIE: You don't need those.

TONY: Ah yes, but this one's a red rider, very rare they are – we'd better keep that.

BILL: How about the other two?

TONY: Well, if we're going to keep one we might as well keep the others. Put them back. Oooh look, here's my dad's medals. Let those who come after him see his name is not forgotten. Oh well, we must keep those. You never know, they might be worth a few bob. Put them back in the drawer. Aah, this is interesting. Four bits of jigsaw puzzle.

A man's earhole, a bit of sky, a bit of ship's flag and a green bit. Do you think it's that 'Drake on Plymouth Hoe' one you bought me when I was in bed with my feet? What happened to that – it was set out on the tea trolley, wasn't it?

BILL: Yeah, it gradually got mixed up with the broken biscuits and sort of slowly disappeared.

TONY: Well, I think we'll keep these. Put them back in the drawer.

HATTIE: What is the point of keeping four bits of stray jigsaw puzzle?

TONY: I'm not convinced the rest of it is missing. Supposing we found the other nine hundred and ninety-six pieces, and we'd thrown these away, I'd never forgive myself. A beautiful stretch of pale blue sky with a hole in it, it'd look horrible. We will keep them until it is ascertained beyond all possible doubt that the rest of it is not in existence. Now what's this? Two French francs. We'll keep those in case we go on holiday.

HATTIE: Well, this can go. This is no possible use to anyone.

TONY: Wait a minute, wait a minute, what is it? Let me see it.

HATTIE: It's a wireless licence for 1936.

TONY: You can't throw that away, have you gone mad? Supposing a gentleman from the BBC comes round and says, 'You didn't pay your wireless licence in 1936,' I've got proof here that I did. I keep all my old bills. You can put that in the loft with all the others.

BILL: We might as well throw these stones out – I don't know how they got there.

TONY: You can't throw my stones away. They're not just ordinary stones, matey. They are from the beach at Bognor Regis. They have tremendous sentimental and intrinsic value. I count them among my most treasured souvenirs. Look at them, worn smooth by countless centuries of eternal battle with the movement of the restless sea. I shall gaze at them when I am old and grey, sitting back in my old rocker, contemplating the wondrous subtlety of the shade in the strata that traverses them, and remembering... remembering the most miserable holiday I ever spent in my entire life.

As the scene developed, Bill Kerr demonstrated a gift for plaintive pauses that rivalled Hancock's:

BILL: I've rolled the string up like you said, Tub.

TONY: Well?

BILL: I can't get it off my fingers now. I think I've rolled it too tight.

TONY: Well, what do you want me to do about it?
BILL: I don't know. I just thought you might have an idea.
TONY: Well, I haven't. You'll just have to work it out for yourself.

…

BILL: Tub, my fingers are turning white.
TONY: Oh?
BILL: Yeah, I think the string's getting tighter.
TONY: You shouldn't have dipped your hand in the water, should you?
BILL: I had to. The string was on fire. I tried to burn it off with my cigarette lighter.
TONY: Oh, what a nincompoop. Cut it off with the scissors.
BILL: Oh yeah, that's a good idea, isn't it?

…

BILL: Tub.
TONY: What?
BILL: I can't get the scissors under the string. I think we'd better do something. My fingers are throbbing and they're turning blue.
TONY: Look, you wound the string round your fingers, right?
BILL: Yeah.
TONY: Well, to get it off, why not try winding it in the opposite direction?
BILL: Oh yeah. I never thought of that.

…

BILL: Tub.
TONY: Oh what?
BILL: Hallo Sid.
SIDNEY: Hallo Bill.
TONY: *(Long pause)* Well?
BILL: Well what?
TONY: You called me.
BILL: Did I?
TONY: Yes. You said, 'Tub.' And I said, 'Oh what?' Then you said, 'Hallo Sid,' and Sid said, 'Hallo Bill.' Then I said, 'Well?' and you said, 'Well, what?' and I said, 'You called me.' Now… I want to know why you called me in the first place.
BILL: Um… er…
TONY: Well, think, man, what was it?
BILL: Um… er…
TONY: Are your shoes hurting you?
BILL: No.

TONY: Are you hungry?

BILL: No.

TONY: Think hard, it'll come, don't get flustered, keep calm. Now what is it?

BILL: Um… er… *(Long pause)* Hallo Sid.

TONY: You've said that. Now stop wasting my time, what did you want? It must have been something.

BILL: Oh, yeah, yeah. I remember what it was. I've got the string off my fingers.

TONY: Oh, good lad. How did you do it?

BILL: Well, I unwound it off my fingers like you said to.

TONY: See, a little bit of thought. What have you done with the string?

BILL: It's wound round my other fingers now. And it's tighter this time, it's hurting twice as much.

TONY: Sid, you can buy him if you like. You'd like a go on Sid's cart, wouldn't you?

BILL: No. I just want to get this string off my fingers. They've gone numb, you know.

TONY: Have they?

BILL: Help me get it off.

TONY: No. You've got to learn to stand on your own two feet. If we keep helping you do things, you'll never learn. Now you go and sit in the corner and work it out for yourself.

…

BILL: Tub.

TONY: Now what?

BILL: I've got the string off me other hand now.

TONY: Congratulations. How did you do it?

BILL: Well, I knew if I tried to unwind it again, I'd just get it back on the hand I had it on first of all, so I thought to myself, I'll be clever, I won't use my hand at all. So I got the end in my teeth and unwound it that way, and it worked.

TONY: Good lad. Where's the string?

BILL: I swallowed it.

The rapport between writers and performers gave Galton and Simpson freedom to experiment. 'We'd just write pauses in the script,' says Ray, 'and left it to the actors to play around with how long they could sustain it.' Hancock could keep it going all night; here he takes his timing from the ticking of an alarm clock:

HANCOCK'S HALF HOUR, fifth series, episode twenty

'THE SLEEPLESS NIGHT'
First broadcast: Tuesday 3 June 1958

TONY: Sleep, sleep, that's all I ask for… sleep, sleep…
SID & BILL: *(Make noises in their sleep… grunts, etc.)*

> EFFECTS: *(Very loud ticking clock)*

TONY: That clock is driving me barmy. I've been lying here for two hours trying to ignore it. But it gets louder every minute. I could hardly hear it at first, but now listen to it. It's thumping away over there like Big Ben. Where is it? Where is it? It wasn't here when I went to bed. I smashed our one. Of course, it's Sid's wristwatch. The one he bought in Port Said for three and nine. There it is on his chair. Glowing away there, mocking me it is. Deliberately keeping me awake. I can hear it… tick tock, tick tock, keep him awake, keep him awake, tick tock, tick tock. Where's me army boot, I'll creep up on it. Softly now, don't let it know you're coming. Quietly.

> EFFECTS: *(Clock ticks louder)*

TONY: One bash, that's all, one little bash. You luminous gargoyle, grinning at me in the dark… take that!

> EFFECTS: *(He bashes the watch with his boot… the chair breaks as well)*

SIDNEY: What was that, what's going on here… Hancock, what are you doing?
TONY: Keep away from me, I've still got the boot.
SIDNEY: What have you done?
TONY: *(Lunatic)* I've killed it. I've killed the watch. I had to, it was driving me mad, so I hit it, it won't tick any more, I'm free, free, nobody'll blame me, I had to kill it, it was self-defence.
SIDNEY: He's bonkers. Hancock, go back to bed, you'll be all right, you're just tired, funny things happen to the mind at night, you go back to bed, get some sleep, you'll be all right in the morning. Get some sleep.
TONY: Yes, yes, sleep, that's what I need. Sleep, must go to sleep. Got to be clear-headed in the morning… sleep, that's all I need, sleep.
SIDNEY: That's it, get into bed.
TONY: Aah, lovely bed, sleep, sleep, sleep, sleep. I'm going, I'm going,

I'm sinking, I can feel it coming over me, lovely sleep, I'm drowsy, any minute now, I'm going, going… I'm going… *(He snores)*

EFFECTS: *(From downstairs, telephone bell rings)*

TONY: *(Wakes at first ring)* What's that? What's that? Fire, fire, women and Hancock first. Man the lifeboat.

The monologues had been dropped from the scripts after the first series, the victim of a relentless focus on realism. Instead, especially in the final radio series, the writers introduced longer passages, flights of fancy that let Hancock soar:

HANCOCK'S HALF HOUR, sixth series, episode two

'THE MEETING' (also known as 'THE CHILDHOOD SWEETHEART')
First broadcast: Tuesday 6 October 1959

TONY: Good grief… why am I standing here chit-chatting with the likes of you? I have an important engagement to keep.
SIDNEY: What engagement?
TONY: Twenty-five years ago today, I made a pact.
BILL: Who with?
TONY: My childhood sweetheart. Olive Locksmith. When we said goodbye in 1934 we pledged to meet again twenty-five years later… and today is the day.
BILL: Where are you meeting her?
TONY: At the same place where we said goodbye… outside Le Café de la Belle Marguerite, Chiswick.

GRAMS: *(Romantic music under)*

TONY: She was beautiful and life was wonderful; we were nine years old and madly in love. I tied a bit of cotton round her finger and we swore our eternal undying love. But it wasn't to be. They tried to tell us we were too young, but that was nonsense. I could have kept her – I was earning good money on the paper round. But no, there was another problem. We didn't understand it… what can two people in love know about such things as… class distinction. You see, my father was only a tram conductor. It was hopeless from the start, you see… her father was a driver. Well, you couldn't cut across barriers like that… there was ten bob a week difference straight away. Oh, they tried to be kind to me about it… my father gave me some advice… stick to your own station in life, son, and don't get hurt, he said. She's not for you. Money marries money, he said… give up this hopeless quest. It was *Room at the Top* all over again. And to make sure we never met again, her parents moved. He got transferred from the 67s at Tottenham to the 34s at Clapham Common. We were heartbroken. It was the end of our world, life held no further meaning for us. I was right off my cornflakes for days. I lost interest in my conkers. I tried to find solace in my fag cards, but it was no good – everywhere I looked, all I could see was her sweet face smiling at me through the misty film that covered my eyes.

SIDNEY: Oh cor blimey.

TONY: Life was an empty shell, an abyss of black despair. Then came the day to part. I put on my best cub's uniform with the red and green woggle and we met secretly. I shall never forget that last meal together. Two bars of chocolate with holes in and a bottle of fizzy cherryade. We kissed goodbye, and she put on her roller skates and was off down the pavement. It was at that last meeting we swore to remain true to each other, remain single and meet again in 1959 to see if we still felt the same way about each other. I have kept my part of the bargain, and today we shall meet again after all these years… You haven't been listening to a word I've been saying, have you?

BILL: Yeah, you were telling us about some bird you were knocking about with… er… she lived on a tram and she was eating chocolate with holes in, on her skates.

TONY: I was talking about Olive, my sweetheart.

SIDNEY: And a load of old rubbish it was too.

TONY: Oh, well, of course. I didn't expect you to understand. How could a man like you ever hope to understand the sensitive world of two children who have discovered the world of innocent love for the first time?

SIDNEY: Innocent young love. If I'd been your old man, I would have given you a thump round the earhole and kicked you up to bed.

TONY: I don't think I have ever met such a crude man in my life. Entirely lacking in any human understanding whatsoever. Not an ounce of poetry in you, is there?

SIDNEY: Oh yes there is. When I was eight, I wrote a poem… more of a lament it was… it was about the first horse I ever backed, came in second. I called it… 'Send Him to the Knacker's Yard'.

Another favourite technique was to set the characters bickering. Instead of long speeches, barely anything here is longer than a single line, as Tony, Sid and Bill wind each other up:

HANCOCK'S HALF HOUR, sixth series, episode three

'THE LAST BUS HOME'
First broadcast: Tuesday 13 October 1959

SIDNEY: Oh, I do hate hanging about in the cold waiting for buses. Where is it?

TONY: It's not due yet. You are a misery, aren't you?

SIDNEY: My feet are cold.

TONY: You shouldn't wear those nylon socks. I told you to get a wool mixture.

SIDNEY: They don't make the wool ones so flashy. I like flashy clocks up the side.

TONY: They look horrible. Pink's not your colour for a start.

SIDNEY: They're not pink. It's called Mediterranean Mauve. The latest colour from Italy, the man said.

TONY: Italy. Birmingham, they come from. They can sell you anything, can't they? I can't understand you. For a man who's so shrewd in business matters, you're a right mug the minute you walk into a clothes shop. They see you coming. Nylon socks, two-tone French winkle-pickers, Frank Sinatra hats, what a mess you look.

SIDNEY: I think I look rather sharp.

TONY: Sharp! It's an education to walk behind you. If you could have only heard the comments as you walked up the balcony stairs tonight. Every time your trouser legs went up and those horrible socks poked out, a buzz went round the cinema.

SIDNEY: Admiration, that was. You're just jealous because you can't dress, that's all.

TONY: Me? Can't dress? Oh well, of course, now you're just being ridiculous…

BILL: Here's the bus coming.

TONY & SIDNEY: Where, where?

BILL: Oh no, it's turned off. Must have been a lorry.

TONY: Why don't you keep your eyes open? Raising our hopes like that. Keep quiet until you can see the whites of its numbers.

SIDNEY: Why don't they put sides on these bus shelters? The wind don't half whistle through.

TONY: Honestly, you're a right drag you are. You haven't stopped moaning since we left home. I'm not going out with you any more. You spoil the whole evening.

SIDNEY: We shouldn't have come all this way out. It takes the whole shine off it when you have to wait hours for a bus home. They only run every half-hour… bringing us right out here in the wilds.

TONY: You're trying to start a row, aren't you? You've been after one all night, haven't you?

SIDNEY: Yes I have.

TONY: You're blaming me.

SIDNEY: Yes I am.

TONY: Good, well, now I know where I stand. That's cleared the air a bit.

SIDNEY: What are you going to do about it?

TONY: Never you mind. Now I know where I stand, that's all I want to know. That's all I'm interested in.

SIDNEY: Well, come on then, what about it?

TONY: No, no, that's all right. As long as I know where I stand, that's all.

SIDNEY: He's going to sulk now.

TONY: No, I'm not. I know where I am now. A stab in the back, most enjoyable. It starts up as a nice evening at the pictures and it finishes up a punch-up at the bus stop. Very nice. Friendship, that is.

SIDNEY: I am not punching you up.

TONY: Get your hand off my shoulder.

SIDNEY: Who are you pushing?

TONY: I am not pushing anybody, just get your hand off my shoulder.

SIDNEY: Are you threatening me?

TONY: Take it how you like.

SIDNEY: Would you like to step out into the kerb?

TONY: Suits me, as long as I know where I stand.

SIDNEY: We'll get it over with, once and for all.

TONY: Certainly. That suits me. Bill, hold my hat. Now then, you've asked for this.

SIDNEY: I'm ready. I've been wanting to poke you one all night.

TONY: Well, now's your chance. Come on then. Now I know where I stand. That's different. Now I know… right… put your fists up.

SIDNEY: They're up.

TONY: Come on then, make the first move. Go on.

SIDNEY: I'm going to.

TONY: Come on then. I'm waiting.

SIDNEY: So am I.

TONY: All right then. Come on, make one move, just touch me once, that's all. It'll be your lot. Come on.

SIDNEY: All right then, come on then.

TONY: Hallo, watch it, get back. Aah, watch it. I'll have you.

SIDNEY: You want a fight then?

TONY: Yes.

SIDNEY: Come on then.

TONY: All right then.

BILL: There's a bus coming.

TONY & SIDNEY: Where, where?

BILL: Oh no. It was another lorry. Well, it looked like a bus, it had the same shaped bonnet.

TONY: You buffoon. And give me my hat back. I said hold it, not put it on.

BILL: Have you finished your fight then?

TONY: Yes we have.

BILL: Who won?

SIDNEY: Mind your own business.

TONY: It was a draw.

BILL: You didn't touch each other.

TONY: We didn't have to. We're two intelligent men, we don't have to resort to violence. We've grown out of the primitive means of settling quarrels, and any more cheek and you'll get a clip round the earhole.

SIDNEY: And you'll get one from me as well.

BILL: I haven't done anything.

TONY: Well, just watch it then.

SIDNEY: Yeah, watch it.

TONY: We'll go by ourselves next week, Sid – leave him behind, eh?

SIDNEY: Yeah, he's a bit of a lumber, isn't he? Oh for crying out loud, how much longer is this bus going to be?

By the end of the fifties, Tony Hancock's focus was entirely on his television series. The final episodes of the radio *Half Hours* were recorded in pairs, months before transmission – a sign of how little importance Hancock now placed on them. His indifference did not reflect Galton and Simpson's attitude. Their scripts were becoming increasingly innovative, rooted now in the rhythms of everyday conversation. It was this naturalism that they would use as the foundation of *Steptoe and Son*:

HANCOCK'S HALF HOUR, sixth series, episode twelve

'HANCOCK IN HOSPITAL'
First broadcast: Tuesday 15 December 1959

TONY: Tell me the news. What's been happening?

BILL: Oh, the news. Oh yeah. What's been happening... Nothing much at all.

TONY: Well, there must be something to talk about. Think, have a think, what's been happening outside?

BILL: Well... um... er...

    EFFECTS: (Tapping on locker... rhythmic, annoying tap)

TONY: *(After a fair pause)* Don't keep tapping on my locker.

SIDNEY: Oh, I'm sorry. *(PAUSE)* Want a fag?

TONY: You can't smoke in here.

SIDNEY: Oh blimey, that's going to be a drag... how much longer is there?

TONY: Another hour and a half.

SIDNEY: Hour and a half... without a fag... oh dear.

    (PAUSE, during which they make various noises. Clearing throats...
    bored stiff noises.)

SIDNEY: What's the time?

TONY: Another hour and twenty-nine minutes.

SIDNEY: Oh.

    (Another PAUSE)

BILL: Here, guess who I saw yesterday.

TONY: Who?

BILL: What's his name... you know... that fellow who used to live round the corner... what's his name... you know him...

TONY: Ginger Williams.

BILL: No, not him. The other one.

TONY: Oh I remember, the tall bloke with the dark hair, who used to go out with that bird from across the...

BILL: No, not him. Oh, what's his name...

TONY: Not that funny bloke who used to live with his mother.

BILL: No. More recent than him... you know him... what's his name...

TONY: Describe him to me.

BILL: Well... shortish... fairish... medium built... oldish... looks younger than that, though... nice fellow... you know him... oh, what's his name... his brother went out with that girl... what's her name... you know her...

TONY: Hilda.

BILL: No... the other one. The little girl who lives down the High Street...

TONY: Ethel.

BILL: No, that's the one who got married. No, I mean the other one... what's her name... well anyway, I saw him yesterday.

TONY: How was he?

BILL: Oh, just the same. He never changes, does he?

TONY: Doesn't he?

BILL: Well, you know him better than I do.

TONY: Do I? Well, what about him?

BILL: Oh nothing. Nothing. I just saw him, that's all.

SIDNEY: What's the time?

TONY: One hour, twenty-six minutes to go.

5 The Missing *Half Hours*

ore than two dozen radio episodes of *Hancock's Half Hour* have
been lost. Because all the shows were pre-recorded, tapes must
have existed at one time in the BBC archives, but twenty-five
shows have been destroyed, taped over, thrown away or misfiled, perhaps
to be rediscovered by happy *Hancock* fans in the future. These lost
episodes are not just the early shows – the last of them, 'Sid James's Dad',
went out during the fourth series, when up to 7 million people were
tuning in each week. The BBC did not have a consistent policy about
preserving the broadcasts. 'It used to drive us up the wall, thinking about
it,' Ray sighed.

Of the twenty-five, three exist as poor quality amateur recordings, the
performers so blurred and muffled that they are indecipherable. In the
days before cassette players, when even reel-to-reel decks were rare, most
fans could not tape the shows.

The recordings are gone, but Galton and Simpson kept copies of every
script. In 2002, they agreed to let the Tony Hancock Appreciation Society
scan every page to computer, for storage in a digital archive: in this way
they have been saved but, with rare exceptions, not published until now.
Here are glimpses of 'the hidden Hancock':

HANCOCK'S HALF HOUR, first series, episode two

'THE POSH ENGAGEMENT RING'
First broadcast: Tuesday 9 November 1954

MOIRA: You nasty, low-down, despicable, twisting, crooked, lying,
cheating – er.... er....
TONY: Scrounging?
MOIRA: Thank you... scrounging, crawling, miserable, little squirt.
TONY: Yes... I think that about covers the lot...

MOIRA: Prison's too good for your type. They should go back to the
olden days. I'd like to see you put on show in a public place so the
people can throw rotten fruit at you.

TONY: Come and see my stage act.

That had Hancock's character summed up early on and by the fifth show
in the first series his pretensions were to the fore:

HANCOCK'S HALF HOUR, first series, episode five

'THE HANCOCK FESTIVAL'
First broadcast: Tuesday 30 November 1954

TONY: Pray forgive this untimely hour, but I have summoned you here
today so that you may be the first to hear the momentous news that
is destined to surprise all my friends.

BILL: You're not starting work?

TONY: You're quite right, I'm not starting work.

MOIRA: Tony, before we go any further, why have you locked yourself in
your room all week?

TONY: I'm coming to that. For the past several and a half days, I have
been giving vent to all the creative histrionic genius that for many
years throughout my young life has been burning inside my tortured
soul like the very clappers. In short, I have been writing. I am now an
author – a litterateur. I have given birth to a book. It will shake the
literary world.

MOIRA: It won't pass unnoticed in the medical world.

TONY: That's it – laugh at me. I don't care. They laughed at Puccini, they
laughed at Mozart, Bach, Beethoven, Chopin and all them other great
painters – but the proof rests in the great work I have produced.
Behold – the fruits of me artistic labour. Me manuscript.

This magnum opus was a collection of ninety-seven short plays for radio,
with the lad himself cast as the hero in every one. The first portrayed him
as a frustrated artist, Paul Goggin – a theme Galton and Simpson would
return to in their final script for Hancock, the 1961 film *The Rebel*. This
scene can be read as the prototype for the movie:

TONY: Quick – me paints – me brushes – to work.
ORCHESTRA: (Link)

BILL: From that day, Paul was a changed man. He painted furiously day and night – working like a man possessed. I shall never forget that fat little figure standing there in his brown smock and bare legs. He looked like a toffee apple with two sticks.

MOIRA: On and on he worked, the deft bold strokes of his brush pouring out all the creative genius that had burned within him for years. Painting, all the time painting. By this time he was working so quickly we couldn't supply him with paint fast enough.

TONY: That tube of green paint you bought this morning – it's no good. I can't paint with it. What's it called?

MOIRA: Let's see. *(Reads)* Chlorophyll toothpaste.

These early programmes would be the inspiration for decades of comedy. By the start of the seventies, comedian and writer Graeme Garden was blending slapstick, sitcom, satire and surrealism in *The Goodies*, but in the fifties he was a schoolboy fan of Tony Hancock. 'Although I admired the later "solo" work like "The Blood Donor",' he said, 'I think my fondest memories are of the early radio shows. The thing I liked was the comedy team, where all the characters were funny. That's what we tried to do later with *The Goodies* too, with very few guest roles being "straight". The later TV *Hancock*s made him the comic focus surrounded by "natural" characters, which puts a great responsibility on the star. So I suppose I preferred my Hancock when he was bouncing around in the midst of Sid James, Bill Kerr, Hattie Jacques and Kenneth Williams on the wireless, where the plots and locations were wilder than on TV.'

By late 1954, with the launch Associated London Scripts, and Galton and Simpson sharing offices with their fellow directors, Eric Sykes and Spike Milligan, the scope for *Hancock's Half Hour* seemed unlimited. It was going to be a good Christmas, and they celebrated in a trio of episodes. All three have been lost; the first saw Hancock threatened with the Labour Exchange:

HANCOCK'S HALF HOUR, first series, episode seven

'THE DEPARTMENT STORE SANTA'
First broadcast: Tuesday 14 December 1954

TONY: Do you realize what this means?

GRAMS: ('Pomp and Circumstance No. 4') (Under)

TONY: Every principle we stand for is in danger. The freedom of the individual to decide for himself where and when he is going to lay down his head without the horrible threat of a job looming over him on his awakening. The right of every man to be unemployed regardless of race, creed, colour. To work or not to work, that is the question. This happy breed of men – this little world – this precious stone set in a silver sea, is now bound in with shame. Alas poor Yorick – I knew him well… worked his head to the bone… and for what? We are being deprived of the basic privilege of every self-respecting layabout. There's nothing so becomes a man as modest stillness and humility – but when the blast of work blows in our ears… it gets dead dodgy. What has happened to the heritage of our freedom-loving island – to our birthright handed down through countless generations? Shirkers of the world unite! Arise! There are too many jobs! There is not enough unemployment to go round! Let it be known here and now that I for one refuse to go to work.

In the same episode, he gets a job as the Father Christmas at a department store:

TONY: Ho, ho, ho, ho, ho. Come and visit old Santa. Season's greetings. Get your lovely Christmas presents here. Have a go at me sack. Tanner a dip. Jolly days. Jingle bells. Winter's here, lots of good cheer. Good King Wenceslas. Roll on half past five. Hallo, here comes another rocket ship full of the little perishers. Ha, ho, ho, ho, ho. Get off. Scat. Shoo. Go home. Git out of it. Hoppit. Take that! Get your thieving hands out of me sack. Aaah!! Who's pulled me eyebrows off? Get down, you. I'll give you a clip round the earhole. Put that train set down! What do you expect for a tanner? Aaaaaaah. All right, that's it – all off.

EFFECTS: (Referee's whistle; kids stop screaming)

TONY: All right, come on. Own up. Who was the little clever dick who set light to me beard? That ugly pimply little herbert with the matches. Come here and I'll… what's that, Madam? Yours. Oh. Ho. Ho. What a nice little chap he is, to be sure. Let me pat him on the head. Where's me sledge?

Hancock clings on to his job until he shows a child how to use a pair of new roller skates:

TONY: I used to be a dab hand at this lark. Let me put 'em on and show you. You place your foot in... like... this – and strap them... round... here. Then you... put the other... one... like that. There. Now you'll notice I have left enough play in the straps to allow me to stand up quite comfortably and allow me to... aaaaaaaaaaaaaaah!

EFFECTS: (Take off on roller skates. Series of loud crashes and bangs as Tony crashes through department. Finish with one almighty crash as he collides with the crockery stand. Give it the lot. This effect can last as long as you like.)

TONY: All right. Which clever little herbert was it who pushed me?

In the third series, Galton and Simpson returned to the Santa theme – but this time Hancock really was Father Christmas:

HANCOCK'S HALF HOUR, third series, episode ten

'THE TRIAL OF FATHER CHRISTMAS'
First broadcast: Wednesday 21 December 1955

EFFECTS: (Jingle of harness on echo. Hold under.)

TONY: *(Calls)* Come on, Donner! Come on, Blitzen! Not far to go. Nearly home. Cor dear me, this job gets harder every year. All these council flats with no chimneys or fireplaces. I don't know how they expect me to crawl in and out of radiator pipes. Still, it's worth it. They're all good kids. Except that one in Stoke-on-Trent who left the fire on. I'll leave him till last next year. Modern children... *and* their parents. Telling their kids I don't exist. My reputation's gone right down these last few years. Four million kids last night thought I was their old man dressed up. I got a right bashing down at the Elephant and Castle. Still, it's all part of the job...

EFFECTS: (Fade in. Helicopter engine.)

TONY: Hallo, there's a helicopter down there. It's the police. I wonder what they want.

EFFECTS: (American police siren)

TONY: That's funny, they're after me. Can't understand it, I'm only doing thirty... and the North Pole's hardly what you'd call a built-up area. Few igloos here and there but... he's definitely after me. He's signalling me to stop. Whoa, Donner! Whoa, Blitzen… Blitzen. I've told you before. When I pull the reins, that means stop. I've had just about enough of you today. I *told* you to whoa over Bombay – and where did you stop… Vladivostok. 'Me hoof slipped on a snowflake.' What sort of a mug do you think I am? You're not coming next year. I'm having Rudolph out instead. I know he's got a red nose… but if we keep him off the bottle, he'll be all right. Now come on, pull up and see what the nice policeman wants. We may have forgotten somebody.

The nice policeman arrests Santa on a charge of neglecting his festive duties. At the trial, the judge is Kenneth Williams; Henry VIII and Charles Dickens are on the jury, and the prosecuting counsel is the Devil… played by Sid James:

KENNETH: Mr Mephistopheles, we don't usually have the likes of you up here, so kindly be on your best behaviour. And put your wig on.
SIDNEY: I can't, it looks stupid balanced on top of me horns. Now, let's have a look round. Hallo, there's one or two lads up here who should be down in my area. Still, don't worry, lads, I won't let on. Nice place you've got here. A bit parky, though, after what I'm used to. Any of you lads want a warm, you can come down any time. Got the new slow-burning grates.
KENNETH: Mr Mephistopheles, will you stop trying to entice our population away from us.
SIDNEY: Have some fun down there too, lads. Plenty of girls. Lucretia Borgia, Cleopatra, Josephine… all that lot.
KENNETH: Mr Mephistopheles, did you hear what I said? Mr Mephistopheles…
SIDNEY: Your honour, when you want to attract my attention, don't do it by pulling my tail, or there'll be trouble.

Hancock conducts his own defence:

KENNETH: You only work one day a year.
TONY: I do not. I'm at it all the year round. Designing new toys. They won't stand for a block of wood and four wheels these days, matey… paint 'em red and call 'em fire engines..? Oh dear me, no. They want radio-controlled flying saucers these days. And they take time. How

would you like to get up at twelve o'clock Christmas night and belt all round the world before morning? And when you get to Australia you're lumbered – it's only Christmas Eve. You've got to hang around in the boiling hot sun with all *this* clobber on. 'Neglect of duty' – I'm not having that.

Kenneth Williams frequently played a judge, with Hancock in the dock. To convey age and pomposity, the twenty-eight-year-old Williams delivered a fusty impersonation of Sir Felix Aylmer, then president of the actors' union Equity:

HANCOCK'S HALF HOUR, first series, episode nine

'THE CHRISTMAS EVE PARTY'
First broadcast: Tuesday 28 December 1954

JUDGE: Is your name Anthony Hancock?
TONY: Yes.
JUDGE: Yes what?
TONY: Yes it is.
JUDGE: Yes it is what?
TONY: Anthony Hancock.
JUDGE: Oh… pleased to meet you.
TONY: Charmed.
JUDGE: Do you come here often?
USHER: Shall I read out the charge, Your Honour?
JUDGE: Proceed.
USHER: It is alleged–
TONY: It's a lie!
USHER: … that on the twenty-fourth of December, the defendant, Anthony Aloysius St John Hancock the Second, did hold a riotous party at his residence and did create a public disturbance by keeping the whole neighbourhood awake until the early hours of the morning.
JUDGE: How do you plead?
TONY: All depends where I cut meself. *(Laughs)* My word, eh? *(Laughs)* Cor dear. That's six months before we start.

In another of the Christmas 1954 episodes, the writers played with a technique which would become a favourite device: like a surgeon in an operating theatre, Tony would run through a list and the others would echo him. Here's Hancock getting dressed:

HANCOCK'S HALF HOUR, first series, episode eight

'CHRISTMAS AT ALDERSHOT'
First broadcast: Tuesday 21 December 1954

> EFFECTS : *(Off mike – knock on door)*

MOIRA: *(Off mike)* Anybody in?
TONY: Ah! It's me beloved Moira. Quick, hair oil.
BILL: Hair oil.
TONY: Aftershave lotion.
BILL: Aftershave lotion.
TONY: Clean shirt.
BILL: Clean shirt.
TONY: Waistcoat.
BILL: Waistcoat.
TONY: Spats.
BILL: Spats.
TONY: Jacket.
BILL: Jacket.
TONY: *(Calls)* Come in.

> EFFECTS: *(Quick door open)*

MOIRA: *(Off mike. Sharp scream.)*
TONY: Trousers.
BILL: Trousers. Hello Moira.

By the end of the episode, they're cooking Christmas lunch for 4,000 at an army barracks, and the cupboards are bare:

MOIRA: I've got an order here. One hundred beans on toast.
TONY: Right. Hundred plates.
BILL: Hundred plates.
TONY: Hundred knives and forks.
BILL: Hundred knives and forks.
TONY: Hundred bits of toast.
BILL: Hundred bits of toast.

MOIRA: Haven't you forgotten something?
TONY: Oh yes. One bean and a book of raffle tickets. Right. Grub up!

This episode also marks the birth of a gag that evolved into Hancock's most celebrated *Half Hour*:

SIDNEY: Squad... halt! Here you are, sir. This lot just came in this morning.
KENNETH: Right you are, Sergeant, I'll take them one at a time for vaccinations. I'll take the fat one first.
SIDNEY: All right, Hancock, fall out... I said out! Not down!
TONY: I just copped the size of that needle.
KENNETH: Now, don't worry, Private, this won't hurt you. Now where's that book? Let's see now. *(Reads in undertone)* Take the hypodermic needle in the right hand, pull plunger back, place against skin and push...
TONY: *(Loud agonizing groans)*
KENNETH: I haven't touched you yet.
TONY: Just practising.
KENNETH: Now – get the needle ready.
TONY: Here, hold on. It looks a bit blunt to me.
KENNETH: *(Happily)* Yes, it's the dartboard that does it.

Here's Hancock trying to wriggle out of a marriage proposal to Moira, after he realizes what the honeymoon will cost:

HANCOCK'S HALF HOUR, first series, episode fifteen

'THE MARRIAGE BUREAU'
First broadcast: Tuesday 8 February 1955

TONY: Look, you don't want to marry me, Moira. I'm not good enough for you.
MOIRA: You are.
TONY: I'm not. I'm fat and ugly.
MOIRA: I like men who are fat and ugly.
TONY: I'm slimming and having beauty treatment.
MOIRA: But Tony, I...

TONY: No, Moira – you're making a big mistake. I can't think why you should possibly want to marry me.

MOIRA: But it was you who wanted to marry me.

TONY: Well, there you are, I'm unreliable. That's the type of man I am. A trifler, a philanderer. No good. Rotten to the core. Forget me, Moira. You'll get over it. Just a girlish infatuation.

MOIRA: But *you* were doing all the passionate courting.

TONY: *(Amazed)* Never trust a man, they're so deceitful.

MOIRA: You said you couldn't live without me.

TONY: No, but I've thought it over, and it'll be cheaper if I try. I'll show you to the door.

MOIRA: Yes but I…

TONY: Run along, Moira, there's a good girl. Sorry I can't marry you this time. Call again. Sorry you've been troubled.

EFFECTS: (Door shut)

The episode also featured a sequence with Peter Sellers as an employer who puts Hancock through an IQ test as part of a job interview. There are no surviving radio recordings of Sellers and Hancock, and they never worked together on TV; both had cameo roles in a 1954 movie called *Orders Are Orders*, but they didn't share any scenes. This fragment hints at a double act that never happened:

PETER: Ahem. Question one was… 'What is an isosceles triangle?' – and you've answered 'Yes'.

TONY: That's it.

PETER: That is not the right answer.

TONY: All right then… 'No'.

PETER: That is not the right answer either.

TONY: Oh, I get your little game… it's a trick question.

On the eve of the second series, Tony Hancock suffered a nervous breakdown. During his act in *Talk of the Town* at the Adelphi he walked off, muttering that the stage was 'too steep', and fled to Rome. With only two days scheduled between recording and transmission, Galton and Simpson had no time to rewrite the first script, and all Hancock's lines were still marked 'TONY', but announcer Adrian Waller made one change to his introduction.

HANCOCK'S HALF HOUR, second series, episode one

'A HOLIDAY IN FRANCE'
First broadcast: Tuesday 19 April 1955

ADRIAN: This is the BBC Light Programme.

(Slight pause)

GRAMS: (Opening signature)

ADRIAN: We present Bill Kerr, Sidney James, Andrée Melly and Kenneth Williams in… *Hancock's Half Hour.*

GRAMS: (Theme up)

ADRIAN: And in place of Tony Hancock who is indisposed – meet Harry Secombe!

Secombe was one of the stars of another huge radio hit produced by Dennis Main Wilson, *The Goon Show.* His fellow Goons, Sellers and Milligan, had already made guest appearances in *Hancock's Half Hour,* but for three weeks Harry Secombe did much more than that: he took control of the show with such confidence that Main Wilson considered installing him as its regular star. Had Secombe accepted, Hancock's career would probably have been shattered: after only one series of his own, he was a long way from the national acclaim he later enjoyed.

All three episodes of '*Harry's Half Hour*', and a fourth in which he signed off from the show, have been lost. In the first, he and Bill board a cross-channel steamer on their way to Southend-on-Sea. Spotting the Eiffel Tower, they assume they're in Blackpool until they are thrown into the Bastille for fare-dodging:

HARRY: What a position to be in. A strange country, couldn't speak the language. A weaker man would have cracked under the strain. But not me. I was determined to show these Frenchies how an Englishman conducts himself… calm, composed, cynical indifference.

EFFECTS: (Echo) (Rattle of chains. Banging on cell door.)

HARRY: *(Echo) (Shouting)* Let me out. Let me out. I'm innocent. I demand to see Her Majesty's representative. You can't keep me here. Let me out. Help!

Evicted from the Bastille for being too noisy, Harry buys a phrase book:

HARRY: Now let's see. Useful phrases. '*Je vais vous embracer*' – I am
    going to kiss you. '*Vous l'essayez et je vous donnerai un coup*' – you
    do and I'll thump you one. End of love section...

But love did come along, when Andrée Melly trod on his foot:

ANDREE: Oooh, *pardon monsieur*...
HARRY: Wait a minute, wait a minute – hold on... 'At the ironmongers'...
    no. Half a mo. 'On the tram'... Oh, how can I tell her? Ah – 'Crockery
    shop' – that'll do. Er... *mes assiettes sont très bien.*
ANDREE: *Assiettes*?
HARRY: *Oui, oui.*
ANDREE: But *monsieur, assiettes* are plates.
HARRY: That's it. Me plates. They're all right. Don't worry.

The twenty-three-year-old actress Andrée Melly, sister of the jazz
singer George Melly, was best known for *The Belles of St Trinians* with
Alistair Sim when she replaced Moira Lister in the *Half Hours*. Alan
explained: 'We put Andrée's character into the show as a French girl,
because of the name really, and we thought, "Oh, it might be a good
gimmick, a bit different." After a while it didn't work and we changed
it. Suddenly, next series, there she was speaking in English. Cut-glass.
Nobody said anything.'

In the Secombe shows, Andrée was still Mademoiselle Melly:

HANCOCK'S HALF HOUR, second series, episode two

'THE CROWN JEWELS'
First broadcast: Tuesday 26 April 1955

ANDREE: *(French accent)* Oh what a wonderful town London is. There is
    so much to see. Where are we now?
HARRY: This is Covent Garden Market.
ANDREE: Oh come on, please let's walk through it.
HARRY: Well, I don't know... how well do you understand English?
ANDREE: I know most words of the language.
BILL: Let's go through, you'll hear the rest.

ANDREE: Oh yes... come on Harry.

HARRY: Well, all right... but on one condition.

ANDREE: What?

HARRY: Well, you see that big man balancing the fifteen baskets on his head?

ANDREE: Yes?

HARRY: And you see that wheelbarrow he's just about to walk into?

ANDREE: Yes.

HARRY: Well, promise me at the moment of impact you'll put your hands over your ears.

BILL: Look out, there he goes.

EFFECTS: (Terrific crash, baskets falling to ground)

KENNETH: *(Precious)* Oh spit, this just isn't my day. That's the third lot of daffs I've dropped this morning. *(Going off)* I might just as well go home, it makes you sick, it does really...

HARRY: And he looks so tough.

BILL: With a voice like that, you've got to be tough.

Harry Secombe's character in *The Goon Show*, Neddie Seagoon, was blithely gullible and trusting. Hancock's gullibility was different: he believed everything he heard himself say. Galton and Simpson decided not to change their style, relying instead on Harry's versatile genius to adapt to their script. Here he is, playing tour guide to Andrée's sight-seer, and demonstrating a grasp of historical detail that was just as deft as Hancock's:

EFFECTS: (River atmosphere. Ship sirens, tug hooters etc.)

HARRY: ... And over there we have the famous Tower Bridge, a remarkable feat of engineering, rendered alas quite useless in 1943 by a bunch of German frogmen who came along one dark night and sawed the thing in half.

BILL: Oh now please, Harry – that's too much... I'm quite prepared to accept that Cleopatra's Needle was that big because she had bad eyes... but Tower Bridge and frogmen...

HARRY: Please yourself... but why else would a perfectly good bridge be sliced across the middle?

BILL: So it can be pulled up to let big boats go through.

HARRY: A likely story... so it can be pulled up to let big boats...

ANDREE: Oooh look – the bridge has been pulled up to let that big boat go through.

Galton and Simpson were not told whether Hancock was expected to return soon, or even where he was: 'We found out, much later, that Dennis Main Wilson knew Tony was in Italy, but nobody informed us,' said Ray. 'Dennis knew Harry Secombe very well, of course, from *The Goon Show*, and he knew Harry would love doing the *Half Hours*. And he did! But looking back, it was an incredible thing for any performer to do... and if Hancock hadn't come back, it could have led anywhere for Harry.'

Because the scripts were written so close to the transmission dates, the writers were able to react to Secombe's performances, even though they had never written for him before. His infectious silliness, a wild contrast to Tony Hancock's neuroses and pessimism, inspired them to surreal heights for the third episode. Bill and Harry buy a racehorse for seven shillings and sixpence: she only has three legs, and one of those is wooden, but Harry is convinced he can win a fortune if dodgy trainer Sid James will take her on:

HANCOCK'S HALF HOUR, second series, episode three

'THE RACEHORSE'
First broadcast: Tuesday 3 May 1955

HARRY: You promised us you'd train her.
SIDNEY: Yes but...
HARRY: Just give her a chance. She's set her heart on becoming a racehorse. She won't let you down.
BILL: A little kindness and affection...
SIDNEY: That won't help. For crying out loud, Billy, she's only got *two good legs*... and *they're* not even level.
ANDREE: You could put a book under one of them.
SIDNEY: That's all right when she's standing still. What about when she races? She'll be lopsided.
HARRY: A definite advantage when she goes round the bends.
SIDNEY: Only right-handed bends.
BILL: Then find her a right-handed racecourse.
SIDNEY: There aren't any. They're all left-handed.
HARRY: Then teach her how to run backwards.

SIDNEY: All right, all right. I'll give her a trial. But don't blame me if she's no good. You can put her in stable four.

ANDREE: Come on, Sabrina, good girl, follow me. You won't regret this, Mr James. She's a born racehorse.

EFFECTS: (Clip-clop-bonk. Clip-clop-bonk. Clip-clop… terrific crash. Tin cans. The lot.)

HARRY: Don't worry, Sid, this won't happen when her glasses arrive.

SIDNEY: What have I done?

The writers were having fun, as always, with the sound effects:

SIDNEY: Well, come on, let's get down to the course. Get Sabrina into the horse box.

ANDREE: I'll do it. Come on, Sabrina. Good girl. Into the box.

EFFECTS: (Clip-clop. Clip-clop. Clip-clop.)

ANDREE: Oh Sabrina, you silly girl, you've forgotten something, haven't you? Go on, go back and get it.

EFFECTS: (Clip-clop-bonk. Clip-clop-bonk. Clip-clop-bonk.)

Harry's optimism deserved a happy ending, and he got one: Sabrina won at 800,000-to-one, and Bill Kerr had wagered threepence on her:

SIDNEY: You put threepence on her?

BILL: Well, I'm a betting man. If you don't speculate, you don't accumulate.

SIDNEY: I know, I know. But where did *you* get threepence from?

BILL: I wired home for it. I asked Granddad could I have my share of the will now.

SIDNEY: Threepence?

BILL: Yeah, I was always his favourite.

The episode also featured the first appearance of Kenneth Williams's 'Snide' voice, a nasal, ingratiating whine which the actor slipped into the show despite the writers' belief that comedy should not rely on funny voices. 'It brought the house down,' said Ray. 'We just looked at each other and said, "Well, so much for funny voices and catch-phrases."'

Hancock's growing resentment of Snide's presence would lead to the destruction of his friendship with Williams, but he was to become one of the most popular characters in the show, and it began with this exchange:

SIDNEY: That'll do for today, Nobbler. Put 'em all back in the stables. We'll have 'em out on the Downs again tomorrow morning.

KENNETH: Righto Guv. 'Ere – Roman History had a nice gallop this morning. Fastest time she's ever done.

SIDNEY: Yeah, amazing what my training and half a pound of Benzedrine does, ain't it? By the way, how's Lord Epping's Fancy Bit?

KENNETH: She's all right, I was snogging with her round the…

SIDNEY: No, his horse. He's worried about it. He says there was a lot of froth round its mouth when it finished yesterday.

KENNETH: That's right, Guvnor.

SIDNEY: What was it?

KENNETH: Brown ale.

SIDNEY: Nobbler, I've told you before… beer slows the horses down.

KENNETH: Well, you said you didn't want it to win.

SIDNEY: I know… but there must be a cheaper way of doing it.

When Tony Hancock returned to England after three weeks – 'Like a little dog, with his tail between his legs,' as Main Wilson put it – he drove to Shrewsbury, where Harry Secombe was appearing in theatre, to thank him for standing in. Galton and Simpson decided Hancock deserved more penance, and sent him down a Welsh mine in search of Harry. The contrite star, aware that he could easily have been sacked, accepted his punishment without complaint and, though he never offered Ray and Alan any apology or explanation, he did not miss another episode of the show:

HANCOCK'S HALF HOUR, second series, episode four

'A VISIT TO SWANSEA'
First broadcast: Tuesday 10 May 1955

TONY: What's that following us?

BILL: Where? Oh, it's one of them pit ponies. Give him a lump of sugar and he'll go away.

TONY: Come on, boy. Here, boy. Chck, chck. There's a good pony. Oh, look at all that hair covering his face up. Poor thing – he can't see where he's going. Here, boy – let's pull it aside for you. That's it.

HARRY: Well, hallo there.

BILL: Harry! We've been looking everywhere for you.

TONY: Good evening, Harold.

HARRY: Hallo Tony, nice to see you again. What are you doing down here in Welsh Wales?

BILL: He came down to thank you, Harry.

HARRY: Thank me…? What for?

TONY: I've prepared a little speech. Ahem. *(Reads)* I'd just like to say on behalf of myself and the assembled cast how much… don't this coal dust get up your nose… how much I appreciate you stepping into my radio show and taking over for me and making it such a big success.

HARRY: Oh Tony, it was nothing.

TONY: Nothing, he says. Flipping nigh ruined me. Well, anyway, thank you.

HARRY: Not at all. It was a pleasure. Any time.

TONY: There won't be any more times. I'll get along to that studio if I have to go in a wheelchair. Never again will I let anybody else take me place. I've learned me lesson. Now if you'll excuse me I must get back to London to do me broadcast… so I'll just say goodbye, Harold, thank you and… Ooooowwwww.

BILL: What's wrong?

TONY: Me back… it's seized up!! Help! Me back. It's the damp. I shouldn't have come down. Get a doctor. Oooowww. I can't move.

HARRY: Oooh, that's a bit of bad luck. The doctor only comes down here once a week.

TONY: But me radio show… it's tonight.

HARRY: Well, don't worry about it, Tony, I'll do it for you. I'll finish up with a song. That'll get them. Come on lads, we'll be late for the show. *(Goes off singing)* 'If I had the heart of a clown…'

TONY: No. Come back. Bill. Sid. Don't let him do it. It's my show. Pick me up…

GRAMS: (Closing signature)

After its rocky start, the second series settled down, and Galton and Simpson were able to develop the key traits of their characters. In 'Prime Minister Hancock', Tony's delusions are rampant as he runs for parliament. The attempt is doomed from the start… Sid James is his election agent:

Tony Hancock

in

"HANCOCK'S HALF HOUR"

No.1
(3rd series)
with

BILL KERR

SIDNEY JAMES

ANDREE MELLY

&

KENNETH WILLIAMS

THEME & INCIDENTAL MUSIC COMPOSED BY
WALLY STOTT & RECORDED BY THE BBC
AUGMENTED REVUE ORCHESTRA CONDUCTED
BY HARRY RABINOWITZ

....

SCRIPT: RAY GALTON & ALAN SIMPSON

....

PRODUCED BY — DENNIS MAIN WILSON

REHEARSALS:	SUNDAY 30th OCTOBER 1955: 11.00am. FORTUNE
RECORDING:	SUNDAY 30th OCTOBER 1955: 7.30-8.15pm. FORTUNE
TRANSMISSION:	WEDNESDAY 2nd NOVEMBER 1955: 8.00-8.30pm. LIGHT
REPEATS:	SUNDAY 6th NOVEMBER 1955: 5.00-5.30pm. LIGHT
	SUNDAY 13th NOVEMBER 1955: 3.15-3.45pm. GOS
	WEDNESDAY 16th NOVEMBER 1955: 10.15-10.45pm. GOS
	SATURDAY 19th NOVEMBER 1955: 10.30-11.00am. GOS
R.P.REF.NO:	TLO 90363

- 5 -

1. TONY: Good lad. Andree, make fifty copies of it and we'll flog them down the street. Now...let's have a look through the list. What have they got that we haven't?

2. BILL: Practically everything. They were ahead of us from the moment the first chair went in.

3. TONY: Never mind about that, read the list out.

4. BILL: Well...there were two crates of crockery, lino, carpets, a coal scuttle, curtains...

5. TONY: Coal scuttle?

6. BILL: Yeah.

7. TONY: That means they have coal.

8. BILL: Yeah.

9. TONY: Thank goodness. I was afraid we'd have to chop down another telegraph pole this winter. What do you mean, we might have to chop them down. I did all the chopping.

Well I helped. Who put the clothes prop in position to keep the wires up? Anyway, that's neither here nor there. What else have they got?

...les, chairs, a radiogram, a lawnmower...

...give 'em a couple of days to settle in, ...have that. What sort of a bloke do you ...ho is?

- 29 -

1. TONY: Never mind about him, what happens in those doorways?

2. KENNETH: Well I shine me torch in and there's couples in there...and oooh...oooh...

3. TONY: Eh? What? Her hair...specially the shoe shop oh...?

4. KENNETH: Oooh yes.

5. TONY: I know, where the windows sort of come out and form a sort of...you can't see 'em from the road...har har...eh...what...I've been there. Oooh dear, you see things there that well...I have to break 'em up and send 'em home. Well, the blokes anyway. Course I'm a bit of a devil meself.

6. KENNETH:

7. TONY: Aren't we all.

8. KENNETH: Yes. I try all the doorways one after the other. You know, sometimes on a good night I don't get back to the station at all. Now what was it you wanted me for.

9. TONY: Wait a minute, I've forgotten....oh yes. Look, we want you to arrest the bloke next door. He's a homicidal maniac. He's got dozens of dead bodies in his house..and he cuts 'em up and burns them in his incinerator, and then goes out and murders some more.

Passages were sometimes cut from the scripts during rehearsals to prevent the shows from over-running. Here are some pages from the original 'The New Neighbour' script (1955), showing the handwritten adjustments made to this episode.

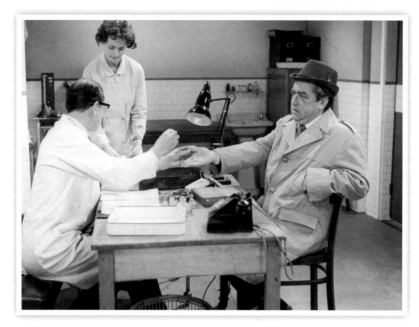

Tony Hancock in one of the most celebrated episodes of the TV series of *Hancock*: 'The Blood Donor' (1961).

At the movies: Hancock (second from left), Ray and Alan (standing) on the set of the first Hancock movie, *The Rebel* (1961).

In 1961, Galton and Simpson were given carte blanche to create their own comedy series: they could write what they liked, for whichever actors they wanted. *Comedy Playhouse* was the result. Here Frankie Howerd stars in 'Have You Read This Notice?' (1963) with Bill Kerr as the customs officer.

It was the second time Galton and Simpson had worked with Howerd – and not the last. Here the three of them discuss Howerd's show *Frankie Howerd*, which the duo wrote in 1964.

Ray and Alan lying on the floor, flat on their backs: their favourite mode when searching for ideas. This is how *Steptoe and Son* first occurred to them. It went on to become the most popular show on television, regularly attracting 24 million viewers.

The scriptwriters on the *Steptoe* set with (from left to right) Harry H. Corbett, producer Duncan Wood and Wilfrid Brambell.

One of Galton and Simpson's innovations was in casting 'real' actors rather than comics, so that the emotion in their storylines didn't play second fiddle to the comedy. This picture shows an anguished Harold in 'A Death in the Family' (1970).

Ray (left) and Alan at work in their office at Associated London Scripts in Bayswater. Alan always did the typing.

A lasting legacy: Galton and Simpson (with Hercules stand-in and cart) at the BBC Television Centre in 2000, toasting their OBEs, which were awarded for services to television.

HANCOCK'S HALF HOUR, second series, episode seven

'PRIME MINISTER HANCOCK'
First broadcast: Tuesday 31 May 1955

BILL: This is your election headquarters?
TONY: Yes, not bad, eh?
BILL: It's a pub.
TONY: *(Amazed)* Is it? I must have a few words with Sidney about this, he
    didn't tell me it was a pub.
BILL: What did you think the bottles inside were?
TONY: He said they contained ballot slips from floating voters.
BILL: Sid must be out of his mind to choose a place like this.
TONY: Oh, I don't know, he's saved some money on the posters. He's just
    pasted 'Hancock' on the ones already here. See. 'My goodness, my
    Hancock.' 'What we want is Hancock.' 'Hancock is good for you.'
    'Hancock for strength.' 'Down with Hancock, then you'll feel better' …
    Mmm, that one didn't work out very well, did it?

Hancock's Half Hour pioneered the use of musical clips to cut between the
scenes. Composer Wally Stott (without ever meeting the stars or the
writers) produced a series of variations on the main theme as links,
labelling each excerpt with a name that hinted at its mood. 'Genevieve
Hancock' was jaunty and optimistic, 'Hancock in Spring' was brighter
still, 'Hancock Rumbled' was ominous and 'Haunted Housecock' was
nightmarish. Galton and Simpson signalled the use of each link with the
word '*GRAMS*':

BILL: Go round kissing all the babies. That'll get the votes.
TONY: Don't be silly, they're too young to vote.
BILL: No, their mothers. A woman's always a sucker for someone who
    takes an interest in her kids. Kiss the babies and the women'll vote
    for you. It never misses…

    GRAMS: ('Genevieve Hancock')

ANDREE: How is he, doctor?
KENNETH: Oh, it's nothing to worry about, just a slight case of measles.
    Plenty of rest, he'll be all right in a week or two. Well, goodbye Mr
    Hancock.
TONY: Goodbye doctor.

KENNETH: *(Off mike)* Look after yourself. Keep away from children, won't you?

TONY: As long as I live.

EFFECTS: *(Door shut)*

TONY: *(Disgusted)* Measles. Whose bright idea was it to go round kissing all the babies?

BILL: Well, I'm sorry, Tub.

TONY: 'Don't forget the one with the freckles,' he says. Aaah... If I get half as many votes as I've got spots, I'll sweep the country.

Throughout the first series, Hancock had been down on his luck. Now the writers were starting to experiment. 'Some weeks he was out of work, a comedian,' said Alan, 'the next week he was an in-work actor or an out-of-work *actah*; some weeks he had money, some weeks he didn't... One week he was a lawyer, QC, in the courtroom. You change it, nobody says, "Oooh, you can't do that."'

'Nobody said a word,' agreed Ray. Revelling in their inventive licence, they cast Tony as a doctor, a gangster, a navy captain and a ninety-three-year-old millionaire... all in the same episode:

HANCOCK'S HALF HOUR, second series, episode ten

'THE THREE SONS'
First broadcast: Tuesday 21 June 1955

KENNETH: This is the story of a family, a rich old man and his three sons. Triplets whom he hadn't seen for over twenty years... finally reunited when he summoned them to his deathbed... The parts of the father and his three sons will all be played by Mr Anthony Hancock. The rest of the cast will have to jump in where they can.

...

KENNETH: Hancock... I'm placing you in command of an ocean-going minesweeper. Can you handle the deep sea stuff?

TONY: Can I handle it? The deep sea stuff? Me? 'High-tide Hancock'? With all due respects, me hearty, I'll have you know that I've wrung more saltwater out of me socks than you've sailed on. I've spent me life on the deep sea stuff. All the long runs – Tower Bridge to Southend and back twice a week. Highly dangerous voyages they

were. Never knew the human frame could stand so much battering
– Arctic winds – waves like mountains…

KENNETH: Yes, well–

TONY: Single men and volunteers only on our run. The dockers used to
line up as we left Tower Bridge and wave goodbye to us. You could
hear them muttering, 'There go the mad fools on the Southend run
– poor devils.' Living hell it was. Oh, but then we was young and
reckless in them days.

KENNETH: Do you mean to say that during the whole of your sea-faring
career you've never been further than Southend?

TONY: Of course not. Nobody has. You can't go any further than
Southend. Get down there and look out to sea and you can see
where it ends… ten miles out. I'm not sailing out there and falling
over the edge for no one.

…

TONY: *(Low and casual)* Hiya Nicky.

BILL: Gideon. Gideon, it's you.

TONY: Yeah. Gideon Hancock, remember? The kid everybody said would
wind up in prison.

BILL: Yeah, how are you doing?

TONY: I just got out.

BILL: You're looking real sharp, Gideon.

TONY: I'm doing all right.

BILL: You must be making a lot of dough.

TONY: Yeah, look.

BILL: Gee, gold teeth.

TONY: That's nothing. Have another look.

BILL: Gee, gold gums.

…

ANDREE: Well, here we are, Sid. 259 Harley St… Doctor A. Hancock,
Physician, Surgeon and Psychiatrist. Hedges cut. Choose your own
shapes. Surgery hours: 9 to 12 and 2.30 to 6.

SIDNEY: I don't like it. He's only open when the pubs are closed.

ANDREE: Go on, ring the doorbell, let's get it over with.

EFFECTS: *(Doorbell rings. Door open.)*

TONY: Yes?

ANDREE: Dr Hancock?

TONY: Are you from the *Lancet*?

ANDREE: No.

TONY: The British Medical Council?
ANDREE: No.
TONY: The Sunday papers?
ANDREE: No.
TONY: Speaking. What can I do for you?
SIDNEY: I'm suffering from insomnia.
TONY: Are you? Well, you've come to the right man, I'll tell you that for
    nothing. No, better not… make it a guinea.

   …

   GRAMS: *(Pastoral theme)*

TONY: *(Old man. Coughing weakly.)* Nurse… nurse.
ANDREE: Mr Hancock, for the last time, I am not going to sit on your bed.
TONY: Where's Meadows?
KENNETH: *(Old man)* Here I am, sir.
TONY: Well… where's me sons? I must see them before I go. Where are
    they?
KENNETH: They're all dead, sir.
TONY: Dead? Me three sons? Gone *before* me?
KENNETH: I'm afraid so, sir.
TONY: Well, there's not much point in hanging about round here now
    then, is there? Might as well go up and join them. Ah, I'm looking
    forward to seeing the three young rascals again. Twenty long years.
    (Sighs) Come on, Meadows, time to go. Lay down.
KENNETH: Very good, sir.
TONY: Goodbye, Meadows.
KENNETH: Goodbye, sir.
TONY: *(Long pause)* You dead yet, Meadows?
KENNETH: No, sir.
TONY: You're not trying, Meadows.
KENNETH: I am, sir.
TONY: Well, hurry up, we haven't got all day. Hold your breath or
    something.
KENNETH: Very good, sir.

As Galton and Simpson strove to build each individual episode around a
consistent storyline, like a half-hour play, the climactic gag would often
be a twist on the opening scene:

HANCOCK'S HALF HOUR, second series, episode twelve

'THE MATADOR'
First broadcast: Tuesday 5 July 1955

KENNETH: All right, Mr Hancock, you can get dressed now.

TONY: Well, doctor, what's the verdict?

KENNETH: Well, I'm not going to beat about the bush, I may as well tell
you straight out – you're a malingerer. Go away.

TONY: Yes doctor.

EFFECTS: (Door shut)

BILL: Well, what did he say, Tub?

TONY: I've got malingery. He said I've got to go away.

BILL: Gee, that's tough. Malingery. And you look so healthy.

TONY: That's always the way, William. A rose is always in its fullest bloom
just before it's plucked. I've suspected something was seriously
wrong with me for some time now. Me strength's going, and I'm right
off me food.

ANDREE: I've never seen you push your plate away.

TONY: There you are, shows you how weak I'm getting. Who'd have
believed it? Me, a malingerer. I'm glad I gave me job up, I wouldn't
want the lads at work to catch it.

ANDREE: Gave up? You haven't done a day's work for twelve years.

TONY: It's not my fault. It's the trade I'm in. It's passing through a slack
period.

BILL: And what *is* your trade?

TONY: I'm an airship builder. But no more. I'm finished. A shell of a man.
Struck down with malingery on the brink of a great career. I was just
waiting for those Zeppelins to come back and I'd have been well
away. But now... *(Breath)*

And at the end of the show, after Sid James has conned Hancock into the
bullring:

KENNETH: Mr Hancock, I take back everything I said about you. I made a
great mistake. You are certainly not a malingerer.

TONY: Oh, what wonderful news. I'm cured. Hear that, Bill? Me
malingery's cured.

KENNETH: After seeing you in the ring, it's obvious to me that you have
got, as the French say, *'un coeur de lion'*.

TONY: Oh no, not that, I've only just got over me malingery. Get me a French doctor. I've got curdy leons! I'll have to go away, the prime of me life and I've got curdy leons. It's not fair, I'm ill, the plague, ting a ling...

GRAMS: (Closing theme)

As already mentioned with reference to 'Sunday Afternoon At Home', passages were often cut from the scripts during rehearsals to prevent the show from overrunning. Happily for comedy, those sections remain in the original copies, excised with a single diagonal line; below is one such passage, with the cut marked in brackets. It is unheard and unread since the day Tony and Bill tried it out:

HANCOCK'S HALF HOUR, third series, episode three

'THE NEW NEIGHBOUR'
First broadcast: Wednesday 2 November 1955

TONY: Close the door, don't let those removals men see you. Did you make the list out?
BILL: Yeah, I got it right here. It's all down. Everything our new neighbours own. I didn't miss a thing.
TONY: Good lad. Andrée, make fifty copies of it and we'll flog them down the street. Now... let's have a look through the list. What have they got that we haven't?
BILL: Practically *everything*. They were ahead of us from the moment the first *chair* went in.

[Cut begins]

TONY: Never mind about that, read the list out.
BILL: Well... there were two crates of crockery, lino, carpets, a coal scuttle, curtains...
TONY: A coal scuttle?
BILL: Yeah.
TONY: That means they have coal.
BILL: Yeah.
TONY: Thank goodness. I was afraid we'd have to chop down another telegraph pole this winter.
BILL: What do you mean, *we* might have to chop them down? I did all the chopping.

TONY: Well, I helped. Who put the clothes prop in position to keep the wires up? Anyway, that's neither here nor there.

[Cut ends]

TONY: What else have they got?

BILL: Tables, chairs, a radiogram, a lawnmower.

TONY: Hmm, give 'em a couple of days to settle in, we'll have that lot.

Even when material had to be cut, the ideas could survive. The following segment, about Hancock's trials in an office elevator, had to be trimmed, but the writers returned to the setting four years later for one of the best-loved episodes of the TV series, 'The Lift'.

HANCOCK'S HALF HOUR, third series, episode five

'THE WINTER HOLIDAY'
First broadcast: Wednesday 16 November 1955

TONY: You sent for me, sir?

KENNETH: Ah yes, Hancock, come in. Sit down. Do you know why I've asked you to come and see me?

TONY: No, I don't, sir. I hope you're satisfied with my work.

KENNETH: Of course. You're easily the best lift attendant we've ever had.

TONY: Thank you, sir. Of course you realize my working for you is only a temporary arrangement. Just to tide me over while I'm resting between stage and film engagements to concentrate on me radio work.

KENNETH: Of course. How long have you been with us now?

TONY: Two years, sir.

KENNETH: Capital. Now let me come to the point. I've been looking through your attendance card and I find you haven't had your annual holiday yet.

TONY: No, sir.

KENNETH: But I don't understand, Hancock. We closed the whole firm down for a fortnight's holiday in July.

TONY: So that's why the place was deserted. Well, well, well, I thought they were all using the stairs.

KENNETH: Anyway, the point is, you are entitled to a fortnight's holiday. I suggest you take it as from next week.

TONY: Er, no – no, if you don't mind, sir, I'd rather not.

KENNETH: Why on earth not?

TONY: I'm having no strangers playing about with Mabel.

KENNETH: Who's Mabel?

TONY: My lift. She's getting on a bit now and she has to be treated gently. I know what would happen if I was to leave her – you'd get one of those kids in. Straight out of school – rocket ship crazy. They'd be up and down that shaft like a jet-propelled yo-yo. She's not up to it.

KENNETH: Don't worry, Hancock, I assure you she'll be in good hands. You go away and enjoy yourself.

TONY: Well… all right then – but don't forget, she has to have her oil changed every two thousand floors… and maximum load three persons. None of that, 'All pile in – we'll miss the last bus' stuff. I've got just about fed up with crawling out onto the roof and shouting for help every other journey.

[Cut begins]

TONY: Oh, and I'd better warn you about those office boys.

KENNETH: What have they been up to now?

TONY: If you don't come as soon as they press the button, they open the gate and slide down the cables.

KENNETH: Oh, we'll have to put a stop to that.

TONY: You will. Sometimes they grab the wrong cable and I go shooting up to the sixth floor – and it's not funny when you've got one leg out on the basement floor.

KENNETH: All right, I'll send a memo round. Is there anything else I should know about?

TONY: Yes – the floor indicator in the lift has gone wrong. The little light says you're on the fifth floor. You step out of the lift with a tray full of tea, and bash… there's another foot and a half to go.

[Cut ends]

The space race between the United States and the Soviet Union had begun, and Britain's comedy writers were inspired to blast their characters into the stratosphere in makeshift rocket ships. Spike Milligan did it in 1957 with the classic *Goon Show* episode, 'The Space Age', but Galton and Simpson got there first, after a blob of red paint on the lens of his telescope convinced Hancock that an intergalactic fireball was about to destroy the Earth:

HANCOCK'S HALF HOUR, third series, episode seven

'THE RED PLANET'
First broadcast: Wednesday 30 November 1955

SIDNEY: Hey... just a minute, where did you get these telescopes?

TONY: Mind your own business. *(Slight pause)* Got a penny, I can't see anything.

SIDNEY: So that's why you went down to Brighton pier last week. You went around pinching all the telescopes.

TONY: I did not pinch them. I bought them. I gave Captain Tom five shillings for each of them.

BILL: Five shillings. But those telescopes are worth pounds.

TONY: They are when they've got lenses in them.

SIDNEY: And how do you expect to see the stars if you haven't got any lenses?

TONY: I've put me own in. I went down to the optician and told him I needed glasses. Well, I haven't had a wig or any teeth or anything, so why shouldn't I? Now shuttup... I wish to examine the heavens. Stand back! I'm about to astron. Where's me charts? Ah, here we are. The night sky in December. Let's see now. The time is five past three. Yes. Well, according to the chart, the North Star should be approximately two foot nine to the left of Mrs Higgins's television aerial. Let's have a look. Yes, there she is. The sailor's friend.

BILL: The North Star.

TONY: Mrs Higgins. Tilt it up a bit. Ah – there's the North Star. Key to the whole sky, that is. Find that first and you can find anything. Now... track down two degrees and we should find the Plough. Yes, there it is. The Plough.

SIDNEY: Oooh, let's have a look, the boys are in there tonight – darts match...

By now, the midpoint of the third series, Bill Kerr's character had evolved into an idiot savant, foreseeing every disaster that loomed over Hancock, and too simple-minded to sound a warning. 'We had those wonderful words to say,' Bill recalled, in a phone interview from his home in Perth, 'and we had to stop ourselves from corpsing all the time because everybody was so terribly, terribly funny. Who else in the world could have written that show – nobody except Ray and Alan. Without them... it all begins and ends with the words, and then if you're lucky enough to be able to interpret those words, boy oh boy, you're home free, as the

Americans say. I feel very privileged to have been able to say all those lovely words.'

BILL: Hey Tub, who left the heap of scrap iron in the garden?

ANDREE: This is Tony's rocket ship.

BILL: Really? Well, well... looks like a lot of dustbins welded together, doesn't it?

TONY: You'll have to forgive him, Sid, he doesn't know much about these things. He's a bit simple. Dustbins.

BILL: How do you get in it?

SIDNEY: You take the lid off.

BILL: Oh.

    EFFECTS: (Clank of dustbin lid)

BILL: Hey, there's a pile of rubbish in here.

SIDNEY: *(To self)* Oh blimey, I forgot to empty them.

BILL: Corned beef tins, baked beans, tomatoes, cabbage leaves...

SIDNEY: Supplies. Haven't forgotten *anything*.

TONY: Well, I suppose I'd better get in and acquaint myself with the mass of complicated machinery and mechanism.

SIDNEY: Oh, you mean the steering wheel.

TONY: Is that all?

SIDNEY: What else do you need? You've only got to shoot off and point it towards Mars.

ANDREE: Which brings us to another little item. Where are the engines?

SIDNEY: There they are... sticking out of the tail.

ANDREE: What, those four bits of blue paper?

SIDNEY: Yeah.

TONY: Well, how do we start it?

SIDNEY: You've got a box of matches, haven't you?

ANDREE: This is too much – Tony, you're being robbed! This thing won't even get off the ground, let alone go to Mars. 'Light the blue paper'...

SIDNEY: Look, lady, they're not ordinary rockets, I assure you. They're atomic. Specially designed by Britain's foremost expert on atomic research – Professor William Penney.

TONY: He's right – it says so on the side. Look – 'Penny Atomic Whizzers'. He's right. That's good enough for me.

In an episode that survives only as a poor quality amateur recording, Tony and Bill visit a Turkish bath. The storyline was echoed in a poignant meeting a dozen years later, as Bill Kerr recounted: 'I saw Tony just before he left for Australia [in 1968]. It was in Jermyn Street, he had his coat collar turned up and he looked for all the world as though he was down on his uppers. His hair was all dishevelled, and he said, "I'm going into the Turkish baths, come and have a Turkish bath with me." I said, "I'd love to, mate, but I've got to get home." We had a couple of little minutes of conversation and that was the last I saw of him… I've often wondered, would anything have changed if I'd had a Turkish bath with him? No, it wouldn't have.'

HANCOCK'S HALF HOUR, third series, episode eight

'THE DIET'
First broadcast: Wednesday 7 December 1955

TONY: Well, if this is a Turkish bath, I don't think much of it. Most unfriendly.
BILL: What do you mean?
TONY: Well, I'd no sooner got in here than some big fellow in a vest and white trousers grabbed hold of me, threw me on a table and started thumping me. And I'd never seen the man before.
BILL: What did you do?
TONY: I hit him back. Well, I'm a peaceful man… but I'm not having that. That's carrying a joke too far. He was laying into me something rotten. 'Course, he had the advantage – surprise. I had me shirt halfway over me head at the time… and I was laying on me back, I couldn't defend meself. Lucky I still had me shoes on. A few crafty digs with me Italian points soon sent him on his way. He won't pick on me again in a hurry.
BILL: You idiot, he was a masseur.
TONY: I don't care what country he comes from, I'm not being knocked about by these Continentals.

A page later, Snide appears:

KENNETH: Trying to lose weight, eh? Well, you've come to the right place. Before I started working here I used to weigh 23 stone. And of course, walking in and out of the steam room all the time, I've lost 15 stone. I reckon in five years' time, I won't be here at all.
TONY: I'll come back then, shall I?
KENNETH: Oooh, you're a card you are, aren't you, eh? A proper comic, aren't you, eh? You should take it up. That made me laugh, that did. And I don't get much to laugh at these days, you know.

TONY: Getaway.

KENNETH: No, I'm very lonely. The other attendants, my mates, you know, all my close friends...

TONY: Yes.

KENNETH: They hate the sight of me. 'Course, they're trying to get rid of me, you know.

TONY: Amazing, isn't it?

KENNETH: I know. And they go about it in nasty, underhand ways. They know the hot rooms steam up my glasses, so they always send me into the hottest room we've got, hoping I'll trip up and fall into the bath... Now come on, let's help get some of that weight off you.

TONY: What are you going to do?

KENNETH: I'm going to pummel you.

TONY: You're not.

KENNETH: I am. I'm going to go slap, slap, slap, slap, slap all over you.

TONY: You do and I'll go bash, bash, bash, bash, bash all over you.

'Hancock's character is of all time,' said Alan. 'There were Hancocks, that character, around 300 years ago. If you read Dickens, Hancock's in there all the time. It's just the language which has changed. A little bit more flowery, a little bit more over-written in a way, but the characters were all there – there's a Hancock in every book.'

And it's not just Dickens – look at Tolstoy, Dostoyevsky, Chekhov...

HANCOCK'S HALF HOUR, third series, episode nine

'A VISIT TO RUSSIA'
First broadcast: Wednesday 14 December 1955

KENNETH: Comrade, will you please state your business.

TONY: Certainly. I and my small band of strolling clowns wish to travel to Moscow and entertain. Tumblers, minstrels, jesters... in one programme we offer a veritable feast of frolic and drollery designed for the merriment of the simple villagers. Kindly arrange to have a droshki, a fresh team of horses and a lantern waiting at the frontier – we will make the city gates by nightfall. Inform the burgomaster of our intended arrival, that he may place at our disposal a suitable inn where we may refresh ourselves and change into clean linen after the tedium of our travels.

KENNETH: Get you.

ANDREE: You must forgive him, comrade, Tony's knowledge of modern Russia never got past page 48 of *Anna Karenina*.

KENNETH: Comrades, am I to understand you wish to journey to the Soviet Union?

SIDNEY: Oh, is that on the way to Russia?

TONY: *(Sotto)* Sid, watch it, don't be so ignorant… that's an insult. Is it on the way to Russia. Illiterate oaf. It's nowhere near it.

Only one script in the *Hancock's Half Hour* archive has never been broadcast. Called 'The Counterfeiter', it also stands out as the only script in which Bill Kerr had the starring role – in several scenes Hancock barely speaks, or does not appear. 'Tony didn't mind other people getting laughs,' Alan said, 'so whether that really had anything to do with why he didn't like it, I don't know.'

The star rarely vetoed anything, let alone a full script: he regarded himself as a serious performer, not an ad-libbing stand-up act. On the rare occasions when he did object to a line, it would usually be one that sounded too much like the punchline to a gag. Much more common were the cuts Main Wilson demanded, to keep the shows within half-hour constraints: the archive scripts reveal that five minutes or more had to be chopped from many episodes. 'We never liked it,' Alan admitted, 'but of course there was no alternative.'

The writers can't be sure which episode they produced at short notice to replace this one, but it's probable that it was the last show of 1955, which went out as a lightly rewritten version of 'Cinderella Hancock' from the first series. That was the only time Galton and Simpson reused one of their scripts… it's also one of the broadcasts which has been lost. It is little consolation that, if Hancock had agreed to perform 'The Counterfeiter', it's probable that no recording would survive:

HANCOCK'S HALF HOUR, unbroadcast episode, originally written to be third series, episode eleven

'THE COUNTERFEITER'
Never broadcast

EFFECTS: *(Door opens)*

SIDNEY: Well, well, well, Hancock and Billy the Kerr. What brings you round here?

TONY: We've come in answer to your advert in the window. Smart lad wanted to learn printing trade. No experience necessary. Anything from fourteen days to six months' holiday a year guaranteed.

SIDNEY: Yes, that's right.

TONY: Well, here's the smart lad.

SIDNEY: What, Billy?

TONY: Yes, I want him to learn an honest trade.

SIDNEY: How right you are.

TONY: What's the money like?

SIDNEY: Perfect. It fools me sometimes.

TONY: Well… what about it, William?

BILL: I don't care what I do as long as I make a lot of money.

SIDNEY: You'll get the push if you don't.

TONY: That's what I like to hear. An employer who insists on his employees having a share in the fruits of his business.

SIDNEY: Certainly. They get some of it in their pay packets.

TONY: I can see you're going to be very happy here, William. I shall leave you to your work. Oh, and Sidney?

SIDNEY: Yeah?

TONY: See he doesn't slack or go to sleep. Keep his head away from anything soft. He'll have his head underneath a newspaper before the bell's stopped ringing.

SIDNEY: Don't worry, I'll watch him. See you.

EFFECTS: (Door shuts)

BILL: Well now, what do I have to do?

SIDNEY: You're going to be a printer.

BILL: Don't I have to serve an apprenticeship?

SIDNEY: Oh er… yes, all right then, if you want to. Here's a press. Put a bit of paper in it.

BILL: Right.

SIDNEY: Turn the handle.

BILL: Right.

EFFECTS: (Clank of handle turning once)

BILL: Right.

SIDNEY: Welcome to the printing trade.

BILL: Now wait a minute, I thought an apprenticeship lasted seven years.

SIDNEY: Well, normally it does, but I don't think we'll stay open that long. Now… all you have to do is turn this handle.

BILL: I've got you.

EFFECTS: (Handle turning)

SIDNEY: That's it. Now all them bits of green paper coming out, you
    bundle them up into hundreds and put 'em in the oven. Regulo one.
BILL: What are they?
SIDNEY: Er… dance tickets.
BILL: Oh. *(PAUSE, then suspiciously)* Hey… wait a minute.

EFFECTS: (Handle stops turning)

BILL: These dance tickets look like pound notes.
SIDNEY: Never mind, you've only just started, you're bound to make a
    few mistakes.
BILL: I know what you're up to. You're a forger. You're making counterfeit
    notes.
SIDNEY: No, Billy, you've got it all wrong.
BILL: Then what are you doing?
SIDNEY: Well, um… er… if I was to tell you they were fourpenny bus
    tickets for conductors with big ticket racks, you wouldn't believe me,
    would you?
BILL: No.
SIDNEY: Then I'll have to think of something else, won't I? No, you see,
    what's really happening is we're printing them for another firm.
BILL: Who?
SIDNEY: The Bank of England.
BILL: Don't give me that, they print their own.
SIDNEY: Yes, but they've had a sudden rush.

Rehearsals for each show started at around 10.30 a.m. on the day of
recording. 'The scripts were doled out,' Alan said, 'and that would be the
first time they'd seen them. So they'd have a first read-through to get
acquainted with it, and this is where the question arose of the ability to
read and get it right the first time. I mean, Hancock would read a line and
do it perfectly, and if it was funny they used to fall about laughing.
Because all four of them, the male members of the cast, were enormous
guffawers. Loud, guffaw laughter. Hancock, he used to roll about on the
floor almost. Sid was a guffawer, Bill was very loud and Ken had his
braying, so if something appealed to them, all four of them would be
roaring with laughter.'

'We didn't really need a public audience there,' Ray added. 'We just
needed those four.'

The timing needed to make the bickering work between Tony and

Bill, such as this New Year's Day scuffle over a sixpence, was crucial. The two men shared a sense of comedic rhythm that has never been equaled on radio:

HANCOCK'S HALF HOUR, third series, episode twelve

'HANCOCK'S NEW YEAR'S RESOLUTIONS'
First broadcast: Wednesday 4 January 1956

TONY: Money means nothing. True contentment and happiness come
    from within. If your soul is pure and shining, it will show through.
    Money, huh! A good, clean, honest life, that's what counts. That to
    money! Abandon this mad desire for wealth, renounce it, cast it
    aside, seek the true happiness, forget about money, it means
    nothing, it…
BILL: Hey – there's a sixpence laying on the floor.
TONY: It's mine. Mine. Give us it here. Mine. I saw it first. Mine.
BILL: Get your foot off my neck. It's mine.
TONY: It's not – it's mine.
BILL: Prove it.
TONY: It's a sixpence.
BILL: Yeah.
TONY: Is it silver, with the queen's head on one side and a coat of arms
    on the other, and writing round the side and a crinkled edge?
BILL: Yeah.
TONY: It's mine. I recognize it. Mine looked just like that.
BILL: Tell us the date.
TONY: Wednesday, give us it.

Like Errol Flynn and John Wayne, Hancock won World War Two single-handed. That's what he claimed to Andrée, anyway, when she caught sight of his 'war wound'. The gag was that he actually got the scar when his braces snapped during a song-and-dance act for troops on the Isle of Wight.

His real war service was just as comical: at eighteen, Anthony Hancock volunteered for the RAF with dreams of becoming a fighter pilot, discovered that his eyesight was too bad (and, he claimed, that his arms were too short) for flying Spitfires, and was transferred to Stranraer on the south-west Scottish coast, where he was in charge of keeping the Nissan hut heaters supplied with coal.

HANCOCK'S HALF HOUR, third series, episode sixteen

'HOW HANCOCK WON THE WAR'
First broadcast: Wednesday 1 February 1956

TONY: By the summer of 1940, I'd been up to the Palace so many times, the sentry at the gate thought I was courting one of the chambermaids. Then came the mission that was the turning point of my army career. Me, Sid and Bill were landed on the coast of North Africa with orders to blow up the three dams on the Rhine.

ANDREE: But the Rhine is in Germany.

TONY: Is it? Oh… well, you see, we'd been issued with tropical kit and it would have looked suspicious if we'd gone straight there. Don't interrupt. Anyway, we had this bomb Barnes Wallis had made for us… and we were standing up to our knees in the sea, practising skimming it across the water to each other when…

ANDREE: Just a minute, Tony – if you were in North Africa, just how did you plan to blow up the dams that were in Germany?

TONY: A very good question. I thought you'd spot that. Well, you see, I worked it out… we were going to sling it into the Med, so it'd bounce across towards Italy, then up past Gracie's place, through the Brenner Pass, roll down the other side, into the Danube, turn left past Vienna into the Rhine, then by horse-pulled barge right up to the dam.

ANDREE: And did it?

TONY: No, we slung it in the Med and the tide brought it back.

ANDREE: But there isn't a tide in the Mediterranean.

TONY: Yes, I know, but you see… well, it was… I mean… Yugoslavia. I was dropped behind the lines to help Tito blow up the *Tirpitz* and…

ANDREE: The *Tirpitz* was in Norway…

TONY: I remember the French campaign as if it were yesterday. The turning point of my army career. We were dug in just outside Paris, 500 miles behind enemy lines, and the Hun was throwing everything at us. Morale was dropping very low, but I was standing firm and…

GRAMS: *(Pitched long-range gun battle. Rumblings. Whine of shells. Muffled explosions. Star shells. Occasional machine guns. The lot.)*

BILL: I've just had a message from HQ, sir.

TONY: Read it.

BILL: It says – Retreat immediately. No hope of relieving you. Signed Monty.

TONY: Send this back – Will never retreat. See you in Berlin. Signed Hanky.

BILL: Sir – if I may be so bold – I think I can safely say that a tactical withdrawal would be very much appreciated by the men.

TONY: What men?

BILL: Me and Sid.

TONY: Is that all we have left?

BILL: That's all we started with. I told you it was too much for the three of us. The 15th and 16th Panzer divisions and a couple of hundred thousand storm troopers.

TONY: It's not too much for me. Remember that, Private Kerr. You're just here to feed the bullets to me.

SIDNEY: I'll feed you one in the back of the nut if you don't get us out of here.

TONY: Hello, hello – a malcontent. Mutiny is a very ugly thing, Private James.

SIDNEY: So are you.

At the height of Beatlemania in the mid-sixties, a story was widely told of a High Court judge who was so out of touch that during one case he asked his clerk, 'Who are The Beatles?' It's apocryphal, of course, the juridical equivalent of an urban legend. But it might have had its beginnings a decade earlier in this scene from one of the last lost episodes. It features Alan Simpson as an extra voice, in probably his longest radio appearance:

HANCOCK'S HALF HOUR, third series, episode fifteen

'THE BREAKFAST CEREAL'
First broadcast: Wednesday 25 January 1956

> EFFECTS: (Courtroom atmosphere. Gavel three times.)

ALAN: Order in court. Order in court. Ahem. My lords, ladies and gentlemen, this is a three-day contest, eight hours each day, between – in this corner, at fourteen stone two…

KENNETH: Please… please, Mr Clerk of the Court.

ALAN: Oh, I'm sorry, me lud. I forgot, that's me evening job, ain't it? Ahem. Silence in court. The case of Hancock versus Crunchyflakes Limited. First day… Presiding Judge – Lord Chief Justice Phillips. Right lads, fags out, wigs on, up on your feet, everyone back to his own bench. His Lordship the Judge.

KENNETH: Thank you, you may be seated.

EFFECTS: (Courtroom sitting down)

KENNETH: Now then... 'Hancock versus Crunchyflakes'. Yes. Is Mr Hancock in court?

TONY: I am, me lud.

KENNETH: And is Mr Crunchyflakes here?

SIDNEY: The name is James, your honour.

KENNETH: Oh, I see – James Crunchyflakes.

SIDNEY: No, no, Sidney James.

KENNETH: Sidney James. Yes, well, we only need one Christian name, I'll call you Sidney Crunchyflakes.

SIDNEY: Oh, blimey, look – my name isn't Crunchyflakes.

KENNETH: Then why don't you mind your own business? Let Mr Crunchyflakes speak for himself.

TONY: With the greatest respect, me lud, this gentleman trades under the name of Crunchyflakes.

KENNETH: Oh, I see. Crunchyflakes... yes. I don't believe I've heard the name before.

TONY: They are a new brand of cornflakes, me lud.

KENNETH: Oh really, how interesting, yes. What are cornflakes? Will the gentlemen of the press please note that question and see that it gets in the papers. Photographs can be taken in my chambers afterwards. Right, next case.

Twenty years later, Kenneth Williams was excused from jury service on the grounds that, as he noted in his diary, he had spent a substantial part of his career sending up judges.

In real life, Tony Hancock kept himself well informed on current affairs. Kenneth Williams's diaries describe how the two men dissected the Suez Crisis of 1956 in several discussions that went on deep into the night. But when Anthony Aloysius St John Hancock the Second joined his ninety-three-year-old Uncle Palmerston at the helm of a Fleet Street journal, he didn't know his masthead from his elbow:

HANCOCK'S HALF HOUR, third series, episode seventeen

'THE NEWSPAPER'
First broadcast: Wednesday 8 February 1956

TONY: Yes, I rather fancy meself as a Fleet Street tycoon. 'Cos I'd have to be raised to the peerage. Lord Beavercock – that'll do.

ANDREE: What sort of a newspaper is it?

TONY: I don't know – I've never read it. Come to that, I never read any of them. Last time I read a newspaper was when we took the lino up. No, no, I tell a lie – I sometimes lean over the counter of the fish and chip shop and screw me head round... but apart from that, nothing. Flook, Jane and Garth... that's me lot.

BILL: Well, you'd better learn something about them before you see your uncle.

TONY: I'll be all right, I know what it's all about, I'm no mug. I've seen it all on the films... 'Hold the front page!' ... 'Give me the City Desk, I've got a story that's going to bust this town wide open!' ... and all those big printing presses pounding away, and the newspaper that turns itself round, and gets bigger and bigger and then stops dead in the middle of the screen so you can read the headlines... I've seen it all, don't worry...

A few pages later, Hancock decides he has cracked the Fleet Street formula:

TONY: Now look, I've been studying this newspaper lark. I've read all today's papers and I've found out the general policy of how to make a successful newspaper. Rule Number One... and the most important thing of all... only put important world news in if you've got nothing else to fill it up with. Secondly... use as few words as you possibly can. Instead... lots of strip cartoons with not too many words in the bubbles. People don't like words these days, it confuses 'em. Keep it simple... you know... crosswords with easy clues and a few letters already put in to help 'em a bit...

BILL: How about pin-up girls?

TONY: Essential, essential. Never do any good if we don't have them in. Golden rule in Fleet Street. Use any excuse to put in a woman showing a lot of herself. If it's been cold, shove in a photo of a girl wearing just a fur muff and a headline – 'Brrrrr... Coldest In 80 Years'.

BILL: And if it's been hot?

TONY: Same photograph but take the muff off and put a watering can in. Now... future policy. In the sports page, I want you to write an article condemning bullfighting as cruel, sadistic, savage and bloodthirsty, 'cos the British don't like that sort of thing. But write it as cruel, sadistic, savage and bloodthirsty as you can, 'cos they love reading about it.

Hancock's family history changed from week to week – not just the heir to a newspaper empire, but the son of a bus driver, remnant of the landed gentry and even the Last of the McHancocks. Bill's lineage never changed: he was the boy from Wagga Wagga, born in the bush ('How old are you? And you still believe that sort of stuff?' mocked Tony). Sid's background was scarcely mentioned... until, in the last of the episodes missing from the BBC archive, his father turned up:

HANCOCK'S HALF HOUR, fourth series, episode three

'*SID JAMES'S DAD*'
First broadcast: Sunday 28 October 1956

TONY: It's just that I'd never thought of you with a mum and dad. You don't look the type.

SIDNEY: Well, I am. I've got a mum and dad same as everybody else.

TONY: Of course you have, I just can't imagine you as a baby, that's all. I don't know though... yes, I can see you now, sitting in your pram filling up your rattle with lead shot and hitting all the other kids over the head with it. Anyway, what about your dad?

SIDNEY: It's his birthday tomorrow. He's eighty-three. And he's coming down to London to spend a holiday with me.

TONY: Very nice too. What's wrong with that?

SIDNEY: Well, I can't let him stay with me.

TONY: Why not?

SIDNEY: Well, it's... it's very difficult... I mean... well, how can I put it... well... he's *honest*.

TONY: Oh, I see.

SIDNEY: He's a nice, kind, harmless old man. And... well, if he found out what I've turned out like, it'd break his heart.

TONY: Hasn't he got any idea then?

SIDNEY: No, I ran away from home when I was fifteen, and we haven't seen each other since.

TONY: What does he think you do for a living then?

SIDNEY: Well, I'm a bit ashamed of it really but... well, you see, he kept reading in the papers that I was appearing in court, so there was only one thing I could do.

TONY: What?

SIDNEY: I told him I was a judge.

6 Hancock on the Television

In July 1956, after his third radio series had commanded audiences of up to 7 million, Tony Hancock made the leap to television with Galton and Simpson. Budgets for TV programmes had risen sharply and producers could now offer fees high enough to tempt the big stars away from the grind of nightly performances on the stage to rehearse a weekly show instead. The broadcasts were live, and rarely recorded – productions were more often restaged than repeated on film.

'It was one of the things we knew we would have to do eventually,' said Ray. 'Television was getting bigger by the month. One of the good things about going from radio to television was that Hancock somehow managed to look like his voice. I don't think people were amazed when they saw him. It seemed to match. We made no concessions to television at all. We were aware that it would be filmed, but we were still writing words. What mattered, what was important, and where all our interest lay, was in the words.'

'Another bonus we were expecting was that the television scripts would be shorter – or so we thought,' added Alan. 'We imagined at first that all the visual business would mean less writing, but in fact we found we had to produce about the same number of pages whether it was thirty minutes on radio, or a *Half Hour* on television. Partly, that's because we always described the action in the script – we didn't leave that to the director or the actors. And partly it's because we tend naturally to write lots of dialogue. It only became a problem when we progressed to film, and we'd discover our screenplay contained so many lines, it would run to about three hours.'

Hancock himself was delighted to make the move: 'I still feel like a visual comic,' he told Philip Purser of the *Sunday Telegraph*. 'When I finally got into radio properly, I really had to work harder than in any other medium. When we changed to television, it was a sigh of relief.'

The TV and radio series ran side by side for the next three years, though audiences on the Light Programme were falling steadily (below 4 million at their lowest) while television ratings soared (up to 8.7 million within the first year). This reflected TV's rapid emergence as the dominant medium, and not any disparity between Hancock on air and Hancock on screen. In fact, the classic cast never did work together on TV – Bill Kerr was left behind, because Galton and Simpson, producer Duncan Wood and Hancock himself all felt the screen was too small to contain the full radio team. Bill was philosophical about it: 'I understood,' he said. 'I didn't mind.' Instead, Bill's role as chief irritant and idler was added to Sid James's character.

All the episodes of the first TV series – and most of the second, third and fourth – have been lost. There seems no possibility that this opening scene could have survived anywhere on tape: the BBC didn't record it, and the most primitive home taping technology was fifteen years away. As soon as the first *Hancock's Half Hour* had been screened, it was lost forever:

HANCOCK'S HALF HOUR (TV), first series, episode one

'NELSON IN HOSPITAL'
First broadcast: Friday 6 July 1956

ANNOUNCER: The next part of our programme, *Hancock's Half Hour*, follows immediately.

(Working class living room. There is a television set facing the camera. Four chairs are arranged round the set. The husband enters. He is in his shirt sleeves and is chewing.)

HUSBAND: *(Calls off)* Come on, Edie, hurry up. Telly'll be on in a minute. You can leave the washing-up till the morning.
WIFE: Coming, Bert. *(She enters drying her hands with the tea towel)* What's on?
HUSBAND: What do you mean, what's on? You've never worried about that before. We just switch it on and sit there till bedtime. With a bit of luck we might enjoy it tonight.
WIFE: Well, I just wondered what was on, that was all.
HUSBAND: What does it matter? Something to do. Saves going out, or reading, or talking, or looking at you.

(While the husband has been talking she has been looking at the Radio Times and has found the appropriate page)

WIFE: Oh, here it is, Bert. Quarter to eight, weather forecast...

HUSBAND: We've missed that... that's you being late in from work. First programme I've missed in three years.

WIFE: Ah, here we are... eight forty-five. *Hancock's Half Hour* starring Tony Hancock.

HUSBAND: Who's he?

WIFE: I'm not sure, Bert. I think he's one of them radio blokes.

HUSBAND: Radio?

WIFE: Yes, you know, one of those things people have in cars.

HUSBAND: Tony Hancock. Hmmm. He hasn't been on the telly before, has he?

WIFE: No. It says this is his first time on BBC television and tonight's the first programme in the series.

HUSBAND: Well, all right then, we'll give him a chance. See what he's like. If we don't like him we can always... we can always... er...

WIFE: Always what?

HUSBAND: Well, we can sit in front of the set. We don't have to watch him, do we? Go on, switch it on, Ede, you never know, he might be all right.

(She switches the TV set on. The announcer appears.)

ANNOUNCER: Good evening.

BOTH: Good evening, Peter.

ANNOUNCER: Tonight we present the first programme in the new television series of *Hancock's Half Hour*. And here to introduce the programme is the star of the show – Tony Hancock.

(Close up of TONY in front of curtain, sitting at a desk. He is wearing a dinner jacket with slim-jim tie.)

TONY: Good evening, and I would like to welcome you to the first programme in my new series. This is of course my first appearance on BBC Television and I'm very thrilled at the chance of at last coming into your homes.

WIFE: I don't think I'm going to like him.

(TONY reacts very slightly)

TONY: This programme will be coming to you once a fortnight and I do hope that you will like what we have in store for you over the next few weeks.

WIFE: I don't like his face.

(TONY reacts a bit more obviously)

TONY: *(Intense and serious)* I do realize of course that this is an entirely new venture for me and I am well aware of the famous names of television that I will be following, and if I can entertain you as well as they have, I shall be happy...

HUSBAND: He hasn't made me laugh yet, look at his face, a right misery.

(TONY jollies himself up. A broad smile. Lots of tooth, gay bubbling laugh.)

TONY: I hope you're going to like me and...

HUSBAND: Rotten teeth he's got. Don't fit very well, do they?

(TONY closes his mouth and tries to talk without opening it)

TONY: I hope you're going to like me and...

WIFE: He ought to get something done about his hair as well.

(TONY covers up his hair with his hand)

TONY: I hope you're going to like me and...

WIFE: He's much fatter than I expected.

(TONY pulls in his cheeks)

TONY: I hope you're going to like me and...

HUSBAND: Well, I wish he'd get off and let somebody else have a go.

TONY: Now I'd like to introduce you to some of the cast. First, I have with me a man whose face you've seen many times on the films, a very fine actor and a close friend of mine... Sidney James.

(Sidney moves into the picture, beaming)

WIFE: Oh yes, I like him. Much better looking, isn't he?

(TONY signals to camera. Signals 'Cut')

TONY: Ha, ha! So much for the cast. Now about the show.

HUSBAND: Cor, it's him again. Let's switch over. He's a right wash-out, he is.

TONY: Well, let's get started.

WIFE: Got no life in him, has he?

(TONY moves gaily about, effervescently, burbling with force)

HUSBAND: Not as good as Arthur, is he? He could learn a few things off Arthur, he could.

(TONY puts on a pair of horn-rimmed spectacles)

TONY: And so, playmates, I'd just like to finish by saying, I thank you.

(Holds his nose and goes down out of screen like Arthur Askey does)

WIFE: I wish it was Norman Wisdom, he's much better.

(TONY comes up again with a cloth cap on, laughing à la Wisdom. He goes to sit down. Misses chair and gets up laughing)

TONY: I fell over. But I'd just like to finish by…
HUSBAND: Terry-Thomas is the boy I like.

(TONY puts a long cigarette holder in his mouth and starts smoking)

TONY: *(Terribly posh)* How do you do. Are you terribly well? Good show.
HUSBAND: Well, I don't fancy his face looking at me for six weeks. Wish I could think of something else to do.

(TONY is getting furious. The next dialogue he looks from one to the other.)

WIFE: He's too old for my liking.
HUSBAND: Very brought down, I am. Not my cup of tea at all – we pay three guineas a year for that.
WIFE: I can't understand it. I heard he was all right on the radio.
HUSBAND: Well, he should have stayed there. He's not going to be any good on telly, I'll tell you that, and I've spotted 'em all. He's a wash-out.
WIFE: I wouldn't mind if he was better looking, but he's so ugly.
HUSBAND: I'd like to know how much he's getting for this. It's a disgrace. A waste of public money. Look, the dog's crawled under the table now, and he'll watch anything. I've never seen a bigger load of rubbish in my life.

(This is the last straw for TONY who has gradually been getting more and more furious. He puts a toy windmill on the table. Moves the arms and spins them.)

TONY: Interlude.

(He gets up and stalks out of camera, leaving an empty screen)

WIFE: Where's he gone now?
HUSBAND: I don't know, but this bit's an improvement.

GRAMS: *(Knock at door)*

HUSBAND: Come in.

(Door opens. Enter TONY in dinner jacket and plus fours. He walks straight up to the television set and puts his foot through the screen.)

GRAMS: (Crashing glass)

(TONY then advances on husband)

TONY: Now… so you don't like the choppers, eh? I'm fat, am I? I see…

(The camera cuts back to SID in the studio, and the next time we see TONY he is lying bandaged and splinted in hospital)

TONY: If only I'd known he was a heavyweight wrestler, I would never have bothered.

Kenneth Williams appeared in only the second television series, and the single example of his 'Snide' character to survive on film is in this episode, where Hancock flies to Switzerland for a skiing holiday and has to share a hotel room with the West Dulwich yodelling champion. In his autobiography, *Just Williams,* the actor claimed Hancock was unhappy with the scene, which included a childlike ritual, making up after an argument by shaking hands with the little fingers only. 'I remember talking to Tony about the success of the Tyrolean piece a few weeks afterwards and he nodded agreement: "Yes, it went very well on the whole but there were complaints from some people; they thought it was a bit poofy… it's the two men in one room, and us doing the little fingers bit… they read things into it, two blokes holding hands."'

HANCOCK'S HALF HOUR (TV), second series, episode one

'THE ALPINE HOLIDAY'
First broadcast: Monday 1 April 1957

KENNETH: Nobody likes me. I don't know what it is, but I seem to get on people's nerves. They think I'm daft.
TONY: I can't understand it.
KENNETH: I mean well.
TONY: I'm sure you do.
KENNETH: People give me photographs. But when they get to know me they ask for them back. Even me mother.
TONY: That's terrible. You've touched me right here. I've gone right off. You poor wretch. Here, have one of mine.

(Takes a photo out of his case and gives it to KENNETH)

KENNETH: *(Looking at photo)* Oooh, thank you, thank you, it's all mine. I think you're nice. Just goes to show, there is kindness left in the world after all. I'll treasure this, you don't know what this means to me, I'll never forget you... aren't you ugly?

(TONY snatches it back)

Sid James, a more experienced film actor than Hancock, used his technical knowledge to enhance his performance, and shared his expertise with the star: 'Sid would keep an eye on the monitors all the time during rehearsals,' Ray said. 'He knew how to make the most of different shots and angles, and he'd suggest bits of direction to Tony – "Tell them you want a close-up before this line, to bring out the reaction." Tony wouldn't have thought of it himself, but he'd seize on these ideas and learn from them. Sid was very unselfish. He'd share what he knew, to make other people look better.' This episode, another of Hancock's narrow escapes from the altar, has been lost, but almost every line invites a close-up of his anguished face:

HANCOCK'S HALF HOUR (TV), fourth series, episode eight

'MATRIMONY – ALMOST'
First broadcast: Friday 13 February 1959

> *(SIDNEY and TONY are both in morning dress with flowers in their buttonholes. SIDNEY is trying to tie TONY's tie. TONY hasn't got his coat on.)*

TONY: Do you think I'm doing the right thing, Sid?
SIDNEY: Of course you are. They're loaded, aren't they?
TONY: I suppose so.
SIDNEY: They must be... place like this, servants... this little do must have cost him a good five thousand nicker. We've got it made, boy, we'll be in clover for the first time in our lives.
TONY: But I'm not sure that I love her.
SIDNEY: Oh cor blimey, do me a favour. This is a wedding – what do you want to drag that into it for? This is a business deal. You keep her happy, she doles out the lob, me and the lads down the track every night, a perfect arrangement.

TONY: That is not the way I am approaching the thing. I always said when I got married it would be for love. And when I met her, I thought, here we are, lad, this might be it.

SIDNEY: Well, this is it. You love her, of course you love her, and she loves you, and we're all going to be very happy. Now come on, get your boots on.

TONY: I'm not sure, Sid. I'm being rushed into this… not only by you but by her as well. And by her parents. I've been swept off my feet. I don't understand it. Why am I so desirable all of a sudden? I've been knocking around thirty-four years and not a nibble, then all of a sudden, wallop. A rich bird cottons on to me and in two weeks it's eyes down for a plateful of wedding cake. Why? That's what I want to know.

SIDNEY: You're fascinating, that's why. She's knocked out with you. It's those great cods' eyes of yours, staring away there, you've transfixed her. It's like a snake and a rabbit.

TONY: I can't say I care very much for your similes.

SIDNEY: You're her Svengali. She's like putty in your hands. Why bother with 'why'? Just collect the money and say nothing.

TONY: Have you been saying anything to her?

SIDNEY: No. I told her you had some money, but then I had to – you didn't want her to think you're a fortune hunter.

TONY: How much money did you tell her I had?

SIDNEY: Oooh, not much, Four or five hundred… thousand.

TONY: What did you want to tell her that for? I haven't got four or five hundred pence.

SIDNEY: It doesn't matter to her. Her family's got more money than they know what to do with.

TONY: But I've deceived her.

SIDNEY: She won't bother. She loves you. You can see the way she behaves… she's potty about you.

TONY: That's true. I suppose she is slightly mad about me. It's understandable, of course. I am quite a fine figure of a man really, in some respects.

SIDNEY: Of course you are.

TONY: Well built, without being obese. A well set-up young lad.

SIDNEY: Yes.

TONY: Not exactly rangy…

SIDNEY: No, no.

TONY: But definitely, er… what would you say… a shortish Gary Cooper?

SIDNEY: Oh yes.

TONY: Of course, the long hair, you see… gives a sort of poet look, a dreamy quality…

SIDNEY: A sort of thinker.

TONY: That's it, you've got it, you've summed me right up there, a thinker… I give one the impression of being pre-occupied with the higher things in life, don't you think?

SIDNEY: Yeah. All you've got to do is keep your trap shut and don't spoil the illusion.

TONY: I've got to talk to her sometimes. She'll be my wife. I can't just sit there and pretend I'm thinking, it'll get monotonous for her. Apart from the fact I get a headache if I concentrate too much.

Sid's character had been evolving and extending throughout the radio run, but on TV it developed fully. Galton and Simpson drew on elements they saw in the actor's own personality – Sid James really was a natural success with women, despite his battered face, and he really did have a taste for dangerous gambles. Hancock's future wife Freddie, who had been working with him as his publicity agent since 1954, remembered Sid's complex private life: 'Sid would have a girlfriend coming to the recording, and the wife was coming, another girlfriend he was getting rid of was coming, they'd be in the circle, the stalls, they'd be all over the place. And part of my job, unofficially, was to make sure that they stayed separate. It's good training for PR.'

Sid's shyster trait had once been part of the Hancock character, as a petty kleptomaniac in *Calling All Forces*, but that early compulsion to pocket anything not bolted to the floorboards was clumsy compared to the artful, heartless, inspired thieving of Sid James in the *Half Hours*. Sid robbed Tony blind with a completeness that was so graceful, it seemed almost poetic. The following handful of extracts from radio and TV show how a one-dimensional (but very funny) comic routine gradually became a complex (and very crooked) human character:

HANCOCK'S HALF HOUR (radio), series one, episode five

'THE HANCOCK FESTIVAL'
First broadcast: Tuesday 30 November 1954

EFFECTS: (Door opens)

SIDNEY: Ah, just the boys I'm looking for.

BILL: Sidney!

TONY: Mr James, what are you doing here? I've told you not to come round here in daylight.

SIDNEY: That's a fine way to talk to your bookmaker. I've got news for you.

TONY: What?

SIDNEY: You know that horse I told you to put thirty quid on – that cast-iron, dead cert, can't lose, sure-fire, odds-on favourite… the one you said wouldn't win?

TONY: Well?

SIDNEY: It didn't. Thirty nicker you owe me.

HANCOCK'S HALF HOUR (radio), series one, episode seven

'THE DEPARTMENT STORE SANTA'
First broadcast: Tuesday 14 December 1954

BILL: Wait a minute. How did you manage to get a job like this, Sid?

SIDNEY: Simple. They said they wanted someone reliable, trustworthy, upright and honest.

BILL: So?

SIDNEY: So I forged some credentials and got the job.

HANCOCK'S HALF HOUR (radio), series one, episode nine

'THE CHRISTMAS EVE PARTY'
First broadcast: Tuesday 28 December 1954

SIDNEY: I would have got here earlier, Billy, but I was delayed. I've been down the shops getting my Christmas presents.

BILL: What took so long?

SIDNEY: Usual things, doors to open, wires to cut, windows to smash, all takes time.

HANCOCK'S HALF HOUR (radio), series two, episode twelve

'THE MATADOR'
First broadcast: Tuesday 5 July 1955

TONY: I don't trust that man. He's always twisting me. Look at those two suits he sold me last week.

BILL: They were a very good fit.

TONY: They *ought* to have been. When I got home, I found me wardrobe was empty.

EFFECTS: (Telephone bell. Receiver up.)

KENNETH: Hallo. Sid James Overseas Enterprises Limited. Edwardian Fred speaking. Oh – half a minute. Hey Sid.

SIDNEY: Hallo.

KENNETH: Long distance call from Spain. It's Barcelona Bertie.

SIDNEY: All right, give us the phone. Hallo. Hallo – Bert? Sid. Como esta you? Good. Who, me? Oh, not so bueno. No. Life's full of trials and tribulations. Yes. Specially the trials. Now look, Bertie, bad news. That English bullfighter I promised to send over. He can't do it. No, he was practising at home yesterday and he got gored. Yeah. His missus stuck a hat rack in him. I'm sorry, Bertie. Yeah, I *know* an English bullfighter's a big draw out there. Yeah, I *know* it'd be a novelty. All right, so you've *found* the biggest bull in Spain for him to fight, there's nothing I can do about it. No, of course I can't find anybody else to take his place. I can't think of anybody who'd be mug enough to risk his life fighting a monster like that.

EFFECTS: (Door open)

TONY: Morning, Sidney.

SIDNEY: Bert, I've just thought of somebody. I'll send him over. Cheerio. And hasta your vista too.

HANCOCK'S HALF HOUR (radio), series three, episode fourteen

'THE STUDENT PRINCE'
First broadcast: Wednesday 18 January 1956

KENNETH: My dear Mr James... let me explain why I am here. I understand you are a man who, for a reasonable price, is prepared to accept certain... er... jobs, with no questions asked.

SIDNEY: Oh no, not me, I do ask questions. I'm going to ask one now... how much are you paying?

KENNETH: Twenty thousand pounds.

SIDNEY: A very good answer. I'll do it.

HANCOCK'S HALF HOUR (radio), series four, episode two

'THE BOLSHOI BALLET'
First broadcast: Sunday 21 October 1956

SIDNEY: Oh dear, don't tell me I sold you the wrong tickets? I just don't
    know what to say.
TONY: How about, 'Here's your money back, and five quid for your
    trouble'?
SIDNEY: No. It wouldn't sound right coming from me, would it?

HANCOCK'S HALF HOUR (radio), series five, episode ten

'THE ELECTION CANDIDATE'
First broadcast: Tuesday 25 March 1958

TONY: You come in here at seven-thirty in the morning and ask for
    breakfast. I suppose you've been out all night again?
SIDNEY: Yeah.
TONY: What have you been doing?
SIDNEY: Working. Do you mind if I put me sack down?

    EFFECTS: (Heavy clank)

SIDNEY: Now, what you got, I'm starving.
TONY: What's in that sack?
SIDNEY: Nothing. A few odds and ends, that's all.
TONY: Show me.

    EFFECTS: (Clinking of metal)

TONY: Odds and ends. Three hundredweight of assorted lead here.
    Sawn-off rain-water pipes. A few curly bits from under somebody's
    sink, all these bits of gas pipe... there won't be a lamp in the High
    Street working tonight.
SIDNEY: I found it all lying on a waste dump down the road.
TONY: No you didn't. You've been creeping around Cheam all night with a
    hacksaw. Every night it's the same. Lead one week, brass the next week,
    copper the next week... this town will fall to bits if you don't turn it in.
SIDNEY: No it won't, they're just odd bits sticking out of walls, I just trim
    'em down a bit.
TONY: You can't go around chopping bits of rain-water pipes off, it's not
    like pruning trees.

SIDNEY: Are you going to give me any breakfast or not? I can pay for it. Here you are, two feet of waste pipe.

EFFECTS: (Clonk)

Tony: Get that off my table.

SIDNEY: That's worth seven and a tanner, that bit.

TONY: I don't care how much it's worth, get it off the table, you come in here trying to barter with your night's pickings, two foot of pipe for some cornflakes and pease pudding, whatever next? It's worth two curly bits and a section of guttering any time, that is.

HANCOCK'S HALF HOUR (TV), series three, episode eleven

'THERE'S AN AIRFIELD AT THE BOTTOM OF MY GARDEN'
First broadcast: Monday 16 December 1957

(In the offices of Sidney James & Co, Estate Agents. An old couple are sitting in front of Sid's desk.)

SID: Look, there's nothing I can do. It's your own fault. You should always have your house insured. You should have insured it against falling into the sea.

OLD MAN: It fell in before we could get there. It's your fault. When you sold it to us, you said it was supposed to be hanging over the cliff. You said it was built that way.

SID: So it was – there was nothing wrong with the house, it was the cliff that wasn't very good.

As Galton and Simpson explored Sid's character, his instinct for a quiet life and an easy ride became as important as his dodgy deals. Here's Sid, driven out of his wits by Hancock's efforts to save money:

HANCOCK'S HALF HOUR (TV), fifth series, episode one

'THE ECONOMY DRIVE'
First broadcast: Friday 25 September 1959

SIDNEY: What a miserable existence this is. You might as well be dead. *(Starts pacing up and down)* No fire, no telly, no fags, nothing to eat, nothing to drink, go to bed as soon as it gets dark, get up as soon as it gets light, don't put the lights on, don't put the fire on, don't turn the tap on, watered-down milk... *(SIDNEY gradually gets worked up. TONY just sits and stares at him.)* Stale bread, it's worse than prison, I can't stand it much longer, do you hear? I can't stand it much longer, halfpenny here, penny there, can't have this, can't have that, don't do this, don't do that, I can't live like this, do you understand, I can't live like this, it's driving me mad, mad, mad, MAD!

TONY: Don't walk up and down, it wears the carpet out.

'We used to ask Sid if he ever thought of starring in a show himself,' said Alan. 'And he insisted, "Not me, mate. Second banana, thank you very much. I don't need that pressure, the world on my shoulders. I like to do my job, go home and let the other fellow take the praise... and all the rest that goes with it."'

'I don't think anyone disliked Sid,' Ray said simply. 'He was one of the most likeable characters in the theatrical world.'

HANCOCK'S HALF HOUR (TV), fifth series, episode two

'THE TWO MURDERERS'
First broadcast: Friday 2 October 1959

(SIDNEY comes in. Looks all round him, suspiciously.)

SIDNEY: Did you have a bird in here?

TONY: That was a very cruel remark if ever I've heard one. You are fully aware of my lack of success with the ladies. There hasn't been a bird in here since Dolly Clackett got married. I shall never forgive her. On the very Saturday when I lashed out – to please her, mark you – one hundred and twenty pounds on an Italian scooter and two skid lids. And you talk about having birds in here. I wouldn't give them houseroom.

SIDNEY: You had the curtains drawn.

TONY: Yes... well... you know how sensitive I am. I just don't like people looking in.

SIDNEY: You were counting your money, weren't you?

TONY: I was not.

SIDNEY: Don't give me that old codswallop, you were counting your money. It's your annual count-up.

TONY: I haven't got any money. I'm a very poor man.

SIDNEY: You've got a fortune stacked away here somewhere. I just don't know where you keep it, that's all.

TONY: And you won't find out either.

SIDNEY: Oh, so you admit it.

TONY: I don't admit anything.

SIDNEY: All right, have it your own way. But listen to me, I have got the hottest business proposition to put to you that has come my way in years.

TONY: No.

SIDNEY: You haven't even heard it yet.

TONY: I don't care. Not a penny.

SIDNEY: But this is a racing certainty.

TONY: They always are.

SIDNEY: Never like this, never like this. This is the chance of a lifetime. A genuine, straightforward, one hundred per cent honest business investment. I can't miss. Are you interested?

TONY: No.

SIDNEY: You fool. You short-sighted fool. You've always been telling me to get an honest business, and this is it. Let me tell you about it. I have made a takeover bid for the most successful shop in Cheam High Street.

TONY: Not the undertakers?

SIDNEY: No, no. All right, the second most successful. Mabel's Fish and Chip Parlour.

TONY: Mabel's Fish and Chip Parlour? Successful? She hasn't got through that bundle of newspapers I sold her last year yet.

SIDNEY: No, you've got it wrong, she's making a bomb. I've seen the books.

TONY: She's cooked them, and that's the only thing she is cooking, believe me.

SIDNEY: All right, that doesn't matter, it's the ideas I've got for it. I've got plans. I'm going to do it up like a coffee bar. I'm having the whole shop done out like an underwater cavern. Tables shaped like big oyster shells… seaweed hanging up the walls… fishing nets, plastic shrimps hanging from the ceiling, and waitresses done up like mermaids, hopping round the tables, see…

TONY: And I suppose you'll have me sitting in a big chair with a long beard, holding a trident.

SIDNEY: I'll clean up. Plate of fish and chips, bread and butter and a pickled onion, four and a tanner. It could be a household name in Cheam… 'El Fish and Chipo'. Look, whoever goes into this with me is going to make a small fortune, and I am giving you first refusal.

TONY: All right, then, I refuse.

SIDNEY: Please, Hancock, please, I'm serious about this. I've put everything I've got into it, but I need some more capital.

TONY: I'm sorry, Sid, I see nothing but disaster in this scheme. Save your money, because you're not getting any of mine.

SIDNEY: That's your last word?

TONY: That is my last word.

SIDNEY: You selfish swine. You know how much this means to me, and you won't lift a finger to help me. I'll remember this, Hancock. You let me down in my hour of need.

TONY: Oh, don't go maudlin.

Tony Hancock campaigned to have the shows pre-recorded, despite the expense of television tapes. In a 1958 article for *Television Annual* he explained his reasons: 'If the programme does not click on the night, though it may have been effective at rehearsal, well – the opportunity to go back and make it click has gone forever. For this reason, I favour the pre-filming of comedy shows. Immediately one says this, one raises that criticism of using "canned" shows as though these were somehow second-hand... [But] if a strived-for effect does not come off properly in filming, you can reshoot... So take me "canned". I think you will get a better return for your viewing time and licence money!'

All of the last three series survive on film because of Hancock's determination to switch to canned.

HANCOCK'S HALF HOUR (TV), fifth series, episode six

'THE CRUISE'
First broadcast: Friday 30 October 1959

(*TONY in a deckchair, alone, on a cruise ship in the Mediterranean. He is reading. A woman, played by HATTIE JACQUES, enters.*)

HATTIE: Hallo, are you on your own?

TONY: Yes thank you. Hoppit.

HATTIE: Would you like me to sit and talk with you?

TONY: No.

HATTIE: I've noticed you. Always on your own, aren't you?

TONY: Yes thank you.

HATTIE: Don't join in anything, do you?

TONY: I enjoy being on my own.

HATTIE: Are you an eccentric?

TONY: No I am not. Leave me alone.

HATTIE: Always reading, aren't you? You'll hurt your eyes, you will.

TONY: I'll hurt yours in a minute. Run along, there's a good girl. There's a bathing beauty competition up the road, go on.

HATTIE: Oooh, you're a cheeky one, you are. What cabin are you in?

TONY: Never you mind.

HATTIE: Well, I thought, we're both on our own, no responsibilities, and we're about the same age.

TONY: I beg your pardon, I resent that.

HATTIE: Something happens to me when I get on a boat.

TONY: Well, it won't happen this time, I assure you.

HATTIE: Cabin 23, B deck.

TONY: What?

HATTIE: No. Cabin 23, B deck.

TONY: How very uninteresting. Do you mind?

HATTIE: About half past twelve, then. I'll meet you under the lifeboat.

TONY: Yes. If I'm not there by sunrise, don't wait.

HATTIE: Oooh… I've been looking forward to this trip… meeting someone like you… you fascinate me, you do.

TONY: Hard luck.

HATTIE: Quiet… dignified… reserved… good-looking in a portly kind of way. Is that your technique then?

TONY: Will you please leave me alone, madam!

HATTIE: That's what I mean… see… hard to get… still, we've got another ten days yet… you'll come round… they always do. Bye bye… cheeky.

(She leaves)

TONY: Cor, stone me… what a fiasco. Two hundred birds on board and she's the only one who goes berserk.

'Galton and Simpson played with language,' said Andrew Collins, who co-wrote the twenty-first-century sitcom *Not Going Out*. 'If someone asked you what Hancock's catchphrase was, there is no answer. "Cor, stone me!" feels like the sort of thing he'd say a lot, but it's not a catchphrase. That's how subtle and nuanced he is: his attitude, his politics, his weaknesses, his vanities, his prejudices, his inconsistencies – these are all the creation of Galton and Simpson. The punchline wasn't the be-all and end-all. The turn of phrase was equally important, and equally funny. The situations were often absurd but their language was always rooted in believable vernacular.'

Despite the insistence of colleagues such as Eric Sykes that television demanded a different kind of writing from radio, Ray and Alan continued to concentrate on dialogue, rather than working physical 'business' and sight gags into the scripts: 'When you have a good situation or a good storyline,' Ray explained, 'the vision takes care of itself. Once we got to the set on a Friday, for the rehearsals, that was when we might see the opportunity for visual jokes and moves, and we could suggest them then.'

'It all evolves, of course,' Alan said. 'You learn as you go along. Towards the end of the series, we were putting in little visual bits, mimes, which Tony loved doing. I remember particularly one in the library where he had to keep quiet – he was being shushed all the time, so he played out the plot of a book in mime, and it worked very well. We learnt by doing it, really, which is the story of our career – when we started, we were virtually paid to learn, which you don't get these days.'

HANCOCK'S HALF HOUR (TV), sixth series, episode two

'THE MISSING PAGE'
First broadcast: Friday 11 March 1960

TONY: Well, you see, this bird is in the room with this bloke when her husband walks in and…

(The readers in the library turn and shush them. TONY now mimes the action of the book to SID, with SID reacting appropriately. TONY describes the girl's shape. Then a man with big shoulders. Does the man kissing her passionately. Jumps back. Opens a door. Does melodramatic step into the room as the husband with the melodramatic 'ha-ha!' The husband has a terrific fight with the lover. Strangling one another, etc. Finally the husband draws a gun and shoots the lover several times. Does the lover doing the death scene. Kicks the body. Jumps on it. Then does the girl pleading on her knees. He throws her on one side. Has a struggle with the gun. The gun gets forced against her. Goes off. Another big death scene from the girl. She dies. The husband is remorseful. He tries to revive her. Jumps up. Puts hand to ear. Turns round and puts hands up as the police come in the door. Holds out hands for handcuffs. Imitates the judge sitting at the bench. Describes the wig with his hands, bows to three sides of the court. Raps gavel three times. Puts black cap on. Grabs back

of collar to indicate being strung up. By now the LIBRARIAN has come onto the scene and has watched the last half of this pantomime. TONY suddenly realizes he is there and with great embarrassment busies himself collecting some books.)

LIBRARIAN: What do you think you're doing?

TONY: And just what do you mean by that?

LIBRARIAN: This is a library, not the Royal Academy of Dramatic Art. I've been watching you. You've been creating a disturbance ever since you came in here.

TONY: I was merely describing to my friend what his book is about.

LIBRARIAN: We get a thousand people a day in here – supposing they all did it? A thousand people a day in here, gesticulating. We can't have that in a public library.

TONY: I was not gesticulating.

LIBRARIAN: You were gesticulating… and I've had complaints. It's very distracting. You'd better get your books stamped up and leave.

When the next TV series was announced, it was renamed simply *Hancock*, and it did not feature Sid James. The decision was Hancock's alone: his insecurities made him fearful of being seen as half of a double act. But he could not bring himself to tell his friend – that was left to the producer. 'Sid was really shocked and heartbroken to be dropped,' said Ray. Determined not to be trapped in a double act, Tony Hancock wanted the freedom of working on his own. Galton and Simpson, though they were sympathetic towards Sid (and even wrote a series for him – *Citizen James* [1960] – as compensation), rose to the challenge of presenting Hancock without a sparring partner.

'The last series we did, without Sid James, we deliberately made the first script a solo performance: Hancock without anybody, Hancock on his own,' Ray said. 'And we were a bit worried about sending it in to him in case he thought we were taking the piss. But we'd said to ourselves: "All right, Hancock, if you want Sid out and you want to be on your own, you will be on your own." We were waiting in trepidation for him to say, "You bastards, what do you think you're doing? You think you're funny, eh?" But as soon as he'd read the script, he phoned up and said, "Wonderful, wonderful, I just hope I can do it justice."'

HANCOCK, first series, episode one

'HANCOCK ALONE'
First broadcast: Friday 26 May 1961

(We discover TONY lying full length on the bed, which is made. He is fully dressed, staring up at the ceiling, smoking a cigarette. Up against the wall is a pole with a nuclear disarmament sign on the top of it. As he is lying there he starts trying to blow smoke rings. He contorts his face as he blows the smoke out but he doesn't succeed. He takes another puff and this time taps his cheek with his finger as the smoke comes out. This doesn't work either. He takes another draw and tries again, but the same thing happens. He takes another draw, but by now the dog-end is so little he burns his lips. Business trying to take the dog-end out of his mouth. He finally stubs it out in the ashtray, and feels his lips gingerly. He takes the cigarette packet to light another cigarette but it is empty. He tosses it away in irritation.)

(He lies there for a few moments. Yawns. Looks around the room slowly. His feet catch his attention. He wiggles them. He then puts one foot vertically with the heel resting on the bed. Then he puts the other foot on top of it with the heel resting on the toes. He takes the bottom foot out and places it on top of the other one with the heel again resting on the toes. He takes the other one from underneath and repeats the operation. Now his two feet are a couple of feet off the bed, one on top of the other, thus causing a strain on his stomach muscles. These give way and his feet collapse on the bed. He rubs his stomach muscles and winces.)

TONY: Getting old.

Without any other actors to play against, Hancock talks to himself:

TONY: I wonder if the milkman's been yet. I haven't heard him. Only I'd like a cup of tea. A – cup – of – tea.

(Now his teeth are showing after the word 'tea'. He has a look at his teeth in the mirror.)

I'll have to stop smoking.

(He fingers one of his front teeth)

Is that loose… or is it my fingers going in and out? I'll have to get that seen to.

(Studies his teeth again)

Not a bad set of choppers really. There's a good few bites left in them yet. It's funny, all the girls have said that. You've got a good set of teeth. They've all said that.

(Smiles with his teeth clenched)

Yes, there's no sweet tooth decay there, mate. I wonder which one's the bicuspid. I've been meaning to find that out for years.

(He tries out the word to savour the sound of it)

Bicuspid. It's a funny word, that is. Bi-cus-pid.

(He says it with different inflections)

Bicuspid. By Cuspid, he's a handsome devil, Sir George.

(Mocking laugh)

Bicuspid. I suppose it's Latin. Bi, meaning two. One each side. Cus… meaning… to swear, I expect… and pid. Pid. I should think that's Greek. Greek for teeth, I should think. That's it then. Bicuspid. Two swearing teeth. Sounds reasonable. I bet I'm not far out anyway.

Even when the phone rings, it's a wrong number. Tony starts chatting to the woman on the other end, hears that she's been stood up by her boyfriend, Fred, and invites her on a date. For a short time his loneliness lifts, as he prepares to go out – and then the phone rings again:

(TONY rushes over and picks up the receiver)

TONY: *(Lazy posh)* Hallo, Earl's Court 3927. The Hancock residence. Mr Hancock? I'll see whether he's at home. Who? Oh Joyce, I'm getting ready. Cancelled? What do you mean, cancelled? I've spent hours getting ready… that is, well that's nice, you might have told me… well earlier then. What am I going to do? I was looking forward to this, I cancelled all my other engagements. What about you, where are you going… perhaps we could… you've found Fred. Oh. Yes, well, I hope you have a nice time. Oh, don't worry about me. I probably would have been bored anyway. No, I'm all right, I've got plenty to do. Lonely? No, no, I like being on my own. I prefer being on my own, I'm just not a gregarious person. Hang on.

(He stands. Picks up dictionary and finds 'gregarious'.)

Hallo? Living in flocks or communities, fond of company, to herd together. No, don't you worry about me, there's something on the Third Programme I want to listen to anyway. It's a talk on Etruscan vases. No, no, think no more of it. Yes, all right, some other time. Of course. Any time, any time.

(He slams the phone down)

Stupid women. Why do they phone in the first place? Why don't they leave you alone?

(Throws himself back on the bed in disgust. Picks up the cigarette packet, opens it. Still nothing in it. Throws it away again.)

(Mimics her) Sorry, it's cancelled. Hope you won't be lonely.

(Normal voice, piqued) Leopardskin tights at her age, what must she look like? I bet she was horrible. She sounded a right crone. That was a lucky escape, I nearly got sucked into a social whirlpool there... diverted from my lofty ideals into a life of debauchery. The fleshpots of West London have been cheated of another victim. Eve has proffered the apple and Adam has slung it right back at her. That'll make a good play... I'll start on that in the morning.

Producer Duncan Wood held Hancock in awe for his ability to convey emotions through flickers of expression. In a BBC interview thirty years later, he said: 'When you went into a close-up on camera, you could see his mind working before he uttered the next sentence... the laugh would frequently come on the close-up before he said the line. You could see it running through his mind: "This man's a bloody idiot, and I'm going to tell him so." It's a marvellous ability to have.'

Galton and Simpson played constantly to Hancock's strengths, fashioning dialogue that gave Hancock the opportunity to telegraph his emotions before he delivered the lines. In the next episode, they cast Hancock as a radio actor – but this was not a return to the 'behind-the-scenes of vaudeville' format. Instead, he was a troublemaker on a rural soap opera. It's a storyline that demonstrates how much more inventive Galton and Simpson could be when they were not hampered by the restrictions of a two-man set-up.

HANCOCK, first series, episode two

'THE BOWMANS'
First broadcast: Friday 2 June 1961

> *(A recording studio, with full cast. TONY walks on mike. He is dressed for the part. Battered old hat, old coat. Corduroys with a strap above his knees. A knobbly stick under his arm.)*

TONY: *(Suffolk, singing)* I've got mangel wurzels in my garden, I've got mangel wurzels in my shed... I've got mangel wurzels in my bathroom and a mangel wurzel for a head.

> *(The actors look puzzled at their scripts at this. An actor playing the dog comes on yapping and snarling.)*

TONY: Down boy, get down, down.
DOG MAN: *(The dog yaps)*
TONY: Back, you black-hearted creature, get down.
DOG MAN: *(The dog snarls ferociously)*
TONY: Get down afore I fetches my stick across you. *(He and the dog are ready to have a go at each other)* Go on, lie down there.

> *(The producer waves frantically at TONY. TONY points to the dog and mouths, 'It's him.')*

...

ANNOUNCER: You have been listening to 'The Bowmans', an everyday story of simple folk. The News and Radio Newsreel follows in a few moments.

> *(The 'on the air' light goes out. The actors relax. They turn on TONY.)*

DAN BOWMAN: *(Actor's own voice)* What do you think you're playing at? Are you trying to ruin the programme?
TONY: It wasn't my fault, it was him, the dog, barking where he wasn't supposed to, he was trying to drown me. I know what he's up to.
DOG MAN: I did not, I barked where I was supposed to bark.
TONY: You did not. It's got down here three yelps and a growl. You were a-barking and a-snarling all over the place. I've never seen such a disgraceful exhibition of drunkenness in all my professional career.
MRS BOWMAN: *(She has a very educated voice in real life)* You shouldn't have poked him with that stick.

TONY: You keep out of this, madam, I am the oldest member of this community, let's have a little respect.

MRS BOWMAN: You may be the oldest member of the village, Mr Hancock, but you are not the oldest member of the cast. Dan and I... that is, Mr Osmington and I were the two originals, you were brought in after us, and you can be taken out.

TONY: What do you mean by that? I've been in this show for five years, and I've got the biggest fan mail of all of you. Twenty-two million people sit by their radio sets at a quarter to seven every night, just waiting to have a giggle at the antics old Joshua gets up to. I carry this programme, it's only me and my bits of earthy philosophy, and my jokes, and my little rhymes, that's what keeps them glued to the set, mate, that's what they're waiting for. Not you moaning all round the house about the weather and your daughter and your rock cakes.

...

TONY: *(Flipping through the script)* Here... what's this? Joshua falls in the threshing machine.

PRODUCER: Oh yes, I've been meaning to have a word with you about that.

TONY: I should think so too.

PRODUCER: Yes, he falls in the machine and is rushed off to hospital.

TONY: Oh. I see. A nice touch of human interest. Yes, old Joshua in hospital, what a good idea. I see I'm on the danger list... hovering between life and death. We could keep this going for months, will he or won't he, how's old Joshua getting on, fighting for his life, twenty million people crying their eyes out, slowly he pulls through, courageous old Joshua, jokes with the doctors, his first day up, chasing the nurses round the ward, until six months later he emerges triumphant from the hospital, stronger than ever.

PRODUCER: Er, well, no. He dies on Tuesday night.

TONY: He dies.

PRODUCER: Without regaining consciousness.

TONY: You must be raving mad. Surely you don't imagine the public are going to stand for this? There'll be a shouting mob outside Broadcasting House slinging bricks through the windows.

...

TONY: It's the writers. They don't know what they're doing. It's the way they've been portraying me. What can I do with the rubbish they've been giving me to say? They've made me unsympathetic. Last week I kicked the dog three times.

PRODUCER: That wasn't in the script.

TONY: Well, no. But he asked for it, shoving in yaps where there weren't any.

Out of work, Tony talks to himself, a scene that in earlier series would have been a dialogue between Sid and Tony:

TONY: Oh, show business is being run by idiots these days. No men of vision left. Oh for the days of the actor manager, own my own theatre, and to all of them… *(puts thumb on nose)* They don't want talent these days, they just want a pretty face. Not that I don't come under that category as well. I'm not a pretty-boy, I agree… Oh, I think I'll turn acting in. Go and live on a barge. It's a facile life anyway. *(Posh voice)* Hello, darling, caught the show last night, loved it, you were absolutely divine. Load of old rubbish. I'll be a missionary, I think. Help the under-privileged people of the world. I hear it pays quite well too, or shall I do away with myself…

The theme of being trapped, central to Galton and Simpson's concept of situation comedy, is played out literally in 'The Lift'. It shows the character at his most irritating and contumacious, and as he drags the other characters into the chaos of his life, there is a sense that they will eventually escape from him… but he can never escape from himself.

HANCOCK, first series, episode four

'THE LIFT'
First broadcast: Friday 16 June 1961

(A girl comes round the corner of the corridor. She presses the button. Stands back and looks at indicator. Goes and stands with the rest of the group. TONY edges up to her.)

TONY: They certainly takes their time, these liftmen, don't they?

GIRL: *(No reaction)*

TONY: They've improved the lifts, but they haven't improved the liftmen, have they?

GIRL: *(No reaction)*

TONY: That's progress for you.

(PAUSE)

TONY: That's the way it goes.

(PAUSE)

TONY: Yes indeed.

(She gets fed up: looks at her watch. Presses lift button again. Stands back to see indicator. Returns to group – stands further away from TONY. TONY reacts. A young man comes round corner. Goes up to group and stands between TONY and girl. TONY reacts. The young man edges up to girl. He looks her up and down. By now TONY has moved in the other side of her and is eyeing the young man with dislike.)

PRODUCER: *(To girl)* Hallo, I haven't noticed you on this floor before. Are you a visitor or do you work for the old firm?
SECRETARY: I'm a secretary: I only started this week.
PRODUCER: Oh, Crichton's the name, producer: *Up You Go, Let's Go Dancing* and *Thursday Magazine.*

(TONY reacts in disgust; the girl, however, is impressed)

SECRETARY: Oh, really. *Thursday Magazine* is one of my favourite programmes. I always stay in to watch it.
PRODUCER: *(Modest)* It's a job, it's not bad, fifteen million viewers, not bad, when I took it over it only had five. Perhaps we might have the opportunity of working together sometime.
SECRETARY: Oh, I do hope so.
PRODUCER: *(Moves a fraction closer)* Well, we'll see what we can do, eh?

(She smiles up at him. Shot of TONY, dead niggled.)

PRODUCER: He's taking his time, isn't he? Has anyone pressed the button?
TONY: We all have.
PRODUCER: It doesn't seem to have done much good, does it? Let me have a go.
TONY: He'll come when he's ready; it's no use to keep buzzing him.

(The producer presses the button. Shot of the indicator board: the arrow starts on its arc as the lift comes up.)

SECRETARY: He's coming up.
PRODUCER: *(Cocky)* Yes, I thought he would.

TONY: Well, there's nothing marvellous in that, he didn't know it was your
finger on the button.
PRODUCER: There's no need to take that attitude, old man.
TONY: I'm not taking any attitude, I just don't see how you can stand
there and take the credit for it. It could just as easily have been me
who pressed it, it just happened that he was ready to come up at that
particular time.
PRODUCER: Yes, all right, there's no need to make a song and dance
about it, old man.
TONY: I'm not making a song and dance about it. I just didn't like your
tone of voice, the way you implied that he only comes up because he
knows you're here, and that we are nothing.
PRODUCER: Well, let's forget about it, shall we? As long as he's coming
up, that's all that matters.

*(The young man shrugs his shoulders to the girl, to imply what a
funny man TONY is)*

TONY: Yes, well.

(He lapses into silence. He looks up at the indicator board.)

TONY: Hallo. He's stopped on the fourth floor.
PRODUCER: That's all right, he's picking somebody up.

(Shot of indicator board with the arrow on four)

TONY: Hallo, he's on the move again.

(The arrow goes to three, then to two, and so on to the ground)

TONY: *(Triumphant)* Har, har, he's gone down again, clever dick. I'll say no
more.

The lift arrives, and gets stuck between floors. The attendant blames
Hancock – the machinery is designed to carry eight people, and he was
the ninth one in:

MRS HUMPHRIES: Oh dear, I think I'm going to faint.
TONY: You can't, dear, there's no room.

*(MRS HUMPHRIES puts her hand up to her face, groans, and swoons
up against her husband)*

DOCTOR: Stand back, stand back, I'm a doctor.

TONY: We know you're a doctor, you've mentioned nothing else since you got here. I can't understand you, I don't go around blabbing about what I am.

DOCTOR: I think we've all reached an opinion as to what you are. Now kindly keep quiet.

...

TONY: Of course this is nothing new to an old submarine hand like me. It's just like the old days. Laying on the bottom, engines off, still, silent. Nobody daring to move. Jerry destroyers dashing about upstairs, trying to find us sitting there, sweating, waiting, joined together in a common bond of mutual peril. Yes, it's all too familiar.

VICAR: I thought you said earlier you were in the army.

TONY: Did I? Oh well, yes, I was. I was attached to a Commando unit being transported by submarines to blow up the heavy water plants in Norway. Very tricky stuff, heavy water... very tricky. Have you ever handled it?

VICAR: No, I can't say I have.

TONY: You don't want to. Very tricky stuff. A cupful of that in your font, blow the roof off it would. Dear oh dear, it's hot in here, isn't it? Stuffy.

VICAR: Yes, it's in the air.

TONY: Yes. Too many people breathing too little air. It's a funny thing, air. You can't see it, you can't touch it, you can't smell it, but it's there. It's just as well we've got it all around us. I mean, supposing you had to carry your own supply round with you... when you were born, they said, 'There you are, there's your lot, drag that around with you.' You'd have to have something the size of the Albert Hall. You'd have to have great wide streets and big doorways to get in and out of. It wouldn't work. I reckon that ants would have taken over by now.

It is impossible to overstate the influence of Galton and Simpson on British TV comedy: 'They were the first writers, outside of the *Monty Python* team, that I knew by name,' said broadcaster and writer Andrew Collins. 'I watched an awful lot of sitcoms as a boy – I grew up on *Dad's Army, Are You Being Served?*, *Some Mothers Do 'Ave 'Em* and *Love Thy Neighbour* – but it was *Hancock's Half Hour* that actually got me interested in the craft of writing. Although it was Hancock himself I adored, I gradually became more and more interested in the idea that these two other men actually wrote the words he said. My favourite lines from Hancock were not the obvious ones – "very nearly an armful" – but more esoteric ones, such as, "Life would be intolerable if we knew everything" (from the cup-of-tea-and-a-biscuit scene in "The Blood Donor") and, "Is that tooth loose… or is it my fingers going in and out?" from "Hancock Alone".What I admired about them was often their brevity, their clarity or the fact that they were not punchlines to set-ups.'

HANCOCK, first series, episode five

'THE BLOOD DONOR'
First broadcast: Friday 23 June 1961

TONY: *(Lying back, fully dressed, on a hospital bed in the recovery area)* It's a funny thing, this blood business.

MAN: Well, I suppose it is.

TONY: It all looks the same and yet… it's all different. Yes, it's very funny stuff, blood.

MAN: Yes. I don't know where we'd be without it.

TONY: That's true. That's very true. Where would we be without it? Yes, it's very important, blood. It circulates right round the body, you know.

MAN: Yes, so I believe.

TONY: Yes, it starts at the heart, it gets pumped right round, goes through the lungs, back into the heart, and round it goes again.

MAN: What for?

TONY: What for. Well, it speaks for itself, doesn't it? I mean, the heart's got to have something to pump round… there's no point in it banging away all day long for no reason at all.

MAN: Well, why have a heart then?

TONY: Well, if you didn't, the blood wouldn't go round, would it? It'd all stay in one place. When you stood up, it'd all sink to the bottom of your legs. It'd be very uncomfortable, wouldn't it? It'd feel like you were walking around with a bootful of water. Your heart saves you having to keep standing on your head and jumping about to keep it moving. It does it for you.

MAN: But I still don't see what good blood is, though.

TONY: Well… your body's full of veins, isn't it?

MAN: Yes.

TONY: Well, you've got to fill them up with something, haven't you?

MAN: Ah yes, I see. Are you a doctor then?

TONY: Well no, not really. I never really bothered.

MAN: Oh.

TONY: Anything else troubling you, any aches and pains?

MAN: No, no. I'm all right.

TONY: Ah well, that's the main thing, isn't it? As long as you've got your health.

MAN: Nothing else matters really, does it?

TONY: No. And the funny thing is, you know, you never appreciate it until you haven't got it any more.

MAN: Yes, some people take their health for granted, don't they?

TONY: Do you know, that could have been me talking. You took the words right out of my mouth. Yes, if you haven't got your health, you haven't got anything.

MAN: Mind you, they do some marvellous things these days.

TOY: Oh yes, it's advanced a lot, medical science. I'm glad they slung away the leeches. That was the turning point. I mean, look at the things they can do these days. New blood, plastic bones, false teeth, glasses, wigs... do you know, there's some people walking around with hardly anything they started out with.

MAN: Yes, what would we do without doctors, eh?

TONY: *(Making a point)* Or, conversely, what would they do without us?

MAN: That's true. That's very shrewd.

TONY: But the main thing is... look after yourself.

MAN: You look after your body and your body will look after you.

TONY: That's very wise. Of course, the Greeks, they knew all this years ago.

MAN: Did they really?

TONY: Oh yes, very advanced people the Greeks were. They had hot and cold water and drains, always washing themselves they were. Of course it all got lost in the wars.

MAN: When Mussolini moved in.

TONY: No, no, before him. They taught it to the Romans, then the Romans came over here...

MAN: Well, of course, you can always learn from other people.

TONY: Of course you can. That's why I'm in favour of the Common Market. You can't ignore the rest of the world.

MAN: That's true. That's very true.

TONY: You can't go through life with your head buried in the sand.

MAN: No man is an island.

TONY: You're right there! I agree. Necessity is the mother of invention.

MAN: It certainly is. Life would be intolerable if we knew everything.

TONY: I should say it would. My goodness yes. Let the shipwrecks of others be your sea marks.

MAN: For things unknown there is no desire.

TONY: Well exactly. A bird in the hand is worth two in the bush.

MAN: It is indeed.

TONY: Do you like winegums?

MAN: Thank you very much.

TONY: Don't take the black one.

MAN: No, all right. Of course they do a tube with all black ones now, you know.

TONY: I know but you can't always get them.

MAN: Well, that's the way it goes.

TONY: Still, as long as we've got our health.

MAN: Yes, that's the main thing.

TONY: Yes, that's the main thing. Ah yes. Yes indeed.

MAN: Well, I think I'm ready now.

TONY: Oh, you're off then.

MAN: Yes, out into the big world.

TONY: Do you live far?

MAN: Just up the road.

TONY: You'll get a bus, then, will you?

MAN: No, I think I'll walk.

TONY: You haven't got far to go, then?

MAN: No, just up the road.

TONY: Oh well, it's not worth it then, is it?

MAN: No, not really.

TONY: Oh… well, I'll say cheerio then.

MAN: Yes, cheerio. Look after yourself.

TONY: Yes, and you.

MAN: I will.

TONY: Don't do anything I wouldn't do, will you? *(Laughs)*

MAN: I won't. Well, cheerio then.

TONY: Cheerio.

(The man leaves)

TONY: Nice man, that, a very nice man. Very intelligent. Good conversationalist… cut above the type you meet down the pub… very nice man. *(Feels in his pocket)* He's walked off with my winegums. I only broke them open for him. Oh what's the use! If you can't trust blood donors, who can you trust? *(Calls)* Nurse, what about some tea down here, you've had my blood, it's not asking for much really. And two spoonfuls of brown sugar… dear oh dear…

The man who took his winegums was Hugh Lloyd, a *Hancock* regular who was often his partner in those exchanges of microscopic small talk.

Hancock's conversation could be achingly banal, but when he was alone, his monologues became flights of the ludicrous and whimsical... or bitter litanies of self-reproach, such as this valediction from the final episode of the series:

HANCOCK, first series, episode six

'TAKING A WIFE'
First broadcast: Friday 30 June 1961

> *(TONY's flat. We discover him looking gloomily out of the window. He stands, looking out for a time, and collapses despondently on the bed.)*

TONY: Oh, the world's gone mad. We've been taken over by the advertisers, that's the trouble. We've been brainwashed. By packets of detergent. That's a good phrase: we've been brainwashed by packets of detergent. I'll come out with that down the coffee bar tomorrow night. We've all got shining white brains. Don't get left behind with a Brand X brain. Four-figure men have their brains washed by the new blue whitener. Are you unsuccessful with women, does the girl of your dreams go out with other men? It's because you're wearing the wrong socks. And we accept all this. If you haven't got your hair glued down with great handfuls of jollop, the birds walk right past you. The board of directors turn round and gasp with admiration as you walk in with your seven-guinea hand-cut suit. *(Aside)* 'Mark that boy down for promotion, just the sort of man we want for our new export branch.' So he buys a box of chocolates and gets married, drinks a cup of hot chocolate every night so he won't lose his job, takes pills when he's over forty so he can mow his lawn quicker than the bloke next door. Well, good luck to him. It's not for me, I don't do any of those things, and look at me. Nothing.

(He gets up and goes over to the wardrobe mirror)

Look at you. Thirty-five years old, over the hump, and what have you achieved? What have you achieved? Two abandoned plays, three lay-downs in Whitehall, a couple of marches and a punch-up with the Empire Loyalists. This Is Your Life. A slim volume indeed. What happened to you? What went wrong? What happened to those dreams you had when you were sixteen? Prime Minister, remember? At twenty-three? Hancock the Younger? What happened? I'll tell you what happened. You went down the billiard hall too much. That's no training for a prime minister. When you're under fire in the Commons over your foreign policy, it's no good saying, 'Ah, but does the Honourable Member for Bournemouth know how to screw the cue ball back on the black after being snookered behind the baulk line?' No, you lost your chance, my old son. You have contributed absolutely nothing to this life. It's been a complete waste of time you being here at all. No plaque for you in Westminster Abbey. The best you can hope for is a few daffodils in a jam jar. A rough-hewn stone bearing the legend, 'He came, and he went. And in between, nothing.' Nobody'll even notice you're not here. About a year afterwards, somebody might say down the pub, 'Here, where's Hancock, I haven't seen him around lately.' 'He's dead.' 'Oh, is he?' Then there'll be threepence in the RAF Benevolent Fund and the darts'll be out. A right *raison d'être* that is.

(He turns away from the mirror and wanders around)

No one will ever know I existed. Nothing to leave behind me, nothing to pass on, nobody to mourn me. That's the bitterest blow of all. But if I had a son, I could teach him, guide him, tell him where I went wrong. Then the name of Hancock would mean something. I'd be remembered then. The old portrait in the picture gallery. 'Who's that old cove?' 'Oh, that's Anthony Hancock, Julian's father.' 'Oh, what a remarkable looking chap.' 'Yes, he was the one who started it all, he'll never be forgotten.' Yes, Julian. Julian Hancock. Or... Simon. Arbuthnot. Bertrand. No, they'll call him Bert. Bert Hancock. Sounds like a house demolisher. Watch it come down, Bert Hancock. Yes, that's the answer, a son. And that means marriage. Well – that's it then.

And that *was* it. Tony Hancock would never perform a Galton and Simpson script on TV or radio again.

7 Cinematic Hancock

I n 1961, *The Rebel* took Galton and Simpson to the movies and gave Hancock his first starring role in the cinema. He had been waiting a long time: the British film industry was at its peak, making international stars of comedians such as Terry-Thomas and Peter Sellers, but the scripts offered to Hancock had never seemed to fit him. When he was approached by the Associated British Picture Corporation at the end of the fifties and a four-picture deal was mooted, the biggest box-office success of the year was *Carry on Nurse* (which co-starred Kenneth Williams and Hattie Jacques). Tony Hancock looked like a certainty for cinema stardom, if only the right script could be found.

Galton and Simpson had never tackled a film script before, and the storyline reflects the journey Hancock's TV persona was making: he begins in a dingy bedsit, makes his escape to a foreign city, wins acclaim and fortune, and finds himself far out of his depth among multi-millionaires and movie stars. *The Rebel* also marked the first time that Ray and Alan collaborated with Hancock on a script: they spent a week thrashing out the plot with him at his flat. The producer, W. A. Whittaker, encouraged them to use 'jeopardy' as a theme – adding layers of danger to the scenario. What begins as an innocent misunderstanding becomes an art fraud that could see Hancock jailed or even killed.

These structural challenges were very different to the problems they faced with every TV script, where the situation had to be set up, developed and resolved in half an hour. A shortage of ideas, however, was not a problem: more than an hour's material had to be cut from the first draft. 'The one fault about our work was that, although we were economical with words in every line, our scripts were always too long,' said Ray. 'We were very reluctant to lose good lines, but when you overwrite, they have to go, one way or another.'

The film had a mixed reception: in England, the *Times* called it a 'gratifying success', but in America, where it was distributed under the off-putting title *Call Me Genius*, the *New York Times* accused Hancock of 'a clumsy pretence of being funny'.

'*The Rebel* is now considered much more favourably than it was at the time, as a satire on the art world,' Alan said. 'At the Royal College of Art, we are told it's regarded as a classic. We have heard Lucian Freud said, supposedly, that it's the best art film ever made. It's very flattering to think that Lucian Freud is taking the mickey out of you!'

THE REBEL (film)

UK release: Thursday 7 March 1961

TONY: *(Surveying his masterpiece, the crouching figure of a grotesque woman, crudely hacked from concrete)* Oh, you temptress. Oh, you voluptuous Jezebel. My Aphrodite. What carnal desires did you stir in the breasts of helpless men? If ever a devil was born without a pair of horns, it was you, Jezebel! It was you. Cor, I've got a winner here, mate. Now, I think we'll just have a couple of chips off the old hooter, eh? You'd like that, wouldn't you? *(Winks)* Good. *(Moves ladder to the sculpture, climbs up and sorts through tool bag)* Let's see now, what have we got? That's it now. *(Chips at face, chuckles)* Don't worry, it's coming, coming beautifully now. A bit off the old bridge of the nose there. *(Steps back)* Nearly finished, my beauty. *(Sits on bed)* Soon you'll be ready to go out into the world and drive men mad with desire. I created you! I'm your master! *(Laughs maniacally)* Cor dear, I nearly went off again, I need some air. *(Runs to window)* I dunno though. *(To Aphrodite)* I think we'll risk it. *(Opens window and goes back to sculpture)* Now then. *(He starts hammering again. Outside, MRS CREVATTE, who is scrubbing the doorstep, looks up at the noise.)*

TONY: Yes, little bit more off the old choppers, I fancy. What do you want, gas or cocaine? Ho ho, we have some laughs, don't we? *(His chisel slips, knocking out a tooth. TONY reaches into the mouth.)* Oh dear. I think she's swallowed it. Never mind, dear, we'll have a plate put in there, nobody'll notice.

(MRS CREVATTE marches upstairs)

MRS CREVATTE: Mr Hancock. *(Bangs on door)* Mr Hancock.
TONY: Hallo, the barbarians are at the gate of Rome.
MRS CREVATTE: Mr Hancock!
TONY: All right, I'm coming.

MRS CREVATTE: Mr Hancock! Mr Hancock!

TONY: *(Opening door)* What?

MRS CREVATTE: Mr Hancock, you're hammering again.

TONY: I know I'm hammering again. Turbanned fool. *(He tries to close the door, but MRS CREVATTE blocks it)*

MRS CREVATTE: Don't be rude. What are you hammering? You know I don't allow alterations to my property.

TONY: I'm well aware of that. This dosshouse hasn't been touched since about 1850. You're waiting for a grant from the National Trust, aren't you? Now go on, push off. I'm busy.

MRS CREVATTE: I don't want any lip. I demand to know what you're hammering. This is a respectable guesthouse. I've got a right to know what's going on in my own rooms.

TONY: What I do in my room is no concern of yours. I pay my rent.

MRS CREVATTE: Only if I sit outside your door. What about this week's for a start? You let me in, pay me my rent.

TONY: You stay here. I'll get it. *(He tries to shut the door but MRS CREVATTE forces her way in)*

TONY: See? Nosy! There's nothing here.

MRS CREVATTE: *(Pointing to bedroom)* What's in there?

TONY: Nothing! You keep out of there.

(MRS CREVATTE bursts into the bedroom)

MRS CREVATTE: Oooh! Wassat?

TONY: What's what?

MRS CREVATTE: That! That great ugly thing here.

TONY: Great ugly thing? That is Aphrodite at the water hole.

MRS CREVATTE: What's it doing in here? Get it out of my house! Get it out of my house!

TONY: It's not doing any harm, it's a work of art – look, she's beautiful.

MRS CREVATTE: I will not have these great hulking lumps of stone in my apartment. A flaming cheek! She's right above my bed, she is. Supposing she fell through the floor?

TONY: Sometimes I wish… Look, Mrs Crevatte.

MRS CREVATTE: How did you get it up here in the first place?

TONY: I brought it up the stairs. It's in 15 bits held together with iron rods. I got them from a breaker's yard. The head is the foundation stone from the Dog and Duck up the road, and the left leg's a bit of the old war memorial, and the rest of it is made up of six chunks of town hall, two bits of railway bridge and a lump of the public library.

MRS CREVATTE: It's disgusting. What is it?

TONY: It's a nude.

MRS CREVATTE: It's not nice. It's got no clothes on.

TONY: Well, of course it hasn't got any clothes on! She's a nymph. What's the point of coming up out of a water hole with clothes on? Oh, you're impossible, madam.

MRS CREVATTE: I got no time for naked women without any clothes on. They're lewd.

TONY: My dear good woman. Artists have been painting and sculpting nude women since the beginning of time. Nude modelling is a very respectable profession these days.

MRS CREVATTE: Here! Have you been having naked women in my establishment?

TONY: Of course I haven't! I can't afford thirty bob an hour. I did that from memory. That is women as I see them.

MRS CREVATTE: Oooh. You poor man. Oooh, fancy knocking around with women like that — I wonder what your kids'll look like.

TONY: Look, I am not one of the realist school of art! I am an impressionist.

MRS CREVATTE: Well, it don't impress me. I think it's vile and prurile and I want it out of the house and I want my stepladder back. Look at it. *(She gestures at the paintings around the walls)* It's all a load of miskellaneous rubbish.

TONY: How can you stand there and say that? Here you are, surrounded by a roomful of *objets d'art*, knocked up over the years through torment and self-denial, and you call it miskellaneous rubbish. What do you know about creative arts?

MRS CREVATTE: *(Looking at a painting above the mantelpiece)* What's this horrible thing?

TONY: That is a self-portrait.

MRS CREVATTE: Who of?

TONY: Laurel and Hardy! Who of? Buffoon...

MRS CREVATTE: *(Now studying a painting of flying ducks)* Oooh crumbs, what's this one supposed to be?

TONY: I call that Ducks In Flight.

MRS CREVATTE: I never seen beetroot-coloured ducks before.

TONY: Well, they fly at a fair lick, those ducks. They're up out of the water and away. You just have to whack on whatever you've got on your brush at the time.

(MRS CREVATTE is now straining her neck to study an abstract painting from all angles, including upside-down)

TONY: Hey, what's all this lark? What's all this business for?

MRS CREVATTE: I'm trying to make out what it is.

TONY: What do you mean, you're trying to make out what it is. Surely it's obvious what it is to anybody with the slightest glimmer of imagination. It's a…

MRS CREVATTE: Yes?

TONY: It's… well, what does it matter what it is? It's a design in shapes and colours. Perhaps now you can see what I'm trying to do with my life. Perhaps now you'll begin to appreciate art.

MRS CREVATTE: Yes. Yes, I think I am.

TONY: Ahh!

MRS CREVATTE: Yes, I think I've just about got the hang of it now.

TONY: Well, that's more like it.

MRS CREVATTE: You take that thing over there. *(She gestures at Aphrodite)* If that's not out of my house by tomorrow night and you with it, I'll call the police and have you evicted. Those are my last words. Out, all of it! Turning my house into a rubbish dump. Flaming cheek. *(She exits)*

TONY: *(Muttering)* 'What's that horrible great thing?' 'It's a self-portrait.' 'Who of?' Who of! 'Miskellaneous rubbish!' Uncultured crone! *(Addressing a print of a Van Gogh self-portrait)* Ah, Vince boy. You had the same trouble, didn't you? You went through it, didn't you, mate? Made you cut your ear off. Why do they persecute we great men? Because they're afraid of us, that's why. Well, they haven't seen the last of my work.

(The sculpture of Aphrodite falls through the floor with a tremendous crash. TONY stares down into the hole.)

TONY: Missed her…

After *The Rebel* (1961), Hancock was eager to make another film. He demanded a script that would have appeal in America and beyond. At first he was enthusiastic about a story with echoes of *Kind Hearts and Coronets*, in which he was the hapless heir who obliterates his family fortune. After that, he embraced and then dismissed the tale of a disastrous holiday cruise. Galton and Simpson decided to focus on the elements that had made the solo series of *Hancock* such a triumph, and during six weeks in early 1961 they wrote an entire movie, *The Day Off*, which followed a hapless bus conductor from the moment he woke up, through an escalation of embarrassments, to a heart-breaking climax where his delusions wreck the best chance of love he might ever get.

Hancock loved the script. Then he ditched it, again demanding something 'more international'. Then, in a move that no one had expected, he split with his agent, Beryl Vertue at Associated London Scripts. By implication he was severing the relationship with Ray and Alan, and they never worked together again. 'I suppose there were a few hard feelings at first, but that didn't last long,' Alan said. 'It led directly to the *Comedy Playhouse* series for us, so the timing was right.'

'He was probably the best we ever worked with,' Ray pointed out. 'We worked with a lot of great comedians and wonderful actors, but for sheer comic mastery there was no one to touch Tony.'

Hancock's career went into a long slide, ending in his suicide, aged forty-four, in Sydney, Australia, in June 1968.

The Day Off is a long script. Shot uncut, it would probably run close to three hours. Instead of trimming it, the writers simply consigned it to their archives. The scenes were never plundered for television, and the story was never offered to any other star; fifty years after it was written, *The Day Off* is Galton and Simpson's unseen, unread treasure – the Holy Grail of comedy. During a search for forgotten scripts in the last drawers of the filing cabinets in Ray Galton's cellar, it was found behind a sheaf of paper folders. The binder is a blue-black, hardboard casing with a sprung spine and a leather facing; there is nothing on the cover to indicate what it contains. Its 109 foolscap pages are crammed with single-spaced typing, including full descriptions of scenes and camera angles, as though the whole movie existed in the writers' heads. But there is no cast list because, apart from Tony Hancock, no actor was ever approached for any of the roles.

When the idea was first suggested of including an extract in this compilation, Ray and Alan were doubtful: they hadn't looked at the script in half a century, and were not even sure if it was good enough to be shown to the public.

It's better than good, of course. It's the lost Hancock masterpiece from the same year that Galton and Simpson wrote 'The Blood Donor' and the first episode of *Steptoe and Son*: until now, most film historians have assumed the script must have been half finished when it was abandoned, or perhaps destroyed. In fact, it is polished, complete, multi-layered and, at the end, achingly sad. The following scene gives a flavour, and underlines that when Hancock parted from his writers, their relationship was at its peak:

THE DAY OFF

Film script, 1961, unmade

   (INTERIOR. SUPERMARKET. DAY)

   (The supermarket is full of customers, mostly women, pushing their trolleys round and collecting their goods. TONY walks in past the entrance where the trolleys are kept. An ASSISTANT stops him. She is a pretty girl.)

ASSISTANT: A trolley, sir?

TONY: No, thank you. I only want a tin of beans and some shredded wheat.

ASSISTANT: Still, you'd be more comfortable with a trolley.

TONY: Yes, all right then, thank you. *(He takes a trolley)* Do you have to take a driving test with these?

   (He laughs at his little joke. The ASSISTANT smiles in duty more than amusement.)

TONY: I live on my own, you know. I'm a bachelor.

ASSISTANT: *(Uninterested)* Really.

TONY: Yes, I'm not married. I'm not even engaged. Only some people think I come round here doing the shopping for the wife, but it's for myself, I always look after myself – well, you have to when you're on your own, don't you? I mean, when there's nobody else. No indeed, that's life, if you don't look after yourself, nobody else will.

   (A woman walks past and takes a trolley)

TONY: It's my day off.

ASSISTANT: *Is* it?

TONY: Yes, I have a day off every week. Well, I expect you do too. When's your day off then?

ASSISTANT: This afternoon, it's early closing day.

TONY: This afternoon. That's a coincidence, isn't it? What with me having a day off as well. Both having the day off to ourselves. I, er... was thinking of doing something this afternoon... you know... get a boat up to Hampton Court or something... it's very pretty round there... or I could fit in with your plans.

ASSISTANT: I doubt it, I'm going out with my boyfriend.

TONY: Oh. He has the day off as well.

ASSISTANT: He works here... that's him over there.

(Cut to a shot of a great beefy young man behind the butcher's counter. He is looking over at TONY and the girl, and cutting up a side of beef with rhythmic chops of a great meat axe.)

TONY: Oh, yes, yes. A strapping young man, isn't he? Yes indeed. Well then, I'd better get my beans and my shredded wheat, hadn't I? This won't get the baby washed. *(Raises his hat)* Good morning.

(He wheels his trolley off into the crowd. He dodges about, trying to find the cereal section. He finds it and is confronted with a tremendous selection of different cereals. He picks up two of them and looks on the back to see what the free gifts are.)

(Close-up of the two packets. One is a detective set and one is a spaceman's outfit. He decides on one of them, drops it into his trolley and puts the other one back. He looks around for the baked beans, dodges about trying to find them and has to retrace his steps against the flow of people. He finds the baked beans, takes a tin down and dodges back to his trolley.)

(He sets off to find the exit, when his eye is taken by a large notice: SPECIAL TODAY. MYSTERY OFFER. TWO FOR 1/9. He wanders over and picks up one of the tins. There is no label on it. He puts it up to his ear and shakes it. Shrugs. Takes another tin and drops it into his trolley.)

(Straight away his eye is caught by another notice: SPECIAL TODAY. SPAGHETTI IN TOMATO SAUCE WITH MEATBALLS. 1/10 [crossed out] TWO FOR 2/6. TONY reacts as if to say, 'That's not bad.' He takes two tins and is just about to put them in his basket when he sees yet another notice: EXCLUSIVE TO THIS STORE. TINNED STEAK. CUT PRICE OFFER.)

(TONY grabs a tin of this and a tin of something else nearby. He looks around him. We see a very quickly cut sequence of various products, luxury goods, exotic mouth-watering items, tins of all shapes and sizes. TONY is getting the buying fever that attacks people in supermarkets on occasion. He starts collecting tins and packets from various sections. Duck in oranges, tinned caviare, York hams, etc. He puts some long French loaves in the trolley, falling over the side. Now he is picking up things by the armful, and then setting off for more. His mouth is watering as he raids the various sections.)

(We see him walking past the cheese counter, now pushing two trolleys loaded up and overflowing with stuff. On the counter is a tray for people to sample the cheeses, with various little bits on salt biscuits. TONY tries one, and immediately puts a large, pre-wrapped chunk of it in his basket. He tries another one, nods with approval and drops half a pound of that one into his basket. He picks up half a pound of another cheese and puts it into his trolley without even bothering to sample it. He thinks again, and tries a taste of it. It is horrible. He grimaces, takes the half pound out of his trolley and puts it back.)

(Over the loudspeaker, on which we have been hearing messages relayed to the staff and music, we now hear a recorded jingle, advertising a dried food product. TONY listens avidly to this. At the end, he goes straight to the shelves where the brand is on display. There is only one packet left. He makes a dash for it at the same time as another shopper. They both grab it.)

TONY: It's mine, I got to it first.
WOMAN: You did not!
TONY: Yes, I think you'll find I did.
WOMAN: I got to it first.
TONY: You did not.

    (Neither of them will let go)

WOMAN: I must have it, I came in here specially to get one.
TONY: I can't help that, I was first. Let go.
WOMAN: You are taking advantage of the fact that you are stronger than me.
TONY: And you, madam, are taking advantage of the fact that I am a gentleman. Now let go.

(They start tugging harder. An assistant comes along with some more of the same product and puts them on the shelf. TONY and the WOMAN stop struggling, but they keep their hands on the packet. Then they both let go, the packet falls to the ground, and they both grab one of the new ones each. They move on, leaving the first packet on the floor.)

(From the cash registers, we see TONY coming down the gangway between two racks of shelves, with his trolleys towards the camera. This is the final leg before paying for the goods. He has now got to the stage where he is taking something from every section as he

goes past: a book, a long-playing record, a brush, clothes pegs, pot scourers, things that are not much good to him which he is taking purely because they are there. He reaches the end of the aisle and joins a queue of customers waiting to check out with their goods.)

(One of the customers in another queue has her young son with her. He is dressed in a cowboy outfit and is playing among the counters, the piles of stacked-up food, the refrigerators, etc. He is hiding behind them and pretending to fire his gun at the shoppers. He creeps up behind TONY and shoots him, shouting a loud gunshot sound at the same time. TONY jumps out of his skin.)

(TONY sees the MOTHER smiling at him and smiles back at her, and nods towards the little boy approvingly. He moves to the cash register, pulling his trolleys with him.)

BOY: Are you a wagon train, mister?

TONY: Yes, that's right. We're on our way to Californ-i-a with supplies for the soldiers. These are the old chuck wagons.

BOY: And I'm a baddie attacking the wagons.

(He dances round TONY, firing his gun. TONY smiles at the MOTHER, who is a good-looking young woman. TONY joins in with the little boy – using his fingers as a gun, and making noises like the ricochet of bullets. The little boy ducks behind a stack of tins, poking his head out to fire at TONY. TONY fires back at him. THE CASHIER is waiting for TONY, who is now next to have his purchases rung up.)

CASHIER: Oi, Maverick. Over here.

(TONY pushes his trolleys to the till. The CASHIER looks at the load of stuff TONY has collected.)

CASHIER: Cor blimey, are you opening a restaurant or something?

(She starts taking the stuff out, one by one, from TONY'S trolleys and totting them up on her register. The little boy continues to play cowboys and Indians. TONY joins in again, enjoying himself if the truth is known. He does an imaginary fast draw and fires at the child. The boy walks towards TONY with TONY firing frantically at him. TONY stops firing.)

TONY: What's the matter?

BOY: You're not playing properly. You've used up all your bullets.

TONY: Have I?

BOY: Yes, you've only got a six-gun, you can't keep firing like that.

TONY: Ah well, I've got some more bullets in my gun belt.

BOY: No, you haven't. I crept up in the middle of the night and stole them.

TONY: Oh well, I didn't hear you, you see. I was asleep.

BOY: *(Points the gun at him)* Stick 'em up.

(TONY raises his hands)

BOY: I'm gonna kill you now, Black Jake.

TONY: I see.

(The CASHIER finishes totting up the goods)

CASHIER: Twenty-eight pounds, twelve and six.

(The BOY fires at TONY, who hasn't heard the CASHIER. TONY pretends to be shot, clasping his hands to his heart.)

CASHIER: Are you all right?

(TONY comes to and realizes the CASHIER is speaking to him. He pulls himself together.)

TONY: Yes, thank you.

CASHIER: I thought you'd had a heart attack when I told you how much it came to.

TONY: No, no. How much does it come to?

CASHIER: Twenty-eight pounds, twelve and six.

TONY: *(Shattered)* How much?

CASHIER: Twenty-eight pounds, twelve and six.

TONY: Oh come now, you've made a mistake. You got your fingers mixed up on the buttons.

(She hands him a long roll of paper with the items and the total on it which she has taken out of the machine)

TONY: This is all very embarrassing, I really hadn't intended to buy all this, I must have got carried away. I only came in here for a tin of beans and some shredded wheat.

CASHIER: What are you talking about, there's no shredded wheat here.

TONY: Well, there you are, that proves it, I was mesmerized. I'm not used to these establishments.

CASHIER: Are you going to pay for this or not?

TONY: I can't.

CASHIER: Then what did you buy it all for?

TONY: I couldn't help it. I didn't realize I had all this stuff, you don't add it up as you go round. There should be a law against these places, tempting people to live beyond their means.

CASHIER: Twenty-eight pounds, twelve and six.

TONY: *(Angrily)* I haven't got twenty-eight pounds, twelve and six.

(The MANAGER of the supermarket comes up)

MANAGER: What seems to be the problem, Miss Williams?

CASHIER: This gentleman has purchased these goods and now refuses to pay for them.

MANAGER: *(Turning to TONY)* Oh? What's wrong with them?

TONY: Nothing's wrong with them – I can't pay for them, I haven't got that much money. Look, let's put them back on the shelves and I'll take a tin of beans and some shredded wheat.

MANAGER: It isn't as easy as that. The goods have been itemized on the cash register. It would throw our whole system of accounts into confusion.

TONY: I refuse to pay for goods I do not intend to take home with me. I am willing to retrace my steps, put the things back, and start again at the entrance. Beyond that I am not prepared to move.

MANAGER: I see. An impasse.

TONY: If you like.

CASHIER: Shall I call the police, Mr Taylor?

MANAGER: No, no, that...

TONY: Yes, yes, go on, send for the law, go on, let's make a test case out of it. Do your store a lot of good, that will. *(Shouts, like a newsboy)* 'Man held to ransom at cash desk!' Very nice. Should bring you in a lot of custom. *(He looks round cockily to get support from the other customers, as if to say, 'There, that told him.')*

(The MANAGER looks at the CASHIER with a withering look)

MANAGER: I'm sure we can settle this amicably without resorting to police action.

TONY: I'm sure we can. We'll put it all back and start again.

MANAGER: No, no, sir, we'll put it back. We value our customers' goodwill above everything. *(Snaps his fingers)* Jones! *(A male ASSISTANT comes over)* Put all this back, and... what was it again, sir?

TONY: *(Smugly)* A tin of baked beans and a packet of shredded wheat.

MANAGER: Large beans or small?

TONY: *(Easy come, easy go attitude)* Er... large.

MANAGER: Thank you very much, sir. *(He waves the ASSISTANT off to get them)*

TONY: Ah, that's a bit more like it. Yes. that's always been the trouble with these self-service places, there's never been anyone to get the stuff for you.

MANAGER: Quite.

TONY: I'm sorry I had to put my foot down, I realize it's not your fault. You've got your rules, I realize that. You've got your job to do and so have I, but there again one has to stand up for one's rights.

MANAGER: Precisely, sir, I quite understand.

TONY: We all make mistakes.

MANAGER: Of course. Ah…

(The ASSISTANT returns, carrying a large tin of beans and a packet of shredded wheat)

MANAGER: There we are, sir, one large beans and a packet of shredded wheat.

TONY: Thank you very much.

MANAGER: *(Snaps his fingers)* A carrier bag for the gentleman, come along now, you can't expect him to carry them in his pockets.

(The ASSISTANT hands a carrier bag over. The manager puts the beans and the packet into it, and hands it to TONY.)

TONY: You don't do deliveries, do you…

MANAGER: Er, no, sir.

TONY: Oh, all right then. *(He takes the carrier bag)*

MANAGER: Ring that up please, Miss er… er… One large beans and a shredded wheat.

(The CASHIER pushes the buttons with bad grace. She tears out the total.)

CASHIER: Two and tenpence.

TONY: Very reasonable.

(He feels in his pocket. There is nothing there. Hands the carrier bag back to the MANAGER and feels in the other pocket. The smile gradually dies on the MANAGER'S face.)

TONY: Two and ten. Yes. Ah… *(He finds some loose change)* Two-and-seven. *(Laughs at the MANAGER, who is not amused)* Isn't that strange? I've come out without any money. I could have sworn I had a couple of notes on me. I'll toss you for the odd threepence.

MANAGER: *(Holding himself in check)* Put these back on the shelves please, Mr Jones. *(He hands the carrier bag to the ASSISTANT and addresses TONY)* I suggest you don't come in here again until you have got some money.

TONY: Yes. Right. I can't think how it happened. *(Backs away towards the exit)* It's my day off, you see, and I always put my best clothes on. I must have left my money in my working clothes… no, I tell a lie, I didn't, I left it on the bedside table, and I forgot to pick it up… I bet I haven't got my street door key either. I'll go and get some money from the post office, I'll see you later then…

(He backs away to the door and out, talking as he goes)

8 *Comedy Playhouse*

Tony Hancock was rumoured at his peak to be earning £30,000 a year with the BBC – a colossal sum for the time, and one that embarrassed and bewildered him. He tried, during his 1960 *Face to Face* interview with John Freeman, to dismiss the figure as inflated, but his protests sounded unconvincing. He also hinted at changes to come in his career. These proved drastic: after the break with Sid James, his agent, and Galton and Simpson, he would not work for the BBC again.

Tom Sloan, the corporation's head of light entertainment, saw his star comic was on the slide, and let him go. He also saw that his star writers were at their peak, and offered them anything they wanted, to stay. Their first demand was modest: they wanted to write for Frankie Howerd.

Sloan turned them down. 'He said, "Frank's finished. His last series was terrible,"' Ray remembered. 'We laughed and said, "Frank? Finished?" but he pressed a buzzer on his desk and said, "Bring in the books." They brought in these bloody great ledgers, all the audience comments and research, and the viewing figures.'

The figures looked bad. Ray and Alan tried to brush them aside, pointing out that Howerd's whole career had been erratic. They argued that his last series had suffered from poor scripts, and asked for the chance to show how good their old friend could be when he had the right material.

Sloan would not be persuaded. He had a more ambitious concept, and he told the writers: 'What I'm proposing is a *Comedy Playhouse* – that's the title I want to give it. I've got ten half-hours free here, and you can write what you like, providing you use my title. You can cast who you like, be in it yourselves if you like, direct it yourselves if you like. Do something different every week.'

The scope of the commission, and the freedom that was being offered, staggered them. Sloan was not even restricting his writers to a format – he made it clear he would welcome sketches, playlets and anything else that fitted the title. 'The extent of his *carte blanche* bowled us over,' Ray said, 'because no one had ever been invited to do anything like that, and I shouldn't think anyone ever will be again.'

Comedy Playhouse went on to run for thirteen years and 120 episodes. Galton and Simpson delivered the first two series, comprising sixteen half-hour shows; ten episodes were written in late 1961 and early 1962, with the second series (shorter because of a quirk of BBC scheduling) being written in early 1963. After that, the roster of writers included Carla Lane, Johnny Speight, Roy Clarke, and Jeremy Lloyd and David Croft. *The Liver Birds, Till Death Us Do Part, Last of the Summer Wine* and *Are You Being Served?* all began as one-offs on *Comedy Playhouse*. Tom Sloan had devised a format that would be the genesis of twenty-eight different series in all, making it easily the richest ever source of television comedy. It became the fount of great sitcoms.

Sloan recognized the gulf between the public's perception – that comedians improvised their dialogue on air – and the reality, that their comic genius stemmed from the writing. In 1961 Galton and Simpson were successful and highly respected, but they would not become household names until their sitcoms belonged unmistakably to them, and not to the performers. Full recognition came with *Steptoe and Son*, which featured actors rather than comedians, but the process began with *Comedy Playhouse*.

From the outset, Ray and Alan were determined to challenge the BBC's unwritten restrictions, and experiment with the nascent sitcom form. They wrote stories within stories, stories where nothing happened, stories set in Moscow and Malaysia and on window ledges and in the middle of the English Channel, stories that took place only in the imagination. And for the first episode, they broached the taboo on black comedy with a script that cast Eric Sykes as a corrupt undertaker.

'It was originally called *Dearlove and Son*, and it was set somewhere like Rye, a small town on the south coast,' Alan said, 'and they told us, "We can't have this... it's funereal, all about death!" They were very unhappy. So we set it in the thirties, which we thought made it more palatable.'

Whatever the era, Sloan was, as Ray put it, 'not at all conciliatory'. So the writers suggested setting it in France. Sloan said, 'Fine! You can do anything you like about France.'

'We called it *Clicquot et Fils*, after the champagne,' Ray said.

The opening scene, featuring Sykes and Barbara Hicks, was darker and more cynical than anything the writers had attempted with Hancock. Presaging the callousness of the Steptoes, it indicated a new direction for Galton and Simpson:

COMEDY PLAYHOUSE, first series, episode one

'CLICQUOT ET FILS'
First broadcast: Friday 15 December 1961

EXT: *(Undertaker's shop window)*

(M. CLICQUOT is looking gloomily out of the window. As he turns back to the shop we cut to inside.)

(He looks at a photo on the wall, adjusts it, dusts it. Moves a bowl of flowers slightly, moves a candlestick an inch to one side. CLICQUOT goes over to his desk and sits down. He picks up a newspaper. Shooting over his shoulder, we see the headline: Famine In China. CLICQUOT reacts to this.)

(A woman comes up to the shop. CLICQUOT opens the door for her.)

M. CLICQUOT: Good morning, Mme. Dupont. Now what can I do for you?

MME. DUPONT: It's about my grandfather.

M. CLICQUOT: Ah yes. Very sad. This must be a very anxious and trying time for you. A wonderful old man. A true son of France.

MME. DUPONT: The doctor came in again this morning and...

M. CLICQUOT: *(Takes her free hand)* Mme. Dupont, words of comfort are inadequate at a time like this. You may feel that a man... in my profession, after all these years, has become hardened... indifferent to the sorrow of others... but you would be wrong. Let me assure you, dear lady, that...

MME. DUPONT: The doctor said he's much better.

M. CLICQUOT: Pardon?

MME. DUPONT: He's getting up this afternoon.

M. CLICQUOT: *(PAUSE while still holding her hand)* I see. *(Lets hand go, forcing a smile)* Well... this is indeed wonderful news. I couldn't be happier for you.

MME. DUPONT: Yes, and after us all thinking that he was going.

M. CLICQUOT: Yes, an amazing old gentleman.

MME. DUPONT: Doctor says he'll be all right... he's got to rest more. Falling off his bike at his age, he ought to know better.

M. CLICQUOT: Quite. *(Smiles sourly)* Well, Mme. Dupont. *(Helps her up. Takes her elbow.)* I'm sure you will want to get back. It must be a great relief to know that he is going to be all right.

MME. DUPONT: There is just one other thing.

M. CLICQUOT: Yes?

MME. DUPONT: *(Embarrassed)* Well... seeing as things have turned out as they have... could we have our deposit back?

One advantage of the *Playhouse* format that Ray and Alan embraced immediately was the freedom it gave them to work with actors instead of comedians. They admired the versatility of John Le Mesurier and Warren Mitchell, both regulars on *Hancock's Half Hour*, and they were quick to send a script to another comic actor and rising TV star, Stanley Baxter. The play was a two-hander, set on a park bench – a duologue between two timid office workers, Baxter and Daphne Anderson, who were clearly attracted to each other but trapped in unhappy marriages to other people. Their conversation was banal and hesitant, a procession of trivial platitudes that hid something much more grave and moving which the couple could not have articulated, even if they had found the courage.

'It was a near disaster,' said Ray. 'Because it was so straight it didn't get any laughs whatsoever. We had a studio audience there, and oh my God! Stanley and Daphne were giving a lovely performance but it was not getting any laughs at all... until we got within about two or three minutes of the end, and at last we got a laugh. Just the one.'

'We wanted to edit it out,' Alan said. 'That laugh gave it away that there was an audience there. But I remember looking at the audience and they weren't looking around and yawning, they were all engrossed in what was going on. Because Stanley and Daphne played it so beautifully and very quietly, and the audience were listening.'

'Lunch in the Park' was the only *Comedy Playhouse* where the dress rehearsal lasted five minutes longer than the performance, because during the run-through the producer, Duncan Wood, allowed time for laughter. Baxter was shaken, and went home fearing that he'd let the production down. 'There was only a solitary laugh, and I was used to playing to audiences that did laugh at what I was doing,' he said, fifty years later. 'I thought maybe I was just the wrong person for it, and I was worried that maybe they thought so too. They're [Galton and Simpson] both charming, lovely people, and quite superb writers.'

The writers were unrepentant. 'We took the view that we'd been given a free hand,' said Alan, 'and we were doing the comedy without any laughs, that's all. It's *Brief Encounter*, basically. You're relying on the imag-ination of the audience and the quality of the acting.' It remains one of their most affecting pieces of writing:

COMEDY PLAYHOUSE, first series, episode two

'LUNCH IN THE PARK'
First broadcast: Friday 22 December 1961

MAN: You make excellent sandwiches. How do you cut the bread so thin?

WOMAN: I buy it already sliced.

MAN: Women make different sandwiches to men, don't they? Look how thick mine are.

WOMAN: I think men should have thick sandwiches. It… it's more manly. I like men who smoke pipes too.

(He half pulls his pipe out of his top pocket, smiles and puts it back. This is an involuntary action on his part.)

WOMAN: Didn't she make them this morning?

MAN: The sandwiches?

WOMAN: Yes.

MAN: No. I left her in bed.

WOMAN: How is she?

MAN: Just the same.

WOMAN: Still her back, is it?

MAN: I think so. I don't know. I didn't ask. I just made my sandwiches and left… I took her a cup of tea up, but she didn't answer, I just let her sleep.

WOMAN: Will she be up when you get home?

MAN: I don't expect so. When she gets backache, she has to stay in bed, otherwise she gets migraine as well.

WOMAN: What does the doctor say?

MAN: He says there's nothing wrong with her. He's refused to come round any more.

WOMAN: Perhaps it's her nerves.

MAN: I took her to a nerve specialist. He said there's nothing wrong with her, too. But she doesn't seem to get any better.

WOMAN: How much older is she than you?

MAN: Three years.

WOMAN: It must be very difficult for you.

MAN: My sister comes round twice a week to clear up.

WOMAN: No, I mean… with her.

MAN: Oh… I don't see much of her really. I've got my television. It's not too bad.

WOMAN: Does she like television?

MAN: Medical programmes. That's all. *Eye on Research*, she used to watch.

WOMAN: That's not on now.

MAN: Very well done, that programme.

WOMAN: Oh yes.

MAN: Did you see the one about the heart operation?

WOMAN: No, I missed it. I saw the brain operation.

MAN: I didn't see that one. Was it good?

WOMAN: Very well done.

MAN: It's amazing what they can do these days, isn't it?

WOMAN: Amazing.

MAN: But they still can't find anything wrong with her.

WOMAN: Perhaps there isn't anything wrong with her.

MAN: That's unkind. You've never said anything unkind before. Did you mean to be unkind? You're usually such a kind person.

WOMAN: I'm sorry. I just don't like to think of you being unhappy. You're so kind and gentle, she takes advantage of it.

MAN: Do you like brisket?

WOMAN: Thank you.

(She takes a sandwich from him. She offers him one of hers. He takes one.)

MAN: Is that your chump chop in there?

WOMAN: *(Looks down at her basket)* Yes, how did you know?

MAN: The blood's coming through. It's lucky you put it on the top. I'd turn that over if I were you. Put the bit where the blood is coming through on top, then it won't stain anything.

WOMAN: Oh, it won't hurt, there are only potatoes underneath.

MAN: It's always best to put the potatoes on the bottom, isn't it? A little trick of the trade, that. I remember once, when I was a boy, I went shopping for my mother and I put the eggs in first – then I went to the greengrocer's and had ten pounds of King Edwards emptied in on top of them.

(They laugh)

MAN: I'll never forget that.

WOMAN: Did you get into trouble?

MAN: I should say I did.

WOMAN: Did your mother hit you often?

MAN: Oh no, she didn't used to hit me at all, she was a very kind woman, my mother, she would never hit me. Never once, in her whole life.

She used to get my father to do it. She wouldn't look. She used to go out of the room. She couldn't bear violence. She would say, 'You wait till your father comes in.' Then she would tell him, and she would have to go out because she didn't like to hear me screaming. She would go down to the church and cry in the back row... I caused her a lot of unhappiness like that. She never reproached me for it though. She was very kind.

By the third episode, Galton and Simpson were beginning to realize that too much choice could be as limiting as too little. 'When the world is your oyster, it's difficult to decide what you're going to do,' Alan said. 'We had a lot of trouble coming up with ideas, even though we could do anything. We realized very quickly that one of the good things about doing a fixed format is that you've got set-ups to fall back on all the time. Familiarity is a great aid for the audience.'

For inspiration, they were drawing now on cinema, especially the new wave of realist film from the continent. 'We were very impressed by films that were being made in Europe, as opposed to America or Britain,' Ray said. 'When we saw *Bicycle Thieves* – my God, this was what we had never seen in our lives before, films that were made for adults, about adult things, about life. That was very influential.'

The *Comedy Playhouses* were short stories, and the writers were conscious that cinema drew on a literary tradition of classic miniatures: *Boule de Suif* by Maupassant, for instance ('a lovely little story that made perfect comedy,' commented Alan), had been the basis for John Ford's *Stagecoach*.

'We did a lot of reading, both contemporary and the older, turn-of-the-century authors, especially Russians, but I don't think we tried to copy in any way what they were writing,' Ray said. 'That would have been madness. It's unconscious, if you are being influenced by somebody you've just read. We didn't think, "Oh God, this is very Chekhovian."'

'We left that to other people,' Alan cut in, drily.

Ray agreed: 'We would have been very flattered... or insulted.'

For their third story, they mirrored a device employed by P. G. Wodehouse – though this was certainly an unconscious borrowing, since neither was a great fan of the anecdote-at-the-club, reminds-me-of-a-fellow-I-knew tales related by characters such as Uckridge or Mr Mulliner. The title was a nod to another upper-class English humorist, Noel Coward, though these *Private Lives* were more sordid. Edward Whiteley, whose story is recounted over drinks by a raconteur at a West

End gentlemen's club, has four mistresses. His women fluctuate with his moods – they include the horsey Lavinia, and Dolly, a chorus girl:

COMEDY PLAYHOUSE, first series, episode three

'THE PRIVATE LIVES OF EDWARD WHITELEY'
First broadcast: Friday 29 December 1961

(In Kensington)

LAVINIA: You look tired, darling, have you had a hard day at the club?

WHITELEY: I should say so. Sixteen straight games, 178 cannons on the trot –how's that?

LAVINIA: Sounds terribly tiring.

WHITELEY: Let me look at you. *(He stands at arm's length from her and admires her)* Beautiful. Exquisite. *(Takes her by the hand)* Ah, Lavinia… I've thought about you all day.

LAVINIA: What, during all those cannon things, oh that is sweet.

WHITELEY: Have you missed me, Lavinia?

LAVINIA: Well, of course I have, darling. Biarritz just wasn't the same without you.

WHITELEY: Ah yes, Biarritz. And how was Biarritz?

LAVINIA: Terribly hot. Of course, everybody was there… the whole of London.

WHITELEY: Did you enjoy yourself?

LAVINIA: *(Not keen)* Yeeesss. I suppose so. As much as one can enjoy oneself in Biarritz. One has to be so terribly careful to avoid the sun… otherwise one goes a ghastly brown colour… one looks no different from those poor wretches working in the fields. Would you like a drink, darling?

(And later, in a private room after a night at the music hall)

WHITELEY: Come here, me proud beauty. *(He takes her hand, pulls her onto his lap, kisses her hand, then works his way up to her shoulder, with her giggling. He kisses her shoulder.)*

DOLLY: Stop biting my shoulder, the audience get jealous.

WHITELEY: I'll drive them raving mad by the time I've finished with you. *(He carries on kissing her)*

DOLLY: Oooh, I'm hungry. *(She takes a piece of toast and starts eating it. WHITELEY continues kissing her ears, her shoulders, while she prattles.)* I had another row with that silly Milly Perkins today. She's always copying me. I can't buy anything without her going out and buying one just like it. There was that hat last week *(She puts another piece of food in her mouth)*… it was a lovely hat, with big feathers; the woman said it was the only one in London – you're tickling – then she walked in the next day wearing one exactly like it. Anyway, the same thing happened today. I bought a new pair of slippers and she had a pair exactly the same, and she said she bought hers before me, and what's more they were the same pair she had on the night Lord Bertie Smythe drank champagne out of them, and she said she'd bet no one has ever drunk champagne out of my slippers. Teddy.

WHITELEY: Hmmm?

DOLLY: Will you drink champagne out of my slipper?

WHITELEY: *(His head comes up like a shot)* Do what?

DOLLY: Well, I can't let her get away with it. I want you to drink champagne out of mine, then I can show her…

WHITELEY: Champagne… out of your…

DOLLY: Everybody does it these days. All the chorus girls have had champagne drunk out of their slippers except me.

WHITELEY: It'll ruin the champagne and the slipper…

DOLLY: You don't love me.

WHITELEY: I do love you.

DOLLY: Then why won't you drink champagne out of my slipper?

WHITELEY: Look, I'll pour some in, then you can show them where it's been.

DOLLY: It's not the same. I'll know you haven't drunk it.

WHITELEY: It'll make your foot wet.

DOLLY: *(Crying)* They were right, you don't love me.

WHITELEY: I do love you.

DOLLY: No, you don't. You just kiss me and cuddle me but when I ask you to do something to prove you really love me, you won't.

WHITELEY: How can drinking champagne out of your slipper prove that…

(DOLLY cries)

WHITELEY: Oh, all right. Give us it here.

DOLLY: You have to take it off. *(Pulls her skirt up)* Be romantic with it.

WHITELEY: *(Bends down and takes her slipper off, muttering)* I don't know. *(He puts the slipper on the table. Takes the champagne bottle. Fills her glass up and goes to pour some into the slipper.)* You realize it's all going to come out of the toes?

DOLLY: Not if you tilt it back properly. Don't be such a misery.

WHITELEY: *(Pouring it into the slipper)* Perfectly good champagne, this is.
    1887. *(He picks up the slipper, carefully trying not to spill any)* Are
    those curtains closed?
DOLLY: Yes.
WHITELEY: Oh well... cheers. *(He touches her glass with the shoe)* Down
    the hatch. *(He drinks from the slipper. DOLLY throws her arms around
    him.)*
DOLLY: Oh Teddy, you do love me.

*(Fade the sound with WHITELEY taking sips from her slipper, Dolly
clasped around his neck)*

NARRATOR: *(Overlaid)* That night he drank twenty-four slippersful of 1887
    Bollinger reserve, and was last seen driving a Hansom cab full speed
    down Brixton High Road at 4.30 in the morning. He was stopped by a
    policeman and gave his name as Ben Hur.

The fourth edition of *Comedy Playhouse* led to *Steptoe and Son*, and is
covered in depth in the next chapter. With the fifth show, Galton and
Simpson used a technique from French farce, where an empty set is gradually filled by a gaggle of characters. Instead of hotel guests and maids,
they brought in burglars, who convene on a country house to raid the
safe, the silver and a collection of porcelain. But the thieves also break
into the drinks cabinet...

'The Reunion' was a rare example of a story where the writers knew
their ending before they started. 'Nine times out of ten we'd get to the
penultimate page,' Alan said, 'and we'd spend a day thinking how to
end it.'

'We always considered it a success if we hadn't got a pay-off,' said Ray,
'and we got to the last page, and we came up with a good one that made
it look as if that was what we were writing towards. Great satisfaction,
that.'

This episode was different: they knew from the outset that their
characters would end up throwing a drunken party that wakes the
neighbourhood and attracts the police. That provided a pretext for a
script that sent up all the stereotypes of vintage crime stories – the
raffish gentleman burglar in dickie-bow and monocle, the curmud-
geonly safe-cracker with an ear that can hear a speck of dust fall, and
the salt-of-the-earth housebreaker with a wife and nine children to
feed. It gave them a chance to use some of their favourite actors,
including Lee Montague as Maurice, Dick Emery as Arthur, and J. G.
Devlin as Paddy:

COMEDY PLAYHOUSE, first series, episode five

'THE REUNION'
First broadcast: Friday 12 January 1962

MAURICE: *(Suddenly)* Shhhh…
ARTHUR: *(Whispers)* What?
MAURICE: *(Whispers)* The lights, quick. Coppers.
ARTHUR: Oh Gawd.

    (ARTHUR switches out the cabinet light and MAURICE the main light)

ARTHUR: *(Whispers)* I didn't hear a car, did you?
MAURICE: *(Whispers)* No, he's probably on his own…

    (We hear the window go up)

ARTHUR: *(Whispers in panic)* He's coming in.
MAURICE: *(Waves to ARTHUR to get one side of the curtains. He goes to the other.)* When he comes in – jump on him.

    (They wait either side of the curtains. The curtains start to part. A hand comes through, holding a lighted torch.)

MAURICE: Now!

    (ARTHUR and MAURICE jump on the figure and roll him up in the curtains. The figure yells.)

PADDY: I give in… don't hit me… it's a fair cop…

    (At this they stop struggling. MAURICE lets go of the figure in the curtains and he comes out. It is PADDY O'HANAHAN.)

PADDY: I haven't touched a thing, you can't do me for breaking, it was already broken… I'm innocent, I…

    (They turn the torch on a very frightened-looking face)

MAURICE: Cor blimey, Paddy O'Hanahan.
PADDY: Who is it… who are you… turn that lamp out…

    (ARTHUR switches the main light on. PADDY sees who his captors are.)

ARTHUR: Paddy.
PADDY: Arthur Clench! Maurice Woolley! Me darlin' boys!

    (They both clasp his hand, delighted to see each other)

PADDY: Oh God, you frightened the life out of me.
MAURICE: We thought you were a rozzer.
PADDY: Me a rozzer, begad, that'll be the day.
MAURICE: Have a drink, warm yourself up.
PADDY: Well now, that's very kind of you.

(They walk over to the decanter. MAURICE pours himself a drink and one each for himself and ARTHUR. They raise their glasses and clink them together.)

PADDY: Success to temperance.
ARTHUR AND MAURICE: Cheers.

(They drink)

PADDY: *(To ARTHUR)* Well, you haven't wasted much time, have you? You only got out yesterday.
ARTHUR: Yeah, well, there's no point in hanging about, is there? You get rusty. It's like motor car accidents, you have to get behind the wheel again, otherwise you lose your nerve.

(They laugh)

PADDY: That's worked out fine… I like a bit of company while I'm working, someone to talk to, because it's a long job getting a safe open.
ARTHUR: We haven't come across the safe yet, Paddy.
PADDY: It's over there, behind that picture.
MAURICE: How do you know?
PADDY: Oh, this is me third visit here. I've been interrupted every time. But I've a feeling I'm going to do it tonight. *(He finishes off his drink)* Well, we're not being paid by the hour, gentlemen, let's get to work.

(PADDY goes to the picture, which is on hinges, and swings it open. There is a wall safe behind it. He flexes his fingers, takes a bit of sandpaper out of his pocket, and gently rubs it across his fingertips. Takes a stethoscope out of his bag, puts it on, places the mike against the safe and starts twiddling the dial. MAURICE carries on wrapping up the silver and ARTHUR goes back to the jade cabinet.)

MAURICE: How's Bridget these days?
PADDY: Fine. And Doris and the kids?
MAURICE: Very well.
PADDY: Oh, that's good.

(MAURICE starts humming to himself)

PADDY: Sssshhhh!

MAURICE: Sorry.

PADDY: *(Listening intently to the tumblers)* Aha, that's one of the little
　　darlings. Ah, won't be long now. *(PADDY relaxes, takes a packet of
　　sandwiches from his pocket)* Anybody want a sandwich?

ARTHUR: What are they?

PADDY: They're made out of genuine Irish soda bread. Flown over fresh
　　from Ireland every morning. Go on, try some real bread for a change.
　　It's better than that sliced rubbish you get over here.

MAURICE: *(Has a look inside the sandwich)* What's this, then, peat and
　　shamrock?

(They laugh)

PADDY: It is not – it's corned beef and watercress. Do you want one or
　　not, Arthur?

ARTHUR: No, thanks.

MAURICE: *(Takes a bite out of his sandwich)* Mmm, they're all right, aren't
　　they? I thought you lot only ate spuds.

PADDY: Well – we do eat the occasional Englishman if he wanders across
　　the border. Do you want a sup of tea? *(He has taken a Thermos flask
　　from under his coat. He undoes the top and pours a cup of tea.)* Go
　　easy with that, there's a drop of the hard stuff in there… keeps the
　　chill out of your bones, in this godforsaken heretic country…

MAURICE: *(Splutters)* Cor blimey, you should put some tea in as well, you
　　know.

PADDY: Oh dear, look at the time. I'll miss *Maigret* tonight again. Still,
　　can't be helped… business first. That's the trouble with our job, you
　　miss so many good programmes.

MAURICE: We haven't got a television.

ARTHUR: Haven't you? I can get you one. There's a bloke next door to
　　me, he nicks them from the warehouse. Twenty nicker for a 21-inch.
　　That's less than a pound an inch, that's not bad, you know.

MAURICE: No, I wouldn't have a nicked one in the house. You don't get
　　no guarantee, it goes wrong and you've had it.

Episode six, 'The Telephone Call', was based on a newspaper cutting:
after the Berlin Wall appeared, an Englishman had phoned the Kremlin
to complain about the Cold War. 'We didn't normally write political or
topical stories, but this bloke actually got through,' Alan said, laughing at

the idea of it half a century on. 'The thought of even being able to dial the number… in those days, you had to book an overseas call two days in advance if you wanted to phone America or Australia, and it was about three pounds a minute. Which is like £30, £60 a minute now.'

The irate caller was Peter Jones, goaded by his wife, June Whitfield. Pat Coombs was the telephone operator:

COMEDY PLAYHOUSE, first series, episode six

'THE TELEPHONE CALL'
First broadcast: Friday 19 January 1962

JOHN: The Government, a right useless lot they are. It's the politicians that's causing all the trouble. They're too busy playing their little games, trying to frighten each other… my bomb's bigger than yours… I've got better rockets than you have… my old man's a policeman. If old Kruschev walked into this kitchen now, I wouldn't be frightened of him… I'd say, 'How do you do?' We'd sit down, have a cup of tea and we'd have the whole thing sorted out in ten minutes.

SANDRA: Oh well, you're clever, aren't you? The Prime Minister, he's a right woodenhead next to you.

JOHN: There's no need to take that attitude, Sandra.

SANDRA: Well, you get on my wick. You're all talk. You never do anything. If you're so worried about the bomb, and Berlin, and Africa, don't moan to me about it, do something, be a man for once in your life, do something, then I might be impressed.

JOHN: *(Gets up)* All right, I will do something.

SANDRA: Go on, then, do something.

JOHN: All right then, I'm going to.

SANDRA: Well, don't just stand there, go and do it.

JOHN: I'm going to, don't you worry.

(He leaves the kitchen. SANDRA carries on reading her magazine. Cut to JOHN, entering the lounge. He locks the door after making sure she isn't following him. He goes over to the telephone. Carefully picks it up so the bell won't ring. He waits for the operator to answer.)

(Cut to LOCAL EXCHANGE. We see the operator putting the plug in.)

OPERATOR: Number please.

JOHN: *(Quietly, so his wife can't hear)* This is Fincham in the Wold 34.

OPERATOR: Yes. Where to?

JOHN: Moscow.

OPERATOR: Moscow… What name are you calling?

JOHN: I want to make a personal call to Mr N. Kruschev *(The OPERATOR writes this down)* at the Kremlin, Moscow.

OPERATOR: *(As she writes)* Mr N. Kruschev, the Kremlin… who?

JOHN: Kruschev. N. Kruschev.

OPERATOR: What, *the* Mr Kruschev?

JOHN: Yes. *The* Mr Kruschev. The Prime Minister.

OPERATOR: Are you having me on?

JOHN: Look, Miss… I'm Mr J. Baxter of 23 The Larches… I want to make a telephone call… a perfectly straightforward telephone call… all you're there for is to connect me with the person I wish to speak to… now will you kindly do so…

OPERATOR: There's no need to adopt that tone of voice, caller. We're all here to help each other. Now… what is the number?

JOHN: I don't know the number, I've never called him before.

OPERATOR: I'll get International. *(She dials)* Is he a friend of yours, then?

JOHN: No, not a friend. No.

OPERATOR: Is he expecting you to phone?

JOHN: I doubt it.

OPERATOR: What are you going to speak to him about then?

JOHN: Mind your own business. Have you got International ringing yet?

OPERATOR: It's ringing. Have you ever phoned Mr Kennedy? I like him… he's a lovely man, isn't he? Mr Macmillan, he's nice too. Hallo International, Moscow please. Person-to-person call from Mr J. Baxter of Fincham in the Wold to Mr N. Kruschev, the Kremlin, Moscow. Yes, Kruschev. Oh, some crank.

JOHN: I am not a crank. I heard that.

OPERATOR: Please do not interrupt, caller. I'm trying to get Moscow for you.

JOHN: Well, hurry up.

OPERATOR: Hallo International… oh, you've got through to the Kremlin? Yes… I see. Yes. Hold the line. Hallo caller.

JOHN: Yes.

OPERATOR: He's out. Will you speak to the first secretary?

JOHN: No, I want to speak to Mr Kruschev. I'm an ordinary citizen who's worried about the world situation.

OPERATOR: Hold the line, caller. Hallo, International… he says no, he wants to speak to Mr Kruschev personally because he's an ordinary citizen and he's very worried about the world situation. Yes. I see. Yes. Hold the line, International. Hallo, caller? They say it is a great honour to get a call from one of the glorious workers of Great Britain and that when he comes in they'll tell him you called, and they've no doubt he'll ring you back.

JOHN: *(Pleased)* Really?

OPERATOR: That's what they said.

JOHN: When are they expecting him back?

OPERATOR: They don't know. He's having lunch at a tractor factory.

Friends of Alan and Ray occasionally provided them with the inspiration for situations. 'The Status Symbol' was a two-hander between a garage mechanic, played by Alfie Marks, and a hopeless fantasist, played by Graham Stark and based on a friend called Spooner. The star of the show was the car, a Rolls-Royce, and the memory of that inspired an exchange between Ray and Alan that hints at how they improvised their characters' dialogue:

RG: The Rolls was the undisputed status symbol for this country. You had to be *somebody* to have a Rolls-Royce. Mind you, I never liked them. I always had Bentleys.

AS: I always had Rolls-Royces. I wasn't as sophisticated as Ray, you see. Ray always said, 'I'm not going to have a Rolls-Royce, everyone will laugh at me.'

RG: Bookmakers have Rolls-Royces.

AS: I was fine, I wanted a Rolls-Royce! I found people like me didn't know what Bentleys were. And the only reason I wanted a car that size was that I wanted people to know I'd done well. Didn't give a toss whether it drove well or not. I got my first Rolls in 1956.

RG: I bought my Bentley before him. And not a Rolls, absolutely.

AS: Too common. No, not common... lairy! Sophisticates had Bentleys.

RG: My first one was a two-door. Rolls-Royce only supplied the engine and the chassis... you could get the body made by a dozen firms. I had a James Young carriage, 1947 two-door, dark olive green.

AS: When I bought my Rolls it was black and silver, but going off a bit, the silver was a bit tarnished. I got talked into having it resprayed, midnight blue, for £200. That was a Silver Cloud, just over two grand it cost me.

RG: People were impressed. Whether you were a bookie or not, they were impressed by the car. I remember once travelling this way from London, and suddenly there was a bang! And some old tramp had chucked a brick at the Bentley. I was outraged, and I stopped the car, and I went, 'Why did you chuck that brick at my car?' And he said, ''Cos it's dirty! 'Bout time you had it cleaned.'

AS: Eric Sykes was the first one I remember to have a personalized number plate: ES900. That's one thing I've never had, a personalized number plate. Even I think that's a bit common. I did look it up once, AS1, to see if I could have got it. In those days all you had to do was buy the vehicle it was on and then you could transfer it. I looked up the vehicle and it was on a farm tractor in Scotland. The bloke was offering it for a hundred grand, so he knew!

RG: The ultimate at that time was Lew Grade.

AS: He had one to ten.

RG: LG1 to LG10; he had ten cars.

COMEDY PLAYHOUSE, first series, episode seven

'THE STATUS SYMBOL'
First broadcast: Friday 26 January 1962

CYRIL: I want every bit of this car to be in working order before it leaves my garage. Don't worry, it won't cost much.

WILFRID: It seems everything keeps going wrong with it.

CYRIL: Well, you must expect a few things. It's an old car. You must expect to spend a few quid on it. I mean, it's not as if you're really spending it. It's more like an investment. You'll be top man around here. When you drive out of here, their eyes will be popping out of their heads... bowing and scraping all over the place... because that's what they do to a Rolls-Royce. The service you get... parking space, winderscreens wiped, you'll never have to open your own door... you'll never get pinched by the coppers in this. They'll be too frightened, they won't know who you are. They don't know if you're the King of Spain or not. You can get away with murder in a Rolls-Royce. There's nobody else round here who's got one. Except the undertaker… and you can't count him. He never used his for pleasure. And the birds… cor…

WILFRID: *(Eager)* Do you think the birds'll like it?

CYRIL: Like it? They'll go potty over you. Have you got a girl?

WILFRID: No.

CYRIL: You will have. Proper rumpo car, this is. Look at all the room in the back there. And it's got blinds. You don't have to wait for the windows to steam up.

WILFRID: *(Worked up)* How much longer do you think it'll take?

CYRIL: Well, that depends on what sort of job you want done. I mean, you don't want it bodged up, do you? You want a proper job done, don't you? Let's get that straight from the start.

WILFRID: Oh no, no, I don't want you to rush it.

CYRIL: Good, because if you want that, you'd better take it somewhere else, 'cos I don't do bodge jobs. It's not in my nature and never will be… I'm a craftsman… I take a pride in my work… I'm thorough… I'd sooner lose money than do a bodge job.

(WILFRED has been jiggling the window as he says this)

WILFRID: This window rattles a bit, doesn't it?

CYRIL: I'll shove a bit of cardboard down there, that'll hold it.

A story set in a hospital on visiting day harked back to Milford Sanatorium; it was also an homage to a Laurel and Hardy short from 1932, *The County Hospital*, in which Ollie lay on his back with a leg in plaster and Stan sat on the end of his bed eating hard-boiled eggs. In 'The Visiting Day', it was Bernard Cribbins in the bed, with Betty Marsden and Wilfrid Brambell as his parents with a box of dates. (*Hancock* obsessives will know that in the final radio series, Bill and Sid bring a bag of winkles when they visit Tony in hospital.)

The impression that the long months on the TB wards made on the two scriptwriters is seen more clearly in this episode than in almost anything else Galton and Simpson wrote. There's a sense of despair pervading the hospital, which is crystallized both in the loneliness Trevor feels when he thinks no one is coming to see him, and the loathing when his parents turn up. 'When we were in the sanatorium,' Alan recalled, 'visiting day was like that for some of the patients – grinding through two hours, because people had nothing in common with their visitors any more. They used to sit there waiting for them to go.'

COMEDY PLAYHOUSE, first series, episode eight

'VISITING DAY'
First broadcast: Friday 2 February 1962

> *(Cut to the entrance of the ward. A middle-aged woman comes in. She is the patient's MOTHER. She is carrying a string bag. Dressed in her Sunday best with a horrible hat. She looks round the ward, then she spots her son, TREVOR.)*

MOTHER: *(Loudly)* Oooh, there he is. *(Calls out behind her)* Oi, Jim… he's in here.

> *(Everybody in the ward stops talking and looks up at the raucous voice. TREVOR'S father comes to the doorway. He is dressed in a long black overcoat, muffler and flat cap.)*

MOTHER: *(Pointing to TREVOR'S bed)* That's him. Come on.

> *(They go up to the bed)*

MOTHER: Oh, poor little perisher, look at him. Hullo, son.

> *(TREVOR hasn't heard her. He has his radio headphones on and his eyes closed.)*

MOTHER: Oi… I'm talking to you.
FATHER: Perhaps he hasn't come round yet.
MOTHER: What, after six weeks?

> *(She pulls the headphones off. TREVOR opens his eyes with a start.)*

TREVOR: Well, Gordon Bennett… what's happened, the house fallen down?
MOTHER: Hullo son… we came round as soon as we could, didn't we, Jim?
TREVOR: Don't give me that… the television's broken down, hasn't it?
MOTHER: How did you know?
TREVOR: I thought so.
MOTHER: Oh, don't he look ill… bless him… don't he look ill, Jim, don't he…

> *(She goes to hug TREVOR. He pushes her away.)*

TREVOR: Now don't start that, Mum… for Gawd's sake.
MOTHER: You're still my little boy, y'know.

TREVOR: Yeah, well, go on, sit down... there's a chair... *(to the old man)* and keep your feet off the bed.

(They sit down)

TREVOR: Well, I didn't expect to see you two.

MOTHER: Well, we thought we ought to pop in and see how you're getting on, didn't we, Jim? Didn't I say we ought to pop round and see how he was getting on. I said that this morning, didn't I, Jim?

TREVOR: I've been here six weeks, why haven't you been in before?

MOTHER: No, well, it's been very difficult... it's your dad... *(lowers her voice)* He hasn't been too well. It's his chest again. *(To FATHER)* You've been ill, haven't you? Haven't you been ill? Tell him what was wrong with you. It was his chest. Terrible chest he's got. Been hawking around the house all night long... haven't you... been hawking around the house all night long... shocking noise he makes... *(to FATHER)* Let him hear how you cough. Go on, let one go.

(The old man coughs chestily)

MOTHER: See what I mean... all night long he goes on like that.

(The FATHER coughs again)

TREVOR: Turn it up, Dad, not in here.

MOTHER: He won't see a doctor.

TREVOR: It's them stinking fags he smokes.

MOTHER: *(To FATHER)* See, I told you. It's them fags... Trevor says it is... and he ought to know, he's in hospital. *(To TREVOR)* Go on, tell him to give it up... go on, he listens to you, he don't take no notice of me.

TREVOR: Oh, leave him alone... let him get on with it. Get his insurance money.

(The old man is rolling a cigarette)

TREVOR: It's no good rolling that, you can't smoke in here.

(The old man thinks for a bit, then gets up to go out)

MOTHER: Where are you going?

FATHER: Out in the corridor to have a smoke.

MOTHER: We've come here to see him. Sit down and keep still.

(The FATHER sits down again. He looks around, not taking much notice of the other two.)

MOTHER: Oooh, I nearly forgot. We brought you something.

TREVOR: *(Mollified)* Oh... oh, thanks very much. What is it?

MOTHER: Here you are. A box of dates.

(She takes a box of dates out of her string bag and hands them to him)

TREVOR: How long have you known me?

MOTHER: Why, what's wrong?

TREVOR: You know I don't like dates. I've never liked dates. Ever since I was a kid, I've hated dates... and what do you bring me? Dates.

MOTHER: *(To FATHER)* There you are, what did I tell you this morning? I said he didn't like dates, didn't I... but you wouldn't have it... take him some dates, you said...

TREVOR: Why didn't you bring me some oranges... or some grapes?

MOTHER: He said bring you some dates.

TREVOR: I don't like dates.

FATHER: I'll have them.

TREVOR: You knew I didn't like dates, didn't you... you had this worked out, didn't you... oh... here you are...

(TREVOR throws the dates across to the old man. The old man opens the box and starts eating the dates. He drops the stones onto the floor as he does so.)

TREVOR: And that's it, is it? That's all you've brought me. Six weeks it's taken you to come here, and when you finally get here, that's it... a box of dates.

MOTHER: It's all we could get.

TREVOR: It's all you had left over from Christmas, you mean.

MOTHER: What sort of Christmas did you have, son?

TREVOR: I don't know, I was unconscious.

MOTHER: *(Sympathizing)* Oh, what a shame. We had a nice time... quiet, you know... but very nice. *(To FATHER)* He was unconscious.

(The old man nods)

MOTHER: Well, so was he, most of the time... how he got home from the Swan, I don't know. Four o'clock he came home... didn't you... four o'clock you came home... while your son was lying here unconscious. You ought to be ashamed of yourself. We thought about you over Christmas... we wondered how you were getting on... didn't we, Jim... We wondered how he was getting on.

TREVOR: You didn't think about coming in to see me.

MOTHER: There didn't seem much point with you unconscious... there was no point in spoiling everybody's Christmas, was there... but we thought about you... it wasn't the same without you. Was it, Jim? Did you think it was the same without him? I didn't. I don't think Jim did, either... did you, Jim? No, of course he didn't. He wouldn't be your dad if he did.

TREVOR: You missed me but you didn't bother to come and see me.

MOTHER: Well, I don't like hospitals.

TREVOR: Well, neither do I! That's why I thought you might come and cheer me up. Cor blimey, it's only for two hours a week.

FATHER: Two hours? I thought it was only half an hour.

TREVOR: You don't have to stay... I've managed all right without you so far...

MOTHER: Oh, don't take any notice of him. *(To FATHER)* Stop upsetting him... you know how sensitive he is...

(The old man carries on eating dates. There is a silence. No one has anything to say. TREVOR sits there fed up. The mother smiles at him now and then, and looks round the ward. The old man picks up the headphones and puts them on, and sits there listening to the programme, with a blank expression. Now and then he eats a date.)

TREVOR: *(Finally he can stand the silence no longer)* Well, say something, somebody, you haven't seen me for six weeks, you must have something to talk about. I'm your son. What's been happening?

MOTHER: Nothing much.

TREVOR: What do you mean, nothing much? Haven't you got any news?

MOTHER: What about?

TREVOR: Well, anything. I don't care. But don't let's just sit here staring at each other... you might as well go home...

MOTHER: We don't want to go home, we only just got here... we came here to see you. Didn't we, Jim, didn't we come here to see him?

(The FATHER takes the headphones off)

FATHER: Eh?

MOTHER: I was saying we've come here to see him, we don't want to go home yet, do we?

FATHER: Oh no. *(To TREVOR)* Here, is there a television set in the ward?

TREVOR: No, there isn't!

FATHER: Oh. *(He puts the headphones back on and lapses back into silence)*

In the most polished *Comedy Playhouses*, the characters were unassuming and the dialogue was realistic, the sound of ordinary people who became self-conscious when they tried to articulate their feelings. These episodes required construction that was so artful it appeared to be spontaneous. The stories seemed simply to happen.

'"Sealed With a Loving Kiss" was one of my favourites,' Alan said, 'a complete little story, a rounded situation where it doesn't just suddenly end with a joke. That's a tight construction, where we had to be careful. The audience had to know the situation while the two protagonists stayed in the dark. It starred Ronnie Fraser and Avril Elgar, who was a Plain Jane type. They've agreed to meet at Paddington Station, on a first date, but he's sent her a photograph of his handsome father, and she's sent him a photograph of a good-looking girl. They get talking to each other, and they never realize that they're each other's date.'

COMEDY PLAYHOUSE, first series, episode nine

'SEALED WITH A LOVING KISS'
First broadcast: Friday 9 February 1962

ARNOLD: Cigarette? *(He takes out a packet of cigarettes)*
FREDA: Oh, thank you. *(She takes one)* I smoke these too.
ARNOLD: Do you?
FREDA: Yes, I save the coupons.
ARNOLD: So do I. That's the only reason I buy them. They're diabolical
    fags. What are you after?
FREDA: The hairdryer.
ARNOLD: Oh... I fancied the automatic tea-maker. *(Lights the two*
    cigarettes) Another hundred packets and I'll have enough coupons.
    (He coughs) Oh, I think I'll settle for the garden fork and turn it in.
    (Coughs) Your... er... your bloke hasn't turned up then.
FREDA: No. I was wondering if something has happened to him.
ARNOLD: No, I expect it's the traffic. He'll turn up... full of apologies... he,
    er... he won't get annoyed, will he, if he sees me talking to you?
FREDA: I shouldn't think so... why should he?
ARNOLD: Oh, well, you know... some blokes get a bit shirty, seeing their
    birds talking to another bloke... you know... I wouldn't want to get
    into any punch-ups.
FREDA: Oh no... he's not like that, I'm sure he's not. He's a very nice person.

(Crowd pass. PAUSE)

ARNOLD: Well... there's not many people about tonight.

FREDA: Yes, well, it's cold, isn't it?

ARNOLD: *(Shivers a bit)* Yes it is, isn't it... how did you get on during the snow?

FREDA: Oh, all right... I don't mind the snow.

ARNOLD: Oh, I don't mind the snow – it's the cold that creases me. Of course, women don't feel the cold like men... well, that's what they say... they don't seem to... I mean, they don't wear very much, do they... underneath...

(FREDA looks at him a bit old-fashioned)

ARNOLD: Well, you know what I mean... compared with us. I mean, we wear... we wear... you know... under our... can I get you a cup of tea?

FREDA: No, thank you.

ARNOLD: I haven't offended you, have I?

FREDA: Over what?

ARNOLD: Well... what I was saying... about women not wearing...

FREDA: No, no, of course not.

ARNOLD: I mean, I don't want you to get the wrong end of the stick, I wasn't trying to be... you know... saucy.

FREDA: That's all right, I'm not offended. I mean, underwear is underwear really, isn't it?

ARNOLD: Well, that's the way I look at it. But I didn't know how you felt about me mentioning it, so to speak.

FREDA: That's all right.

ARNOLD: And you wouldn't like a cup of tea?

FREDA: No, thank you.

ARNOLD: It's not the sort of a night to be hanging about, is it?

FREDA: All right then... perhaps I will. Have a cup of tea. If it's no bother.

ARNOLD: No, no, you stop here and I'll get it off the trolley.

FREDA: *(She undoes her purse)* Here you are, let me...

ARNOLD: No, no, that's all right... I'll get them.

FREDA: No, I insist on paying for mine.

ARNOLD: No, I won't hear of it... it's only threepence or fourpence... you stay here, I won't be long.

FREDA: *(Shouts)* If your friend turns up... you just go... don't worry about the tea...

ARNOLD: How many sugars?

FREDA: Six.

ARNOLD: How many?

FREDA: I've got a sweet tooth.

ARNOLD: Yes, you have, haven't you? I won't be long.

> *(He goes away. FREDA stands there looking about the station. Cut to ARNOLD going up to a tea trolley.)*

ARNOLD: Two teas, please, miss.

> *(The TROLLEY GIRL pours the two teas out. He puts six spoonfuls into one of them. She watches him. After the fourth one, he realizes she's looking at him. He stops after the sixth one.)*

TROLLEY GIRL: Do you want any help to stir it?

ARNOLD: *(Stares balefully at her)* Just tell me how much it is, that's all.

TROLLEY GIRL: One and eight, please.

ARNOLD: Oh… that's a bit expensive, isn't it? *(He feels in his pocket and gives her a two-shilling piece)*

TROLLEY GIRL: Sugar's not so cheap either.

There's one moment when Arnold shows a spark of passion, in an unexpected monologue about his name. The sense of grievance echoes Hancock, and the touch of surreal invention – that idea that solemn names are something we should put on when we leave school, like suits – is worthy of Harold Steptoe. It's a quintessential piece of Galton and Simpson:

ARNOLD: Archibald. Now there is a rotten name. I mean, how can you call a baby Archibald? A little, three-week-old baby… Archibald. There are some names that just don't fit little babies. I mean… George. You can't call a baby George. There should be grown-up names and kids' names. You change over when you get older. Nobody under fifteen should be called George. Or Archibald. Or Arnold, come to that. Sam, there's another one. And Bert… a little kid, laying in a cot with napkins on… 'How's Bert getting on?' It's not right.

The last of the series featured a couple of spivs in a rowing boat, urging on a dim-witted swimmer who is trying to beat the speed record for a Channel crossing. He's wearing a waterproof watch (it stopped working when he forgot to take it off in the shower) and a pair of ergonomic trunks (that keep slipping round his ankles) and his agents couldn't care if he drowns, provided they pocket the sponsorship money. As a satire, the piece is more relevant than ever, but Ray and Alan never felt satisfied with it – partly because they had written it with Sid James in mind, and he wasn't available.

'It was a failure completely,' Ray said. 'It didn't work.'

'Technically it was difficult to do,' Alan agreed. 'Instead of Sid, we finished up with a fairly late alternative, Sidney Tafler. He was a very dapper man who used to play in Ealing comedies. He got a lot of work – all the films that Sid James didn't want to do.'

Tafler was Lionel, the crooked manager, with Warren Mitchell as his nervous sidekick and Michael Brennan as the lummox in the trunks. In the first scene they are bickering in a Normandy hotel; later, in a scene that was almost impossible to shoot, they are bobbing about on rough water in the English Channel:

COMEDY PLAYHOUSE, first series, episode ten

'THE CHANNEL SWIMMER'
First broadcast: Friday 16 February 1962

LIONEL: Look, we can't hang about here any longer, a fortnight we've been waiting for the storm to die down... this is as good as we'll ever have it. A fortnight here with his appetite... look at him.

(Shot of CLIVE wolfing back the food)

LIONEL: He's costing us a fortune.
AUSTIN: Let's wait till tomorrow. The Channel might be a bit calmer.
LIONEL: Look, if we wait much longer he won't need to swim it, he'll be able to walk through the tunnel. We'll ask him. *(Calls over to Clive)* Oi, Clive.

(CLIVE looks up from his dinner)

LIONEL: Do you fancy going tonight?
CLIVE: *(Cheerfully)* I don't mind.

(LIONEL turns back to AUSTIN)

LIONEL: That settles it, we're off.
AUSTIN: You can't take any notice of him, he's an idiot. He said 'yes' last night... three ships ran aground.
LIONEL: Look, Austin, what are we here for? Why are we trying to swim the Channel?
AUSTIN: Well... to make some money.

LIONEL: Exactly. And we're not making any, stuck in here with him noshing all the funds. We got too much invested to turn it in now. We got to go. We're on to a fortune here. We got the wristwatch people; we got the swimming trunk people; we got the glucose people, all waiting on the other side. It's no good to them to say, 'This is what Clive Bonser would have used had he swum the Channel.' They're not going to pay for that. They want to see him crawling out of the water with the swimming trunks still on, the wristwatch still going and full of energy. What it boils down to is, no swim, no loot.

AUSTIN: All the more reason to wait till the weather clears up and make sure he gets there.

(The MANAGER of the hotel comes up to them)

MANAGER: Excuse me, monsieur. About the bill, it is a fortnight now, I would appreciate it if you could, er…

LIONEL: Give it to us. *(He takes the slip of paper from the MANAGER. Opens it.)* Gorblimey. That settles it, we're off tonight. *(Shows it to AUSTIN)* That's him and his grub. This is the last time I manage a Channel swimmer. Flyweight boxers for me after this. Come on, phone up Dover, ask them to send a boat across, a pilot and officials.

MANAGER: Excuse me, but you're not thinking of setting out tonight?

LIONEL: We are.

MANAGER: *(Shaking his head)* Tch, tch, tch, tch, tch.

LIONEL: Look, mate, you've been tutting for a fortnight. You're trying to keep us here till the holiday season starts, aren't you? I'm on to you. Well, we're off tonight. We could have gone the first day if we hadn't listened to you. You and your 'Take no notice of the weather forecasts, I've lived here twenty-five years'.

MANAGER: I think it will be very dangerous tonight.

LIONEL: Look, mate, we've all got to make a living, but you're not making yours out of us. We're off. *Compris*? Right. *(Hands him a pile of notes)* And let's have the change.

(The MANAGER leaves)

LIONEL: Money-grabbers. Cash in on anything. Money mad, these French.

(Fade up: the boat at night-time)

LIONEL: *(Calls overboard)* Are you all right?

CLIVE: *(Off)* Yes.

LIONEL: He's all right.

AUSTIN: I don't feel very well.

LIONEL: Oh cor, we've only just started. What's wrong with you?

AUSTIN: I feel seasick.

LIONEL: How can you feel seasick a hundred yards off the beach?

AUSTIN: It's still sea, isn't it? We're going up and down, ain't we? I want to go back.

LIONEL: Well, we're not going back.

AUSTIN: But I'm ill.

LIONEL: Well, hard luck. You'll have to put up with it.

(AUSTIN groans)

LIONEL: Oh, don't keep groaning. You'll put him off.

AUSTIN: Well, it keeps going up and down.

LIONEL: It's a boat, it's supposed to go up and down. Boats have always gone up and down, ever since they invented them they've gone up and down. I've never seen a boat that didn't go up and down.

AUSTIN: Don't keep saying 'up and down'.

LIONEL: Well, you get on my wick. There's a man here with umpteen foot of water under him, depending on us. Supposing we all started moaning and groaning, what good would that be to him? He gets cramp and we're all laying on the bottom of the boat moaning. You should have thought of that before you came... here, it is going up and down, isn't it. *(Holds his stomach)* Oh, that was nasty. Here, have some of these.

(He takes a bottle and pours out some pills, then hands the bottle to AUSTIN)

AUSTIN: What are they?

LIONEL: Seasick pills. Go on, they'll sort you out.

(AUSTIN swallows some. LIONEL swallows some.)

AUSTIN: They were supposed to be for him, weren't they?

LIONEL: Yeah.

AUSTIN: There's no more left.

LIONEL: *(Takes the bottle, shakes it)* Oh well, he's had it then, hasn't he?

(LIONEL tosses the bottle overboard)

CLIVE: *(Yells)*

LIONEL: *(Over the side)* Sorry.

CLIVE: What was that?

LIONEL: Nothing... where did it hit you?

CLIVE: On my head.

LIONEL: Oh, that's all right then. Keep going.

AUSTIN: How's he doing?

LIONEL: Marvellous. He's doing about 36 arms to the minute, four legs to each arm.

AUSTIN: What are you talking about?

LIONEL: That's his rate of swimming. You don't know nothing about this lark, do you? You've never showed any interest, have you? You don't know what it's all about, do you? I've had to pick it all up, you just haven't bothered. Same as that long-distance walker we had last year. You didn't know anything about him. You didn't know why he stuck his backside out while he was walking. You didn't know why it kept going up and down. You thought he had one leg shorter than the other, didn't you? You didn't know.

AUSTIN: Well, I just…

LIONEL: You can't keep relying on me, and then criticizing me all the time. You must take an interest in the people we're managing. Find out about them. Thirty-six arm strokes to the minute, four leg beats to each stroke. That's very good. If he keeps that up he'll break the record.

AUSTIN: What is the record?

LIONEL: Ten hours, fifty minutes. At this rate he'll be across in five hours.

AUSTIN: He'll never keep that speed up, it's impossible.

LIONEL: That's up to him, we're keeping that speed up. It's amazing how fast their arms go when they see the boat disappearing into the distance.

The second collection of *Comedy Playhouses* was screened in spring 1963, after the first six-part series of *Steptoe and Son* had enjoyed an emphatic success. Galton and Simpson, reluctant to accept the constraints of a series of *Steptoes*, were determined not to give up the freedom of the *Playhouses* – but the first episode, about a diplomat and a defector, roused an unexpected controversy.

Alan explained: 'We called it "Our Man in Moscow", after Graham Greene's *Our Man in Havana*. At the time, the director-general of the BBC was Hugh Carleton Greene, Graham's brother. The show was scheduled, and Graham Greene didn't get in touch with us or our agent, but he protested violently to his brother that we were doing a skit on his title. He was outraged. I was disappointed, because I was a great admirer of Greene and I thought he'd be far above that reaction, but apparently his brother told him not to be so stupid and sent him off with a flea in his ear.'

'I'd always admired him as a man of great intellect, a great writer and a very funny writer,' Ray added. '*Our Man in Moscow* epitomized the kind of thing we were trying to do – we were using Robert Morley, who was one of the biggest names we'd ever worked with. And we had a lovely cast, including Patrick Wymark, who was then a very big name in television drama.'

Morley was Sir William, Wymark was Nicolai and Frank Thornton was the unctuous under-secretary, Mortimer:

COMEDY PLAYHOUSE, second series, episode one

'OUR MAN IN MOSCOW'
First broadcast: Friday 1 March 1963

> *(Scene: the magnificent embassy hallway. SIR WILLIAM is just about to go up the stairs when there is a frantic banging on the front door.)*

SIR WILLIAM: Perkins! Perkins! There's someone at the door. *(He goes up one more step)* Perkins! Oh, good lord. I'm a servant in my own embassy.

> *(He goes to the front door and opens it. The door is forced back and a man pushes his way in. He is a Russian of middle age carrying a tuba. He is NICOLAI ROMANOVITCH.)*

NICOLAI: Close the door, close the door. *(He forces the door shut)*
SIR WILLIAM: How dare you come barging in here like this? May I remind you this is British territory? Who are you? What do you want?
NICOLAI: You must help me. Sanctuary. Sanctuary.
SIR WILLIAM: What are you talking about, sanctuary?
NICOLAI: *(Looks through the curtains)* I think they have followed me.
SIR WILLIAM: Who's followed you?
NICOLAI: They have. Don't stand there arguing with me, I demand to see the British ambassador. Don't let them in. Go on, go and tell the ambassador I am here.
SIR WILLIAM: I, sir, am the British ambassador.
NICOLAI: You open your own doors?
SIR WILLIAM: Yes, well… we are a democracy, of course. Now what is all this about?
NICOLAI: *(Looks through the curtains)* They're still there. *(SIR WILLIAM*

looks out) I, Nicolai Alexandrovitch Romanovitch, third tuba player of the Moscow State Symphony Orchestra, wish to apply for British citizenship. Long Live Queen Victoria!

SIR WILLIAM: Yes, well, you're a bit late as far as she's concerned. In any case, you can't become a British citizen just like that. It takes years. You have to be sponsored and everything… there are forms to fill in.

NICOLAI: No, no, you do not understand. I have not got time for forms or sponsors… I wish to apply for political asylum.

SIR WILLIAM: Oh no, not political asylum.

NICOLAI: Yes please. Where is my room?

SIR WILLIAM: Now just a minute… you can't come in… please, I'm afraid… *(calls)* Mortimer! We must talk about this. Now be calm. Why do you want political asylum? Are you a criminal?

NICOLAI: No, no, no, I am a tuba player.

SIR WILLIAM: What's that got to do with it? You can be a criminal and a tuba player.

NICOLAI: No, I am just a tuba player, no criminal. I just want to leave Russia and come to live and work in your glorious country.

SIR WILLIAM: Oh, it's not so glorious… now stay where you are. *(yells)* Mortimer! Now, what have you done, why are you being followed, who is that man out there?

NICOLAI: He is the triangle player.

SIR WILLIAM: He doesn't want to go as well, does he?

NICOLAI: No, he has been sent to see that I do not go. He is not really a triangle player. He is the political musician of the orchestra.

SIR WILLIAM: Oh, the shop steward?

NICOLAI: Please?

SIR WILLIAM: The trade union man? You've fallen behind with your dues? Well, I'm sure we can sort this out, you don't want political asylum for that… I mean, there's no need to cause trouble between our two countries. I mean, everything's going so well, and I don't want a political asylum right on top of the trawler trouble… I'll have a word with him.

(He tries to open the door but Nicolai slams it)

NICOLAI: Comrade Ambassador, you do not understand. He is a political policeman who watches us, to see that we do not deviate. That is why he is made the triangle player – he has more time to watch us.

SIR WILLIAM: Look, I am a great personal friend of your Minister of Culture. I'm sure if I had a chat with him, we could sort all this out quite amicably.

NICOLAI: I will not go back.

SIR WILLIAM: You can't stay here.

NICOLAI: I will not go back.

SIR WILLIAM: *(Bellows)* Mortimer!

> *(Mortimer is standing right behind him and receives the full blast of the shout)*

MORTIMER: You called, sir?

SIR WILLIAM: Where have you been? I've had to open the door myself, there's nobody on guard, this gentleman was allowed to walk straight in.

MORTIMER: What's the problem, sir?

SIR WILLIAM: He wants political asylum.

MORTIMER: *(Pleased)* Oh really. Oh jolly good. That'll make a good piece of propaganda for us.

SIR WILLIAM: To hell with the propaganda… this man is the third tuba player from the Moscow State Symphony Orchestra.

MORTIMER: That's even better, what a capture. *(He outlines the headlines of a newspaper)* 'Leading Russian musician defects to the West'. Oh yes, what a coup. Immense value for our side. Well done, sir.

SIR WILLIAM: What do you mean, well done? I don't want him. Look, the Minister of Culture is coming round tomorrow night for cocktails and a game of chess. How do you think he's going to feel with one of his tuba players locked away upstairs? No, it's out of the question. Tell him to go away.

MORTIMER: You can't deny a man political asylum, sir. I mean, the land of the free and all that. One of our basic principles.

SIR WILLIAM: I don't care. I'm not giving political asylum to any tuba player that happens to wander in here.

NICOLAI: *(To MORTIMER)* Comrade, sir. You seem to be a man of great wisdom and understanding. Permit me to explain my case to you.

MORTIMER: *(Preens himself)* Certainly, by all means.

SIR WILLIAM: Look, I'm the ambassador, I'm the one you explain things to. He's only a secretary, a mere nothing.

MORTIMER: Oh thank you.

SIR WILLIAM: I didn't mean it like that, Mortimer, no offence meant – to explain to a foreigner, one tends to oversimplify.

MORTIMER: *(Coldly)* I understand, sir.

SIR WILLIAM: I'm trying to apologize, Mortimer.

MORTIMER: There's no need to, sir. You're the ambassador, as you pointed out.

SIR WILLIAM: Look, Mortimer...

NICOLAI: Please. Comrades. There is no problem. I stay here overnight, then tomorrow you disguise me and smuggle me out of the country to England.

SIR WILLIAM: Look, I am the British ambassador, not the Scarlet Pimpernel.

MORTIMER: With all due respects, sir. It is our duty to consider all requests for asylum seriously.

SIR WILLIAM: Look, what is this man? A musician. Temperamental. He's had a row with the conductor, probably accused of playing a wrong note, he flares up, walks out in a huff, straight round here, political asylum. A lot of trouble, diplomatic crisis, letters passing to and fro, after three days he'll be homesick and want to get back to his borscht and samovar. Well, I'm sorry, but I don't think it's worth the trouble...

NICOLAI: So... you refuse my request.

SIR WILLIAM: I'm very sorry.

NICOLAI: Then I kill myself.

SIR WILLIAM: Not here you won't. There you are, what did I tell you about musicians? He's mad. Mortimer, stop him.

MORTIMER: Why don't we all sit down and get to the bottom of it? Let's find out what it's all about.

SIR WILLIAM: Good idea. Good thinking, Mortimer. Come into the study. Ring down for some tea.

(They all go into the study. SIR WILLIAM sits at his desk. MORTIMER pulls a chair up for NICOLAI, who puts his tuba down and sits. MORTIMER stands by the desk.)

SIR WILLIAM: Now, take notes, Mortimer. Name?

NICOLAI: Nicolai Alexandrovitch Romanovitch.

SIR WILLIAM: Profession... tuba player, we know that. Reason for application for asylum... Are you being persecuted?

NICOLAI: No.

SIR WILLIAM: Won't they let you practice your religion?

NICOLAI: I don't believe in religion, I am a good communist.

SIR WILLIAM: Well, you don't want to go to England, you'll get persecuted in England if you're a communist, I'm telling you.

NICOLAI: England is free.

SIR WILLIAM: Well... to a certain degree, yes, I suppose so.

MORTIMER: Perhaps you don't feel you are rewarded enough for your talent?

NICOLAI: I have the Order of Lenin, a flat in Moscow, a car and 300 roubles a week.

SIR WILLIAM: That's not bad, is it. That's more than he gets. *(He points to MORTIMER)* You should be a very contented man. I'm afraid I can't see any reason for granting you asylum, can you, Mortimer?

MORTIMER: Why do you want to leave Russia?

NICOLAI: I want artistic freedom to play on my tuba any music I like.

SIR WILLIAM: Oh, that's nonsense, you have to play what's written like all the others.

NICOLAI: No, no, listen to me, comrade. For thirty years I have been the third tuba player in the Moscow State Symphony Orchestra. For thirty years I have played Shostakovich, symphonies in praise of the seven years forestation plan, symphonies in praise of the coal miners' output in Siberia, the steelworkers' concerto, requiem for dead tractor drivers in the virgin territories. I have had enough – I cannot go on. *(Pleading)* I want to play Strauss.

SIR WILLIAM: He wants to play Strauss.

NICOLAI: I want to play waltzes and polkas. Oom pa pa, oom pap pa. *(He dreamily conducts a waltz with his hands)*

SIR WILLIAM: I'm not giving you political asylum just because you want to play waltzes. I've never heard anything like it. I'm sorry, it's out of the question. Really, Mortimer, you must see this...

(NICOLAI carries on humming a Strauss waltz)

MORTIMER: Well, I don't know, sir. We do have precedents.

SIR WILLIAM: Nonsense, we've had nothing like this... it would make us a laughing stock. *(To Nicolai)* Do you mind... we're trying to discuss your future.

(NICOLAI stops conducting)

MORTIMER: Well, if he'd been a writer, sir, and he wanted to, say, write a romantic novel in praise of the previous regime, we would have granted him asylum, wouldn't we, sir?

SIR WILLIAM: Well, yes, but that's political dynamite... that's freedom of speech.

MORTIMER: Well, this is freedom of tuba playing...

SIR WILLIAM: No, no, it's too ridiculous... we can't do it... I can see the cartoons now... no, no, no, the whole situation is farcical. Look, this is my first ambassadorship – I'm not starting off like this, it would follow me wherever it went. 'There he goes, the champion of tuba players...' I mean, there's no dignity attached to it... It's such a silly instrument... I mean, if he was a violin virtuoso, yes, maybe, but not a tuba player.

MORTIMER: With all due respects, you can't really hold his instrument against him... I mean, he's just as much entitled to his human rights as a violin player. After all, he must be quite good on the tuba to be in the orchestra in the first place...

SIR WILLIAM: I realize that, I had no intention of casting any slurs on his technical ability. I'm sure he's very clever – it's just that the image is all wrong.

NICOLAI: Am I staying or not?

SIR WILLIAM: We haven't decided. Look, Nicolai... be reasonable, it's not that we don't want you in England. I'm sure you'd be a great asset to our cultural life, but what I can't understand is – why choose us? I mean, there's all the other embassies to choose from. Why pick on us?

MORTIMER: Yes, I mean, Strauss isn't even English... he's Austrian.

SIR WILLIAM: That's it! Well done, Mortimer, good thinking. Austria, that's the place for you. The home of the Viennese waltz... la-de-dah-da, la-de-dah-da... you'd be much happier there... the great marble ballrooms, the officers in their fur-trimmed cloaks... yes, that's what you're looking for. You go round to the Austrian embassy, I'm sure they'd accommodate you. I know the Austrian ambassador. He's a doctor, he's very musical, he plays the recorder. I'll have a word with him. *(He picks up the telephone)*

NICOLAI: No. *(He puts his hand on the receiver rest)*

SIR WILLIAM: Why not?

NICOLAI: I do not want to go to Austria. I want to go to England.

SIR WILLIAM: What's wrong with Austria?

NICOLAI: They haven't got a king and queen.

SIR WILLIAM: What's that got to do with it?

NICOLAI: For years I have been dreaming of playing Strauss, but where there is Strauss there should also be kings and queens and princesses, beautiful gowned women, handsome officers... without that, what is Strauss? It's just not the same.

MORTIMER: He's got a point there, sir.

SIR WILLIAM: He hasn't got a point. I've done the old-fashioned waltz all over the world, it's got nothing to do with it. Really, Mortimer, you're as reactionary as he is. Oh, I don't know what to do.

MORTIMER: You have no choice, sir. If he won't change his mind, then it must be referred to London for an official decision.

SIR WILLIAM: Yes, you're right. Get through to the Foreign Office and ask for instructions. Now, you go away and come back tomorrow, and we'll let you know.

NICOLAI: I am not leaving here.

SIR WILLIAM: Are you frightened of the secret police or something?

NICOLAI: Secret police! What is this secret police? There are no secret police. This is Russia, the country of the workers. We are our own masters, we have no need for secret police. That is Western propaganda... Do not think it is easy for me to leave my Mother Russia – I am very happy here, it is a magnificent example of Soviet co-operation. It's just that...

SIR WILLIAM: I know, you haven't got a king and queen.

MORTIMER: And you want to play waltzes.

SIR WILLIAM: I don't understand him. What are his politics?

MORTIMER: It's quite simple, sir. He's obviously a Romantic Marxist Monarchist.

SIR WILLIAM: I wouldn't have thought so. I see him more as a Communist Constitutional Royalist.

MORTIMER: We can't say that to London.

SIR WILLIAM: Tell them he's a Liberal, then.

A playful nod to Graham Greene was followed by a pastiche of another master of short stories, Somerset Maugham. Eric Barker starred as a district commissioner in the Malaysian jungle, with Terence Alexander and Erica Rogers.

COMEDY PLAYHOUSE, second series, episode two

'AND HERE, ALL THE WAY FROM...'
Broadcast: Friday 8 March 1963

LAWRENCE: Would you care for a drink before you turn in, Ampleforth?

AMPLEFORTH: Thank you, sir. After you, sir.

(They go up the steps onto the verandah. MRS LAWRENCE comes out to join them. She is young and attractive, dressed in a short cocktail dress. She is holding a highball glass.)

LAWRENCE: Hello darling. *(He pecks her on the cheek)* Had a hard day?

MRS LAWRENCE: Yes I have. Do you know, I had to run my own bath this morning?

LAWRENCE: Oh dear, that won't do. We can't have that sort of thing. I'll have a word with the servants in the morning.
AMPLEFORTH: You must be tired, Mrs Lawrence, have a chair.
MRS LAWRENCE: Thank you, Robin.

(As they cross behind LAWRENCE'S back, AMPLEFORTH takes her hand and they mouth a kiss to each other surreptitiously. LAWRENCE doesn't see this. She sits down and AMPLEFORTH pulls up a chair from somewhere else and sits with them. LAWRENCE claps his hands.)

LAWRENCE: *(Yells)* Boy!

(A very old Malay servant comes out. He is dressed in a white jacket and sarong.)

LAWRENCE: Two large whiskies and water, and… darling?
MRS LAWRENCE: White rum and lime.
LAWRENCE: White rum and lime. Chop! chop!

(The old servant bows and hurries back into the house)

LAWRENCE: Any letters for me today, darling?
MRS LAWRENCE: *(Uninterested)* I don't know, I haven't looked.
LAWRENCE: Oh. I suppose you've been too busy.
AMPLEFORTH: I'll have a look, sir. *(Jumps up)*
LAWRENCE: Oh thank you, Ampleforth.

(Ampleforth goes to the door leading in to the house. Turns and mouths a kiss to MRS LAWRENCE. He goes inside the house.)

LAWRENCE: Damn good fellow, Ampleforth. Make a good district commissioner one day… if we've got anywhere left to district commission in.

One of Ray and Alan's favourite anecdotes is about 'The Script That Wrote Itself':

AS: Sometimes it takes three weeks to write a script, or it can take four hours, but the thing is when you read the four-hour script you can't tell any difference from the three-week script. That's the technique of writing: even though, as Flaubert said, 'Every word is torn from my body.' Those scripts can be a bastard to write but at the end of the day, it reads just as fluidly as the ones that wrote themselves. It's an art in itself, that's what you've got to learn.

RG: The scripts never wrote themselves. Occasionally one would be easier than the others. Our classic story about that is 'Impasse'. We couldn't think of anything for several days, and we were getting near the deadline. By Friday, we were desperate. We told our secretary not to let anyone in, but at the end of the afternoon, when we were still drawing blanks, she phoned upstairs and said Graham Stark wanted to see us.

AS: Graham was an old friend, we'd been working together since the beginning when he played Hancock's straight man, so we said, 'Why not? Send him up. It's not as if he's going to stop us working, because we haven't got an idea to work on!' So Graham came into the office with a copy of the *Evening Standard*. He said, 'I've got to show you this, it's in the stop press – there's these two blokes get stuck driving their cars, one going one way and the other going the other way, in this little lane in Cornwall.

RG: We said, 'Thank you very much, that's the story,' and retired to the pub. Next morning we came in at nine o'clock, and at one o'clock it was finished. We wrote it in three and a half hours.

AS: Normally speaking we would allow six months to do a series of seven. Because there's always some that take two or three weeks to do. But 'Impasse' wrote itself, once we'd got the initial idea.

RG: Alan finished in time for the football.

AS: My shoulders ached for a week afterwards. I've never typed so fast.

The episode starred Leslie Phillips and Georgina Cookson as the couple in the Rolls, and Bernard Cribbins and Yootha Joyce as the people in the Ford:

COMEDY PLAYHOUSE, second series, episode three

'IMPASSE'

First broadcast: Friday 15 March 1963

FERRIS: *(In the driver's seat of his Rolls-Royce)* No, I won't back up. I don't like his attitude. Besides, I'm further up the lane than he is. No, I'm sorry, Celia, there is a principle involved here – I will not be browbeaten by the likes of him.

MRS FERRIS: Oh, don't be so childish.

FERRIS: I'm not being childish. If I back up, it will be a victory for him and his rudeness and lack of road manners.

MRS FERRIS: It won't, it'll be a victory for you and common sense.

FERRIS: He wouldn't see it like that.

MRS FERRIS: There's a lay-by just behind us, what does it matter?

FERRIS: It matters to me.

MRS FERRIS: So we're going to stop here all day.

FERRIS: If needs be, yes.

MRS FERRIS: Oh really, you're making us both look ridiculous, you and your stupid pride – you always have to be in the right, don't you?

FERRIS: Celia, you don't drive, you don't understand the principles of motoring, so please sit there and be quiet. I know how to deal with his type. Leave it up to me.

(He gets out of his car)
(Cut to the Ford)

MRS SPOONER: See, you've started something now. He's getting out of his car. There's going to be trouble.

SPOONER: Well, I'm ready for it. I'm not frightened of him just because he's got a big car, it don't impress me.

(FERRIS comes up to the window of the Ford. He leans on it.)

FERRIS: Now look here, this has gone far enough…

SPOONER: Don't lean on my car.

FERRIS: I'm not leaning on your car, I just rested my hand on the window frame.

SPOONER: Well, don't. Don't touch the car. I don't like people touching my car. Now… you've got something to say?

FERRIS: Yes, I have. Now let's be sensible about this…

SPOONER: I'm being perfectly sensible.

FERRIS: It would be much easier for you to back up your car than it would be for me to back up mine.

SPOONER: Oh? How do you work that one out?

FERRIS: Because your car is smaller than mine. It's easier to reverse a small car, in a narrow lane like this.

SPOONER: Well then, that's your fault, ain't it? You've got no right coming up a lane like this in a great car that size.

FERRIS: I'm entitled to take my car where I please.

SPOONER: You're a roadhog, that's what you are. You want all the road, don't you? You think because you've got a Rolls-Royce, you own the road. We've all got to drive up into the bushes to let you

get by. Well, I'm sorry, those days have gone, mate... we all pay
our road tax.

FERRIS: Oh, I see... that's it, is it? You have an inferiority complex. You
resent the fact that I have a Rolls-Royce while you have a... what is
it?

SPOONER: It don't matter what it is... it's stopping you, ain't it!

FERRIS: Good heavens... if I hadn't heard it with my own ears, I wouldn't
have believed it still existed.

SPOONER: What are you rabbiting about now?

FERRIS: Resentment, that's all it is. You're not really bothered about
backing up, that's not the main issue with you, is it? You just can't
stand me having a better car than you.

SPOONER: Better car? What, that?

FERRIS: Yes, that.

SPOONER: You're joking. I wouldn't have one of them if you gave it to
me. That ain't a car, that's a sex symbol, that's all it is.

FERRIS: How dare you.

SPOONER: What's the matter, you got an inferiority complex, is that why
you need it? Can't impress people on your own? You got to be
surrounded by one of them things, is that it? I feel sorry for blokes
like you. Me, I don't need one of them – people are impressed by
me. Me!

FERRIS: Are you going to back up this heap of old tin, or am I going to
have to push you back?

SPOONER: (Getting slowly out of his car) What did you call my car?

MRS SPOONER: Albert, now don't start anything.

SPOONER: You keep out of this. This is between us. What did you call my
car?

FERRIS: (Deliberately) A heap of old tin. Which, if necessary, I shall drive
up to, and push back, right the way down to the other end of the lane.

SPOONER: (His face close to Ferris) (Quietly) And if you do, I shall push
your teeth right the way down to the other end of your throat.

That name 'Spooner' belonged, of course, to a friend of Ray and Alan;
they'd used it once before, and would borrow it again in 1977, for the irritating know-all in a *Galton and Simpson Playhouse* episode called 'I Tell
You It's Burt Reynolds'.

By 1963, another friend, Frankie Howerd, was reviving his flagging
career with a comeback that started at Peter Cook's satirical comedy club,
the Establishment in Soho. Galton and Simpson celebrated his resurgence

(and reminded the BBC's head of light entertainment of his original promise to them) by casting Howerd as a fretful amateur smuggler who doesn't have the nerve to face the customs check at London Airport:

COMEDY PLAYHOUSE, second series, episode four

'HAVE YOU READ THIS NOTICE?'
First broadcast: Friday 29 March 1963

FOX: *(Looking out of the aircraft window)* The French coast… already. Not long now. Half an hour to sort something out. Concentrate. Concentrate. The watch… you could swallow it. Very funny. Ha ha. Concentrate, you fool. In a minute they'll ask us to strap ourselves in, then I've had it. One last chance. I've got it. Next to the body. Of course. They won't strip me. They wouldn't dare.

(The flight attendant passes. He leans over and grabs her arm.)

FOX: Miss… miss…
PASSENGER: *(FOX is leaning across him)* Do you mind?
FOX: I'm terribly sorry. Miss…
FLIGHT ATTENDANT: What's wrong, sir?
FOX: Can I have some sticky tape?
FLIGHT ATTENDANT: Sticky tape?
FOX: Yes, sticky tape. Sticky paper. Adhesive plaster, anything.
FLIGHT ATTENDANT: Have you cut yourself, sir?
FOX: No, I haven't cut myself. I just want some sticky tape. Have you got any or not? If you haven't got any, I'll ask someone else.
FLIGHT ATTENDANT: Yes, I'm sure I could find some somewhere.
FOX: Well, hurry up, will you… please.

(FOX flops back in his seat, on edge and fidgeting. Track in on his face as he starts imagining…)

(Cut to customs hall at London airport. FOX saunters in. Full of quiet confidence. He picks up his luggage from the conveyor belt and strolls over to the customs counter. He puts his case on the counter. The CUSTOMS OFFICER comes up to him.)

CUSTOMS OFFICER: Good afternoon, sir.
FOX: *(Quietly, with a slight smile)* Good afternoon.
CUSTOMS OFFICER: Is this your luggage, sir?
FOX: Uh-huh.

CUSTOMS OFFICER: Have you read this notice, sir?

FOX: *(Glancing at it casually, hardly taking his eyes off the CUSTOMS OFFICER)* Uh-huh.

CUSTOMS OFFICER: Have you anything to declare?

FOX: Yes I have. Let me see now... 200 fags... off the plane... don't know why I buy them, I don't smoke, but you know how it is, I can't resist a bargain...

CUSTOMS OFFICER: Is that all?

FOX: Ah, half a bottle of brandy, I forgot all about that... I've got half a bottle of brandy off the plane... I'm glad you reminded me of that...

CUSTOMS OFFICER: Yes sir... anything else?

FOX: Let me think... I've got a little chalet you lift the lid off and it plays 'Silent Night'...

CUSTOMS OFFICER: How much did you pay for that, sir?

FOX: Twelve and six. And then one of those glass things, you know... it's got Mont Blanc inside... or would it be Zermatt... anyway, it snows when you turn it upside-down... one and nine, I think that was... oh, and an ashtray.

CUSTOMS OFFICER: And that's all you purchased.

FOX: Er... yes... that's all.. yes, that's the lot...

CUSTOMS OFFICER: Do you possess a watch, sir?

FOX: A watch. Me. No, I never use them. *(Pulls back both sleeves)* No, I'm not a clock-watcher, me. They soon tell you the time when you're in a pub, don't they? *(Laughs)* Whatever made you ask me that?

CUSTOMS OFFICER: We've had a tip-off.

FOX: Tip-off... what tip-off?

CUSTOMS OFFICER: You asked for some sticky tape on the aircraft, I believe. From the flight attendant.

FOX: I can explain that... my book was torn. I have nothing to hide.

CUSTOMS OFFICER: In which case, you won't mind stepping into that room.

FOX: Well, really... I must protest.

CUSTOMS OFFICER: This way, sir. *(He leads FOX into a side room and shuts the door)* Would you mind undressing, please sir?

FOX: Take my clothes off? This is outrageous. I shall speak to my MP about this.

CUSTOMS OFFICER: That's your privilege, sir. If you don't mind.

FOX: I do this under extreme protest.

(He takes off his jacket and hands it to the CUSTOMS OFFICER, who throws it to a second official, who proceeds to rip the lining out and tear the sleeves off, etc.)

CUSTOMS OFFICER: The trousers, if you don't mind, sir.

FOX: You can't do this… that's my best suit… I don't have to put up with this sort of treatment.

CUSTOMS OFFICER: The trousers, please.

(FOX takes his trousers off and hands them to the CUSTOMS OFFICER, who throws them to the second official. He rips them apart, exactly as he did with the jacket.)

FOX: You haven't heard the last of this.

CUSTOMS OFFICER: Your shirt, please.

FOX: Really, this is going too far.

CUSTOMS OFFICER: The shirt?

FOX: *(He takes off his shirt and tears it to pieces himself)* Save you the trouble. *(He is now standing in his vest and boxer shorts)*

CUSTOMS OFFICER: Would you remove your vest please, sir?

FOX: I refuse to take any further part in this farce. I have co-operated just as far as I'm prepared to.

CUSTOMS OFFICER: I must warn you, sir. I am empowered to insist that your vest is removed… by force if necessary.

(The second official moves close to FOX, menacingly. FOX is now completely shattered. He removes his vest. A watch is taped to his stomach. The watch face is over his belly button.)

CUSTOMS OFFICER: Well, I see the time by your navel is 3.35.

FOX: Yes… it's slow.

(Cut back to FOX, sitting in the aircraft. He is in a complete panic, fidgeting, mopping his brow.)

FOX: *(Thoughts overlaid)* I can't go through with it, I can't go through with it…

One of the shared enthusiasms that united Ray and Alan in the sanatorium was modern jazz. 'It's the craftsmanship I admire,' Alan said. 'You cannot play modern jazz without being a master of the instrument, whereas you can play rock and roll without being able to read music. Most sixties chart music left me cold.'

'One of the reasons why we never took part in the Swinging London scene, apart from the fact we were too busy writing, was that we didn't like pop music very much,' Ray added. 'We loved Coleman Hawkins, Stan Getz, Bill Evans. And we shared that with John Le Mesurier, who was such a big jazz fan that he used to go down to Ronnie Scott's and sit by the legs of the piano till the small hours of the morning.'

Le Mesurier starred in 'A Clerical Error', as a conman who impersonates vicars. Much of the episode was played out on the window ledge of a seedy hotel, but the opening part was a poignant, and understated, domestic scene. Le Mesurier's mother was Amy Dalby, who regularly played old ladies in *Dixon of Dock Green*:

COMEDY PLAYHOUSE, second series, episode five

'A CLERICAL ERROR'
First broadcast: Friday 12 April 1963

> (*The front of Wormwood Scrubs prison. Cut to the archway of the prison. The door in the front gate opens, and CALEB BULLRUSH steps out. He is carrying a brown paper parcel under his arm and is dressed in a prison handout suit. He turns and puts his hand through the door, and shakes hands with a hand on the other side. He gives a slight smile as he does so. The door shuts, and CALEB turns to face the world. He sets off down the road. Walks past a church. Stops and reads the wayside pulpit text for the day: 'I will restore to you the years that the locusts hath eaten' – Joel, ii, 25. CALEB smiles, and looks back to the prison.*)

> (*Dissolve to hallway of a terraced Victorian house. The doorbell rings. MRS BULLRUSH, CALEB'S mother, comes out into the passage and opens the door. CALEB is standing there.*)

CALEB: Hallo Mother.
MRS BULLRUSH: Oh, it's you. You're out again, are you? Well, I suppose you'd better come in.

> (*CALEB enters the house. She shuts the door.*)

MRS BULLRUSH: Where were you this time?
CALEB: The Scrubs.
MRS BULLRUSH: Oh. You haven't been there before, have you?
CALEB: No.
MRS BULLRUSH: What was it like?
CALEB: Quite nice.
MRS BULLRUSH: I went down to Brixton just before Christmas but you weren't there, so I came home. I haven't been out since, what with the weather…

CALEB: That's all right, Mother. I didn't expect to see you, not in all that snow.

MRS BULLRUSH: How long were you in for?

CALEB: Three months, that was all. Full remission.

MRS BULLRUSH: Three months... doesn't time fly.

CALEB: Have you been keeping well, Mother?

MRS BULLRUSH: Oh yes, I keep going, there's nothing wrong with me. Your stepfather's dead, though.

CALEB: Oh dear, I am sorry.

MRS BULLRUSH: Yes, a month ago tomorrow he went. Just like that.

CALEB: Did he suffer?

MRS BULLRUSH: No, went in his sleep. I had the shock of my life when I woke up in the morning. We were going to the pictures that afternoon. Shame, he was looking forward to it. He left you his cufflinks.

CALEB: Oh, that was very nice of him.

MRS BULLRUSH: I've given his clothes away. They wouldn't have fitted you.

CALEB: No.

MRS BULLRUSH: There's his umbrella, you might as well have that. *(She takes the umbrella out of the hall stand and gives it to him)*

CALEB: Thank you.

MRS BULLRUSH: Your room's just the same as you left it, I haven't touched anything.

CALEB: Thank you, Mother.

MRS BULLRUSH: I don't like to go in there, because I know you don't like it.

CALEB: That's all right, Mother, I have nothing to hide from you.

MRS BULLRUSH: No, no one's going to accuse me of poking my nose. What you get up to is your own affair, it's nothing to do with me, you're over twenty-one, you're old enough to know what you're doing... only do try and stay out a bit longer this time.

CALEB: I'll do my best, Mother.

MRS BULLRUSH: Well, I can't stop... I'm cutting some furballs off the cat. I don't want to leave the door open, in case he gets out. I've got his legs tied down, but you know how strong he is. Last time I have a fluffy cat.

CALEB: I'll be up in my room, if you need me, Mother. I must get out of this horrible prison suit.

MRS BULLRUSH: Will you be in for tea?

CALEB: No, I'll be going out shortly... on business.

MRS BULLRUSH: Oh, here we go again. *(She turns and goes back into the kitchen)*

The last of the Galton and Simpson *Comedy Playhouses* harked back to the Hancock era: one of their unrealized movie concepts had been based on a film starring the French comic Fernandel, called *Le Mouton à Cinq Pattes (The Sheep Has Five Legs)*. Hancock was to play an incompetent with four successful brothers, whose lives he destroys in turn. Only one section was written before Hancock scotched the idea; it became the basis of this *Playhouse*, starring Alfred Marks as Lionel, a handyman who takes a job at a health farm and soon starts an eggs-and-bacon cafe in the boiler room.

COMEDY PLAYHOUSE, second series, episode six

'THE HANDYMAN'
First broadcast: Friday 5 April 1963

(LIONEL takes out a packet of fags and sticks one in his mouth. He offers the packet to the gatekeeper.)

LIONEL: Fag?

(The GATEKEEPER snatches the packet from LIONEL'S hand)

LIONEL: Here, I said one.

(The GATEKEEPER grabs the cigarette out of LIONEL'S mouth and drops the packet and the cigarette into the basket)

GATEKEEPER: Don't ever let me see you with those again. Smoking cigarettes is strictly forbidden here – it is disgusting and harmful. Have you got any idea what it does to your bronchial tubes?
LIONEL: How should I know what it does to your bronchial tubes? It's hard enough looking at your tonsils.
GATEKEEPER: Every cigarette you smoke is like rubbing a sheet of emery paper up and down them, wearing them away, scraping the surface off them, rubbing them red… raw… and horrible… till you can't breathe and you suffocate with bronchitis – or worse.
LIONEL: Yeah, but it's nice to have one with a cup of tea, isn't it?

Memories of the writers' time at Milford pervade the imaginary health farm. 'Under a bed on our ward, we used to keep an electric stove and frying pan,'

Ray said. 'If we didn't fancy what was for dinner, we'd get in some eggs and bacon and have a fry-up. You weren't supposed to do this, but the matron would come round and sniff the air and say, "Oh, it does smell nice."'

(Cut to inside of the boiler room. Close-up on a great fry-up in the frying pan on the boiler. Steak, eggs, sausages, potatoes, a great plate of bread and butter. LIONEL is gleefully supervising the cooking of it. Camera pans upwards with the steam from the pan to the ventilator grille.)

(Dissolve to another ventilator, then pan down. We are now in the patients' recreation room, with a group of patients engaged in various activities. An old lady is knitting a Fair Isle pullover. Suddenly her nose starts twitching. She sniffs and looks round her. She carries on knitting, but her mind isn't on what she's doing.)

(Cut to a group of card players, playing whist. One plays a card. The second is about to play when he starts sniffing. He looks round to see where the smell is coming from.)

FIRST PLAYER: Come along, come along.
SECOND PLAYER: Eggs and bacon.
FIRST PLAYER: Pardon.
SECOND PLAYER: I can smell eggs and bacon.
FIRST PLAYER: Oh, don't be ridiculous. In this place? It's the diet. You're not used to it. It produces hallucinations. A sort of nose mirage. Play your card.

(The SECOND PLAYER lays down a card)

THIRD PLAYER: Mushrooms.
FOURTH PLAYER: Pardon?
THIRD PLAYER: Mushrooms. With sausages.
SECOND PLAYER: Steak and chips.
FIRST PLAYER: Tomatoes and fried bread.
THIRD PLAYER: What's been lead?
FIRST PLAYER: The nine of mushrooms. Er, no...

(Cut to the old lady, who is now knitting furiously and haphazardly, her mind not on the job, her nose twitching. She is licking her lips.)

(Cut to two patients talking, GENERAL BOOTH and LADY MELCHILD)

BOOTH: *(Conspiratorially)* I wouldn't tell this to another soul, but I've had three fruit drops this week.

MELCHILD: Really, general, for a man brought up on iron discipline, it shows a remarkable lack of moral fibre.

BOOTH: I know, it's unforgivable... rank cowardice, really. I'll just have to try and break myself of the filthy habit. It's just that one gets so damnably hungry...

(He breaks off and starts sniffing. LADY MELCHILD looks surprised; then she catches the aroma and starts sniffing.)

(Cut to two patients playing snooker. One starts sniffing, plays his shot and misses the ball altogether.)

(Cut to a general shot of the room. Gradually the patients get up in ones and twos and small groups, and make their way to the doors and out into the corridor, sniffing. The card players go, General Booth and Lady Melchild, the snooker players and finally the old lady drops her knitting and hurries out after them.)

Galton and Simpson did not return to the BBC's *Comedy Playhouse* series after their two seasons, but a host of other sitcom writers made their breakthrough there: Marty Feldman and Barry Took, Johnny Speight, John Law, Ken Hoare, Christopher Bond, and John Esmonde and Bob Larbey were among the first to take advantage of the opportunity. This comedy space race is one of the reasons that Ray and Alan are held in such high regard by generations of writers: they built a fail-safe format, a launch pad for success, and then, without any professional jealousy, they handed it over to delighted colleagues.

ITV attempted to emulate the success of the series in 1969, with *Galton and Simpson Comedy*; almost a decade later Yorkshire Television revived the format with *Galton and Simpson Playhouse*. Neither of these could be called pioneering, because Ray and Alan had already blazed their own trail, but both collections are packed with sublimely clever comedies. Once again they had an open brief, able to write about anything they liked and cast whomever they wanted. By now, however, the colossal success of *Steptoe and Son* had made their own names instantly recognizable; something the TV channels were keen to capitalize on.

It had never been Ray and Alan's ambition to see their own names in the titles of their series, however: with their usual, self-deprecating humour, they brushed aside the appeal to their egos. 'By the late sixties, we had been to Hollywood,' Alan pointed out. 'We knew we weren't stars; we were in the wrong job for that. There was a gag doing the rounds in

Los Angeles – "Did you hear about the actress who was so dumb, she slept with the scriptwriters?"'

For almost the only time, Ray and Alan introduced a note of religious farce with the *Galton and Simpson Comedy* episode 'Friends in High Places' (1969). Almost all their scripts include elements of political philosophy – they send up social inequalities and class – but they never raise spiritual issues. The explanation lies in their own religious beliefs: both are lifelong atheists.

'I haven't "believed" since I was a choirboy,' Alan said. 'I remember standing in church, singing, when I was about twelve or thirteen, and I had a sort of epiphany. I thought, "What is all this nonsense? What am I doing here?" I used to sing in the choir to earn a bit of money – you got a shilling for weddings, though I used to prefer funerals… you got two bob for funerals, double bubble. But I was standing there and suddenly realized what a load of old nonsense I was chanting.'

'As long as I can remember,' Ray added, 'I've always been an atheist. Certainly since I was about nine years old. My brother was in the Communist Party. As he was my hero, and he didn't believe because the Communists didn't believe, I suppose I didn't believe. I didn't join the Party – but I remember being very affected by the Spanish Civil War, and the religious elements in that. I was probably nine when it finished. All those things conspired to make me an atheist.'

In this cynical look at heaven, three angels – played by Frank Williams, Arthur English and Richard O'Sullivan – are spying on Earth:

GALTON AND SIMPSON COMEDY, series one, episode two

'FRIENDS IN HIGH PLACES'
First broadcast: Saturday 26 April 1969

(SCENE: A cloud)

(Dissolve to two male angels dressed in white, with large wings. They are sitting in two white, high-backed chairs. Clouds are swirling round their feet. One of them is playing a harp, very badly. A third chair is empty. The other angel is looking through a telescope on a tripod, also white. The backdrop is space.)

FIRST ANGEL: Clarence, don't keep playing that thing, there's a good chap.
SECOND ANGEL: You got to practise, ain't you?

FIRST ANGEL: You've been practising for 25,000 years to my knowledge, and you still haven't improved.

SECOND ANGEL: Well, if He'd let me have a saxophone like I asked for, I'd have been all right by now. My fingers are too fat for this thing.

FIRST ANGEL: Well, just give it a rest, it's most disconcerting. Besides, you're not supposed to play when you're on duty. We are supposed to be watching the Earth.

SECOND ANGEL: There's nothing worth watching down there. They're a load of berks.

FIRST ANGEL: *(Pointing upwards)* If He heard you talking like that about His creation, He'd be very upset.

SECOND ANGEL: Well, let's face it, He's done better, ain't He? I prefer them great big scaly things with two heads and ten arms out on Pluto. Now they've done well, they have, and they're nice with it, but that lot down there, a right load of old rubbish. He ought to turn that lot in.

FIRST ANGEL: Yes, I must say I'm inclined to agree. They have made rather a mess of themselves. But there you are, He's got a soft spot for them. They were His first creation.

(He has another look through the telescope. A third angel comes on carrying a tray with Greek-style drinking vessels and a silver salver with a lid on it. He puts it on a table.)

THIRD ANGEL: Grub up, lads.

SECOND ANGEL: What we got today? *(He lifts up the lid)* Oh Gawd blimey, ambrosia and nectar again. I'm sick and tired of that. I've been shoving that stuff down me till it's coming out of my earholes. I'm surprised at Him, a man with His upbringing. I thought we would have been on the old salt beef and lutkas.

THIRD ANGEL: You get fish on Fridays.

SECOND ANGEL: I'm fed up. What's the point of being immortal if you can't have a bit of what you fancy now and then? What wouldn't I give to get me choppers into a nice steak and kidney pudding! Now that's one thing that does look good down there.

THIRD ANGEL: *(Checking a report sheet)* Anything to report?

FIRST ANGEL: Oh, the usual. Wars, murders, suicides.

THIRD ANGEL: Any mass starvation?

FIRST ANGEL: Oh yes, the usual places.

THIRD ANGEL: If they go on breeding like they are, they'll all be starving.

SECOND ANGEL: Pathetic, ain't they? I wouldn't give you two penn'orth of cold tea for any of them.

Perhaps the most popular sitcom on British TV in the seventies was *Dad's Army*, which ran from 1968 to 1977. One of its main stars, Arthur Lowe, was a favourite actor of Ray and Alan. They admired his combination of pomposity and delicacy, and after Tony Hancock's death, they considered reviving the *Half Hours*, with Lowe as Hancock and James Beck as Sid James. The actors were interested, and by 1973 a pilot show seemed set to go ahead. But Beck, who played Private Walker in *Dad's Army*, died unexpectedly in August 1973. He was just forty-four years old.

Lowe revealed a superstitious streak: these deaths happened in threes, he said. Hancock was dead, and now Beck. He didn't want to be next, so he pulled out of the remake.

Undeterred, Ray and Alan wrote 'Car Along the Pass' for Lowe, in their final *Playhouse*-style series, broadcast in 1977. It's a pitch-perfect satire of Little England, all the better for being set 4,000 feet above a Swiss mountainside:

GALTON AND SIMPSON PLAYHOUSE, series one, episode one

'CAR ALONG THE PASS'
First broadcast: Thursday 17 February 1977

(SCENE: Interior of a cable car)
HENRY: I'll be glad to get out of this country. The worst holiday I've ever had in my life. You wait till I see that travel agent. A cheap walking holiday, he said. Huh! We brought most of our own provisions, we've lived in a tent for a fortnight, and we've still spent over £18 each. Never again.

(ETHEL has opened a collapsible picnic table and is preparing some French bread and a box of camembert cheese, with some tomatoes)

ETHEL: I enjoyed it.
HENRY: Oh well, you would. You didn't have to pay for it.

(ETHEL hands him some bread and cheese and a tomato)

HENRY: What's this?
ETHEL: Camembert.
HENRY: Where's the Cheddar?
ETHEL: It's all gone.
HENRY: *(Smelling the cheese)* Oh dear, oh dear. That's terrible. That could break up a demonstration in Cairo, that could.

(HENRY takes off his glasses and wipes his eyes)

ETHEL: We'll have to buy some more food at the next shop we see.

HENRY: We are not spending any more money on food. We'll get fed on the aeroplane.

ETHEL: But that's not until tomorrow afternoon.

HENRY: That's all right, it'll give us an appetite.

ETHEL: Can't we eat in the hotel tonight?

HENRY: Hotel?

ETHEL: Aren't we staying in a hotel?

HENRY: Certainly not. We've got the tent, woman.

ETHEL: You can't put a tent up in the middle of Geneva. It's a big city.

HENRY: If it's a big city, it's got parks.

ETHEL: I was looking forward to a bed and a bath on our last night.

HENRY: You can have a bath. There's a lake there. *(He taps his map)* Look. It's enormous. Miles of it. Oh, I'll be glad to get home. Any tea?

(ETHEL hands him a mug and pours some tea from a Thermos. They sit there eating. HENRY spills some tea on the luggage belonging to the people next to him, a German businessman and his wife. The German wipes it off with his handkerchief. ETHEL is looking out of the window.)

ETHEL: It's very pretty, isn't it?

HENRY: It's all right.

ETHEL: Beautiful scenery.

HENRY: Not bad. If you like that sort of thing.

ETHEL: So high up.

HENRY: Yes. You'd have a marvellous view if it wasn't for the mountains. Oh, can't these things go any faster?

(The German businessman, HEINZ, leans over)

HEINZ: Excuse me for butting in, old chap, but I could not help overhearing. You have not enjoyed your holiday?

HENRY: *(Coldly)* Have we met?

HEINZ: Excuse me. Permit me to introduce myself. Heinz Stahlmaker.

HENRY: A German.

HEINZ: *Ja.*

HENRY: *(Not keen)* I see.

HEINZ: From Baden-Baden. And you?

HENRY: Henry Duckworth, from Twickenham Twickenham.

HEINZ: Ah. Twickenham. Rugger.

HENRY: What do you know about rugger? Germans don't play rugger.

HEINZ: I played it in my school in England.

HENRY: Actually, one doesn't play it *in* the school, one plays it *at* the school.

HEINZ: *Ja, ja,* of course, *at,* yes, I am sorry. Forgive me.

HENRY: Quite all right, a small mistake. I always make a point of correcting foreigners, otherwise they never learn.

HEINZ: Thank you. This is my wife, Hilda.

HILDA: *Guten Tag, mein Herr.*

HENRY: Good afternoon.

HEINZ: Hilda, I'm afraid, does not talk English very...

HENRY: *Speak.*

HEINZ: Please?

HENRY: *Speak* English. Only parrots *talk.*

HEINZ: *Ja, ja.* Speak English. Thank you.

HENRY: *(Warming to him)* So you went to school in England, eh? Jolly good.

HEINZ: And this is your wife?

HENRY: Who? Oh yes, that's her. Whereabouts in England?

HEINZ: Don't you recognize the tie? Haileybury.

HENRY: Oh. Haileybury, yes. Quite good.

HEINZ: Are you public school?

HENRY: Um... er... not the sort of question we ask each other in England. We just... know.

HEINZ: Duckworth. I bet they called you 'quack-quack'.

HENRY: How did you know? They certainly did not!

HEINZ: We may have met on the rugger field, *hein*?

HENRY: Yes, yes, more than likely.

ETHEL: You didn't play rugby at Whitton Grammar, you played football.

HENRY: *(Looking at her sourly)* They played football, I played rugby. Why don't you look out the window, these mountains have cost a lot of money. Make the most of them. *(He hands her his camera)* Take some photographs of something.

HEINZ: This is your first time in the Swiss Alps?

HENRY: And the last.

HEINZ: You must try Germany next time.

HENRY: I've been there before.

HEINZ: Really?

HENRY: Forty-five. Just before you surrendered. Lieutenant, Army Education Corps.

HEINZ: Ah, teaching your soldiers to speak German.

HENRY: I was trying to teach them to speak English half the time.

HEINZ: I too was in the war. Luftwaffe. Hermann Goering squadron.

HENRY: Luftwaffe, eh? Dropped a few on England, did you? I suppose that's why they sent you to school there, get the lie of the land. Cycling round the countryside, taking photographs of the gasworks and the level crossing, I know.

HEINZ: No, no, please, do not let us fight old battles. I love England. In any case, I did not agree with the war.

HENRY: No. None of you did after it was over. I didn't meet one. I don't know how he got an army together. There must have been only half a dozen of you.

HEINZ: Come now, let us forget about the war. We are on holiday.

HENRY: I've finished mine, thank God.

HEINZ: You are on your way back to England?

HENRY: I certainly am. I can't wait to see those white cliffs. Tomorrow afternoon I shall set foot on English soil, never to leave it again.

ETHEL: Look, Henry, mountain goats.

HENRY: Fascinating. It's been the most miserable fortnight of my entire life. Nothing but snow. Freezing cold. And as for the food! Well, I'm sorry, but dipping bits of bread into a potful of boiling cheese is not my idea of a gastronomic experience. What a disastrous trip. We were dug out of an avalanche at Zermatt, we were knocked down by a skier in Villars... in the middle of the high street, I might add. Our tent was trampled underfoot by a herd of cows. I was rendered unconscious by one of the bells that hang underneath their necks and had to spend three days in hospital being treated for frostbite. I tell you, all it needs is for this thing to stop halfway across, and that'll put the tin hat on it.

(CUT TO: Film clip of the cable car going along, halfway across the valley. It stops. After a few minutes of muted worry, HENRY decides to appoint himself as leader of the group.)

HENRY: Oh well, if we're going to be up here for a long time, we'd better get ourselves organized. We can't have a leaderless rabble. *(Stands up)* Attention. Attention, *s'il vous plaît*. My name is Lieutenant Duckworth, British Army. We seem to be in a bit of a hole. Well, not yet. But it's best to recognize the situation and prepare ourselves. It could be all right, but then again it could be dangerous. The eyes and the ears of the world will be upon us, so let us conduct ourselves with courage and dignity. So let's sort ourselves out, shall we? See where we are. Hands up all those who are British.

(ETHEL, HENRY and one other traveller, a mild little man, put their hands up)

HENRY: Oh. Is that all? Oh dear, that's a shame. Oh well, never mind. If we do plunge 4,000ft to our deaths, at least most of us will be foreigners.

…

(HENRY gets up and stamps his feet. HEINZ taps him on the shoulder.)

HENRY: Don't poke me, old man.
HEINZ: I should like to know by what virtue you have assumed command.
HENRY: Quite simple. Senior ranking officer.
HEINZ: Lieutenant?
HENRY: Precisely.
HEINZ: My dear chap, I was a Luftwaffegeschwadergefuhrer.
HENRY: You can't fool me with long words. Flashy labels on empty luggage. What does it mean, anyway?
HEINZ: Squadron leader.
HENRY: Yes. Well. It doesn't cut any ice up here. This is an army job.
HEINZ: We are up in the air.
HENRY: We are attached at each end to the land.
HEINZ: I am the senior ranking officer.
HENRY: One of your generals surrendered to me at Schleswig Holstein.
HEINZ: I didn't.
HENRY: I've still got his wristwatch. And his binoculars.
HEINZ: I am a squadron leader, you are only a lieutenant.

(A FRENCHMAN stands up and pulls them apart, and stands between them)

FRENCHMAN: Silence! This is a stupid argument. Who cares what either of you were?
HENRY: Who asked you to join in? Who are you?
FRENCHMAN: Le Viscomte de Valence, General, l'Armé de la France. The senior ranking officer!
HENRY: General? Huh! Vichy, no doubt. Collaborator. Doesn't count. Sit down.

9 *Steptoe and Son*

The fourth episode in the first *Comedy Playhouse* series was a two-hander called 'The Offer'. It was born during an all-day trawl for inspiration, when both Ray and Alan were lying on the floor, flat on their backs – their favourite mode when searching for ideas, and possibly a legacy of their years in the sanatorium. 'We had a very good bit of carpet in the office,' Ray said, 'and when we were stuck for ideas, me especially, we'd lie down.'

When either man had a thought that seemed to offer even faint promise, he would speak it out loud. If it was met with silence, he'd know it wasn't worth much. That morning in 1961, Ray Galton proposed: 'There's these two rag-and-bone men.' The suggestion failed to raise a spark. Three hours later, still combing the air for ideas, Alan Simpson said, 'What was that, there were two rag-and-bone men?' They began to improvise a dialogue, and it quickly became obvious that their characters couldn't stand each other. This raised two questions: why would they keep working together, and who were they anyway? Father and son; they were father and son. That answered both questions.

Harold was desperate to escape – from his demanding father, from poverty, from a job that offered no prospects but hard physical labour. He had worked on the cart since he was twelve; now he was nearly forty, and still unmarried. Albert was thirty years older, lonely and in poor health, and bitterly afraid of seeing his only son move away. The situation was coarse and real and all too commonplace; it would have been tragic, except that Harold's optimism could never be doused for long. Albert, though he was maudlin, bigoted, petty and foul-mouthed, possessed a streak of cunning which had kept him alive since his days in the trenches of the First World War. That cunning was more than a match for Harold's naive efforts to better himself.

'The Offer' ended with Harold struggling to push a cart laden with his ramshackle belongings, and unable to budge it while his father asked, with an innocent smirk, 'I'll go and open the gates, shall I?'

'For "The Offer", we were determined to use a pair of serious character actors,' Alan said. 'The material wouldn't have worked with comedians in the roles. We had used Eric Sykes and Stanley Baxter earlier in the *Playhouse* series, but a well-loved comic would have had completely the wrong effect in "The Offer". People know them, and that changes their expectations. With a comic, you're waiting for the laugh. We wanted to convey the reality of this situation, and for that we needed actors.'

The writers knew before the script was finished which actors they wanted for the parts – Harry H. Corbett as the son and Wilfred Brambell as his father. Corbett had earned a name in fringe theatre, including the Langham Experimental Group and Joan Littlewood's Theatre Workshop company at Stratford East, but his reputation had not yet made him a household name; Wilfrid Brambell had been impressive as an old tramp in a television play by Clive Exton called *No Fixed Abode*. This was the final break from the music-hall tradition of comedy: these were real actors, who breathed life into the lines and didn't stop to count the laughs. 'Ray and I went to the rehearsals, and we couldn't believe what we were seeing,' Alan remembered. 'In the final scene, when Harold breaks down over his cart, Ray turned to me and said, "Those are real tears. He's really crying." We were used to comedians screwing up their faces and going "boo-hoo".'

Corbett had already met Ray and Alan briefly, as he revealed in an interview, later included in a BBC *Arena* documentary: 'I told them how much I really admired their work. I really did, and I said if they ever felt like writing anything... I looked at television and all I saw that was making any kind of good social comment was the Hancocks, the Eric Sykes... Oh, I did envy them. So, this thing about the rag-and-bone men thumped through the door. I read it and immediately wired back: "Delicious, delighted, cannot wait to work on it." I thought, this is brilliant. Good work is always easy. You don't even have to learn the lines. They're there, they're right, and they're the lines you should say.'

STEPTOE AND SON, first series, episode one

'THE OFFER'
First broadcast (as a Comedy Playhouse*): Friday 5 January 1962*
First broadcast (as the opening episode of Steptoe and Son*): Thursday 7 June 1962*

(In the junk yard)

HAROLD: Your precious horse... I tell you, he's useless... he's old... he's slow... I don't know why you don't take him round the knacker's yard and have him melted down.

ALBERT: You don't like that horse, do you? Come on, admit it, you've never liked him, have you?

HAROLD: Well, seeing as how you've brought it up... no, I don't. He's vicious. He lunged at me again today.

ALBERT: He's no fool, he knows when he's not liked. You got to handle him right. Like I handle him. He don't lunge at me.

HAROLD: Course he don't. He knows when he's onto a good thing, the way you treat him. Giving him sweets and lumps of sugar all the time. His teeth have gone rotten through you. I don't call that being kind to a horse, making his teeth go rotten.

ALBERT: It's not the sweets, he's getting old. That's why his teeth are rotten.

HAROLD: He's rotten all over. Glue, that's all he's good for.

Father and son are rag-and-bone men, junk collectors who go 'totting' for old clothes and broken furniture around Shepherd's Bush, the west London suburb where the BBC studios were based. They scratch a living by stripping the scrap metal from what they find, by passing cloth for recycling to the rag trade, and by selling 'antiques' from the yard outside their tumbledown house. They have no van, and without their horse, Hercules, to pull the cart, they would be out of business.

HAROLD: *(Gets annoyed)* Here, look, you moan about the way I treat the horse, you moan about the way I go totting... *you* go out with the cart. Go on, you go out... I'll stay here in the yard... I wouldn't mind sitting round the fire drinking tea all day long. Go on, you get up on the plank, you're so good at it... I'm sick and tired of sitting up there staring at that great backside all day long. You go out tomorrow.

ALBERT: You know I can't take the cart out any more... with my legs.

HAROLD: Yeah, well, that's it then, ain't it? You don't want to say anything, do you? Otherwise, I'm liable to turn this lot in and be off. I'm sick to death of you, the yard, the cart and the horse.

ALBERT: Dah, what do you know? What could you do?

HAROLD: Look, mate, don't you worry about me, I can look after myself, I'll be all right. I've had an offer.

ALBERT: Get out of it.

HAROLD: Oh yes I have. And it don't include you or that rotten horse. See? OK? All right? Well, watch it then.

ALBERT: What offer? Who from?

HAROLD: Never you mind. I'll go and feed the horse.

ALBERT: You don't want to go taking no offers, we've got a good business here.

HAROLD: You're worried now, ain't you?

ALBERT: You don't want to go taking no offers. Young fellow like you. There's plenty of opportunities here, there's not many young lads of your age with a partnership in a thriving business like this.

HAROLD: I'm thirty-seven, Dad.

ALBERT: Well, that's young, ain't it? If I was thirty-seven I'd be out with that horse.

HAROLD: If you were thirty-seven you wouldn't be out with that horse, because that horse wouldn't have been born. You would have been out with the horse we had before, and it was a much better horse than that rotten one I have to go round with.

ALBERT: That's it, go on, blame the horse. All bad workmen blame their tools. You've had it too easy, you have. My dad made me come up the hard way, that's where I gone wrong. I brought you straight into the business. You didn't have to work your way up… straight onto the cart you went. With your own horse. And your name on the gate.

HAROLD: My name ain't on the gate… it's got, 'And Son'.

ALBERT: That's you, ain't it?

HAROLD: No, it ain't, it's you. It was your dad who had that sign painted.

ALBERT: Yeah, well, it's an old firm, there's no point in wasting money keep changing the sign. It'll all come to you one day, when I'm dead and buried… and I don't suppose it'll be long…

HAROLD: Oh Gawd, here we go…

The sitcom's dynamic was fuelled by fear – the old man's terror that his son would leave him and that he would die alone, and Harold's dread of being trapped in Oil Drum Lane until he became a broken-down decrepit like his father.

ALBERT: You don't want to go taking no offers. I've built this business up for you, son. It's yours when I'm gone. Then when *your* son comes along, you won't have to change the sign either… Steptoe and Son, only it'll be you and your son.

HAROLD: But I ain't got no son, have I? I ain't even got a wife.

ALBERT: Well, go out and get one.

HAROLD: Look, I ain't going to get married, Dad. As soon as I meet a bird and she says what do I do and I say I'm a rag-and-bone man, she don't want to know.

ALBERT: And what's wrong with rag-and-bone men? It's an honourable profession. Very useful members of the community, we are. You tell them that, next time they turn their noses up.

'The Offer' was conceived as a self-contained playlet, but the open-ended final scene, when Harold has loaded his cart and is preparing to leave, implied this drama would be played out again. Producer Tom Sloan recognized the potential, and even before the episode was screened he was urging Galton and Simpson to write a series around the characters of Harold and Albert. 'We didn't fancy it,' said Ray. 'We'd tasted freedom with *Comedy Playhouse*, and we wanted to keep doing that. But Tom Sloan kept on, so in the end we thought we'd shut him up by saying, "We'll do a series of *Steptoe and Son*, if you can get Harry and Wilfrid to agree." We were sure they'd never say yes… and they jumped at it.'

HAROLD: If there's anything else I need, I'll come back and get it. Well… that's it… I'll be off now, then. Go and get the horse.

ALBERT: You're not having the horse.

HAROLD: I want the horse…

ALBERT: The horse is mine, I'm not giving it to you.

HAROLD: I only want to borrow him, I want to get me stuff moved out.

ALBERT: No, you're not having him. You never liked him… you never had one good word to say for him all the time we've had him.

HAROLD: I got to have the horse, how am I going to get the stuff out?

ALBERT: That's your problem, ain't it? You're not having the horse.

HAROLD: All right, keep your stinking horse. That ain't going to bother me. I'll move it myself. I don't want any favours from you, mate. I've never had any in the past, I don't want none now. It's another good reason for going. I'll soon have this lot on the move.

(He gets in between the shafts)

HAROLD: Well, I'll be off then. I'm sorry it had to end this way. I'll come and see you… when the pressure's off a bit. Cheerio.

ALBERT: Cheerio.

(HAROLD strains at the shafts. Nothing happens.)

HAROLD: Is that brake off?
ALBERT: Yeah.
HAROLD: Right. Well, I'll be off then. Cheerio.

(He strains again. The cart doesn't budge.)

ALBERT: Cheerio.
HAROLD: No hard feelings.
ALBERT: No.
HAROLD: It's the only way. If you don't look out for yourself, you don't
    deserve to get on. I was in a rut, you see. If I don't go now, I'll never
    go.
ALBERT: No. Cheerio then.
HAROLD: Cheerio.

(He strains harder and harder to get the cart moving)

ALBERT: I'll go and open the gates, shall I?
HAROLD: Yeah, yeah, all right.

*(He strains and strains, and gradually gets weaker. He relaxes and
has another go. He is panting with effort.)*

HAROLD: *(Almost crying)* Move, you rotten, stinking cart... move... I got
    to go... I got to get away. Move... move...

*(The cart doesn't move. HAROLD gradually breaks down. Finally he
slumps over the shafts. ALBERT comes up and stands looking at him
for a moment. He then puts a hand out, onto HAROLD's shoulder. He
helps him up and puts an arm round him.)*

ALBERT: I'll go and put the kettle on and we'll have a cup of tea. I'll get
    the old sausages going – you like sausages, don't you?

(He leads HAROLD towards the room)

ALBERT: It's a bit late to go anywhere now, ain't it? It's dark now, you'd
    have to have lights on.
HAROLD: I'm still going... I'm not staying.
ALBERT: 'Course you're not... you can go another day... on Sunday,
    when there's not so much traffic about. We'll get the cart unloaded in
    the morning... don't you worry about it.

(They walk off across the yard to the door into the room)

HAROLD: I'm going, I'm not staying here. I'm taking that offer.

ALBERT: 'Course you are. You can go another day. He'll keep the offer open for you, if he reckons as much as you say he does. Or you could stay here with your old dad and wait till a better offer comes along... I mean, the way you're building up your stock here... you'll be more of a power to be reckoned with. I mean, the more you can put in, the better offer you're going to get...

(They reach the door and go into the room)

The name Steptoe harked back to the beginning of Ray and Alan's career when they, and a group of friends, rented a flat in Richmond. 'Opposite this flat,' said Ray, 'there was a photographic shop called Steptoe and Figge, and we always thought that was a funny name. "Figge and Son" wouldn't have worked. "Steptoe" was perfect.'

Once Brambell and Corbett had agreed to return for the series, five more episodes that developed their characters were scripted. In the first, Albert's scheming to keep his son at home is shown to be first wheedling, and then callous and ruthless:

STEPTOE AND SON, first series, episode two

'THE BIRD'
First broadcast: Thursday 14 June 1962

ALBERT: What are you getting ready for?

HAROLD: I'm going out.

ALBERT: What, again?

HAROLD: Yes... again.

ALBERT: You went out last night.

HAROLD: I know I went out last night... and I'm going out tonight as well... and I wouldn't be surprised if I went out tomorrow night. All right?

ALBERT: Where are you going then?

HAROLD: Just out.

ALBERT: Yeah, but where?

HAROLD: Nowhere... just out, that's all.

ALBERT: Well, you can't go out without going anywhere.

HAROLD: Well, I can... and I'm going... out.

ALBERT: What time will you be in?

HAROLD: I don't know. I might be late. I might be very late.

ALBERT: What are you going to do then?

HAROLD: Look, I'm your thirty-seven-year-old son… I'm not your sixteen-year-old daughter. Nobody's going to try anything on me. I mean, nobody's going to get me up a dark alleyway. Nobody's going to drug me up with vintage cider and have a go at me. I'm not a Judy, Dad… I'm a bloke. You're worrying like I was a Judy or something… it's not natural… it's daft.

(He tucks his shirt collar in and starts washing himself, in his shirtsleeves. The old man surveys him.)

ALBERT: You know *Perry Mason*'s on tonight. I thought you would be staying in to watch it. I thought you liked *Perry Mason*. Why don't you stay in and watch him?

HAROLD: I don't want to… I happen to have made arrangements to go out.

ALBERT: Oh, you *are* meeting somebody then?

HAROLD: So now you know… I'm meeting somebody.

ALBERT: Oh. Where will you be, if I want to get in touch with you? In case something happens. You know…

HAROLD: *(He has lathered his face. Stops.)* You're fishing, aren't you?

ALBERT: No, I'm not. It's important… I'm not a young man any more. You never know when I might have to get in touch with you. *(Puts his hand to his chest)* My heart being what it is. Where will you be?

HAROLD: Oh, I don't know… you could try the Silver Grill at the Savoy… or the American Bar at the Ritz… I haven't made my mind up yet.

(He starts shaving)

ALBERT: You're having a shave then.

(HAROLD ignores him, carries on shaving)

ALBERT: You had a shave yesterday.

(HAROLD still ignores him)

ALBERT: I've never known you have two shaves in a week before. *(HAROLD carries on shaving)* Must be someone special if you have to have a shave.

HAROLD: *(Stops shaving)* Look, don't keep on talking to me when I'm shaving. This is sharp… I've just honed it. I don't want to go out with a bird with bits of fag paper stuck all over my face, do I?

ALBERT: *(Realizing)* Oh. You're going out with a bird, are you? So that's what you're getting all tarted up for. Oh, I see. That's the way the wind's blowing. Birds now, is it?

HAROLD: All right, so now you know. I'm going out with a bird. Is that all right with you, Dad? Can I go out with a girl, Dad? I won't be late home, Dad... I won't get her into trouble, Dad. Is that all right, can I go out, please Dad?

ALBERT: Less of your lip.

Later, Albert seems to have accepted the fact that his son has a steady girlfriend, and suggests they invite her round for a fish supper. But the old man's selfishness has not abated and as they wait for the woman, the fish goes cold and the chips congeal:

(HAROLD looks out of the window)

ALBERT: Is she coming?

HAROLD: Can't see her.

ALBERT: I reckon she's given you the elbow. She ain't coming. Let's start.

HAROLD: 'Course she's coming. She ain't very late.

ALBERT: Nearly an hour... cor dear... she's got you on a bit of string, ain't she? I wouldn't let her make a mug of me... I know what I'd do if I was you.

HAROLD: What?

ALBERT: I'd have the soup for a start.

HAROLD: Look... eat a roll and shut up.

(ALBERT gets stuck into the roll)

ALBERT: I bet those fish and chips are getting dried up. *(PAUSE) (ALBERT sniffs)* Is that soup burning?

HAROLD: No.

ALBERT: We'll need some more candles in here soon. Can I have some wine?

HAROLD: No.

ALBERT: I must say you've gone to a lot of trouble... for a bird who hasn't turned up. You sure she ain't out with another bloke?

HAROLD: *(Controlling himself)* Be quiet, Dad... I know what you're trying to do.

ALBERT: I ain't trying to do anything, son.

HAROLD: Well, keep quiet about it then. *(PAUSE)* Who said she's out with another bloke?

ALBERT: Well... she ain't here, is she? I mean, if she was so keen on you, she'd be here, wouldn't she? I mean, she should be here, shouldn't she? It just seems a shame... a fine boy like you... if you let her treat you like this now, what's it going to be like later on? Your life won't be your own. She'll twist you round her little finger. A boy like you deserves something better than that. Not a bird who doesn't turn up... going out with other blokes.

(HAROLD turns away from the window. He can't control himself any longer.)

HAROLD: *(Shouts)* All right. All right. Go and get the dinner in.

(ALBERT is delighted. He scampers into the kitchen. HAROLD sits down at the table.)

HAROLD: If she didn't want to come, why didn't she say so? She didn't have to humiliate me. She only had to say...

(ALBERT comes scurrying back holding two bowls of soup)

ALBERT: Here we are... just as well, there's all the more for us.

(ALBERT puts one bowl in front of HAROLD and one in front of himself)

HAROLD: Who do they think they are?

(He sweeps his soup onto the floor. ALBERT is startled.)

HAROLD: Who do they think they are?

(He brings his fist down on the table and Albert's soup goes flying)

ALBERT: What are you doing? That was my soup... I...
HAROLD: No wonder these girls get themselves duffed up. *(He clenches his fist)* I could do her myself...
ALBERT: I'll go and get the fish and chips.

(ALBERT is a bit frightened at this turn of events. He scampers into the kitchen.)

HAROLD: Made a right berk of myself... candles...

(He sweeps the candles off the table. ALBERT, in the kitchen, takes two plates of fish and chips out of the oven. He goes into the other room carrying the two plates. As he enters, a plate just misses his head and hits the wall.)

ALBERT: Fish and chips... sit down, lad... forget about her... eat your dinner. I've split hers up, half each.

HAROLD: I don't want any dinner.

(HAROLD knocks the plate of fish and chips, and hurls it across the room)

ALBERT: Don't let her upset you, she's not worth it.

HAROLD: You're just as bad as she is...

(HAROLD hits ALBERT's plate and hurls the food across the room)

ALBERT: *(Trying to stop him slinging it)* No, don't... don't... that was my dinner!

(ALBERT scampers over on his hands and knees, and starts picking up the fish and chips from the floor. HAROLD pulls the tablecloth off and sends everything else on the table flying.)

HAROLD: I spent good money on her... she's got no right to do this... who does she think she is...

(There is a knock at the door. They freeze.)

ALBERT: It's her... don't let her in yet. I'll get her dinner ready.

(He crawls about the room, putting fish and chips onto the plate. HAROLD goes to the door and opens it slightly. There is a woman of about thirty-four standing there.)

HAROLD: Well?

WOMAN: Hallo, Harold.

HAROLD: You're a bit late, aren't you?

WOMAN: Am I?

HAROLD: Yeah, you are.

WOMAN: Well, just a few minutes, perhaps. Aren't you going to let me in?

HAROLD: What for?

WOMAN: Well, you asked me round for dinner.

(ALBERT goes to the door and stands behind HAROLD with the plate of fish and chips. Taps HAROLD on shoulder. Shows him the plate. HAROLD takes the plate and hands it to the woman.)

HAROLD: Well, here it is. I hope you enjoy it.

(HAROLD slams the door in her face. We hear her shouting outside.)

WOMAN: What are you playing at? Open the door! Let me in! Put the light on! I can't see...

(HAROLD and ALBERT steal away)

HAROLD: *(In hall. Shouts to her.)* Shut up... and don't come round here again. *(He slams shut the door of the living room and cuts off her shouts)*

ALBERT: *(Cackles)* That's the way to treat them... I'm proud of you, son... we don't need any women. We're better off on our own. Come on, let's watch *Perry Mason. (He starts fussing around HAROLD)* You sit here... take your boots off... make yourself comfortable... have a fag... I'll get you a drink... what would you like? I'll open the bottle of hock... you stay there, I'll go and get it.

HAROLD: Who did she think she was?

ALBERT: Well, there you are... that's women for you.

(As ALBERT goes past the grandfather clock, he looks craftily at HAROLD, who is staring out of the window. Without being seen, ALBERT puts the hands of the clock back an hour. He smiles to himself and goes on into the kitchen.)

Thirty years earlier, Stan Laurel and Oliver Hardy had made their most celebrated two-reeler, *The Music Box.* They are a pair of delivery men who have to carry a piano up a flight of stairs to a house on top of a hill: the film won an Oscar, and made Laurel and Hardy the most famous comedy duo in Hollywood. The confidence Galton and Simpson displayed in taking this archetypal comic premise and reworking it was matched by the brilliance of the script, which made the idea seem brand new. Harold and Albert have agreed to collect a piano from an apartment at the top of a block of flats – but before they tackle the stairs, they have to get it out of the door:

STEPTOE AND SON, first series, episode three

'THE PIANO'
First broadcast: Thursday 21 June 1962

ALBERT: Well, come on, are we going to get this carpet rolled up or not? Ready?

HAROLD: Right.

(HAROLD lifts the piano again. ALBERT continues rolling the carpet. ALBERT reaches a leg.)

ALBERT: Up a bit higher.

HAROLD: Oh Gawd.

(HAROLD strains and lifts it up a bit higher. ALBERT manages to get the rolled carpet under the leg. HAROLD puts the piano down. Then he goes to another leg and lifts it up. ALBERT starts rolling again.)

HAROLD: Look… if you keep rolling it, by the time it gets to the leg it'll be four foot high. I can't lift it up four foot. Pull it, don't roll it. Use a bit of common, Dad, please. Honest, you wouldn't survive five minutes without me.

(ALBERT pulls the carpet along and gets it under the leg, so that now the piano is off the carpet. HAROLD lowers the piano. He is exhausted.)

HAROLD: Right, now give it a shove.

(They get behind the piano and start shoving. It rolls slowly over towards the door.)

ALBERT: It ain't going to go through the door.

HAROLD: Of course it's going to go through the door. They got it through the door when they brought it in. How do you think they got it in… do you think they built the flat around it? If it went in, it'll come out. First rule of geometry.

(HAROLD goes round to the front of the piano so that ALBERT is pushing and HAROLD is pulling. HAROLD backs through the door pulling the piano with him. The piano gets stuck in the door. They can't budge it. Now HAROLD is in one room and ALBERT in the other.)

ALBERT: Told you… it ain't going to go through, is it? Geometry or no geometry.

HAROLD: You didn't think I thought it would go through like this. I mean, obviously you can't get something that's six foot wide through a three-foot aperture. I mean, everybody knows that. I have manoeuvred it into this position so that we can now turn it on its side and wiggle it through.

ALBERT: I ain't lifting it. It's too heavy. My lungs wouldn't stand it.

HAROLD: We ain't lifting it. We're just turning it over.

ALBERT: You can't turn it over without lifting it.

HAROLD: Don't keep arguing. I know what I'm doing. Take the strain.

(They get hold of the piano, one at each end)

HAROLD: Lift.

ALBERT: *(Straightens up)* You said we don't have to lift.

HAROLD: What I meant was we don't have to lift the whole piano off the floor at the same time. We just lift one side of it, and turn it over. It's like a racehorse, not all of its legs are off the ground at any given time.

ALBERT: What about when he's jumping?

HAROLD: What's that got to do with it? Why do you have to complicate everything? This is a piano.

ALBERT: Well, you started talking about racehorses, not me.

HAROLD: Only because I was trying to explain the principle to you in simple terms that you would understand.

ALBERT: Look... are we lifting it or not?

HAROLD: We are upending it. There is a subtle difference. We are upending it – and then we are wiggling it... *(Makes a wiggling movement with his hand)*

ALBERT: *(Puzzled)* Wiggling it?

HAROLD: Wiggling it. Right... take the strain.

(FADE... FADE UP)

(The piano is now stuck with its keyboard against the study door)

ALBERT: Well, we've upended it, we've wiggled it, we've turned it round... and we still ain't got no further.

HAROLD: It is going to go... it came in... it's going out.

ALBERT: If they had another door, or if that wall wasn't there, it'd be easy. We could bring it round in a ninety-degree arc.

HAROLD: What are you talking about? Shut up.

ALBERT: I'm only trying to help.

HAROLD: Well, don't.

ALBERT: Well, it ain't going to go through this way.

HAROLD: *(Controlled fury)* I know it ain't.

ALBERT: Well, what are you hanging about for... look at the time... they're open!

Wilfrid Brambell, aka Albert, who was nearly two decades younger than his character, was a meticulously groomed man in real life. 'Nobody recognized him when he left the set,' said Alan. 'He was immaculately dressed, with his perfectly pressed trousers, an expensive shirt and tie, gleaming shoes… nothing like Albert's filthy clothes and blackened teeth. Harry, on the other hand, was better dressed on the set than he was in his own clothes, and of course all the fans would recognize him immediately.'

Sudden fame came as a shock to both actors. The first series of *Steptoe* was repeated as soon as the six-show run ended, and viewing figures for the repeats were astronomical: half the country was tuning in. Ray and Alan had taken a driving holiday in southern Europe, and were not aware of the series' success until Harry Corbett phoned them: 'He told us, "You've got no idea what's happening here, it's madness. I can't go outside my door,"' Alan said.

The critical acclaim, and the BBC's delight at their hit, made a second series inevitable. Despite their initial reluctance to be tied to another long-running show, after seven years of *Hancock's Half Hour*, Ray and Alan were aware that the Steptoes gave them an opportunity no other show could ever rival: the chance to write scenes and situations that were wholly built on dialogue – scenes such as this one:

STEPTOE AND SON, first series, episode five

'THE DIPLOMA'
First broadcast: Thursday 5 July 1962

> *(ALBERT unloads the cart. Throws the piping onto a pile and takes the saucepan out.)*

ALBERT: How much do you think we're going to get on this lot?
HAROLD: Look… if you want a row… let's have one… here and now, 'cos I'm in the mood for one, I'll tell you. Don't think I enjoy flogging my guts out all day for a saucepan and a couple of yards of pipe.
ALBERT: Flogging your guts out… sitting in the caff all day… drinking tea with your mates, putting tanners in machines, that's what you've been doing.
HAROLD: Is that what you think I been doing? Stuck in the caff. Is that what you think? Has it been raining today or hasn't it?
ALBERT: Yes. 'Course it's been raining.
HAROLD: Right… feel my coat… go on… feel it.
ALBERT: *(Feels the coat)* It's wet.
HAROLD: That's right… it's wet. So is my shirt… so is my vest… and so am I. Wet… wet… now how do you think I got wet, eh?

ALBERT: Well… you probably been out in the rain.

HAROLD: That's right… I been out in the rain… I been out in the bleeding rain all day long… I been in the caff for half an hour. To have me dinner. That's when it stopped raining. It stopped when I went in… and started again when I came out.

ALBERT: Daah!

Just as Wally Stott's theme for *Hancock* had become a national institution, so too the music for *Steptoe* became instantly recognizable. The composer was Ron Grainer, who also wrote the themes for *Doctor Who* and *Tales of the Unexpected*. It followed the actors for the rest of their careers – both Corbett and Brambell appeared in *Carry On* movies, for instance; Corbett starred in *Carry on Screaming* (1966) and Brambell had a cameo in *Carry on Again Doctor* (1969), and in both cases they appeared to the strains of 'Old Ned'.

For the last episode of the first series, Galton and Simpson introduced a theme that increased the pathos of Harold's situation: he is terrified to leave his father, in case the old man dies without him… yet he knows that if he doesn't break free, he will die alone and lonely himself. The fact that Albert knows this and exploits it doesn't make it any less true, or poignant. This thread ran through all eight series, culminating in the penultimate show, where Albert is bedridden and Harold is reduced to carrying him to the toilet. To begin with, though, Albert's phantom heart attacks are psychosomatic:

STEPTOE AND SON, first series, episode six

'THE HOLIDAY'
First broadcast: Thursday 12 July 1962

(A loud groan from ALBERT in the bedroom. HAROLD listens in the sitting room.)

HAROLD: Oh Gawd, here we go. What's it this time, his legs, his heart, his lungs or his guts?

ALBERT: *(OFF: Groans)*

HAROLD: Hark at him going away. Shuttup.

ALBERT: *(OFF)* Harold…

HAROLD: I'm busy… don't start that lark, I know what you're up to. I'm going away on my own.

ALBERT: *(OFF)* Harold… I'm not well…

HAROLD: Hard luck.

ALBERT: *(OFF)* It's my heart.

HAROLD: I thought it would be, it's about time.

ALBERT: *(OFF)* It keeps jumping.

HAROLD: You'd better lay still and keep quiet then.

ALBERT: *(OFF)* I can't get my breath.

HAROLD: Stop shouting then, you won't use so much.

ALBERT: *(OFF)* Harold… call the doctor… I'm going, Harold… call the doctor.

HAROLD: *(Waving goodbye)* I should think he can hear you.

(Cut to the bedroom. ALBERT is sitting up in bed, wearing a striped nightshirt and his cap.)

ALBERT: Harold… Harold… I'm going, Harold… I'm not joking this time.

(ALBERT cocks his head and listens to see if it is having any effect)

ALBERT: Harold… Harold… oooh my chest… can you hear me, Harold? Harold…

(There is no reaction from HAROLD. ALBERT gets fed up with this. He gets out of bed, looks round. Goes over to the bedside cabinet, deliberately knocks it over with a clatter, then lies down on the floor, moaning and groaning.)

(CUT to HAROLD. He jumps at the noise. For the first time he is worried. He runs to the bedroom. He sees ALBERT on the floor.)

HAROLD: Dad… Dad, are you all right? Dad!

(HAROLD raises the old man's head and cradles it against his shoulder)

HAROLD: Dad… If you're mucking about, I'll wallop you… Dad… *(Very worried)* What's wrong, Dad? What happened? Oh, come on, Dad, stop playing about… Dad, Dad…

ALBERT: *(Groans weakly)*

HAROLD: This is no time for joking, Dad… I'm warning you, Dad… if you're having me on, I'll… I'll… if there's nothing wrong with you… it'll be the last you see of me… I'll skin you… so help me, I'll skin you… Dad, are you all right? Dad… Dad…

(FADE)

(FADE UP on the sitting room. HAROLD is pacing up and down, very worried. The bedroom door slams. HAROLD goes into the hall and meets the DOCTOR.)

HAROLD: How is he, Doctor?

DOCTOR: He's resting quietly. I've given him a sedative.

HAROLD: Is he going to be all right?

DOCTOR: Oh yes, I should think so. There's never very much wrong with him, is there?

(HAROLD is furious. He starts towards the bedroom. The DOCTOR holds his arm.)

HAROLD: I thought so... I'll smash his head in...

DOCTOR: Now wait a minute.

HAROLD: You know he's a malingerer... he's always having you round here, and there's nothing wrong with him. Why don't you tell him there's nothing wrong with him?

DOCTOR: I've told him... you see, your father's condition is not physical... it's a mental condition.

HAROLD: I agree with you there... he's raving bonkers...

DOCTOR: I think we ought to have a chat about your father.

HAROLD: Go on...

(HAROLD wanders over to the sideboard with the drinks on. Pours two whiskies.)

DOCTOR: When does your father get these so-called heart attacks?

HAROLD: When he can't get his own way. When I want to do something and he doesn't want me to do it.

DOCTOR: Exactly... typical...

HAROLD: Drink?

DOCTOR: Oh, thank you.

(The DOCTOR takes the drink, sips it, reacts slightly and looks at it)

HAROLD: It's whisky... blended.

DOCTOR: You see, your father is an old man... he's frightened of being alone... a common enough fear with people of his age... you're the only relative, I take it?

HAROLD: Yeah.

DOCTOR: Yes... well, there it is... he tells me you're planning to take separate holidays this year.

HAROLD: I'm going on my own... it's the first time in my life... well, Gawd blimey, it's only for a fortnight.

DOCTOR: I sympathize with you... but old folk aren't rational about these things... he thinks you don't want him.

HAROLD: I don't... at least, not on my holiday.

DOCTOR: Well, it's up to you. As a doctor, there's nothing more I can do. We have no medicine for loneliness, Harold.

HAROLD: But it's only for a fortnight... I only want to be on my own for a fortnight... I've been looking forward to this... don't my health count? I'll send him a card every day... two cards...

DOCTOR: Well, that's hardly the same thing, is it? As you say, it's the first time, and I'm a little worried that something may happen to him while you're away... they can wish these illnesses on themselves, you know.

HAROLD: So I'm trapped, that's what it amounts to, don't it? I'm trapped... I'm doomed to be a nursemaid to him all my life.

DOCTOR: I wouldn't put it like that... after all, we're all trapped by something or other. We all have responsibilities... one day you'll be old yourself.

HAROLD: Yeah, but I've been looking after him all my life. I ain't had time to get married and have kids to look after me... *(shocked)*... I *will* be on my own.

It wasn't just Albert who could throw a sickie. Hercules, the Steptoes' elderly carthorse, was also adept at winning sympathy. Hercules was a real rag-and-bone man's horse, loaned to the BBC for the show by two totters who worked the streets around Notting Hill – Arthur and Chris Arnold. 'Years later,' Alan said, 'Chris told me that they earned more from six weeks filming with the horse than they did during the whole of the rest of the year on their round.'

Hercules was often heard but never seen in the yard; his appearances were confined to filmed segments, on the west London streets. 'Nobody ever noticed that he was actually a mare,' Ray says. 'And she wasn't "Hercules", of course... she was "Dolly".'

Harold professed to loathe the horse; to Albert, Hercules was his only friend. At the beginning of the second series, the horse collapsed and the vet was called, provoking one of Harold's bitterest monologues:

STEPTOE AND SON, second series, episode one

'WALLAH-WALLAH CATSMEAT'
First broadcast: Thursday 3 January 1963

> *(ALBERT and HAROLD are waiting outside the stable. ALBERT is standing still, looking miserable. HAROLD is pacing up and down, smoking.)*

HAROLD: He's been in there long enough, hasn't he? He ought to know what's wrong with him by now. What's keeping him so long? I'm going in there.

ALBERT: There's nothing you can do. It's no good walking up and down here like a pregnant father. He's in good hands. Come inside and let's have a cup of tea.

HAROLD: Tea? At a time like this? Tea?

ALBERT: It'll do you good. Calm your nerves.

HAROLD: Oh, ain't it pathetic! Your faith in the healing powers of a cup of tea. That's your answer to everything, ain't it? Have a nice cup of tea. The Englishman's panacea. Mother just died? Oh, what a shame, have a cup of tea. Just been run over, never mind, have a cup of tea. I have been offered tea for disasters, funerals, operations, floods, wars, Dunkirk, the Blitz, piles, coronations, hunger marches, hysteria and insomnia – a nice mug of tea in one hand and thumbs up to the camera with the other. Britain can take it! Well, they can have it. I am sick and tired of being a cheerful chirpy Cockney sparrow... I am as entitled to be depressed and miserable as anybody else, so you can stick your cup of tea... right back down the spout.

The bonds between Harold and Albert were twisting under tension. At first it had been the son who was desperate to marry and escape. With this next episode, Galton and Simpson showed that Albert also wanted to find a wife to relieve his loneliness, even if that meant sullying Harold's memories of his own mother, who had died when he was a small boy. This gave the writers an opportunity to explore a fascinating relationship that was always implied but never seen: Albert's married life.

'One of the most interesting things about developing the characters was talking about the mother, who never appeared,' Alan said. 'She'd been dead thirty years, since Harold was six years old. When we first started, we referred to her but we never quite knew who she was. Then we made her a teacher, and it came out she had been a bit more middle class than the old man. So why did she marry him?'

'Had she been alive,' Ray said, 'he [Harold] would have got a proper schooling, he might have gone on and been something in the world. In one episode, we revealed she had been in the Salvation Army, and the old man said, "I soon knocked that out of her."'

The claustrophobic intensity of the show meant neither character could better their situation. Progress was impossible; all their efforts could achieve was a deeper misery. Harold would never escape from poverty or find a lasting love; Albert was incapable of finding anyone to mitigate his loneliness. Their clam-shell existence might be prised open a crack at the start of each episode, but it would snap shut at the end. For Galton and Simpson, this meant every story arc must lead straight back to the beginning. The technical challenge this presented had largely been solved with the first episode, 'The Offer': that storyline began at a crisis in the relationship between father and son, with the implication that this had been building up for a long time. By the same token, viewers sensed that, when Albert announces in the following extract that he is planning to marry again, the old man has been nursing his hopes for a long time... and now they are about to be crushed:

STEPTOE AND SON, second series, episode three

'THE STEPMOTHER'
First broadcast: Thursday 17 January 1963

HAROLD: You're not bringing her back here.
ALBERT: Why not?
HAROLD: You and that woman. Upstairs. In my mum's bedroom. Oh no, I'm not standing for that.
ALBERT: What are you talking about?
HAROLD: I can't stop you getting married, but I'll stop you bringing another woman into this house. I'd sooner burn it down. This is my mother's house. Haven't you got no respect at all?
ALBERT: Your mother's been dead thirty years. Anybody would think we only just put her away.
HAROLD: You may have forgotten her, but I haven't. She was my mother, remember. How am I supposed to feel... you, my dad, upstairs in my mother's bed with another woman?
ALBERT: She'll be my wife... it'll be church and holy. There's going to be

nothing funny about our arrangements. In thirty years I ain't done nothing against your mother's memory. I never looked at another woman. And I was still a young man in my prime... I had my chances... but no... I was faithful to her. I haven't forgotten her. I pay two pounds twelve and six a year to have her grave kept up.

HAROLD: Who paid for the headstone? You didn't, I did. She would have been unmarked if it had been left up to you. It's me who puts the dahlias in the vase on her birthday... You... you never set foot round there.

ALBERT: It's in January... I can't go out in January... it creases me, January does. She wouldn't have expected it.

HAROLD: Wouldn't it have meant more to her, knowing that it was you up above there with the old clippers keeping the grass down? But you... what do you do... as soon as she's gone, you're bringing strange birds back here.

ALBERT: I don't call thirty years as soon as she's gone.

HAROLD: Thirty years... it could have been yesterday... you see, Dad, I remember her.

ALBERT: I loved your mother.

HAROLD: You said you love this one.

ALBERT: Well, I do, I love both of them.

HAROLD: You can't have it both ways. It might be very convenient while you're down here alive... chopping and changing your affections... but what happens when you and this new one go... they don't allow that sort of thing up there, mate. They're very particular up there.

ALBERT: The vicar said it was all right. Thousands of people get married twice... three times...

HAROLD: Not to my mum, they don't.

Steven Gerrard, a lecturer in film studies at Lampeter University in Wales, who has made a study of *Steptoe and Son*'s influence on society, highlights Galton and Simpson's use of language: 'All that Cockney rhyming slang and argot – I'd never heard that before,' he commented. 'I love the way that they use "bleedin'", "bloomin'", "berk"... which is rhyming slang, a shortened form of Berkshire, or Berkshire Hunt. Galton and Simpson have had a real impact on the English language. Such dense layers of verbal imagery, I think it's brilliant. *Steptoe* is almost the perfect sitcom, incredibly influential on other sitcoms after it. And also it has become infused into the British psyche.'

It is not only academics who take the show seriously; its actors did too.

'The Steptoes are real to us,' Harry Corbett told the *Radio Times* in 1962, 'and because, like all human beings, they're so complex, we'll never be able to say we've fully explored them. All we can do is take snippets and present them one at a time – touching on certain facets of character, giving clues which different people will see in a different light, as they always do when assessing other people. I don't tell my friends about the Steptoes, they tell me.'

Ray and Alan were constantly exploring the differences between the old man and his son. Albert and Harold had nothing in common: the restaurants, the shows, the movies, even the bars that the younger man liked were despised by his father. Their tastes in music, like everything else, were poles apart:

STEPTOE AND SON, second series, episode five

'THE MUSICAL EVENING'
First broadcast: Thursday 31 January 1963

ALBERT: What are they?
HAROLD: Gramophone records.
ALBERT: Oh no, not more gramophone records.
HAROLD: Yes, more gramophone records.
ALBERT: You got gramophone records, what do you want more for?
HAROLD: I am trying to build up a comprehensive library of classical
    music.
ALBERT: Oh Gawd, I suppose we're going to have you sitting there with
    your hand over your eyes for a fortnight now. Ain't you got enough of
    them classical bits already?
HAROLD: No, I haven't. There are thousands of compositions I haven't
    even touched upon yet.
ALBERT: Are they all classical?
HAROLD: I haven't sorted them out yet, I bought them as a job lot. I don't
    suppose they'll all be suitable. But I'm hoping there may be one or
    two items I'm looking for.
ALBERT: Have you got any twist records in there?
HAROLD: I sincerely hope not. I bought these from a very select lady. Her
    husband is a doctor, and doctors have a very cultivated taste in
    music. I shall be most surprised if there is anything ropier than
    Rachmaninoff in here, mate. With a bit of luck I may even have side
    one and two of Beethoven's Fifth, I've been looking for them for

months. I'm fed up with starting halfway through the first movement. Do you know, I have not heard Beethoven's Fifth right the way through since September. That was your fault. You ruined them. That and four sides of Finlandia. Using them as table mats.

ALBERT: I was only trying to protect the table.

HAROLD: What about my symphonies? Curled right up, they did. Great steaming teapot stuck right in the middle of them. I've been trying to replace them ever since.

'Because we watch TV in the home, it has more resonance than cinema,' film studies lecturer Steven Gerrard pointed out. 'The world of the Steptoes becomes our world: you enter into it willingly, through television. We begin to pick up on these linguistic traits and repeat them back. And they weren't the stiff upper lip or the upper middle classes, they were us. They were real people.

'I've been influenced by these characters so much, because they're so important in British culture. I think they're very much part of the tradition of failures going right the way back through Shakespeare, but they're very much of their time as well, reflecting the collapse of the British Empire, the Women's Lib movement, the Pill... the male is bombarded from all sides by conflict. And Harold is a failure: he was in the Army, and what did he come back to? Life as a humdrum rag'n'bone man. That's part of the love of Harold and Albert: if we had characters who were successful and entrepreneurial and good-looking, then it wouldn't work.'

Every *Steptoe* plot was meticulously constructed, and the writers were implacable in their determination never to repeat a storyline. The penultimate show of the second series, for instance, was the only time Harold invited a group of friends round for a card school, the type of innocuous plot device other writers might have milked regularly. Because all the situations were unique, the dialogue was endlessly fresh and inspired:

STEPTOE AND SON, second series, episode six

'FULL HOUSE'
First broadcast: Thursday 7 February 1963

ALBERT: What about me? I'm hungry. I've got nothing to eat.

HAROLD: That's your fault, ain't it?

ALBERT: It's not my fault. It's Tuesday. You always bring in fish and chips on a Tuesday. I haven't had a bite to eat all day. I was looking forward to the fish and chips.

HAROLD: Oh for Gawd's sake, get off my back, Dad, please. Here you are –here's a packet of crisps. Eat them and shuttup – go and sit in the corner and keep quiet.

ALBERT: That's going to keep me alive, ain't it, a bag of crisps.

HAROLD: That's all you're getting. Now be quiet, I'm busy.

(ALBERT sits down in his armchair and opens his packet of crisps. HAROLD starts unwrapping the cheeses and arranges them carefully on a cheese dish while ALBERT moans in the armchair.)

ALBERT: Old man like me needs his nourishment… not just a bag of crisps. There's no salt in them either. I'm all skin and bone as it is. If the welfare officer ever found out about me, you'd be in dead trouble.

(HAROLD reacts)

ALBERT: They'd send the Meals on Wheels round here, that'd be a disgrace for you. You'd be put in prison, I wouldn't be surprised. Can't even bother to feed his old dad properly. Strangers, yes. Come in, have some cheese, and onions and wine… not his father, though. Here you are, have a bag of crisps and shut up. Very nice. It wouldn't hurt you, a bit of cheese, you got plenty there.

HAROLD: All right… you want a bit of cheese… here you are, have a bit of cheese. *(He picks up a lump of Camembert)* Here you are, eat that.

(HAROLD puts the cheese under the old man's nose. ALBERT is nearly sick with the smell.)

ALBERT: Oh my Gawd, what's that? Get it away… ugh…

HAROLD: It's Camembert. Nice runny Camembert. Go on, eat it.

ALBERT: Get it away… it's bad…

HAROLD: It ain't bad, it's ripe…

ALBERT: Take it away… rotten smelly foreign cheeses… put it in the dustbin…

HAROLD: It's perfectly good cheese… you wanted cheese, now eat it.

ALBERT: Take it away, get it out of my house.

HAROLD: Eat it. *(HAROLD tries to stuff it in the old man's mouth. ALBERT wriggles his head to avoid it.)* Go on, eat it, you're the cheese-lover… open your mouth.

ALBERT: *(Mouth shut)* No!

(HAROLD lets him go, walks away)

HAROLD: *(Coolly)* Right then. Don't say I didn't offer it to you. *(He places the cheese carefully back on the cheese dish. Cuts a small sliver and eats it.)* A very choice piece of Camembert, that, very nice.

ALBERT: I hope it poisons you.

HAROLD: I wouldn't expect a coarse palate like yours to appreciate the delicacy of a prize Camembert.

ALBERT: Delicacy!

HAROLD: Yes, I think my guests will enjoy it… now, what wine should I serve to complement it? *(Looks along his row of bottles)* Something full-bodied, I fancy, to bring out the full flavour of the cheese… I've got a 1961 Beaujolais Superieur… or a 1959 Macon Ordinaire… oh dear, it's a problem, isn't it? You're a man of the world, you spent four years in France – what would you suggest to go with the cheese?

ALBERT: What about a 1939 gas mask? *(Laughs)*

HAROLD: Oh, very droll. Go and make the tea. The kettle's boiling its guts out… make a decent cup, I'll give you a bit of Cheddar and a cream cracker.

ALBERT: And an onion.

HAROLD: All right.

(Albert goes out into the kitchen)

HAROLD: I do hope he goes to bed early. *(He selects a bottle of wine. The cork is halfway out.)* Oh, I forgot I had this. Chambolle-Musigny, 1957… *(He holds the bottle up to the light)* There's nearly half a bottle there. *(He pours a little into a glass, sniffs it, sips it, rolls it round his mouth and swallows it)* Yes, very pleasant. I must get some more of this. *(Calls out)* Dad, can you remember where we got the Chambolle-Musigny from?

(ALBERT comes in with tray, teapot and two tin mugs to go on it)

ALBERT: Do what?

HAROLD: Where did we get the Chambolle-Musigny? It's not dregs, is it?

ALBERT: No, that's the real stuff, that is. That's a good 'un. That waiter at that French restaurant. That's one of my contacts, that is.

HAROLD: How much does he charge?

ALBERT: Depends how much the customers leave in the bottle. Three and six he charged me for that one.

HAROLD: That's not bad, is it? Half a bottle of Chambolle… three and a tanner… and it hasn't gone off. I shall serve that.

'Bits about our childhood would creep in to Harold's childhood, and attitudes the old man had would be our senior relatives' attitudes,' Alan explained. 'I remember one story about one of my uncles, which we got into a script – when he was in his teens, he stole a horse and milkcart and ran it into a lamppost. Knocked the lamppost over. The milkman was off in one of the houses; getting his end away, I suppose. We put that into a sequence where the old man claimed that one time he'd got the wheel caught in a tramline. Which is what my uncle did. But we took it a step further and Albert had to go all the way down to the tram depot before he could turn round. Whereas, in my uncle's case, he just crashed!'

In the last episode of the second series, Harold falls heavily for one of his customers, the erotomanic wife of a politician. Harold is convinced she is attracted to his intellect; as far as Albert's concerned, he is just 'off in one of the houses, getting his end away':

STEPTOE AND SON, second series, episode seven

'IS THAT YOUR HORSE OUTSIDE?'
First broadcast: Thursday 14 February 1963

ALBERT: I'm no mug, mate… I haven't just fallen off the Christmas tree, you know… I know what's going on… putting your best suit on… shaving… give yourself away, don't you? I know you of old. It's birds… birds is the only thing you ponce yourself up for.
HAROLD: All right, so I spent the day with a bird. Breaks the monotony a bit, don't it? Anyway, what's it got to do with you? I'm over twenty-one, I can do as I like. Mind your own business. Now – let's have some tea.
ALBERT: You'll get no tea from me. You get tea when you work for it. You want tea, ask your fancy bit for some. Or did you get turfed out before her old man came home? Is she married?
HAROLD: I don't know, I didn't ask.
ALBERT: You keep away from her. I'm going to give you some advice.
HAROLD: Advice. That ought to be good. A bit late in life, but nevertheless welcome. Come on then, let's have it, let's hear these pearls of wisdom.
ALBERT: Look, son, I'm a lot older than you.
HAROLD: My God, I wish you'd told me that when I was a boy. What a difference it would have made to my way of life. My dad is older than me. I'm overcome.

ALBERT: Listen to me. I've seen a lot more of life than you have. I'm telling you, no good will come out of this.

HAROLD: Well, it's done me a lot of good already. *(He stretches himself luxuriously)* It's restored my self-confidence for a start. It's very nice to know when you're pushing forty that the birds still fancy you. Maybe when I'm as old as you are, and I'm past it, I shall start moralizing and tut-tutting, but at the moment I'm not complaining.

ALBERT: I'm not moralizing, son, I'm trying to explain something to you.

HAROLD: There's nothing to explain, Dad. I'm just still desirable, that's all.

ALBERT: Listen to me, Harold, I know what I'm talking about. This bird, she lives in a posh house, she's not a bit of old brass, is she? Have you stopped to ask yourself why a bird like that should fancy a load of old tat like you?

HAROLD: That's a nice way of talking about your own son, isn't it? A load of old tat. An unpolished diamond, maybe.

ALBERT: You know what I mean. She's got the pick of the land. Why bother with you?

HAROLD: She just fancies me, that's all. And she fancied me for myself… it made no difference to her, me being a rag-and-bone man.

ALBERT: You great berk, she fancies you because you *are* a rag-and-bone man.

HAROLD: What's that supposed to mean?

ALBERT: She doesn't fancy you for yourself, it's because you're common. Oh, you got a lot to learn. If you think there's anything in this, you're going to be hurt. She won't want to know you tomorrow, she's had her bit of fun. She's amusing herself with you, can't you see that?

HAROLD: Well, I'm having a bit of a giggle myself.

ALBERT: Ah, but it goes deeper with you, don't it? I know you. You've been waiting for something like this to happen. You've given up trying to get out of this business under your own steam. You're hoping some rich woman's going to come along and take you out. Well, they won't. I don't want to see you hurt, son. I've seen it all before. They're all the same, these posh birds. Their old man's out for the day, they're bored, they've tried everything, they're jaded, they're looking for something new and different. So they have a dabble with a bit of rough.

HAROLD: Don't keep calling me a bit of rough.

With around 24 million viewers tuning in every week, *Steptoe and Son* had become a national talking point. When a general election was held in

October 1964, Labour Party organizers asked the BBC to postpone a *Steptoe* repeat, fearing that working-class voters would stay in to watch the show instead of going out to vote (the BBC, obstinate and incorruptible, broadcast the episode; Labour was elected anyway).

Though the show didn't divide British viewers down class lines, Galton and Simpson believed the sympathies of *Steptoe* fans were determined by their age: younger people sided with Harold, while Albert's anxieties would be more easily understood by an older generation. On the whole, though, the old man's unsanitary, selfish and devious ways were easier to condemn than his son's pretentious delusions.

The first episode of series three took those sympathies and turned them inside out. 'When Harold puts his father in an old people's home,' Ray said, 'you would have to be made of stone not to be affected. There was a zoom shot of the old man, looking out of the window at Harry going away, and then he sits down on the bed and starts to cry. There wouldn't be too many people on the side of Harry at that moment.'

STEPTOE AND SON, third series, episode one

'HOMES FIT FOR HEROES'
First broadcast: Thursday 12 December 1963

(The living room. ALBERT stalks in, followed by HAROLD)

ALBERT: I might have known you were up to something this morning… bringing me breakfast up on a tray. Slimy, that's what you are. Conniving. Crafty. Just like your mother, God rest her soul.

HAROLD: Dad, I had no idea.

ALBERT: You haven't got the guts to say it to my face, have you? Can you look me straight in the eye and deny that you're trying to get me put in an old people's home?

(HAROLD looks him straight in the eye. They stare at each other. After a few seconds, HAROLD's gaze weakens and he averts his eyes. ALBERT, realizing that it's true, sinks into his chair. HAROLD is embarrassed. He goes over to his cocktail cabinet and pours himself a drink.)

HAROLD: Would you like a drink?

(ALBERT doesn't reply. He just stares at HAROLD.)

HAROLD: Don't look at me like that. Look, it's not my fault. It's like what they said in the Guardian the other week. You are a victim of the failure of Western society in not knowing how to take care of their old people.

ALBERT: I'm not old. I could still have you over.

HAROLD: All right then, let's say they're senior citizens. You see, they don't have this problem in the East. The family unit is still very strong out there, they've managed to solve the problem, it's all tied up with Shinto, they worship their ancestors. But we ain't wogs, Dad, we're English.

ALBERT: Oh, it's religion now, is it? All right then. What about honour thy father and thy mother?

HAROLD: Believe me, Dad, I'm only thinking of you. I haven't come to this decision lightly. If there was any other way out, I'd take it. But I'm afraid there is no other solution. I'm very sorry, but there it is. You've got to go.

ALBERT: Why?

HARLD: Because I shall be going away very shortly and you'll be left here on your own.

ALBERT: (Alarmed) Going away?

HAROLD: Yeah.

ALBERT: Where are you going?

HAROLD: I'm going round the world on a sloop.

ALBERT: You're doing what?

HAROLD: I'm going round the world on a sloop.

(ALBERT starts laughing)

HAROLD: (Angry) What are you laughing at?

ALBERT: (Laughing) Oh Gawd. Oh dear, oh dear.

HAROLD: I don't see what's funny about that. Lots of people do it. It's adventure. It's… it's doing something…

ALBERT: (Weak with laughter) Oh stop it. No, stop it, Harold. Oooh me heart. Oh dear.

HAROLD: Stop it. Stop laughing.

(ALBERT gradually subsides. Occasionally he chuckles. He almost starts to go off again, but stops himself. Wipes his eyes.)

HAROLD: If you think by ridiculing me you're going to make me change my mind you've got another think coming. There is nothing you can do about it. I am going round the world on a sloop and that is all there is to it.

ALBERT: So that's what you bought a new suit for.

HAROLD: Yeah.

ALBERT: (He has stopped laughing) You're not serious.

HAROLD: I am dead serious, mate.

ALBERT: In that case it's you should be going into a home, not me. You great big berk, you want your brains tested.

HAROLD: I know what's wrong with you – you're jealous, aren't you? Just because you ain't been nowhere, you don't want me to go.

ALBERT: I've travelled, mate.

HAROLD: Travelled? Bognor every year, peering out of the bay window of a boarding house for fourteen days.

ALBERT: I been abroad. France.

HAROLD: Oh yes, I forgot about that. Four years in a trench and a fortnight in Bognor. A world authority on travel. A proper little Marco Polo, ain't you?

ALBERT: I've travelled enough to know it's all the same.

HAROLD: How can it be the same? How can India be the same as this? I want to see it, mate. Before I die, I want to see the dawn come up like thunder, I don't want to read about it, I want to hear it. I want to sit round the campfire with a bunch of sheikhs, sorting through the rice for a couple of sheep's eyes.

ALBERT: Ugh.

HAROLD: The Taj Mahal, the Barrier Reef, the Seven Pillars of Wisdom, the Grapes of Wrath... It's just the same, ain't it, yeah, you can see all that down the bingo hall, can't you?

ALBERT: Dah!

HAROLD: I don't want to get as old as you and look back and think, 'What have I done? – nothing... Where have I been? – nowhere...' I want to be able to look back and say, 'Oh yeah, 1964, that was when I was a gaucho on the pampas, rounding up steers...' I want to see their eyes light up when I tell them about going round the Horn with everything lashed down... calling in at some tropical island for fresh water, garlands hung round my neck by dusky, slant-eyed maidens... stretched out on some palm-fringed beach eating breadfruit... pearl fishing in the Coral Sea... ivory smuggling up the coast of Africa... Whale-hunting off Antarctica... (He is now gazing into the distance)

ALBERT: Shipwrecked off Southend... that's about as far as you'll get.

By the third series, *Steptoe and Son* had taken its creators far beyond the standards of realism they had set themselves with *Hancock*. Part of that stemmed from the relationship between father and son, intensified by the claustrophobic set. 'We certainly didn't have that ebb and flow of sympathy between the characters on the *Hancock* show,' Alan remarked.

Ray Galton felt the series had begun as a drama, whose comic potential they had exploited: 'When we wrote the pilot, we weren't caring at all whether it got laughs or not. As a drama, it has a slight edge of comedy, and we were perfectly happy about that. It was when we agreed to write a series, that's when we had to think about laughs as well, and that changed us and our writing. The situation always was there, which was just what we wanted – they were constantly confronting each other. We didn't care much about bringing in other people. It was a locked-in world.'

Each series took four or five months to write, and was largely completed in advance of filming. This pattern, less frenetic than the weekly explosions of creativity that fuelled *Hancock's Half Hour*, gave the writers time to perfect each script. Cuts were more rare now, and lines were seldom changed, because they could not be improved.

STEPTOE AND SON, third series, episode five

SUNDAY FOR SEVEN DAYS
First broadcast: Tuesday 4 February 1964

HAROLD: Now, let's see. What's on at the Rembrandt? *The Monster from the Black Bog.*

ALBERT: Seen it.

HAROLD: Seen it? When?

ALBERT: Yesterday afternoon. The old people's matinee. Cor, you should have heard them old birds screaming. Good film, though. There's this great thing, 200 foot high, comes out of the bog, dripping with slime. Radioactive, he was. He tramples through London, knocking all the buildings down, then he picks up this bird and bites her head off…

(HAROLD reacts in disgust)

ALBERT: Just like eating a jelly baby, it was. Talk about laugh.

HAROLD: Why was he radioactive?

ALBERT: Ah, well… they'd been dumping all this atomic waste from the power station into the bog… and it brought him back to life.

HAROLD: How did it finish?

ALBERT: I don't know. Some silly old cow next to me complained to the manager and I got thrown out.

HAROLD: You got thrown out.

ALBERT: I didn't do anything. I dropped my glasses, that's all. Skinny legs she had, anyway – I'd sooner have had a go at the monster.

HAROLD: Oh well, that's the Rembrandt crossed off our list, isn't it? We can't go back there again. *(He looks at the paper)* The Majestic – *Jason and the Argonauts.*

ALBERT: Seen it.

HAROLD: When did you see that?

ALBERT: Monday afternoon.

HAROLD: You're supposed to be working while I'm on the round.

ALBERT: I get fed up, stuck in here on my own.

HAROLD: Oh, you poor old devil. Well, that's it, ain't it? There's nothing else round here. That means we've got to go up to Hammersmith now, don't it? *(He turns a page of the paper)* Oh cor... *(despairingly)* the Argosy... *Nudes of 1964.*

ALBERT: I ain't seen them.

HAROLD: You're not going to, either.

ALBERT: Why?

HAROLD: Well, blimey, if you get slung out at *The Monster from the Black Bog*, Gawd knows what'll happen in there.

ALBERT: Oh go on, Harold, let's go and see it.

HAROLD: Pater, I don't go to see films like that. The cinema, to me, is an art form, not a tawdry peepshow. You don't imagine I could be seen queueing up outside there, do you? Quite apart from the embarrassment of sneaking out afterwards, hoping nobody recognizes you.

Though the characters were evolving, the writers were not deliberately forcing the pace of development. Because the situation had to remain unchanged, it was not possible to permit them any radical personal insights. Both Harold and Albert knew as much about themselves, and each other, as they would ever be able to grasp. But for Galton and Simpson, the process of discovery was endless.

'We were learning more with each series,' said Alan. 'With Hancock it didn't really matter so much: he could be a comedian in one episode, then a doctor, then a lawyer – obviously you couldn't do that with Steptoe. It had to be more like a soap opera. It was much more real than *Hancock's Half Hour*, because that was a vehicle for a comedian. *Steptoe* was about two people and they had to be consistent. Within that frame-work, more and more ideas will come out of the relationship. It was a real relationship, but in some respects the Steptoe relationship is an extension of the Hancock/Sid James relationship. By now, though, we could get into more serious areas.'

STEPTOE AND SON, third series, episode seven

'THE LODGER'
First broadcast: Tuesday 18 February 1964

HAROLD: Traitor. Traitor to the working class.

ALBERT: Who is? I ain't no worker, mate. I'm a capitalist. Always have been. I got my own business. I ain't going to be nationalized.

HAROLD: Why didn't you have a revolution in 1926, that's what I want to know. The General Strike. Why didn't you take your opportunity and overthrow them? We could have had it, equality for all, I would have had a chance in this world and we wouldn't be sitting here worrying about bills. Why didn't you revolt, Dad, where were you?

ALBERT: Me? I was making a fortune. 1926 – selling everything, they were, give-away prices... we never had it so good. Oh, if only we'd had a pawnshop – that's where the money was made. Still, you can't have everything.

HAROLD: Oh, what's the point? Since we live in a capitalist society, much as it goes against my dialectic principles, we must solve our problems by applying capitalist methods. We must see what assets we've got and temporarily put them to other uses. Right?

ALBERT: I don't know.

HAROLD: Right. Assets. There's the house, the stock, the horse, the cart and me.

ALBERT: And me.

HAROLD: I said assets. You go and stand over there with the bills. Let's take them one by one. Me. Well, I'm the brains of whatever we go in for, so that's me taken care of. The stock. Well, obviously we can't flog that, otherwise we wouldn't be facing this problem. The house. We could sell that and buy a tent, I suppose. That's about all we'd get for it.

ALBERT: I ain't living in a tent.

HAROLD: Well, that's not the sort of response I expected from an ex Boy Scout. One of Baden Powell's originals.

ALBERT: I'm sixty-six.

HAROLD: The spirit soon dies, don't it... you're a disgrace to your woggle. So that leaves us the horse. Of course, the horse. Our problems are solved. We shall put Hercules out to stud. Yes, I'll get in touch with Captain Boyd Rochfort first thing in the morning. Oh, the Bloodstock Club'll go potty when they hear about this. Oh yes, that's the Grand National taken care of for the next five years. I can just see his offspring now... dragging themselves round Aintree, eating their way through the jumps.

ALBERT: *(Angry)* Is that all you've got to offer? I thought you were being serious.

HAROLD: Serious? Don't make me laugh. That's what I was trying to tell you. We got nothing, mate. Nothing. We're derelicts. We've had it. We're doomed. Look at us. Dregs, that's what we are. Dregs. The lower depths. Straight out of Gorki. He could have been writing about us. Dead Gorki, we are.

ALBERT: Well, it ain't going to get any better with you just sitting there sneering. Do you know what's in the larder?

HAROLD: Don't tell me, let me guess. Skinny mice.

ALBERT: Very funny. You have me in stitches, you do.

After the third series, Wilfrid Brambell announced he was leaving Britain to star in a musical comedy on Broadway. *Kelly* was expected to run for two years, which put the BBC in a dilemma – since they could not expect the public to accept a new actor in Albert's role, they would be forced to cancel the most popular and innovative comedy in television history, unless the writers could invent some other solution.

The Galton and Simpson response was to keep the Steptoe name, but to kill off Albert. They decided that the fourth series would open at the graveside, with Harold grieving for his father. A young man would appear at his shoulder, introduce himself, and explain that his mother had always told him to seek out Harold Steptoe if he ever found himself in trouble... because Harold was the father he had never known. David Hemmings was pencilled in as the young actor who would become the 'son' in *Steptoe and Son*, when a call came from New York: *Kelly* had flopped on its first night. There hadn't been a second. Wilfrid Brambell was coming back to England, and when were rehearsals starting?

The off-screen farce mirrored the comedy that viewers saw: just when a change seemed to glimmer, it was snuffed out. It was both a relief and a disappointment to the writers: the perfect formula would not be disturbed, but an opportunity had been lost. They exorcised their frustrations by introducing, for the first time, the whole of the Steptoe family at the start of the new series:

STEPTOE AND SON, fourth series, episode one

'AND AFTERWARDS AT…'
First broadcast: Monday 4 October 1965

(There is a knock on the front door)

ALBERT: It's the door.
HAROLD: I know it's the door.
ALBERT: Well…
HAROLD: Well what?
ALBERT: Well, shall I open it?
HAROLD: You may open it… but don't let anyone in. I am incommunicado, right?
ALBERT: Right. Yeah, leave it to me.

(He goes out. HAROLD sighs heavily as he picks up a sandwich and nibbles it moodily. ALBERT enters.)

ALBERT: Here, Harold, look who it is. It's Auntie Ethel and Uncle Ted.
HAROLD: *(Wearily)* Dad, I thought I told you…

(Four miserable, self-conscious-looking relatives come in. MAN, WOMAN and a teenage BOY and GIRL. The WOMAN sniffs and goes over to HAROLD, puts her arms round him.)

AUNTIE ETHEL: Oh, you poor boy. What a terrible thing to happen. You should have your mother here on a day like this. Only a mother understands.
HAROLD: Don't worry, Auntie Ethel, I'll be all right.
AUNTIE ETHEL: Well, if she ever sets foot in Cairo Road, she'll get a mouthful… from one end of the street to the other. If you'd like to come and stay with us for a few days, you know you're welcome…
HAROLD: I'll be all right, Auntie Ethel.
AUNTIE ETHEL: It'll be no trouble… will it, Ted?
UNCLE TED: Eh? … Oh… no…
AUNTIE ETHEL: You don't want to stay here with old faceache at a time like this… He'd put the mockers on anybody.

(ALBERT glares at her. We hear another knock at the door.)

ALBERT: What did you call me?
HAROLD: Dad… the door…

(ALBERT goes out to open the door)

HAROLD: Have a drink while you're here, Auntie Ethel.

AUNTIE ETHEL: Oh no, I couldn't, not under the circumstances... we only came to pay our respects... we don't want to impose ourselves in your hour of need... all right, I'll have a small gin. Ted'll have a brown ale.

(ALBERT re-enters with four more relatives)

AUNTIE MAY: I knew it, I knew it, I'm not surprised... I said at the time, didn't I say, Ethel, only last night, at the Skinners Arms, didn't I say to you I'll be very surprised if that lasts. I knew she wasn't any good... I said that wouldn't last, but nobody takes any notice of me, they think I've got a vicious tongue. Oh Harold, you poor boy, I can't tell you how sorry we are...

HAROLD: Thank you, Auntie May, you're very kind...

AUNTIE MAY: Well, don't forget you're welcome to come and stay with us, get away from old misery-guts for a few days.

(ALBERT reacts)

AUNTIE MAY: We can always put you in the spare room...

AUNTIE ETHEL: I've already asked him...

AUNTIE MAY: Ah yes, but we've got more room at our place, you'll have a room to yourself... you can stay in there all day without anybody interfering with you...

AUNTIE ETHEL: ... we wouldn't interfere with him at our place...

AUNTIE MAY: Yes, but you'd be on top of him. All I'm suggesting is...

AUNTIE ETHEL: That your place is bigger than our place...

AUNTIE MAY: You've never forgiven me for moving away from Cairo Road, have you, Ethel?

AUNTIE ETHEL: You left me with Mother, didn't you...

AUNTIE MAY: We had no choice. I've told you before, when Herbert became an inspector we had to move nearer the garage.

HAROLD: Look... Auntie May, Auntie Ethel... please... it's very kind of you both, but I'd rather stop here with Dad... I'll be all right... have a drink and... *(He is about to say 'hoppit' but stops himself)* ... don't start a family history for Gawd's sake...

(We hear a knock on the door)

ALBERT: *(Calls)* The door's open.

(Six more relatives enter, all looking sad. UNCLE ARTHUR goes up to HAROLD, claps him sadly on the shoulder.)

UNCLE ARTHUR: Harold... my boy... words fail me... I just don't know what to say. I felt for you up there, my boy, I really did. I thought to myself, he must feel a right berk up there.

HAROLD: Yes... yes, I did...

UNCLE ARTHUR: A terrible tragedy for the whole Steptoe family.

HAROLD: Yes.

UNCLE ARTHUR: You haven't heard from her then?

HAROLD: No... no, I haven't.

UNCLE ARTHUR: What happens if she turns up again?

ALBERT: She gets a kick up the backside if I'm anywhere around.

UNCLE ARTHUR: No. No. Yes. Well then... er... what will you be doing with the mixer, then?

HAROLD: The what?

UNCLE ARTHUR: The mixer. The kitchen mixer. The wedding present... what me and Deborah gave you. You did have a look at it, didn't you?

HAROLD: Oh yes, of course. Lovely. Yes... thank you very much, it was just what we wanted.

UNCLE ARTHUR: Well, you did... I mean, it's not much use to you now, is it?

HAROLD: No, no, of course not... I hadn't thought about it, what with all that's happened – my life being ruined and that.

UNCLE ARTHUR: No, no, of course not. But as we're here... I mean, I don't want you to think that's why we dropped in... it's just that, well, we won't be seeing you for a long time, I suppose, and... well...

ALBERT: Are you asking for it back?

UNCLE ARTHUR: No, no, Albert, no, no. We were just wondering... you know... I mean, we haven't got one... and well... thirty quid's thirty quid... and well, supposing he gets another bird... he'll be expecting something else, won't he... I mean... you know...

AUNTIE ETHEL: Well, come to mention it... we were wondering about the sheets and pillow cases... because what with my Elsie getting engaged... I mean, if they're not going to be used, there's no point in wasting them...

HAROLD: Well, I wasn't trying to hang on to them... I mean, I've only got back from the church a quarter of an hour... I would have got round to it... you know, I'm a bit sort of shell-shocked...

AUNTIE MAY: The fish knives and forks are ours... and the wooden salad bowl...

AUNTIE ETHEL: The stainless steel gherkin and peanut bowls are from Jim and Edie.

AUNTIE MAY: I'll take those… when I drop in to give them the news.

(The others crowd round the present table, as if it's a church bazaar)

FIRST WOMAN: Is our toaster there, Bert?
BERT: I can't see it.
FIRST MAN: *(Picks up an electric blanket)* Whose is the electric blanket?
SECOND MAN: Over here, Charlie.
FIRST MAN: Coffee spoons?
SECOND WOMAN: They're ours.

(Two of the women, Freda and Daphne, start arguing over some tea towels)

FREDA: Here, they're our tea towels, we gave him them.
DAPHNE: You didn't give him these tea towels. These are Irish linen. Those cheap ones over there, they're about your mark.
FREDA: We did not give him cheap ones.
DAPHNE: Here's the card. *(Shows her a card)* 'Love from Daphne and Trevor'. Satisfied?
FREDA: Well, where's ours then… where's our tea towels? *(She starts sorting through all the linen)* They're not here… Harold, where's our tea towels?
HAROLD: I don't know, Freda, they should be there… all the presents are there.
FREDA: They're not here… they should be on display with the rest of the presents… or perhaps you thought they weren't good enough?
HAROLD: No, it wasn't that, Freda… Dad, have you seen Freda's tea towels?
ALBERT: Red-and-yellow check…
FREDA: Yes.
ALBERT: Yeah. We did the wiping up with them.
FREDA: Oh, that's nice. Using the presents before you get married. Very nice. That's that, then, I won't be able to take them back to the shop, will I? And while we're about it, I am your mother's sister… and I was put into the fourth car. *And* I was put at the back of the church. And yet there were other people – who aren't even family, mark you, who…
ALBERT: Oh for Gawd's sake, Freda, give your ears a chance…
FREDA: Oh, I realize we were lucky to be invited at all… if he *had* got married, that would have been the last we would have seen of him. I haven't even been offered a drink yet.

(All the others agree: 'Neither have I,' 'Nor have we,' etc. HAROLD has been twitching and building up his anger until it finally explodes.)

HAROLD: Shut up… the lot of you.

(They are shocked into silence)

HAROLD: I have never, never seen such a mean, callous, hateful, selfish load of unsympathetic bleeders in all my life. Well, I don't want you or your presents in my house one minute longer.

(HAROLD lifts up the window behind the table. Picks up a steam iron.)

HAROLD: One steam iron.
FIRST WOMAN: That's ours.

(HAROLD tosses it out of the window. The MAN and WOMAN who gave it run out of the room.)

HAROLD: One coffee pot.

(HAROLD throws it out of the window. Two others leave. ALBERT joins in.)

ALBERT: One fruit bowl. *(Throws it out of the window)* One tea service…

(ALBERT throws the tea service out, one piece at a time. UNCLE ARTHUR and his wife run out. HAROLD and ALBERT sling out the presents.)

HAROLD: Three flying ducks… table napkins…
ALBERT: One vase. *(We hear a scream)* Got her.

(HAROLD picks up a large box)

SECOND WOMAN: No, don't. That's our dinner service.

(HAROLD makes to throw it at them. Everybody left now panics and runs out. HAROLD slings it out of window. The room is now empty save for HAROLD and ALBERT.)

ALBERT: I enjoyed that.

The public imagined that Brambell and Corbett must have bickered offstage as ceaselessly as they did on camera. That misconception persisted for decades: in 2008, BBC4 broadcast *The Curse of Steptoe*, a drama that purported to reveal a genuine animosity between the actors.

Both Ray and Alan dismiss the allegations as nonsense. Harry Corbett and Wilfrid Brambell were professionals with little in common but their respect for each other's talent as actors.

Ray Galton felt there was only one cause of friction between them: 'Don't take this too seriously, but I think it got on Wilfrid's nerves a bit when Harry would start telling him what the episode was really about that week. Get him in the corner and start on – I think he resented it slightly, but it certainly didn't cause a permanent rift between them. And though Harry didn't change his overall characterization every time, he would experiment with certain lines, on how to say them. He seemed to have a harder job than Wilfrid, who wouldn't really have any choice: once he'd got that voice and everyone knew what the character was about, his performance had to be straight down the line.'

STEPTOE AND SON, fourth series, episode two

'CROSSED SWORDS'
First broadcast: Monday 11 October 1965

HAROLD: You twit. You stupid, wrinkled, dirty, toothless, brainless old
    twit… That's your trouble, you been going too long. Why don't you…
ALBERT: What? Go on, say it.
HAROLD: Oh, nothing.
ALBERT: Die – that's what you were going to say, wasn't it? Why don't
    you die?
HAROLD: No, I wasn't.
ALBERT: Yes, you were… you can't wait to hear the first shovelful of dirt
    hit the coffin, can you? I wouldn't be mourned, I know that… you'd be
    dancing on my grave… well, I can tell you it'll be a relief to go, to get
    away from this hellhole.
HAROLD: You, die? Don't make me laugh. You'll get your telegram from
    the Queen, don't worry.

'Harry Corbett had this reputation for being a Method actor,' Alan said, 'a reputation for bringing something to whatever he played. But after *Steptoe* he did hardly any more straight acting – just a couple of plays, and a film in 1963 with Edward G. Robinson called *Sammy Going South*, which was a straight drama. For the most part, he couldn't do it, because people didn't believe it. They'd laugh… whereas the old man never had that problem, because he was so obviously acting a part in *Steptoe*. He was quite posh in real life. He played Paul McCartney's grandfather in *A Hard Day's Night,* where the gag was, "He's a very clean old man".'

STEPTOE AND SON, fourth series, episode four

'THE SIEGE OF STEPTOE STREET'
First broadcast: Monday 25 October 1965

HAROLD: What's this? More bills?
ALBERT: Give me my purse back.

> *(HAROLD takes a paper from the purse)*

HAROLD: *(Reads)* Harold Steptoe, age twelve. Position in class, 47th. Number in class, 48. History, C minus, does not try... Sums, C minus, shows no aptitude... English, C, does not concentrate... Geography, C minus, an improvement... Science, C minus, have given up, recommend woodwork... Headmaster's remarks: Harold does not seem to grasp anything that is taught him. He is a very difficult and worrying child, and is in danger of becoming backward. G. Bristow, Headmaster. *(HAROLD is shattered at this. He picks up another.)* Are they all like this?
ALBERT: I meant to burn them. I'd forgotten all about them.
HAROLD: I was never as bad as all that. They hated me, all them masters, because of you. All the kids took the mickey out of me 'cos I was a rag-and-bone man's son. I hated that school. I told you to take me away from it.
ALBERT: Well, I did.
HAROLD: Yeah, but you should have sent me to another one.
ALBERT: Dah, you learnt more from me here, Harold.
HAROLD: Yeah, like how to be bankrupt at thirty-eight.

Five years younger than Harold, Ray and Alan were more celebrated and successful than they had ever been. They were going to Claridges for their haircuts now, and seemed to see John Profumo, the former Defence Secretary, in there on every visit – they suspected he went in daily, to main-tain his impeccable appearance. The two celebrated writers, on the other hand, still felt out of place. 'The manager approached me one day,' Ray said, 'and he asked me, "Mr Galton, could you please ask Mr Simpson to have a shave before he comes in?" I said, "But that's what we come in for." He didn't like how we were walking through Claridges unshaven.'

This was the era of the Profumo Affair, and Britain was agog for scandal. At the grand offices of Associated London Scripts in Orme Court, overlooking Hyde Park, where they had been based since 1958, the writers were surprised to discover that one of their neighbours offered the kind of personal services that would guarantee newspaper headlines. One afternoon they saw an elderly man emerge from a chauffeured car, followed by their neighbour, who had a bundle of canes under her arm. 'We had our ears pressed to glasses against the wall,' said Ray, 'listening for evidence, but we couldn't hear a thing. The walls were too thick.'

All of Britain had sex on the mind, and Harold more than most:

STEPTOE AND SON, fourth series, episode five

'A BOX IN TOWN'
First broadcast: Monday 1 November 1965

HAROLD: I might just as well go and live in a monastery, the amount of crumpet I get. I'd feel better at the end of the day as well... I ought to get a place of my own.

ALBERT: *(Worried)* A place of your own?

HAROLD: Yeah. It's the only way, Dad. I just haven't got any privacy here. I'll just come to work every day – then in the evening when I've finished, I shall go home... like anybody else.

ALBERT: So I'll be stuck here on my own then.

HAROLD: I'll see you every day.

ALBERT: It's the evenings that are the worst. That's when you need somebody, in the evenings. I've only kept going because of you... I've got no other reason for living.

HAROLD: Oh Gawd, here we go. You've got your television and your bingo. It'll be better for you as well, Dad. We won't get on each other's nerves so much. And I'll be a much pleasanter person when I'm getting my share. I won't be so neurotic. It's just not natural, a bloke of my age living at home.

ALBERT: *(He has slumped visibly. Pouring the pathos on.)* I suppose it happens to everybody. That's where we make our mistake, I suppose. We devote the whole of our lives to our children, then when you really need them, they're off. We never think that in the twilight years... we'll be sitting alone at home, just waiting... that's all... waiting, the flickering candle getting weaker and weaker... till one day, it suddenly splutters and goes out... forever. *(Sniffs)*

HAROLD: Laying there, stiff and cold... unwanted, unmourned, unloved...
that is word for word what you said twelve years ago when I wanted
to join the Merchant Navy. Well, I'm not falling for it again. We're all in
the same boat. I'm getting old as well. We're all dying. It starts the
minute you're born. You've had your life – I ain't even started yet.
ALBERT: You've got a funny idea about life. There's more to life than
getting birds.
HAROLD: Is there? Well, when I've got one, I'll start investigating.

The bickering between Harold and Albert had become so subtle that the
writers could strengthen the characters now by seeming to mock them.
When the old man proudly took out his trenches uniform, his son
sneered, but the joke was on two generations of working-class men who
had defended their country and been betrayed by its leaders.

'The First World War has always fascinated me, more than the Second
World War,' Ray said. 'The sheer horror of it. I don't think people have
forgotten it. It's how those poor buggers put up with it – how there wasn't
a revolution in the trenches in 1917 when they found out the Russians
were doing it, I don't know. There should have been – but they didn't.

'Albert was proud of having fought. I suppose the only thing that
doesn't ring true, though it would be known to hardly anybody now, is
that these men almost never spoke about what happened. It wasn't till the
late twenties when books came out about it that anybody started to speak
of it – they were so traumatized that they just wanted to put it behind
them, forget about the whole thing.'

STEPTOE AND SON, fourth series, episode seven

'PILGRIM'S PROGRESS'
First broadcast: Monday 15 November 1965

HAROLD: I just thought you might like to know, the Armistice has been
signed. It's all quiet on the Western Front. You can go home now,
Tommy. There are homes fit for heroes waiting for you. It's going to
be a new world, lad. It's all going to be different. Why, there's going
to be two or three years of full employment waiting for you, what
about that? Don't turn Bolshevik, lad, go home to Blighty and work
hard to keep the upper classes in the manner to which they are
accustomed. Don't forget to turn your rifle in, lad. They'll need that to
turn against you when you go on strike in 1926. But never mind, the

means test is coming, so don't forget – altogether now: (*Singing*)
Pack up your troubles in your old kit bag and smile, smile, smile…
come on, lad, sing up…

ALBERT: Shuttup. Stop it. Stop it.

(*ALBERT turns his rifle on HAROLD. HAROLD puts his hands up.*)

HAROLD: Kamerad, kamerad. I'm sorry. You're quite right. It wasn't your
fault. You didn't stand a chance, did you? They got me as well in the
next lot. I went, same as you. Just as young, just as gullible. I came
back to a new world too… I'm still living in the same house they were
going to knock down after your lot. Never mind… it won't happen
again. When all the top people come out of their atomic shelters after
the next one, they're going to have to build their own bleeding
houses. We'll all be dead.

And while we're on the subject of the war… Galton and Simpson wrote
the following ten-minute short as part of a variety special, broadcast on
BBC1 on Christmas evening, in the year that the first series of *Steptoe* was
broadcast. Poignant and understated – the old man does not stir from his
chair throughout the scene – it depicts Harold at his most desperate, and
reveals how bitterly manipulative Albert could be, a streak that was
usually blurred by comedy. There is no laugh at the end, just a lump in
the throat…

This is one of the few remaining gaps in the *Steptoe* film archive – if a
copy does exist, it has been forgotten. The script was republished in the
Christmas 1965 edition of the *Radio Times*, but since then it has not been
screened or reprinted:

CHRISTMAS NIGHT WITH THE STARS

'THE CHRISTMAS PARTY INVITATION'
First broadcast: Tuesday 25 December 1962

GRAMS: (*Open to the strains of 'God Rest Ye Merry, Gentlemen'*)

(*The phone rings in the hallway. HAROLD comes out, picks up the
phone. He is wearing a paper hat.*)

HAROLD: Steptoe and Son. Harold Steptoe speaking. Oh, hallo Olive.
No, miserable. It's him. Yeah, just the two of us, same as last year…
same as every year. How many have you got over there? How

many? Here, you're not drunk, are you? No, well, you sound a bit, you know... Is Neville there? *(Flat)* Oh. Well, watch him, you know. I know your mum's there. But it's a big house. All right, you're a free agent, yes, so am I. I just said watch him, that's all. You know what he's like when he's got a few drinks inside him. No, he won't come. I can't leave him, can I? I have asked him. He just wants to sit here. You know what he's like at Christmas. Of course I want to come. Do you think I like it, sitting here with him all day long? But it's Christmas. I can't leave him. Yeah, all right, I'll ask him again. But he won't come. Yeah, all right. Here, Olive... what's going on there... who was that... you said 'stop it'. Yes, you did, I heard you. Was that Neville? Let me have a word with him. Olive. What's he doing? I'm warning you, Olive. No, all right, I'm not warning you, I'm asking you. Look, I'll try and get round, I'll really try. Right. Cheerio. You keep away from Neville, or anybody else who's there. Love to your mum. Oh, and thanks for the cravat. It's very nice. Did you get my present? Well, I guessed the size. *(Laughs leeringly)* Ta ta then. I might see you later.

(He hangs the phone up. Miserable. He goes into the living room. The table is laid for Christmas dinner. In front of HAROLD's chair is a half-eaten dinner, pushed to one side. ALBERT is still eating his. There are some tins of food on the table with the lids opened and sticking up. ALBERT has a paper hat on. The room is decorated with home-made paper chains, paper bells, etc. A tatty tree is standing in one corner. HAROLD sits down.)

ALBERT: Who was that?

HAROLD: Olive.

ALBERT: Oh, her. What did she want?

HAROLD: She's having a party round her place. We're invited, if we'd like to go.

ALBERT: No, I'm not going round there.

HAROLD: Why not?

ALBERT: Because it's Christmas. Everybody should spend Christmas quietly with their family.

HAROLD: But we ain't got no family.

ALBERT: There's you and me. We're family, ain't we?

HAROLD: Well, we could go round there as a family and have a good time.

ALBERT: I'm having a good time here, I don't want to go round there. Have some more pudding.

(He pushes a tin of Christmas pudding over to HAROLD)

HAROLD: I don't want any more pudding.

ALBERT: Why, what's wrong with it?

HAROLD: I don't like tinned pudding.

ALBERT: You didn't finish your dinner.

HAROLD: I know I didn't finish the dinner. What sort of a Christmas dinner do you call this? Do you realize we've had tinned soup, tinned turkey, tinned peas, tinned beans and tinned pudding with tinned cream? It's a wonder we ain't got bleeding metal poisoning.

ALBERT: Now stop that swearing, it's Christmas Day.

HAROLD: Yeah, Christmas Day in the junkyard, the rain was falling fast…

ALBERT: All right, that's enough of that.

HAROLD: Come on, Dad, let's clear these things away and go round Olive's.

ALBERT: No. I'm not going out. The Queen's speech is on at three o'clock. I never miss the Queen's speech.

HAROLD: We can see it round Olive's.

ALBERT: No, it's not the same. I like to hear it in my own house, it's sort of more personal that way. Like she's talking just to me. Sort of family to family.

HAROLD: Yeah, but we're not going to stay here all day, are we?

ALBERT: Why not? It's only for one day of the year. It's not too much to ask you to stay in with me for one day of the year, is it?

HAROLD: No, but what's the point? You know the way it's going to go. It's the same every year, we sit here all day long, staring at each other, just the two of us, for twelve hours, with these daft hats stuck on our heads, then when it's all over, we go to bed. What's all that about?

ALBERT: I'd sooner spend it like this instead of going to some drunken party.

HAROLD: Well, I wouldn't.

ALBERT: Well, you'd better go then, if that's how you feel. If you'd sooner spend Christmas with someone else than with your own father, you go then. I'm not stopping you.

HAROLD: I'm not going unless you come with me. That's what I can't understand. I'm not going off on my own, we can spend Christmas together round at Olive's place. I'm asking you to come with me.

ALBERT: And I've said no. Let's pull another cracker.

(HAROLD loses his temper and throws the proffered cracker away)

HAROLD: I don't want to pull another cracker, I want to go out and enjoy myself.

ALBERT: Well, go on then.

HAROLD: You come with me.

ALBERT: No.

HAROLD: Right then. I'll go on my own. You can't say I haven't asked you. Right then. I'll go and have a good time on my own. Right then. *(He puts his coat on and goes to the door. He opens the door and then turns back.)* Oh Dad… what's the difference between spending Christmas round here and spending it round there?

ALBERT: If there's no difference, what do you want to go for?

HAROLD: Well, there is a difference, but it's the same as spending it here… except we'd enjoy it much better. Lots of people and drink and games…

ALBERT: I like Christmas to be quiet… peaceful… spent in my own home. If you'd spent as many Christmases away from home as I have, you wouldn't want to go spending it nowhere else. Did I ever tell you about the Christmas Day I spent in the trenches in France?

HAROLD: Yes.

ALBERT: When the truce was called…

HAROLD: Yeah…

ALBERT: That was in the first year of the war, of course, when it was still gentlemen fighting gentlemen… there wasn't a gun being fired along the whole of the front.

HAROLD: Yeah. You told me.

ALBERT: Then all of a sudden, like as if a signal had been given, we looked over the top of our trench…

HAROLD: And they looked over the top of theirs…

ALBERT: And they looked over the top of theirs… and then we sort of waved…

HAROLD: And they waved…

ALBERT: And they waved. And we climbed out of our trenches with our Christmas puddings from home and we slowly walked over towards their trenches… right out in the middle of no-man's land…

HAROLD: Yeah, and they brought their sausages and sauerkraut and bottles of wine…

ALBERT: And we met in the middle of no-man's land, and we had our Christmas dinner together… in the midst of death there was peace, that's what our padre said… he was right too… me and this German bloke… we prayed together, drank together, showed each other pictures of our families… I drank from his bottle and he drank from my bottle… because it was Christmas… we weren't enemies, we were men… and then we went back to our trenches…

HAROLD: And you shot him.

ALBERT: Yeah. And his mate. We advanced twenty-five yards on the Boxing Day and we only lost 7,000 men – it wasn't bad, was it? And that's why I like to spend Christmas Day on my own.

(HAROLD is at a complete loss to say anything. He starts, but can't think of anything.)

HAROLD: Look, I'm going round to Olive's. Are you coming?

ALBERT: No.

HAROLD: Well, I'm going then… all right?

ALBERT: Yes, you carry on… if you must.

HAROLD: Yeah, well, I'm not sticking in here all day… I got to get out… you're sure you won't come?

ALBERT: No, I'm staying here.

HAROLD: Right. Cheerio then.

ALBERT: Cheerio.

(HAROLD stands in the doorway)

HAROLD: Shall I turn the telly on for you? Only she'll be on in a minute.

ALBERT: No, I'll turn it on. You get off… you don't want to be late.

HAROLD: No, right. Right. I'll be off then.

ALBERT: Cheerio.

HAROLD: I'll wait for you, if you want to come… I don't mind waiting till after the speech.

ALBERT: No, I'll stop here, thank you.

HAROLD: They'll have it on round there. Oh well… I'll see you later then. Cheerio.

ALBERT: Cheerio.

HAROLD: I mean, I'm only popping round there, I'm coming back. You know… wish them Happy Christmas.

ALBERT: Don't hurry back for me, I'll be all right.

HAROLD: Well… ta ta then. *(HAROLD goes out of sight, then comes back)* You can help yourself to my cocktail cabinet if you want.

ALBERT: Oh, thanks.

HAROLD: So you're definitely not coming then?

ALBERT: No thanks.

HAROLD: Right. Well, I'll see you later then.

ALBERT: Cheerio. Have a good time.

(HAROLD goes out into the hallway. Puts his new cravat on. The phone rings. He picks it up.)

HAROLD: Hallo, Steptoe and Son. Harold Steptoe speaking. Oh, Neville. Merry Christmas. Tell Olive I'm just... eh? She asked you to phone me... why, why couldn't she phone me herself? She's frightened to tell me what? *(His face drops as he listens)* Oh. Congratulations. Yeah, I hope you'll both be very happy. No, no hard feelings... why should there be? We had an arrangement. You knew her longer than I did, anyway. Oh no, I won't be coming round, it's Christmas Day. I always spend Christmas Day with my father. Oh no, I wouldn't dream of leaving him... after all, Christmas Day should be spent with the family, I always say. If you see Olive... well, of course you will now... give her my regards. Look after her.

(Puts the phone down. Shattered. He goes slowly back into the living room. Takes his cravat off. Puts his paper hat back on. Goes and sits down. The old man offers him a cracker. They pull it.)

GRAMS: *(All this with a gay version of 'God Rest Ye Merry, Gentlemen' over it)*

(HAROLD reaches over, turns the television on, and they lean forward to watch the Queen's speech. HAROLD spoons bits of Xmas pudding out of the tin.)

Epilogue

Steptoe ran for four seasons in the sixties, and established sitcom as the most popular genre on TV. But sitcom was not all that Galton and Simpson were doing. By the time they shut up the junkyard in 1965, Ray and Alan had also written a variety series for Frankie Howerd, a mixture of stand-up and sketches – exactly the show they had offered to BBC producer Tom Sloan before *Comedy Playhouse*.

They wrote for cinema, too, with *The Wrong Arm of the Law* (1963, starring Peter Sellers), *The Bargee* (1964, starring Harry H. Corbett) and *The Spy with a Cold Nose* (1966, starring Laurence Harvey). They put together a 'Wild West' Broadway show, *The Wind in the Sassafras Trees* (1968), and adapted Joe Orton's *Loot* (1972) for film. A series of one-off sitcoms for London Weekend Television, *Galton and Simpson Comedy*, followed the *Comedy Playhouse* template, before they agreed to return to *Steptoe and Son* in 1970.

The characters seemed to have grown while they were resting – though their enmity was even deeper and more bitter, and their humour often coarser and more cruel, they had also cracked the claustrophobic shell that contained them. Other people entered their world more often now – not only girlfriends and customers, but local gangsters, am dram groups, reporters, politicians, clergymen and even a clairvoyant medium.

The next four series of *Steptoe* were shot in colour, though the BBC wiped almost half the episodes and they survive only as black-and-white recordings from Ray Galton's home video machine. The colour shows that do survive (and are often shown on comedy cable channels) include 'Divided We Stand' (the one where Albert and Harold build a barricade through their house, to keep each other out) and 'The Desperate Hours' (the one in which Leonard Rossiter and J. G. Devlin play escaped convicts who take shelter in Oil Drum Lane).

These are classic comedies, but it cannot be argued that, in the early seventies, they were seminal sitcoms. The purpose of this book is to showcase the pioneering work, the series that were the foundation of situation comedy, and the writers who invented it. By the time Prime Minister Ted Heath was struggling to keep the lights on, the genre had long taken root and was spreading in every direction – there were sitcoms about bus conductors and dustbin men, Home Guard brigades and department stores, racist neighbours and abusive husbands, nasty landlords and lonely flatmates, young men who wouldn't grow up and pensioners who never grew old. Galton and Simpson started it all.

It would be too harsh, though, to end this anthology, this celebration, without a farewell to *Steptoe and Son*. So here are a couple of parting shots. The first, a scene with a TB nurse, harks back to the sanatorium; the second, a glimpse of Albert in his coffin, comes from the second of the two *Steptoe* movies (*Steptoe and Son* was *the* British box-office comedy of 1973, though *Steptoe and Son Ride Again* was somewhat less successful the following year):

STEPTOE AND SON, fifth series, episode six

'T.B. or not T.B.?'
First broadcast: Friday 10 April 1970

>   *(HAROLD and ALBERT, walking towards the Mobile X-Ray Unit. As they reach it, ALBERT turns to go back. HAROLD grabs his arm and pushes him up the steps into the van. Inside the van, an attractive receptionist is sitting at a desk.)*

RECEPTIONIST: Good morning.
HAROLD: Good morning. We have come for the mass x-rays.
ALBERT: Mass x-rays? You said it was just one… on the chest. I'm not having them all over. I'm off.

>   *(He turns to go. HAROLD pulls him back.)*

HAROLD: Come back here.
ALBERT: They're not strapping me down and shooting all that electricity through me. It's not natural. I'll turn into a monster.
HAROLD: What do you mean – turn? *(To RECEPTIONIST)* I must apologize for my father. He's been watching too many of them late-night Frankenstein pictures. *(To ALBERT)* Nobody's going to strap you down. Mass, in this case, means everybody. You have one tiny little x-ray. Now behave yourself. *(To RECEPTIONIST)* I beg your pardon.

RECEPTIONIST: That's all right. *(To ALBERT)* There's nothing to worry about, sir, I can assure you — it does no harm at all. Now we'll just fill these cards in. Name?

ALBERT: Steptoe. Albert Edward Ladysmith Steptoe.

RECEPTIONIST: Age?

ALBERT: Sixty-three.

HAROLD: You liar. He's sixty-nine.

ALBERT: Why don't you mind your own business?

HAROLD: How can you be sensitive about your age at your time of life?

ALBERT: *(Glowers at HAROLD)* Dah!

RECEPTIONIST: Sixty-nine. *(She writes it down)* Address?

ALBERT: The Mews Cottage, Oil Drum Lane, Shepherd's Bush.

RECEPTIONIST: Are you suffering from any illness?

ALBERT: No. Never had a day's illness in my life. I'm as fit as a fiddle. What are you doing tonight?

HAROLD: Dad, please. *(To RECEPTIONIST)* I'm terribly sorry.

RECEPTIONIST: Oh, that's all right. I'm sure he doesn't mean anything.

HAROLD: He does, don't you worry. *(To ALBERT)* You mind your manners. Answer the questions.

RECEPTIONIST: Do you cough at all?

ALBERT: No. Never.

(HAROLD reacts in amazement)

RECEPTIONIST: When was the last time you were x-rayed?

ALBERT: I've never been x-rayed. There's never been any need. There's nothing wrong with me.

RECEPTIONIST: Good! Have you ever received any other medical treatment?

ALBERT: Yes. I had some white powder squirted down my trousers when I came out of the trenches.

RECEPTIONIST: Well, I don't think we'll count that. Right, give that to the nurse. *(She hands him the card)*

ALBERT: I'll wait for him.

RECEPTIONIST: Name?

HAROLD: Steptoe. Harold Albert Kitchener.

RECEPTIONIST: Age?

HAROLD: Thirty-four.

ALBERT: He's forty-one.

HAROLD: *(Angrily)* I'm thirty-nine.

RECEPTIONIST: Which is it? Thirty-four, thirty-nine or forty-one?

HAROLD: Thirty-nine.

ALBERT: Nearly forty.

HAROLD: You'll need an x-ray on your nose if you don't keep it out of my form.

RECEPTIONIST: Address.

HAROLD: Same as his… unfortunately.

RECEPTIONIST: Are you suffering from any illness?

HAROLD: Not to my knowledge. I do keep myself in pretty good physical condition.

RECEPTIONIST: Any cough?

HAROLD: A slight irritation of the bronchial trachea first thing in the morning, but nothing to worry about.

RECEPTIONIST: Any sputum?

HAROLD: Pardon?

ALBERT: Gold watches.

HAROLD: Oh no, nothing like that.

RECEPTIONIST: Have you been x-rayed before?

HAROLD: *(Embarrassed)* Er… no.

ALBERT: Yes you have. Two years ago. When the horse kicked you in the cobblers. *(HAROLD is terribly embarrassed)* It's nothing to be ashamed of. You got over it, didn't you? *(To RECEPTIONIST)* He can still enjoy himself.

HAROLD: *(Clenched)* Dad, it's something I'd rather not talk about in mixed company.

ALBERT: It's all right, she's a medical lady, she's heard worse than that. I think you ought to put it down – x-rayed, gentiles.

RECEPTIONIST: Nothing else?

HAROLD: No.

RECEPTIONIST: That's all, I think. Give that to the nurse through there.
    (She hands HAROLD the card)

HAROLD: Come on, you.

(HAROLD and ALBERT go down a small corridor to the x-ray department)

ALBERT: What did you want to tell her I was sixty-nine for? I would have been all right there. Tasty, wasn't she? She's got T.B.

HAROLD: Has she?

ALBERT: *(Laughs)* Yeah. Two Beauties.

STEPTOE AND SON RIDE AGAIN

UK release: July 1973

> GRAMS: *(Church organ music)*
>
> *(A coffin stands on a trestle in the bare front room. The dog howls softly. HAROLD enters. He sniffs sadly, then gives a whistle.)*

HAROLD: Oi! All right?

> *(ALBERT sits up in the coffin)*

ALBERT: Yeah, not bad. Nice and roomy. Very comfortable.

HAROLD: Well, you can stay in there if you like. I don't mind.

ALBERT: Yeah, it's very nice. Could have been made for me.

HAROLD: I've got news for you. It was. I had it hidden out in the yard for a couple of years, waiting for you to shoot off. I had a bit of spare cash handy, so I thought I'd get in before the prices went up.

ALBERT: You had a bit of spare cash handy, so you bought me a coffin?

HAROLD: Yeah.

ALBERT: Oh, that's nice, that's very nice. What was it for, me birthday or Christmas?

HAROLD: Well, if you don't like it, the man said I could always change it when the time comes.

ALBERT: Morbid, aren't you? Other sons buy their fathers gold watches and cigarette cases – you give me a coffin.

HAROLD: Well, at least I got you a good one. Look at that. Beautiful. Solid teak, that is. It's silk-lined.

ALBERT: That's not teak, it's oak.

HAROLD: Well, at least it's not plastic. Had your name put on the coffin lid as well. 'Albert L. Steptoe, February tenth, nineteen-nought-one… dash.' I can get the other date put in now. 'Deeply mourned by his loving son Harold'.

ALBERT: *(Moved)* Deeply mourned… loving son Harold.

HAROLD: Yeah. I had that put on the tombstone as well.

ALBERT: What tombstone?

HAROLD: Well, I thought I'd get the tombstone done at the same time. He was having a sale, so I thought I'd get the lot and have done with it. You didn't turn your nose up at the Green Shield stamps, did you?

ALBERT: I didn't know it was my own funeral, did I?

> *(HAROLD gestures for ALBERT to climb out of the coffin)*

HAROLD: Come on, out. Oh Gawd, that's disgusting... Just look at the
mess. You've only had it five minutes and it's full of mud, fag ash,
boiled sweets... Dirty. I mean, Dracula's coffin's cleaner than this, and
he's in and out all day long.

The writers achieved a long-standing ambition in 1972 by adapting
Clochemerle, Gabriel Chevallier's satirical novel, for the small screen; it
starred Roy Dotrice and Wendy Hiller. The following year they sent up
the trend for racy television with *Casanova 73*, which starred Leslie
Phillips as a blundering lover. The eighth and final TV series of *Steptoe*
ended in 1974, and Galton and Simpson went on to write a series for Les
Dawson, *Dawson's Weekly*. It was his only sitcom, in which he played a
character who seemed a cousin of Hancock... though he wore a skid lid
instead of a homburg.

Galton and Simpson Playhouse followed for Yorkshire Television in
1977: six superb situation comedies that seemed a deliberate challenge to
other writers. And there the partnership stopped. Alan Simpson decided
to take a year off, to travel and concentrate on other interests, and he
never returned to his typewriter, except to work on existing scripts and
adaptations. Ray Galton continued working with other people, including
Johnny Speight and John Antrobus.

There was a farewell note, however, a short movie called *Le Petomane*
(1979): it starred Leonard Rossiter as a Parisian music-hall artist from the
turn of the century, who made an art form of flatulence. It's a scatolog-
ical joy, but fart jokes never translate well to the page. Instead, let's return
to that creased, defeated face on the front of my dad's *Hancock* LP.

If only life always ran as happily as dialogue by Galton and Simpson...

HANCOCK'S HALF HOUR (TV), fifth series, episode eight

'THE TYCOON'
First broadcast: Friday 13 November 1959

*(TONY jumps up, rushes over to the window and starts clambering
out. SID rushes after him and grabs him.)*

SIDNEY: Come back.
TONY: Let me go, I can't face the world any more – I demand you let me
jump. Leave me alone and mind your own business.
SIDNEY: It's not the end of the world.

340/ The Masters of Sitcom

TONY: It is. Go away.

SIDNEY: All right then... go on... jump.

> *(SIDNEY lets go of him)*

SIDNEY: Go on. It's all yours. Go on, jump.

TONY: All right, I will.

SIDNEY: Go on then, I'm waiting for you.

TONY: All right, I'm going. You don't have to worry about me, I'm going.

SIDNEY: Go on then, get it over with, go on, go on.

TONY: I intend to. You're not going to stop me.

SIDNEY: I don't want to stop you.

TONY: Well, that's all right then, isn't it?

SIDNEY: Yes.

TONY: Right. Now I know where I stand.

> *(Has a look down out of the window)*

SIDNEY: Want a push?

TONY: No, I don't want a push. I'm quite capable of looking after myself.
Well... I'll be off now then.

SIDNEY: Ta ta.

TONY: It's no use trying to stop me. *(PAUSE)* I've made up my mind.
(PAUSE) All the talking in the world won't stop me. *(PAUSE)* I've
thought it over and I've decided this way is best for everybody.

> *(SID loses interest and goes over to the table and starts reading.
> TONY is still on the windowsill.)*

TONY: Well, I mean, what's the point in carrying on under the
circumstances? *(PAUSE)* I mean, you look at it from my point of view.
There's nothing left to live for, is there? *(PAUSE)* No, there's nothing
more to be said. I've made up my mind. *(PAUSE)* Well, I'll be off now
then. *(PAUSE)*

SIDNEY: *(Uninterested and without looking up)* Ta ta.

TONY: It's no use trying to talk me out of it. It won't do any good. *(PAUSE)*
Well, I'll be off now.

> *(Makes a move as if to go right out onto the window ledge. Turns
> back to previous position.)*

TONY: Did you say anything?

SIDNEY: No.

TONY: Oh, I thought you were going to argue with me.

SIDNEY: No, no.

TONY: Because it wouldn't have done any good.

SIDNEY: I realize that.

TONY: It would have to be a very good argument to make me change my mind now.

SIDNEY: Well, I haven't got one.

TONY: Yes, but supposing you had. Supposing you were to say, 'Think about your family, and how you'd be missed down the club, and how young you are, and how talented you are, and what a crime it would be to throw your life away at a time like this…' If you were to put it strongly enough, it might make me change my mind.

SIDNEY: Oh, come in and put the kettle on.

TONY: All right then.

(He comes into the room)

TONY: By heavens, that was a near thing.

Bibliography

The main source of this book is, of course, the archive of scripts and papers held by Ray Galton and Alan Simpson. Almost all these scripts have been made and broadcast; more than half of the recordings have been lost. Many of those which survive have been made available on cassette, video and DVD, as well as being replayed countless times on television and radio. All the extracts in this book are taken directly from the archived scripts, and not from the broadcasts. Other books consulted include:

Davies, Russell (ed.), *The Kenneth Williams Diaries*, HarperCollins, London 1993

Fisher, John, *Tony Hancock: The Definitive Biography*, HarperCollins, London 2008

Hancock, Freddie and Nathan, David, *Hancock*, Ariel BBC, London 1969

Lewisohn, Mark, *Radio Times Guide to TV Comedy*, BBC Worldwide, London 1998

McCann, Graham, *Spike & Co*, Hodder and Stoughton, London 2006

Webber, Richard, *Fifty Years of Hancock's Half Hour*, Century, London 2004

More information is to be found at www.galtonandsimpson.com.

Acknowledgements

This book would not have been possible without the tireless efforts and constant help of Tessa Le Bars, who started work with Associated London Scripts in the sixties, as a teenage assistant, and became Galton and Simpson's agent and manager – the role in which she continues to work with them.

A great debt of thanks is also due to Malcolm Chapman, the unofficial historian of British comedy, who collated the entire Galton & Simpson script archive and assembled it in chronological order, imposing order on dozens of filing cabinets stacked with typescripts, film scripts, shooting copies, recording scripts, handwritten notes, newspaper cuttings and printouts.

The Tony Hancock Appreciation Society played a large part in making digital copies of sections of the archive; special thanks are due to Dan Peat and Keith Mason. Many of the older scripts were painstakingly scanned and copied onto CD-ROM by Martin Gibbons and Ashley Hoare. Sarah Nicholson, the Communications Officer at Surrey Community Health, and Paul Osborne at Greenfield TV provided invaluable help with tracking down Ray and Alan's earliest writing.

Warm thanks also to the performers who talked vividly of working with Galton and Simpson: Stanley Baxter, Fenella Fielding, Bill Kerr, Andrée Melly and Graham Stark. Many thanks as well to Andrew Collins, Graeme Garden and Freddie Ross Hancock, and Dr Steven Gerrard at Lampeter University, for their generosity with their time and their insights.

Special thanks to the team at Michael O'Mara Books, especially the commissioning editor Kate Moore, copyeditor Rodney Burbeck and head of publicity and marketing Ana McLaughlin. Great thanks to Heather Holden-Brown and the indefatigable Elly Cornwall at hhb agency.

Christopher Stevens would like to thank his family most of all – his wife Nicky, and sons James and David.

General Index

Index of Scripts

Key:

Comedy Playhouse – CP

Hancock's Half Hour – HHH (all radio episodes unless 'TV' is indicated in brackets)

Steptoe and Son – SAS

The Roman numerals denote the series and episode.